Encountering Things

Design and Theories of Things

Edited by
Leslie Atzmon and Prasad Boradkar

Bloomsbury Academic
An imprint of Bloomsbury Publishing Plc

B L O O M S B U R Y
LONDON · OXFORD · NEW YORK · NEW DELHI · SYDNEY

Bloomsbury Academic
An imprint of Bloomsbury Publishing Plc

50 Bedford Square	1385 Broadway
London	New York
WC1B 3DP	NY 10018
UK	USA

www.bloomsbury.com

BLOOMSBURY and the Diana logo are trademarks of Bloomsbury Publishing Plc

First published 2017

© Introductions and editorial content, Leslie Atzmon and Prasad Boradkar, 2017

© Individual chapters, their authors, 2017

Leslie Atzmon and Prasad Boradkar have asserted their right under the Copyright, Designs and Patents Act, 1988, to be identified as Author of this work.

Every effort has been made to trace copyright holders of images and to obtain their permission for the use of copyright material. The publisher apologizes for any errors or omissions in copyright acknowledgement and would be grateful if notified of any corrections that should be incorporated in future reprints or editions of this book.

All rights reserved. No part of this publication may be reproduced or transmitted in any form or by any means, electronic or mechanical, including photocopying, recording, or any information storage or retrieval system, without prior permission in writing from the publishers.

No responsibility for loss caused to any individual or organization acting on or refraining from action as a result of the material in this publication can be accepted by Bloomsbury or the author.

British Library Cataloguing-in-Publication Data
A catalogue record for this book is available from the British Library.

ISBN: HB: 9780857857828
PB: 9780857855640
ePDF: 9780857856012
ePub: 9780857856548

Library of Congress Cataloging-in-Publication Data
A catalogue record for this book is available from the Library of Congress.

Cover design Stephanie Coral
Cover image Stephanie Coral

Typeset by Fakenham Prepress Solutions, Fakenham, Norfolk NR21 8NN
Printed and bound in India

CONTENTS

List of illustrations vii
List of contributors ix

    Introduction: Design and theories of things 1
    Leslie Atzmon and Prasad Boradkar

1 Filled with wonder: The enchanting android from cams to algorithms 19
   Betti Marenko

2 When objects fail: Unconcealing things in design writing and criticism 35
   Peter Hall

3 The practically living weight of convenient things 47
   Cameron Tonkinwise

4 Big things: The vibrant culture of boomboxes 59
   Prasad Boradkar and Lyle Owerko

5 Theorizing the *hari kuyō*: The ritual disposal of needles in early modern Japan 65
   Christine M. E. Guth

6 Nothingness in April Greiman's *Does It Make Sense?* 81
   Elizabeth Guffey

7 Making things, things 95
   Nina Rappaport

8 Distributing stresses: The development and use of the Eames Dining Chair Metal (DCM) 109
   Michael J. Golec

9 What design tells us about objects and things 123
    Giorgio De Michelis

10 The modern American telephone as a contested technological thing, 1920–39 133
    Jan Hadlaw

11 Memory, materiality, and the Montreal Signs Project 149
    Matt Soar

12 Connecting things: Broadening design to include systems, platforms, and product-service ecologies 153
    Hugh Dubberly

13 Designing things as "poor" substitutes 167
    Carl Knappett

14 The graphic thing: Ambiguity, dysfunction, and excess in designed objects 179
    Phil Jones

15 Agency and counteragency of materials: A story of copper 191
    Prasad Boradkar

Afterword: Encountering design 203
Bill Brown

Index 213

LIST OF ILLUSTRATIONS

Plates

1. The Promax Boombox from the set of the film *Do the Right Thing*
2. The JVC RC-M90 Boombox which appeared on the cover of "Radio" by LL Cool J
3. The Sharp GF-777 Boombox
4. The Conion CF-100 Boombox
5. Sheinart's (family-owned women's clothing store near Atwater Market, Montréal). Sign installed 1995; removed in 2013 with closure of store. Welded stainless steel; "bastard" script lettering
6. La Belle Province Meat Co. (Boulevard St. Laurent, Montréal). Handpainted on galvanized sheet metal with a wood frame. Late 1960s; discovered in situ in 2013
7. Librarie Guérin (Bookstore, Rue St-Denis, Montréal). Panned acrylic with fluorescent interior lighting. Installed 1973; removed in 2014 with closure of store
8. Café Navarino (Avenue du Parc, Montréal). Panned acrylic with fluorescent interior lighting. Installed 1969; removed in 2010 during renovations
9. *Tambat Ali* in Pune, India
10. Craftsman Shantaram Ambre hammering copper products in *Tambat Ali*
11. Hammertone texture on a utensil
12. Finished copper vessels with the hammertone texture, designed by Rashmi Ranade, stored on a shelf in the factory of Bhalchandra Kadu
13. Learning the hammertone technique from craftsmen Shantaram Ambre (center) and Ganesh Lanjrekar (right)
14. Copper sheets in Bhalchandra Kadu's factory in *Tambat Ali*
15. Specialized hammers for *matharkam* in Bhalchandra Kadu's factory in *Tambat Ali*
16. The Water Bearer, designed by Rashmi Ranade
17. The cup in one of its primary shapes during the manufacturing process. Product designed by Rashmi Ranade
18. The process of creating hammered copper artifacts

Figures

1.1 The Scribe, Pierre Jaquet-Droz's automaton (1721–90), 1770 21
1.2 Difference Engine woodcut. Charles Babbage's Difference Engine No. 1, c. 1830s 26

1.3   Difference Engine Cogs details. Demonstration model of Babbage's Difference Engine No. 1, nineteenth century 27
2.1   Installation view of the exhibition "Good Design." November 27, 1951–January 27, 1952, MoMA, New York 37
2.2   Node Chair 42
5.1   Needle makers from *Jinrin kinmō zui* 69
5.2   Sewing equipment from *Joyō jinrin kinmō zui* 70
5.3   Preliminary steps in needle making from *Tiankong kaiwu* 72
5.4   Final steps in needle making from *Tiankong kaiwu* 74
5.5   Itinerant monks with portable shrines collecting offerings to forge a bell from *Jinrin kinmō zui* 76
6.1   April Greiman, *Does It Make Sense?*, 1986 81
6.2   April Greiman interview with Archie Boston, stills from 20 Outstanding Graphic Designers in Los Angeles, 1986 86
6.3   April Greiman, *Does It Make Sense?* (Det), 1986 87
7.1   Bicycle Manufacturer, 1880 97
7.2   Oyonnax, France, steam-power building 102
7.3   Spiraloop designed by Rama Chorpash 104
7.4   Worker at Steinway Piano, Astoria, Queens 105
8.1   Charles Eames, "Chair," United States Patent Number 150,685 (1947–8) 110
8.2   Charles Eames, "Furniture Shock Mount Construction," United States Patent Number 2,649,136 (1947–53) 116
10.1 AT&T Candlestick Telephone, 1910 136
10.2 "The Efficient Minute." AT&T advertising proof, 1910 138
10.3 "When Mrs. Marshall Uses the Telephone …" advertisement, 1928 140
10.4 Bell's WE "200 Series" telephone, 1928 141
10.5 Telephones designed for Bell's 1929 design competition by (clockwise starting at top left) Lucian Bernhardt, Gustav Jenson, Réne Clarke, and John Vassos 142
10.6 Bell's WE "200 Series" telephone with elliptical base and dial, 1930 144
10.7 Bell's WE #302 introduced in 1939. It was a "combined set" with the ringer integrated into the telephone housing 145
13.1 Male figurine from Petsophas 168
13.2 Male figurine from Petsophas 168
13.3 The Palaikastro kouros 169
13.4 Detail of the Palaikastro kouros 170
14.1 Found Font, Paul Elliman 183
14.2 Krazy Kaps, Mervyn Kurlansky, 1977 184
14.3 Undergraduate project, Stephen Johnson 185

LIST OF CONTRIBUTORS

Leslie Atzmon is Professor of Graphic Design and Design History at Eastern Michigan University (EMU) in Ypsilanti, Michigan. She has both an MFA in graphic design and a PhD in design history. Atzmon has published essays in *Communication Design*, *Design Issues*, *Design and Culture*, and *Eye*. Her collection, *Visual Rhetoric and the Eloquence of Design* (Parlor Press 2011), explores design as a set of persuasive, subliminal cultural beliefs. Atzmon is currently co-editing the anthology *The Graphic Design Reader* (2018), with Teal Triggs, and is an editor of the journal *Communication Design*. She was awarded a Fulbright fellowship to London in 2016 to do research on how Darwin used design thinking to conceptualize evolutionary principles. Along with her colleague Ryan Molloy, she was granted a National Endowment of the Arts (NEA) ArtWorks Design grant to support The Open Book Project, which includes a series of experimental book workshops, and the design and production of *The Open Book Project*.

Prasad Boradkar is Professor in Industrial Design at Arizona State University (ASU) in Tempe. He is the Director of InnovationSpace, a transdisciplinary laboratory at ASU, where faculty and students from design, business, sustainability, and engineering partner with corporations to develop product concepts that hold societal benefit and minimize impacts on the environment. He also serves as the Co-Director of the Biomimicry Center at ASU, an organization dedicated to the exploration of biologically inspired solutions to problems of sustainability. Boradkar is the author of *Designing Things: A Critical Introduction to the Culture of Objects* (2010), and is currently working on a book on Indian design.

Betti Marenko's work is located at the intersection of design and philosophy, with particular focus on Gilles Deleuze and Félix Guattari. Her research examines the tensions between design as way of speculating on, and instigating, the future, and thought that addresses materiality, affect, the virtual, and the non-human. Her current research focuses on computation, non-human philosophy and design by critically examining the new contingent logics of digital computation, whose discontinuities are best captured by intuition and minor practices. By examining what she calls "digital uncertainty," Marenko speculates on how algorithm-driven patterns of differentiation and instability are inducing a cognitive shift in what it means to be human. She has worked extensively on the relationship between technologies and magic, and researches animism as a post-human, post-user, post-cognitive narrative of reframing interaction with digital objects in terms of human-non-human relationality. In collaboration with Phil van Allen, Professor of Interaction Design and Media Design Practice at the MFA program Art Center College of Design Pasadena, she has developed the notion of "animistic design" as a key narrative to explore alternative models of interaction with the non-humanity of digital objects. Her work has been published in *Digital Creativity*, *Design Studies*, *Design and Culture*. Marenko is regularly invited to speak around the world. She has lectured at MIT,

CCA San Francisco, IDE Zurich, University of Belgrade, and the University of Urbino. She is Research Leader in the Product, Ceramic and Industrial Design Programme, and Contextual Studies Leader in the BA (Hons.) Product Design at Central Saint Martins (CSM), University of the Arts London. She is co-editor, with J. Brassett, of *Deleuze and Design* (2015).

Peter Hall is a design writer whose research focuses on critical visualization and mapping as a design process. He is Senior Lecturer and Course Leader, BA (Hons) Graphic Design at Central Saint Martins (CSM), University of the Arts London. Prior to moving back to London, Hall was program director of the Design and Design Futures program at Griffith University Queensland College of Art in Australia, and a Senior Lecturer at the University of Texas at Austin. Hall teaches design history and methods and has written and lectured widely on mapping as a metaphor for a spatial approach to design criticism and history, including a TEDx appearance, lectures and seminars at Parsons The New School for Design, New York, and a video in RMIT's Design Futures 10 x 10 symposium, Australia. He also taught at Yale University School of Art, and worked at the University of Minnesota Design Institute, where he wrote and co-edited with Janet Abrams the book *Else/Where: Mapping—New Cartographies of Networks and Territories*. He is one of the founders and a board member of DesignInquiry, a non-profit educational organization devoted to researching design issues at intensive team-based gatherings, based in Maine. He has been a contributing writer for *Metropolis* magazine, and has written widely about design and design education in its various forms for such publications as *Design and Culture*, *Design Philosophy Papers*, *Eye*, *I.D. Magazine*, *The New York Times*, and *The Guardian*. His other books include *Tibor Kalman: Perverse Optimist*, and *Sagmeister: Made You Look*. Between 2012 and 2016, he was a visitor to the Information Security Group at RHUL, where he joined a team researching participatory mapping in cyber security and new approaches to visualizing networks of trust and resilience.

Cameron Tonkinwise is the Professor of Design at the University of New South Wales Art and Design. Previously, he was the Director of Design Studies and Doctoral Studies at Carnegie Mellon University's School of Design. Before that, Tonkinwise was Associate Dean Sustainability at Parsons The New School for Design, New York, and Director of Design Studies at the University of Technology, Sydney. He has a background in continental philosophy and continues to research what designers can learn from philosophies of making, material culture studies, and sociologies of technology. His primary area of research is sustainable design. In particular, Tonkinwise is widely published on the ways in which Service Design can advance Social Sustainability by decoupling use and ownership—what these days is referred to as the "Sharing Economy." He has also been a strong advocate for the importance of critical practice-based design research. Tonkinwise's current focus, in collaboration with colleagues at CMU and an international network of scholar-practitioners, is Transition Design—design-enabled multi-level, multi-stage structural change toward more sustainable futures.

Lyle Owerko is a photojournalist, artist, and filmmaker. Lyle Owerko has documented a diverse range of subjects, from early 80s' neon colored BMX Bikes. However, his most iconic image is the 2001 photograph *The Second Plane*, capturing Flight 175 as it struck the second tower of the World Trade Center on September 11, which appeared on the cover of the September 14, 2001 issue of *Time* magazine, stands as an iconic record of a national tragedy. Often working with human rights organizations, such as Charity: Water and the United Nations Millennium Promise, Owerko frequently merges art with a social mission in his work. His seminal body of work, *The Boombox Project* began in 2005 as documentation of vintage portable stereos and now includes a series of sculptures and a documentary on the subject. In 2010, Abrams Image published a book of those photos, which included a foreword by Spike Lee and interviews of some of the most distinct contributors of that era. Owerko's work is included in the permanent collection of the Library of Congress, and has been exhibited at the Victoria & Albert Museum in London, among other galleries and institutions.

Christine Guth was a Senior Tutor in Asian design in the Victoria and Albert Museum/Royal College of Art postgraduate History of Design Programme in London from 2007 to 2016. She has written widely about the visual and material culture of Japan and its transnational dimensions in publications including *Art, Tea and Industry: Masuda Takashi and the Mitsui Circle* (1993); *Longfellow's Tattoos: Tourism, Collecting and Japan* (2004); and *Hokusai's Great Wave: Biography of a Global Icon* (2015). In her current project, she returns to the study of early modern era, treated in *Art of Edo Japan: The Artist and the City 1615–1868* (1996, 2010), from the perspective of material culture. Projected as a book-length study, "Making Things: Craft in Early Modern Japan" investigates the use of materials, processes of making, and the role of artifacts in social relations during a period that saw the dramatic rise of consumption of all kinds—from needles to tatami mats. The essay in this volume aims to bring both a historically grounded and theoretical perspective to thinking about the needle, an easily overlooked but critical thing that became widely available during this era.

Elizabeth Guffey is Professor of Art and Design History at the State University of New York, Purchase, where she directs the MA in Modern and Contemporary Art, Criticism and Theory. Her area of specialization is nineteenth-, twentieth-, and twenty-first-century art and design history. Her book *Designing Disability: Spaces, Symbols and Signs* (2017) explores the problematic history of the International Symbol of Access (the "disability sign"). Her book, *Posters: A Global History* (2015), reexamines the poster's roots in the nineteenth century, and explores the relevance that it still possesses in the age of digital media. She is also the author of *Retro: The Culture of Revival* (2006). Guffey is the author of numerous articles on design, and is also the founding editor of the peer-reviewed journal *Design and Culture*.

Nina Rappaport is an architectural critic, curator, historian, and educator. She focuses on the intersection of industry, architecture, and infrastructure and the role of the factory worker. She directs *Vertical Urban Factory*, a think tank, which includes a book with Actar of the same name and a consultancy. The project began with an architecture studio at Parsons School of Design in 2008 and a traveling exhibition in 2011 (New York, Detroit, Toronto, London, Brooklyn, Lausanne) that continues to travel. Her exhibition, *A Worker's Lunchbox,* of her films of interviews with factory workers in Philadelphia, was initiated at the Slought Foundation at the University of Pennsylvania in spring 2017. For eighteen years, she has been publications director at Yale School of Architecture, for which she edits the bi-annual magazine *Constructs*, exhibition catalogs, and the studio book series. As a curator she organized the exhibitions *Ezra Stoller: Photographer* in Washington, D.C.; *The Swiss Section* at the Van Alen Institute in New York; and she co-curated *Saving Corporate Modernism* at Yale. She is co-editor of the book, *Ezra Stoller: Photographer,* author of the book, *Support and Resist: Structural Engineers and Design Innovation,* and co-author of the book, *Long Island City: Connecting the Arts* with the Design Trust for Public Space. She has taught industrial urbanism, urban design theory, and architecture studios at Syracuse New York City, Kean University, Parsons School of Design,

Barnard College, City College, and Yale School of Architecture. She has written numerous essays for international journals and magazines and she lectures widely.

Michael J. Golec is Associate Professor of the History of Design at The School of the Art Institute of Chicago. His scholarship focuses on graphic visualization, image theory, and print materiality. He is the author of *Brillo Box Archive: Aesthetics, Art, and Design* (2008), and co-editor of *Relearning from Las Vegas* (2009). Golec has published articles and reviews in *Design and Culture*, the *Journal of Design History*, *Design Issues*, *Senses and Society*, *Cultural Critique*, *American Quarterly*, and *Home Cultures*. His most recent publications include "Re(in)forming Image Space with 'Touch: Sorting Out Desire,'" in *Ultrashort Hyperframe*, and "Facts Between Pictographs and Photographs," in *Zeitschrift für* Ästhetik *und Allgemeine Kunstwissenschaft*.

Giorgio De Michelis is Full Professor of Informatics at the University of Milano–Bicocca, where he teaches Interaction Design and Informatics for Organizations. He served as Head of the Dipartimento di Informatica, Sistemistica e Comunicazione (DISCo) from October 2001 to September 2007. He researches models of concurrent systems (Petri Nets), Computer Supported Cooperative Work, interaction design, and ubiquitous computing. De Michelis is working to understand how Information and Communication Technology (ICT) can contribute to social innovation and economic sustainability, and designing innovative systems in Ubiquitous Computing and the Internet of Things. De Michelis is member of the editorial board of *Computer Supported Cooperative Work: The Journal of Collaborative Computing*, *ACM Computers in Entertainment*, and *Studi Organizzativi*. He is a member of the European Academy of Science and the Istituto di Studi Superiori dell'Insubria Gerolamo Cardano. De Michelis is among the founding members of EUSSET, the European Society for Socially Embedded Technologies, which promotes people-centered design in ICT. De Michelis is Vice-President of Fondazione IRSO, a private Italian research institution that specializes in innovation processes in industry and government, with particular attention to their organizational and technological aspects. He co-directed research on "The Italian Way of Doing Industry" for Fondazione IRSO. Since April 2008, he has been engaged in the design and development of itsme, a radically new Linux-based operating system for workstations, which is part of the "Situated Computing" perspective. De Michelis has authored over two hundred scientific papers and five books. He is co-author of *Design Things*, with Thomas Binder, Pelle Ehn, Giulio Jacucci, Per Linde, and Ina Wagner (2011).

Jan Hadlaw is a historian of technology, communications, and design at York University, Toronto, Canada. She is an Associate Professor in the Department of Design, and holds appointments in the Communications & Culture, Science & Technology Studies, and Art History & Visual Culture graduate programs. Her research interests focus on modern technologies and the imaginaries that have shaped their design and meaning. She is especially interested in twentieth-century technological artifacts, their representation in popular culture, and the roles they played in shaping and advancing modern conceptions of time, space, and identity. Publications include: "'Mysteries of the New Phone Explained': Introducing Dial Telephones and Automatic Service to Bell Canada Subscribers in the 1920s," in E. Imhotep-Jones and T. Adcock (eds), *Science, Technology, and the Modern in Canada* (2018); "Saving Time and Annihilating Space: Discourses of Speed in AT&T Advertising, 1909–1929," *Space and Culture* 14 (2) (2011): 85–113; "The London Underground Map: Imagining Modern

Time and Space," *Design Issues* 19 (1) (2003): 28–35. Hadlaw is a co-editor of *Theories of the Mobile Internet: Materialities and Imaginaries* (2014). She is currently working on research projects examining the interconnections of technology, design, and Canadian national identity.

Matt Soar is Associate Professor and BA Programs Director in the Department of Communication Studies at Concordia University, Montreal. His professional background, prior to entering grad school, was in graphic design and art direction. Since then, he has written extensively about design, visual communication, and cultural production for scholarly and professional audiences. He was the editor of a special issue of *Design & Culture* on Signs and the City (Summer 2010), and co-editor, with Dr. Monika Kin Gagnon, of *Database|Narrative|Archive: An anthology of Seven Interactive Essays on Digital Nonlinear Storytelling* (2013). Recent articles include: "26 ways of thinking about a graphic advocacy poster," in E. Resnick (ed. 2015) *Graphic Advocacy: International Posters for the Digital Age (2001–2012)*, and "Making (with) the Korsakow System: Database documentaries as articulation and assemblage" in C. Summerhayes, C. Hight and K. Nash (2014) *New Documentary Ecologies: Emerging Platforms, Practices and Discourses*. Soar's writing on graphic design has also been published in *Eye*, *Design Observer*, *AIGA Journal of Design*, and *Looking Closer 4*. In terms of research, Lost Leaders (2011 onward) is an archival, scholarly, and artistic exploration of the histories of US film leader standards. Outcomes have included cameraless animations, interactive works, video microscopy, 3-D modeling, and stained glass. Some of this work has screened at *ATA/Other Cinema* (2015), *Poetics & Politics* documentary symposium (2015), the *Montreal Underground Film Festival* (2014), the *Orphan Film Symposium* (Amsterdam 2014, Culpeper VA 2016), and *FUSE #2: Mobile Interactive Microcinema* (Ann Arbor, 2014). Soar is the founding director of the Montreal Signs Project, centered on a growing collection of commercial and wayfinding signs from around the city. Currently he is adapting two "Solari" flight indicators from Mirabel airport for a gallery installation exploring issues of human migration. From 2008 to 2016, Soar was co-developer of the Korsakow System, an opensource software application for digital nonlinear storytelling, particularly web documentaries.

Hugh Dubberly is a partner in Dubberly Design Office (DDO), a San Francisco consultancy that makes platforms and integrated systems of hardware, networked software, and human services easier to use. The practice offers interaction design, service design, and systems design, as well as data visualization. DDO designs and develops software that runs across a range of consumer electronics, handheld devices, and computers. Before forming DDO, Dubberly was Vice President for Design at AOL/Netscape where he managed teams of designers, engineers, editors, and producers creating content and applications for AOL, Netscape, and other AOL properties. At Netscape, he managed daily operation of the company's web site and helped build and manage the team that transformed the web site from a software distribution tool into the first web "portal"—a $150 million business. At Apple from 1985 to 1994, Dubberly managed cross-functional design teams and went on to manage Creative Services, including corporate identity for the entire company. While at Apple, he wrote and produced *Knowledge Navigator*, the first vision video, and a half a dozen of other technology-forecast videos illustrating the future of mobile, networked computers. Dubberly has also held positions as Director of Interface Design for Times-Mirror and Design Director for Wang Laboratories. He also served on Samsung's Global Design Advisor Board. Dubberly has published numerous articles on systems, design methods, human-computer interaction, and service design and wrote a bi-monthly column for ACM's journal, *Interactions*. He also frequently lectures and teaches. He founded and chaired the Computer Graphics Department (now Media Design) at Art Center College of Design in Pasadena. He has taught at San Jose State, IIT/ID, RISD, CMU, CCA, Northeastern (where he is Professor of Practice teaching design theory), and for six years co-taught a systems design course for grad students in the HCI Group in Stanford's Computer Science Department. Dubberly has served on the AIGA's national board, chaired the 1995 ACD Living Surfaces Conference, and co-chaired the 1990 SIGGRAPH Conference Design Committee. In 2012, he was elected to the ACM CHI Academy. He received a BFA in Graphic Design from RISD and an MFA from Yale.

Carl Knappett teaches in the Department of Art at the University of Toronto, where he holds the Walter Graham/Homer Thompson Chair in Aegean Prehistory. He is an archaeologist interested in how things generate meaning through their creation and use. While the things of the Aegean Bronze Age are his main focus, particularly the pottery of Minoan Crete, he attempts to integrate insights from the study of things in ethnographic, ethnoarchaeological and sociological contexts with a view to developing a broad-based approach to materiality in society. Knappett's publications include: *Thinking Through Material Culture* (2005), *An Archaeology of Interaction* (2011), and *Network Analysis in Archaeology* (2013). He conducts fieldwork at various Bronze Age sites across the Aegean, and directs the new excavations at the Minoan town of Palaikastro in east Crete.

Phil Jones is a Principal Lecturer at the Arts University Bournemouth in the United Kingdom. He is Course Leader for both MA and BA(Hons) Graphic Design courses. Jones is an experienced designer who has produced design work for major national and international clients such as Glaxo Welcome and Canon UK, more recently he has designed catalogues, publicity material and books for the University, such as *Word Matters 3*, which was circulated at the Venice Biennale. His practice has involved working across many design disciplines including publishing, corporate design, exhibition design, branding and new media. He is currently investigating ways in which the cognitive-linguistic enterprise, including conceptual metaphor theory and conceptual blending theory, can be applied to graphic design practice—particularly ways in which conceptual metaphors and schematic structure can be instantiated in graphic artifacts. His ongoing practice-based Ph.D. project is entitled "The Bones of the Book: Schematic Structure and Meaning Made from Books." He has served as an external panel member at Course Reviews and is an External Examiner. Jones has contributed to *The Phaidon Archive of Graphic Design* and has published papers on typography and metaphoricity in *Book 2.0*, *Design and Culture*, *Visible Language* and the *Journal of Research Practice*. He has presented papers at international conferences such as "Beyond the Margins," Clare College Cambridge, and "Cognitive Futures in the Humanities," Bangor University. He was a keynote speaker at Paradox in Grenada, and contributed to the Interregional Culture-led Regeneration Interregnum. Jones is a Fellow of the Royal Society of the Arts.

Bill Brown is the Karla Scherer Distinguished Service Professor in American Culture at the University of Chicago, where he teaches in the Department of English Language and Literature, the Department of Visual Arts, the Chicago Center for Contemporary Theory, and the College. He currently serves as Deputy Provost for the Arts, and he has been a co-editor of *Critical Inquiry* since 1993. He published *The Material Unconscious: American Amusement, Stephen Crane, and the Economies of Play* in 1996; edited a special issue of *Critical Inquiry* on "Things" in 2001, with an introductory essay on "thing theory"; and published *A Sense* *of Things: The Object Matter of American Literature* in 2003. His most recent book, *Other Things* (2015), tracks the role of objects among the visual, plastic, and literary arts, and in the fields of anthropology, phenomenology, psychoanalysis, and aesthetics; it analyzes the impact of particular objects, from mechanical banks of the nineteenth century to 9/11 kitsch, from Man Ray's photographs to Dan Flavin's installations and Brian Jungen's assemblages. He is currently at work on "Re-assemblage," developing a relationship between assemblage theory in social and political theory, on the one hand, and assemblage as an art practice, on the other.

Introduction

Design and theories of things

Leslie Atzmon and Prasad Boradkar

Do we really need anything like Thing Theory the way we need narrative theory or cultural theory, queer theory or discourse theory? Why not let things alone?
BILL BROWN 2001: 1

Can one have a theory of things where "things" stand for the most evident category of artifacts both tangible and lasting? Certainly I confess that when I took up a post as a professional academic in the field of material culture studies in 1981, this seemed to be the limit to the ambition of those studies.
DANIEL MILLER 2005: 4

Introduction

As the epigraphs above indicate, we are not certain about why and how we ought to think about the things with which we spend our lives. Things seem to confound us, as do the ideas we conjure to understand them, and the words we use to describe them. Questions of what things are, what they do, how we perceive them and what they mean to us have dogged thinkers at least since the pre-Socratic Greek philosopher Anaximander (c. 610–545 BCE).

The theoretical examination of things is not new, but it seems to have gathered renewed attention in a variety of disciplines, especially in philosophy, anthropology, art and design history, sociology, and literary criticism. Contemporary theories about things are part of "the material turn," a recent groundswell of scholarship about materiality that explores fundamental questions of what things are, what they do, how they relate to each other and to us, how should they be analyzed, and ultimately, why it is worthwhile studying them.

The essays in this anthology are critical examinations of designed objects located in a larger nexus of theories of things. Our intention is to help make theory accessible and relevant to design practitioners, design educators, and design scholars. In order to do so, we put design front and center in the theoretical examination of things. Most of the essays in this collection feature design case studies, which are crucial to our project because they ensure that theoretical principles emerge from, and are rooted in, discussions of design. In these case studies, theory is presented through accessible real-world scenarios to which designers and design scholars can relate.

This book is not just geared to a design audience, however: the essays in *Encountering Things* can inform scholarship in a range of disciplines that engage in the study of objects. Scholars from other disciplines write about things, but they don't typically engage *design*. What does design have to offer theories of things? Literary critic Bill Brown points out that new discourses of material things grew, in fact, not through interest in the things themselves, but by hitching a ride on attendant historical, sociological, or anthropological themes in material culture studies (2001: 6). These investigations typically scrutinize the lives of things in the context of extrinsic factors. Probing the *design* of things, however, susses out the intrinsic qualities of the designer-thing-user-environment complex. In other words, *things and objects* are the central, inevitable media of design; design is, therefore, particularly consequential to theories about things. Investigating the fertile processes through which designed things come into being, and the ways that designed things and objects resonate with those who use them, will provide scholars from other disciplines access to untapped insights into how things operate.

Our intention in this collection is to examine what theories of things mean, *to*, *for*, and *in* design. *Encountering Things* is built on the premise that it is valuable for design to wrestle with theoretical concepts such as agency, networks and biographies of things—concepts that we will explain later in this introduction. Using design case studies, the essays in this collection reveal theoretical insights into the interactions between people and things during design creation and use processes, and after disposal.

Encountering things

In the burgeoning interdisciplinary scholarship about things, Bill Brown's seminal essay "Thing Theory," in the special issue of *Critical Inquiry* (2001), in particular, advanced the fascination with objects across the academy. "Things are what we encounter, ideas are what we project," he writes, quoting Leo Stein in this essay, and referring to the suddenness, presence, and power with which things assert themselves. He offers examples of how we encounter things: "you cut your finger on a sheet of paper, you trip over some toy, you get bopped on the head by a falling nut" (Brown 2001: 3–4). And it is in these moments that the "physicality of things" asserts itself. In this collection, we are inspired by Brown's use of the term "encounter" to explain the relationship between people and things. The root of the word encounter can be traced to Middle English *incounter* and French *encontre*, which are based on Latin terms *in* (in) + *contra* (against). The word "encounter" suggests entities in a relational dynamic with one another, and it is precisely those relationships that this book considers.

Designers are engaged in imagining and materializing encounters between people and products, graphics, buildings, and cities. How someone holds a toothbrush, reads a sign, walks into a building or navigates a city, therefore, are encounters that inform the design process. Designers also devise objects in accordance with certain implicit and explicit intentions, and people use designed objects in their own particular ways. Through these sorts of encounters, design mediates relationships between technology and society, production and consumption—and people and things. Understanding the nature of the mediations between people and things—making sense of these encounters—can help guide design practice. More important, understanding how design mediates such encounters reveals the roles that designers can play in shaping the interactions between people and things.

We feel it is important to point out that the sorts of encounters described here also occur between people and things in the natural world. The "non-human turn," for example, emphasizes relational dynamics among "animals ... bodies, organic and geophysical systems" and humans (Grusin 2015: 1). Human relationships with non-human beings, like animals and forests—like human encounters with designed objects—are encounters that "force us to recognize the fact that seeing, representing, and perhaps knowing, even thinking, are not exclusively human affairs" (Kohn 2013: 1). Although the non-human turn is a fascinating direction, it is beyond the scope of this book. *Encountering Things* limits itself to conversations about non-living things; it excludes non-living natural entities, living organisms (other than people), and large natural systems like forests and ecosystems. The focus here is on the designed things that emerge from active processes of human agency in acts of transformation of ideas into finished products.

Turning to material

Since the Enlightenment, in the West we have tended to divide the world ideologically along material and non-material lines. Western culture has positioned objects: things and bodies—or material entities—as both inferior to and in service to subjects: words, ideas, and the mind—or non-material entities, in an object-subject polarity. The material turn, though, suggests that objects need no longer be deemed secondary to subjects. It asks a crucial question, moreover: if contrast with subjects is no longer a defining characteristic of objects, how do we reconceive objects in their own right? Contemporary theories push for the agency of things and reimagine the roles of material objects in social systems by questioning the object-subject polarity. In "Beyond the Dualist Paradigm," anthropologist Susanne Küchler advises that we may need "a synthesis of opposites, as here between mind and matter, which draws attention to a potentially new way of perceiving the world" (2008: 101).

New investigations that question the object–subject dichotomy have moved toward "the erasure of the familiar conceptual distinctions between the natural and the social, the human and the non-human, and the material and the cultural, divisions that are all in the first place, predicated on the immaterial/material divide" (Joyce and Bennett 2010: 4). Brown asks if we can lift things above the object–subject fray—if we can take them beyond theory—through a new expansive form of object studies, suggesting that things be understood as artifacts with their own substantive currency, and that they be evaluated for more than just their cultural exchange value. Objects are what we "look *through*"; things are what we encounter. Brown equates objects to windows through which we peer to learn what we can about ourselves, our society, our culture, our histories. Things, on the other hand, cannot be looked through; in our encounters, they establish and assert their physicality upon us (as they bop us on the head). In *Other Things* (2015), Brown further develops the notion of thingness and explains it as "amorphous matter, primal stuff, sensations" that exist before the distinction between subject and object appears, and before individual objects such as tables and chairs start to emerge. A thing, according to Brown, "is the outcome of an interaction (beyond their mutual constitution) between subject and object" (2015: 22). The object and subject mutually create each other, and it is in this encounter that the thing emerges. In a very physical sense, things emerge as a result of encounters between the subjects and objects (designers and the artifacts they create while designing) that are engaged in the design process. Most of the essays in this collection revolve around this notion of things and objects in design. Giorgio de Michelis, though, presents an especially rich description of the evolving nature of objects and things as they progress through the design process in his essay for this volume.

Agency and networks

Recent scholarship suggests that things possess power "in their own right as a consequence of their specific material properties ..." (Joyce and Bennett 2010: 5), and that they possess agency (Hoskins 2006; Hicks and Beaudry 2010; Verbeek 2005; Latour 2005; Knappett and Malafouris 2008). Simply expressed, an agent is one who *acts*. The power granted or effected through that action is the quality of *agency*. Archaeologist Chris Gosden, in fact, paints a portrait of how the visual and material forms of things participate in this project: For an object to be socially powerful," he writes, "the *form* [authors' emphasis] of the object lays down certain rules of use which influence the sensory and emotional impacts of the object" (Gosden, 2005). Gosden stresses that the visual and physical forms of things play a critical role in their agency—that is, in shaping people and culture—and in the social lives of things. And design activity, as a process that shapes the very visual and physical forms of things, is a form of cultural practice. Max Bill, director of the legendary German design school *Hochschule für Gestaltung* in Ulm, once explained that design's task is "to participate in the making of a new culture—from a spoon to a city" (Lindinger 1991: 10). In other words, design shapes many of the physical aspects of our living environment, and in this process, contributes in the creation of a material culture.

In addition to being agents, things don't exist in isolation, but instead function in interconnected and dynamic networks as discussed above. In other words, things are not inanimate, discrete objects, but vital entities that possess power to effect change through their material, formal, and functional properties. Imagine things, therefore, not as mute objects, but as active participants that change us and are likewise changed by us during our interactions with them. Apprehending things as dynamic actors that operate within networks of people, other things, and specific situations can offer new insights into the ways designers make and users employ designed objects. This approach adds to our understanding of the interplay between designer and thing: that is, how a thing moves from an idea to an object-in-the-making to a designed object. It emphasizes the dynamic role of all of the actors: the designer and other people who are involved, the constellation of things that are part of the making process, and the environment in which this process unfolds. This approach also encourages investigation of how the aesthetic, material, and functional properties of objects and things play out in a communicative dance with those who use them.

This communication between people and things is reciprocal. Daniel Miller explains that "in material culture we are concerned at least as much with how things make people as the other way around" (Miller 2013: 43). Brown suggests that a new materialism should ask questions about what things do rather than what things are. He quotes Bruno Latour, who proclaims that "things do not exist without being full of people" (Brown 2001: 12). Brown and Miller (and Latour) refer to the reciprocity of agency—the fact that people and things configure each other. The word "configure," derived from Latin *con*, which means with, and *figurare*, which means to shape, suggests that the encounters between humans and non-humans mold each other. What then, is the role of design in this reciprocal relationship in which people and things shape each other? This association between people and things spans across and evolves through processes of production and consumption. As makers of things, designers play a vital role in producing things through processes of researching needs, understanding constraints, generating concepts, refining ideas, finalizing solutions, and manufacturing/constructing finished goods. Consumers play an essential role while consuming things: paying attention to advertising, shopping, and interacting with and then discarding stuff at the end of its "life."

Defined simply, design shapes problems into solutions by translating needs into things and giving form to function. Designers exercise their agency in this process, crafting their intentions into reality in the forms of typefaces, graphic design, products, buildings, landscapes and cities. During design processes, ideas often evolve from sketches to models to prototypes and eventually emerge as things into the world, fully formed with usable features and functions. While a sketch may demonstrate what a building might look like, a model might explain how a person could navigate through that building. While a digital illustration might show the colors and type treatment of a book cover, a printed mockup might give a tangible sense of what it would feel like to hold and read the book. While a virtual rendering of a product simulated using modeling software might show how a product opens and closes, a functional prototype allows consumers to interact with it and get feedback in return. These illustrations and prototypes are design representations, and the higher their fidelity, the closer they are to becoming things. As their features and functions become operational (buildings become habitable, signs readable, products usable), their agency gets activated and their power becomes palpable. This is when they enter people's lives. It is through this process of designing, of configuring, that the agency of things emerges. While a sheet of copper, a pile of bricks and a drum of asphalt have limited agency, it is when they are configured into pots, houses and roads that their agency becomes fully manifest. Design breathes agency into materials through its practice, transforming those materials into things.

As things are configured through the process of design and manufacturing, they gain value. "Value exists because it is generated by a relational act between an object (a thing) that is being evaluated, and a subject (a person) engaged in the process of evaluation" (Boradkar 2010: 49). Value is not a fixed property of things; it is a fluid rather than a static entity; it has multiple meanings rather than a singular one, and therefore it should instead be imagined as aggregate and relational in nature. This implies that it has several components: the value of things can be financial, aesthetic, historical, symbolic, utilitarian, emotional, and so on. Social-cultural anthropologist Arjun Appadurai suggests that "objects circulate in different *regimes of value* in space and time" (Appadurai 1988: 4), so that value is constructed socially by human agency through a series of encounters and interactions over the life of the objects. As things evolve over time, through processes of production, distribution and consumption, their value changes.

In his discussion of the social lives of things, Appadurai suggests that like people, things have social lives and therefore have life stories and biographies (1986). Tracing the trajectory of designed objects and their shifting values throughout their life stories demonstrates that things' journeys from raw materials, to design concepts, to usable products, to landfill waste are complex. Examining these journeys can give us insights into what things mean to people. "Biographies of things can make salient what might otherwise remain obscure" (Kopytoff 1986: 67). Anthropologist Igor Kopytoff recommends that we interrogate things in the same ways we would interrogate people. He suggests that we query things' birth places, their travel through cities, and the nature of their relationships with people and other things as a means of discovering their life stories. These life stories unearth the critical cultural meanings of things.

Theories of things and design

As we noted earlier, scholars from the social sciences and the humanities have been theorizing about objects and things, but not about *design*. In *Things that Talk: Object Lessons from Art and Science*, for example, editor Lorraine Daston lists the things examined in the volume: "Hieronymus Bosch's drawing *The Treeman*, the eighteenth century freestanding column, Peacock Island and the Prussian river Havel, soap bubbles, early photographs entered as courtroom evidence, the Glass Flowers at Harvard, Rorschach blots, newspaper clippings, and certain paintings by Jackson Pollock as seen by critic Clement Greenberg" (2004: 10). It is puzzling that few of these things emerge from processes of design; most are art objects (drawings and photographs) and natural things (rivers and bubbles). Even though the activity of design is clearly central to the lives of objects and things, design is practically absent from contemporary discourse about things. And on those occasions when design is considered in this work, it is usually categorized as "art." Daston, for example, lumps the eighteenth-century freestanding column together with Jackson Pollock paintings. She observes that "thing-making may be rich in surprises relevant to … questions about … significance and salience" (2004: 10) without distinguishing between the complexions of art-making and design-making processes. The authors in her collection also gloss over the fertile possibilities contained in the interactions that take place among objects, things, designers, design processes, and users.

Design and theories of things

Things tend to be generally under-theorized in design and design scholarship. If the objective of design studies (and of design research) is to be self-reflexive, and to critique its practice and its products, then theories of things deserve further investigation in design studies.

Design practitioners often tiptoe around the edge of theory, but rarely jump in. Designing may be understood as a networked activity that includes designers, objects, institutions, machines, and users, and it often begins with a reasonably well-defined design process. Though they may not verbalize it, design practitioners are invariably aware while designing that objects and things float in transient, in-between states. These liminal, amorphous entities are shaped in part by the designers' interactions with the people, environments and materials that in turn become part of the process. Practitioners typically understand that these transient forms that take shape while working are important to a productive design process. Design practitioners are also trained to consider how users will interact with the objects they've designed, and how objects may influence users. These user–object interactions are what Brown and Appadurai characterize as human actors who "encode things with significance" and "things-in-motion that illuminate their human and social context" (Brown 2001: 6). It is clear that there is an unfortunate disconnect between the essential aspects of design practice described above and the thrust of contemporary theory about objects and things. Practitioners typically do not theorize these processes. We hope that engaging with the essays in this collection, which interweave design case studies with theoretical principles, will reveal how theories of things and design can coalesce in practice.

Design scholars and theorists also have frequently sidestepped theories about things, although they have championed the "linguistic" or "cultural" theoretical turns that emerged in art history. Beginning in the late 1980s, art historians rejected nineteenth-century "reflectionist," object-focused art historical models. Jessica Evans and Stuart Hall argue that the "linguistic turn," or "cultural turn," in the social sciences meant that those scholars who analyze visual objects would never return "to the pre-semiotic assumptions of reflectionism" (1999: 2). The evaluation of the aestheticized object in art history, Evans and Hall further explain, has been superseded by theoretical analysis of "visual metaphors and terminologies of looking and seeing" (1999: 2). Design scholars and writers followed suit, fully embracing these tenets of visual theory, and repudiating the "aestheticized object." The linguistic and cultural turns—which claimed that objects are for the most part a collection of user perceptions and responses—led to a repudiation in theoretical discourse of objects in favor of users and their experiences. Design scholars who focus on users and their experiences, then, have yet to address the fertile interrelationships between design and theories of things.

There is burgeoning interest in materiality and the "material turn" in design studies. If designers are to understand the full import of their activity in a blatantly material sense, however, then they need to engage theories of things. It is critical to note that generating a single, comprehensive theory of things is problematic. As anthropologist Christopher Tilley explains, "There is not, and can never be, one 'correct' or 'right' theoretical position which we may choose to study material forms or to exhaust their potential for informing us about the constitution of culture and society" (2006: 10). Research that explores how theoretical examination of things can influence design studies and design practice should be interdisciplinary, and it ought to be situated within the larger domain of social and cultural theory. This interdisciplinary approach will advance design's recognition of the social and cultural significance of the material world; it can also stimulate design's self-reflexivity, and encourage designers to think of things as physical artifacts that are social beings. We decided to edit this collection, in part, because we want to encourage scholars from other fields who write about objects and things to consider design. But we especially want this project to inspire design practitioners and design scholars to immerse themselves in contemporary ideas about objects and things. As Brown asks, "What habits have prevented us—prevented you—from thinking about objects, let alone things?" (2001: 7).

The essays

Things are changing. Building on the new interest in materiality in design studies, this collection foregrounds designed objects—objects conceived and produced through design processes—and designed things—things that are shaped through their interaction with human and non-human forces within a culture. We are not suggesting here that design scholars stress things and objects instead of subjects and experiences. Rather, by emphasizing the roles that things and objects play in thinking, making, and using design, we hope to expand the methods by which we make sense of things and experiences, objects and subjects.

We asked our authors to address the interplay among objects, things, designers, design processes, and users in the context of theory. It occurred to us that the best way to do so was to invite scholars and practitioners to discuss design in the context of theories of things and theories of things in the context of design. Following Bill Brown's provocative suggestion that "thinking and thingness" may not be as distinct as we imagine, the essays in this collection intend to catalyze theory and design practice in new and unexpected ways, and in the process to coalesce thinking and thingness. Things take shape in the interstitial spaces that develop among designers, design processes, design environments and user experiences. We have aimed to offer our readers thought-provoking perspectives on the meanings of things as they emerge during processes of production, distribution and consumption.

Designers, design critics, and design historians often question how theory applies to non-theoretical research or work. We feel that designers tend to spurn theory either because the writing style is too thick and inaccessible or because they fail to see its relevance to their work—or both. We argue above that in design theory, emphasizing "design" is frequently passed over in favor of literary or social scientific theory. Much of this theory, however, subordinates aesthetic and material qualities of objects and things—and the processes by which objects and things are created and used—to concerns such as the exchange of goods, the function of cognitive processes, or the structures of written or spoken language.

In this collection we foreground the constitutive aspects of the aesthetic and material properties of design. We selected a group of international authors with varied backgrounds, across design disciplines, for *Encountering Things*. Our contributors are educators, practitioners, and scholars. They are designers, design critics, photographers, design historians, theorists, philosophers, and anthropologists. All are interested in how theoretical propositions can offer new insights into the processes by which design is created, produced, and consumed. The authors are also drawn to the ways that design can inform and reshape the theoretical principles that describe what things are.

Betti Marenko inaugurates the collection. In her essay, "Filled with wonder: The enchanting androids from cams to algorithms," Marenko examines how people interact with inanimate objects that seem to think or act like sentient creatures. She compares eighteenth-century automatons and contemporary Android devices—both actors in what she describes as an imaginative material genealogy of technology. Whether they are mechanical or digital, Marenko argues, these devices provoke questions about both the artificiality of life and the intelligence of machines. For Marenko, mechanical and digital devices juxtapose the intellectual capabilities of machines against the artificial nature of human life. These automatons were devices that sparked debates about and experiments on the boundaries between living and non-living beings in the eighteenth century.

Marenko next discusses the idea of automatons as so-called "thick things," which, she argues, embody the multiple divergent perspectives of those who design, produce, and use them. As "thick things" both eighteenth-century androids and contemporary Android devices enmesh materiality and meanings. During the Enlightenment, Marenko writes, the metaphor for technological innovation was philosopher Rene Descartes' notion that the whole universe—including the human body—works like a clock and, and like a clock, depends solely on mechanical functioning. Today's pervasive computational metaphor of processing speed and miniaturization, she continues, has become the byword for technology. It's also a common model for the brain in the neurosciences and cognitive sciences. Marenko points out that as we shape technology, technology also shapes us.

Androids from the eighteenth century and today's Android smartphone share a name, but they have yet another kinship: the capacity of machines to have lives of their own that in turn impact our lives. Whether by mechanical or digital means—by cams or by codes—they both exemplify how fluid the boundary is between human and machine. Eighteenth-century androids brought up philosophical questions about living and non-living beings; the contemporary Android device does not simulate life—rather it underpins everyday living in the digital age. However, if eighteenth-century androids were experimental animated objects that prompted questions about humanity, Marenko speculates, then today's Androids must be more than just indispensable connectivity devices. They too, she writes, are experimental animated objects that embody a dazzling manifestation of enchantment in our machine-permeated culture.

In "When objects fail: Unconcealing things in design writing and criticism," Peter Hall brings to life the significance of designed objects and things that are unable to perform to our expectations. He points out that despite the longstanding discussion about the discrepancies between things and objects, design discourse typically presents isolated static objects in magazines and exhibitions without any consideration of their thingly aspects. Hall suggests that one way to put theories of things to use in design criticism is to investigate failed objects. He draws upon ideas from Bruno Latour, Michel Serres, and Martin Heidegger, as well as from Brown's observation that we can look *through* objects, but that things that fail us "can hardly function as a window." When we investigate why design fails, Hall argues, design criticism moves away from its obsession with design styles and designer biographies toward forms of analysis that divulge the design thing (see Chapter 2). Hall suggests that design writing's focus on style can be traced to three factors: form, the separation between object and subject, and admiration for the present. Hall then asks how we might move design away from its interest in current styles, and instead stress and affirm the thingly aspects of objects. Hall's essay pushes design criticism to consider objects not merely at the moment that they are freshly unwrapped, but as things throughout their lives—especially when they fail.

To begin to tackle these questions, Hall turns to Latour's *We Have Never Been Modern* (1993). Our ways of understanding the world in the West since the Enlightenment have separated the human sphere from the non-human sphere. According to Latour, matters of fact attain objectivity through human and non-human actors who come together to negotiate their interests. Negotiation strengthens the alliance among these actors. When the human sphere is disengaged from the non-human sphere, Hall points out, we end up forfeiting vital information that comes out of the relationships between human behavior and the behavior of the world of things.

Using case studies of design failures—the Challenger and Columbia space shuttle disasters, the Aramis personal rapid transit system, the Concorde airplane, and the Node chair—Hall sidesteps the three delimiting factors mentioned above in order to extricate the things from the objects under discussion. He concludes by pointing out that fundamentally social and technological matters are not separate.

Giorgio De Michelis also relates social matters with objects and things through actor networks in "What design tells us about objects and things." He builds upon Heidegger's explanation of the English word "thing," and its ancient Germanic root "Ding," which means governing assembly. Assemblies, according to Heidegger, operate as things. But, says De Michelis, in order to understand how assemblies function as things, first we need to distinguish between objects and things, and design offers a mechanism by which to understand this distinction. Design presents a unique opportunity to comprehend the thing/object problem, because when design starts, the thing is yet to come into being. For De Michelis, this is when the thing is in the background, as designers are creating objects. The design object can be envisioned as an evolving web of things created, imported or modified by designers. Turning to Bruno Latour and John Law's Actor Network Theory (ANT), De Michelis argues that thingness doesn't emerge in opposition to objectness. He explains that objects and things emerge together, and that we can't perceive one without the other coming up. In other words, we become aware of thingness when we perceive the complexity of objects—thingness brings about the complexity of objects.

As a case study, De Michelis cites a scene from the film *Apollo 13* in which a dangerous technical failure forces the team to contrive a method to make the command module's square filters work in the lunar module's round receptacles. The Earth and space teams, in essence, become an actor network that together solves the life-threatening situation. De Michelis ends by reaffirming the notion that, like the Apollo 13 team, designers first imagine new possibilities and then find ways to frame them. In doing so, they access the things behind familiar objects, and these things suggest new ways of acting and interacting.

Prasad Boradkar and Lyle Owerko's "Big things: The vibrant culture of boomboxes" also deals with ways of acting and interacting. This visual essay features striking images of boomboxes—which are 1990s' portable cassette and radio players with carrying handles—from Owerko's personal collection. Because they could be carried, boomboxes could bring together people as a community—as in Heidegger's sense of a thing as a gathering. Boomboxes were designed to be visible, and to be played loudly and publicly. Often large in size and outfitted with amplifiers to generate high volume, these devices offered the individuals who used them, and who participated in a community of listeners, a sense of empowerment. Boomboxes, Boradkar and Owerko argue, are not dead objects but are rather, borrowing Jane Bennett's term, "vibrant things." Both their designs and their uses gave boomboxes vitality and agency. In other words, they possessed power, agency, and a life of their own, but they also gave the people who used them a sense of power and aliveness. The authors wrap up the essay by noting that, unlike the boomboxes of the 1980s, contemporary portable audio devices are small and private. Contemporary music consumption is largely individualized: listeners use digital audio players, smartphones, and earbuds. The highly social and socialized boomboxes that were used on the street are now secluded silent things held in collections.

Like Boradkar and Owerko, Christine Guth considers the interconnectedness of social matters and technology in "Theorizing the *hari kuyō*: The ritual disposal of needles in early modern Japan." Guth argues that thing theory's Western-derived form of ontological distinction between subject and object doesn't apply well to the character of relationships between people and things in Japan. She argues that, according to Brown, the failure of a design object accentuates the distinction between thing and user, while in Japanese culture the failure of a design object draws attention to the animistic qualities that liken the thing to the user. Guth explains that this cultural attitude comes out of the syncretic Shinto-Buddhist belief system that humans and non-humans are in a repetitive cycle of birth, death, and rebirth.

Guth uses Latour's Actor Network Theory (ANT) to explicate needle disposal rituals—or *hari kuyō*—and the creation and use processes of needles in Japan. She presents the needles as dynamic instruments that participate in networked interactions including the materials from which they are made and their manufacturing processes, how they are used and disposed, as well as the cultural discourses around them. In this discussion of the social lives of needles, Guth demonstrates how needles share the gendered and hierarchical social spaces and potentialities of sentient beings. She considers the needle as a technology and a designed object at once. ANT, she concludes, draws out discursive meanings about the needle's materials, production, and uses. ANT chronicles the needles' complex relationships to those who make them and use them, and it discloses the social life of a mundane thing.

In her essay, "Making things, things," architectural critic Nina Rappaport reveals the complex relationships and social lives of things in the factory. Rappaport's essay focuses on production. And in factory production, she explains, ANT plays out as an orchestration among designers, production engineers, workers, things, and machines—human and non-human actors that are involved in processes of making. Production also relies on interaction and feedback among all of these actors. Appadurai examines how the meanings of things "are inscribed in their forms" (Appadurai 1986: 5). Things evolve, according to Appadurai, so that they are given value by those who are involved in making them—a notion that enhances the roles of designers and workers in the production of things, according to Rappaport.

Although long-distance mass production has for quite some time been the typical manufacturing paradigm, in the twenty-first century the manufacturing process is becoming more collaborative and localized. Many industrial designers have intensified their involvement with local production, strengthening the divide between creating and making. Designers are engaging factory workers and manufacturers in new ways and as collaborative partners through processes of conceptualization, planning and production. The workers utilize various areas of expertise that then become a part of what they are making. Rappaport argues that worker innovations typically occur in the gaps between the original design, the manufacturing process, and the product's circulation in society. She presents several interesting examples, including New York-based industrial designer Rama Chorpash's wire potato masher project, as well as the Long Island City, New York Steinway piano factory's "continuous improvement" processes, during which industrial engineers routinely bring in a group of workers for discussions of issues and opportunities.

Rappaport then questions why most workers aren't recognized for the production of things, and asks how workers may gain agency in an actor network. She wonders what happens if a design is improved by the fabricator, or if the prototype is different from the original thing. Finally, she wonders if a thing that is created by a designer can be what the designer intended it to be if the manufacturing process changes it. The workers' input is a commodity that increases labor-value, Rappaport concludes, but it's also a representation of a new ethical consciousness about where things come from and where they go.

Michael Golec examines the interdisciplinary collaboration that led to Ray and Charles Eames's innovative designs for World War II laminated orthopedic splints and subsequent laminated seats in "Distributing stresses: The development and use of the Eames dining chair metal." The Eames laminated seats supported the postwar "American body" and psyche, paralleling how their laminated splints supported wounded bodies in World War II. Golec describes this process as an alliance between "aesthetics, medics, and therapeutics."

Focusing on the how things become transformative when they are enlisted into environmental services in life, Golec foregrounds the idea of "media in action." He argues that material culture studies has overlooked essential ideas that theories of things have laid bare about the lives of things: that things carry meaning and significance that embody human thinking and belief systems. In particular, Golec considers the addition of rubber shock mounts to both splints and chairs as things that function in these three ways. Thanks to the shock mount, he writes, wood and tubular metal can be as pliable as the human body. His essay demonstrates the alliances between splints and chairs as designs that shared rubber shock mounts, and as designs that attended to both wartime and postwar healing. These splints and chairs have agency—they are things that reveal the realm of human interaction, and they therefore comprise missing material in the production of social spheres.

Cameron Tonkinwise likewise considers the claim that things have agency in "The practically living weight of convenient things." He offers an "anticipatory" response to the statement "things have agency" suggesting that things are more than inert entities, and that they also have traits that are like agency. He considers three aspects of the anticipatory claim that things have agency:

a) Animating: The motivations behind and processes by which designers make agential things.

b) Practicing: The everyday activities that interconnect things in ways that give them agency.

c) Gravity: Recharacterizing a) and b) using a … material metaphor in order to escape a language-dominated version of the agency of things.

In the section on animating, Tonkinwise asks why humans make useful things. He disengages the notion that objects increase efficiency for their users from the inherently inefficient process of conceiving and making objects. Tonkinwise discusses how scholar Elaine Scarry portrays making as an animistic process that takes place in two stages: Making-Up and Making-Real. Animism is the agency of made-up then made-real things—created in reaction to severe pain—that makes living less painful, according to Scarry. Making a chair, for example, is a material response to the pain associated with continuous standing or walking. In the section on practicing, Tonkinwise argues that minor "pains" (such as water dribbling onto a person from the lip of a cup), and severe "pain" (such as torture using common household implements) are actually equal provocations for creating "convenient things."

Tonkinwise contends that "convenient things" are "made-real" as part of a regularized practice in which users collaborate with things that "come alive" and participate. Convenient things have force once they are located in a collection of people and things. Things that offer convenient ways of operating are not neutral, they attract users. He wraps up his essay by reaffirming that making convenient things that have agency is the purview of design, and that designed things function jointly with humans. The result, he contends, is a "convenient practice," a series of routinized cooperative acts between people and convenient things.

Both Brown and Latour call attention to quality of thingness and agency when objects fail physically. In "The modern american telephone as a contested technological thing, 1920–39," Jan Hadlaw argues that, along with physical breakdowns—such as falling off a desk or succumbing to mechanical fatigue—things can also fail aesthetically or as objects of status. In this case, the cultural and social usefulness of an object declines. In the early twentieth century, this is precisely what happened with telephones in the United States.

Hadlaw contends that the Bell candlestick telephone is a thing that is understood one way by the engineers who designed it, and a thing that is understood in a very different way by the consumers who used it. She explains that devices have multiple states of being, and can be therefore be considered or perceived in myriad ways as a range of different things. To Bell engineers, the candlestick phone's "sober machinic appearance" represented serious technological form and function. This phone was a scientific instrument—another component in the network of cables and transmitters, along with Bell employees. Consumers, on the other hand, Hadlaw points out, saw their phones as desk accessories, and they felt that the candlestick phone was ungainly and "ugly." Although it was against the lease terms for Bell service, consumers bought and used what they felt to be visually attractive non-Bell phones. Yet Bell resisted changing the visual aspects of their phone. This conflict persisted, however; Bell ultimately hired industrial designer Henry Dreyfuss to create a new phone under very tight constraints that were imposed by Bell engineers. Hadlaw concludes by applying Latour's notion that designing artifacts requires understanding them as "complex assemblies of contradictory issues." Her essay shows how, in the early twentieth century, the Bell candlestick telephone offered two sets of contested meanings that ultimately had to be negotiated.

Matt Soar's visual essay, "Memory, materiality, and the Montreal Signs Project" negotiates memorable, archived, or rescued signage in Montreal. His project, a research undertaking that is dedicated to investigating and rescuing defunct signage, presents Concordia University's Monsieur Hot Dog lounge, named after a sign hanging nearby that once was used for a closed poutine joint. He also discusses signs that once belonged to the Monkland Tavern in the Notre-Dame-de-Grâce church neighborhood, Warshaw's Supermarket from the formerly working class, residential the Plateau neighborhood, and signage from the 1975 Montréal-Mirabel International Airport that was designed by Papineau-Gérin-Lajoie. To Soar, the project is not merely about signs. Instead, it is an attempt to consider signs in new ways, to use them as mechanisms to aid memory, recall the past and reveal unexpected cultural connotations. Soar's essay also features images of other signs from the Project: Sheinart's family-owned women's clothing store near Atwater Market, Montreal from 1995, La Belle Province Meat Co. from the late 1960s, Librarie Guérin bookstore from 1973, and Café Navarino from 1969. Soar explains that this project is about dematerialization, about absence or lack, as much as it is about materiality and physical presence. And the signs he collects and holds testify to the notion that the meanings we glean from things need to be understood in context rather than as stand-alone objects.

In "Connecting things: Broadening design to include systems, platforms, and product-service ecologies," Hugh Dubberly discusses how contemporary design processes have "dematerialized" by shifting from making things to creating value out of networks of things. While cultural studies is turning toward material objects, design practice is shifting in a direction that can be referred to as an *immaterial turn* which is less interested in physical things and more interested in the connections between them. Dubberly considers situations in which:

1. Organizations are finding that opportunities for creating new value lie primarily in connecting products to services and experiences.
2. Design discourse increasingly recognizes that things are connected to ideas; that artifacts are tied to use, meaning, and context; and that design practice is bound up in language and conversation. And
3. New technologies are connecting things to data networks and complex systems that analyze the data, learn from it, and act on what they learn.

The essay begins with a historical outline of the ways in which objects have shifted from being scarce artifacts to abundant identical commodities. Dubberly argues that when products become commodities there is a push by manufacturers to find ways to make them unique. Services have recently become a way to make products stand out and increase their value. Dubberly cites several examples of product-service systems ecologies, including Apple's iPhone and Amazon's Kindle-Reader-Whispernet-Store system, systems that gather people, devices, software applications, and services. These product-service gatherings, the author points out, need to be designed. Designing isn't just making things, then, it also requires building in what designers learn though trial and error that both involves a constellation of things, and also has clear ultimate goals.

Dubberly observes that, over the past fifty years, design practice has shifted away from giving form to objects to a focus on design thinking. Practice has moved from producing designed objects for clients to collaborative discussions about what should be made. Customers are also beginning to participate in platforms with businesses, organizations, and other customers through which they can engage to consider products and policies. Dubberly cites mathematician Danny Hillis's notion of the "Age of Entanglement," a contemporary cultural paradigm under which technology moves from methods that control single-variable problems to processes that consider complex, multivariate problems. Designing systems and product-service ecologies means that things will need to be connected and that designers must think in systematic terms. Dubberly explains in his conclusion that designers must consider the relationships among all participants when designing systems, and they will also need to be able to design platforms that others can then use to design relationships.

Carl Knappett writes about the design of relationships between ineffable entities and their material substitutes in "Designing things as 'poor' substitutes." He discusses three anthropomorphic 4,000-year-old male figurines from a site in Palaikastro, Crete. Two of the figurines, found in a mountain sanctuary, are small and "crude" representations of worshippers. Based on its exotic materials, exquisite craftsmanship, and relative scale, the third figure likely represents a male deity. Called a "kouros," it was found at the settlement of Palaikastro, rather than at the peak sanctuary.

All of these figurines, Knappett argues, work as material substitutes for invisible forces. He ponders the two different calibers of figurines, asking if the third figure is a well-designed substitute, while the first two are just sloppy, 'poor' substitutes. The answer, Knappett suggests, can be found in design, which he characterizes as human ability to conceive, plan, and make products that are used by people. Knappett argues that the potency of both sorts of figurines comes from the ways that they are designed objects that function as surrogates. According to philosopher Andy Clark's "extended mind" hypothesis—in which objects in the environment function as a part of the mind—"surrogate situations" are real objects that stand in for aspects of other specific situations or things. In this manner, surrogacy helps people comprehend conceptual phenomena, by piggy-backing them onto a real-world structure. As an example of surrogacy from design, Knappett cites yet-to-be realized buildings, which are commonly represented by material surrogates such as architectural models. Prototypes, sketches, or storyboards that are seemingly unfinished or rough, he argues, are commonly utilized as steps toward an outcome, but they also represent aspects of that outcome.

Knappett next considers surrogate religious artifacts that represent fundamentally ineffable entities. The Bronze-age figurines that are investigated in this essay, he argues, should be understood as religious artifacts that play a "substitutional role" in "surrogate situations." The worshippers utilized them as material objects that evoked their gods in a cognitive process that parallels the ways that design prototypes function as cognitive props for a future object. Drawing on Clark's ideas, Knappett concludes that the most effective design prototypes and religious artifacts represent the objects for which they are substitutes by eliminating concrete detail. This lack of detail seems to enable the kind of abstract human thought that connects surrogate objects to the yet-to-be-produced things or ineffable entities that they represent.

Phil Jones likewise focuses on how design artifacts enable human thought and action in "The graphic thing: Ambiguity, dysfunction, and excess in designed objects." Jones interprets Brown's definition of things and objects through the lens of George Lakoff and Mark Johnson's "embodied realism," in which our bodies mediate the production of meaning. Jones thus presents both things—entities that we cannot perceive or know directly—and objects—entities that we can know and interpret—as embodied mental formulations. The ambiguity of things, Jones argues, may be partly due to how "thingness" in graphic design objects correlates to perception of a thing's materiality and transparency. Jones presents examples that flesh out his ideas, including Paul Elliman's typeface *Bits*, Mervyn Kurlansky's *Krazy Kaps*, Stephen Johnson's undergraduate project on emergence, Richard Olsen's book *Double Bind*, and Muji objects. *Double Bind* is designed so that both the book spine and fore-edge—the page edges— are sealed, which keeps the user from accessing the book's interior. This inherent dysfunction calls attention to the book as a thing.

Jones ends by arguing that there can be issues around thingness in human perception, for example, where there is dysfunction or contradiction, or where there is not enough sensorimotor data to resolve the thing at hand; or conversely, when there is too much sensorimotor data so that the thing becomes overwhelming. He also points out that that things call attention to themselves because they resist clear characterization, but things also become the focus of attention when they interrupt human activity. Things and thingness can therefore, according to Jones, be understood as by-products of perception—of meaning construction processes—rather than as qualities that exist independent of human agency.

Elizabeth Guffey also considers meaning construction processes in her essay "Nothingness in April Greiman's *Does It Make Sense?*". She contemplates meanings in both the creation and use of Greiman's revolutionary poster, which was commissioned for issue number 133 of the journal *Design Quarterly* in 1986 (DQ 133). Graphic designer Greiman, Guffey argues, used what was brand-new computer technology in 1986 as a tool to investigate notions of materialization and dematerialization. The designer also explores "thingness"—and what Guffey calls "no-thingness"—through the poster's format and content.

In a 1987 interview, Greiman takes great pains to emphasize that *Does It Make Sense?* was designed as a three-dimensional thing, which was clearly important to the design, Guffey notes, yet design historians have ignored both the slipcase and they ways that users access the piece as it is unfolded. When the piece is photographed flat, only on one side, it loses palpable content. Guffey details how—as the poster is unfolded—the visual content is revealed piece-by-piece. This whole experience, beginning with the slipcase and moving to the poster, reveals thingly parts of the content and a thingly experience of the piece.

Greiman "dematerialized" things to make this poster: she began with photographs or videos of physical things. When these things became electronic blips and pulses, Guffey writes, they gave up their physical forms. The project, though, returned to physical form once again. It was finally composed physically using "tiling"—which entails digitally dividing up a large project into pieces so that each "section" fits on smaller sheets of printer paper. The project was tiled so that it could be printed piece-by-piece on Greiman's Image Writer II dot-matrix printer: the first draft of the poster was printed on individual letter-sized pages. The pieces were assembled by a professional offset printer for the final photostat photography, resulting in the finished 76 x 26-inch camera-ready art that would be used to offset print the final poster.

In any format, this poster should be a pivotal marker for histories of digital media, but seen in person, Guffey explains, it also bridges a key moment in our understanding of materiality and immateriality. Read appropriately, as an early attempt to understand material and immaterial things, and the concept of digital "no-thingness," Greiman's poster continues to make good sense. The real question, Guffey asks, is how can it be understood so it makes the best sense?

Prasad Boradkar wraps up the essays with "Agency and counteragency of materials: A story of copper." The essay ventures into *tambat ali* (coppersmith lane), situated in the heart of the city of Pune in western India, where a small craft community has resided for over 300 years. In *tambat ali* people and things, humans and non-humans, are entangled in a complex web of social and technological interactions. The humans are craftspeople, who over several generations have been fabricating a variety of things like coins, vessels, and religious statues from copper; and the artifacts, tools, machines, and factories make up the non-humans of the "community." Copper appears in the name of the community (*tamba* means copper in the local language Marathi), but it is also essential to the identity and survival of the members of this crafts cluster. Using hand tools and powered machines, the craftspeople exercise their creative agency on the copper to shape it into beautiful and useful things, while the material responds with a counter-agency that partially resists their efforts. Copper is too hard to be easily bent into a desired form simply by hand, but soft enough to be shaped into vessels and other goods when subjected to the concentrated and exaggerated force of tools and machines. Copper also exercises its own agency in the absence of humans—it propels heat and electricity through its body, it reveals a luster of its own, it binds with oxygen under the right conditions to form a green patina, it resists bacterial growth, and it is believed to impart medicinal properties to things with which it comes in contact.

The *tambats* know copper; they know how it resists and responds to their hands and tools; they have learned the mechanisms by which they can coax it into the things they intend it to become. It is in the interaction between human agency and material counteragency that things emerge. In a series of highly specialized processes, and in the deft hands of the craftspeople in *tambat ali*, flat sheets of copper are transformed into vessels and other everyday things of use. It is this chain of operations in all its sociotechnical complexity, often referred to as *chaîne opératoire*, that gives the finished copper goods a form, a biography, a history, a social life. Boradkar's essay then presents a brief visual and verbal exposition of the agency and counter-agency of copper through the biography of one unique vessel, a water carafe.

Conclusion

Things and objects—and the rich relationships between them and us—demand theoretical scrutiny from the discipline of design. It turns out that thinking about how objects interact with human subjects, and how they change, reconfigure, and refashion each other enriches how we designers experience our perpetual dance with the things and objects in our orbits. The process of theorizing things needs to draw from design, and the benefits of this effort can extend across other disciplines as well. Media and cultural studies can supplement their analyses of the production of media forms with knowledge of design processes. In their study of everyday life and culture, anthropology and material culture can gain a better understanding of the roles played by design and designed goods in processes of production, exchange and consumption. Theories of things generated in close conversation with design studies can complement and build upon those in the humanities and social sciences, further advancing the increasing engagement between all disciplines engaged in the examination of matter.

If we imagine the lives of things progressing through production, distribution, and consumption cycles, then the humanities and social sciences intercept them in the last stage when they enter everyday use. In other words, things typically have been interpreted as objects of consumption, post-production and post-distribution. Much of the work on things and objects from these disciplines, though, makes scant (if any) references to design. Design research, on the other hand, also examines things in the earlier stages of their lives—during production and distribution. In order to produce comprehensive cultural biographies of things, we need to study them through their entire lifecycles (of production, distribution, and consumption) as well as through a variety of disciplinary lenses. Scholarship about things, therefore, needs to be interdisciplinary; and it needs to inhabit the space of inquiry in which the humanities, social sciences and design studies intersect. Our hope is that the essays in this collection will make theories of things accessible and relevant to design practitioners, educators, and scholars. We also intend that this volume demonstrates the kinds of inquiry that designers can offer those engaged with theories of things.

Bibliography

Appadurai, A. (1986), "Introduction: Commodities and the Politics of Value," in Arjun Appadurai (ed.), *The Social Life of Things*, Cambridge: Cambridge University Press.

Appadurai, A. (ed.) (1986), *The Social Life of Things: Commodities in Cultural Perspective*, Cambridge: Cambridge University Press.

Bennett, J. (2010), *Vibrant Matter: A Political Ecology of Things*, Durham, North Carolina: Duke University Press.

Bennett, T. and P. Joyce (2010), "Material Powers: An Introduction," in T. Bennett and P. Joyce. (eds), *Material Powers: Cultural Studies, History, and the Material Turn*, London: Routledge.

Boradkar, P. (2010), *Designing Things: A Critical Introduction to the Culture of Objects*, Oxford: Berg Press.

Brown, B. (2001), "Thing Theory," *Critical Inquiry* 28 (1): 1–22.

Brown, B. (2016), *Other Things*, Chicago: University of Chicago Press.

Daston, L. (2004), *Things that Talk: Object Lessons from Art and Science*, New York: Zone Books.

Evans, J. and S. Hall, (eds) (1999), *Visual Culture: The Reader*, New York: The Open University.

Gosden, C. (2005), "What Do Objects Want?," *Journal of Archaeological Method and Theory* (12) 3: 193–211.

Grusin, R. (2015), *The Nonhuman Turn* (21st Century Studies), Minneapolis: University of Minnesota Press.

Harmon, G. (2005), *Guerilla Metaphysics: Phenomenology and the Carpentry of Things*, Chicago: Open Court.

Henare, A., M. Holbraad, and S. Wastel (2007) *Thinking through Things: Theorizing Artefacts Ethnographically*, London: Routledge.

Hicks, D. and M. C. Beaudry (2010), "Introduction. Material Culture Studies: A Reactionary View," in D. Hicks and M. C. Beaudry (eds), *The Oxford Handbook of Material Culture Studies*, 1–21, Oxford: Oxford University Press.

Knappett, C. and L. Malafouris (2008), *Material Agency: Towards a Non-Anthropocentric Approach*, New York: Springer Science+Business Media LLC.

Kohn, E. (2013), *How Forests Think: Toward an Anthropology Beyond the Human*, Berkeley: University of California Press.

Kopytoff, I. 1986. "The Cultural Biography of Things: Commoditization as Process," in A. Appadurai (ed.), *The Social Life of Things: Commodities in Cultural Perspective*, Cambridge: Cambridge University Press.

Küchler, S. (2008), "Technological Materiality: Beyond the Dualist Paradigm," *Theory Culture Society*, 25: 101–20.

Lamb, J. (2011), *The Things Things Say*, Princeton, NJ: Princeton University Press.

Latour, B. (2005), "From Realpolitik to Dingpolitik: How to Make Things Public," in B. Latour and P. Weibel (eds), *Making Things Public: Atmospheres of Democracy*, 14–41, Cambridge, MA: MIT Press.

Law, J. (1992), "Notes on the Theory of the Actor-Network: Ordering, Strategy and Heterogeneity," *Systems Practice* 5: 379–93.
Lindinger, H. (1991), *Hochschule für gestaltung (Ulm, Germany)*, trans. David Britt, Cambridge, MA: MIT Press.
Miller, D. (1994), *Material Culture and Mass Consumption*, Oxford: Blackwell.
Miller, D. (2005), "Materiality: An Introduction," in D. Miller (ed.), *Materiality*, Durham: Duke University Press.
Miller, D. (2013), *Stuff*, Cambridge: Polity.
Tilley, C. (2006), "Theoretical Perspectives," in C. Tilley, K. Webb, S. Kuechler, M. Rowlands, and P. Spyer (eds), *Handbook of Material Culture*, London: Sage.
Verbeek, P. (2005), *What Things Do: Philosophical Reflections on Technology, Agency, and Design*, University Park, PA: Pennsylvania State University Press.
Williams, R. (1989), *The Politics of Modernism: Against the New Conformists*, London: Verso.

1

Filled with wonder

The enchanting android from cams to algorithms

Betti Marenko

Instruments have a life of their own. They do not merely follow theory; often they determine theory, because instruments determine what is possible, and what is possible determines to a large extent what can be thought.
HANKINS AND SILVERMAN, *INSTRUMENTS AND THE IMAGINATION* (1995)

We are the androids
PIERRE JAQUET DROZ'S WRITING AUTOMATON (1770S)

Introduction

In the eighteenth century, androids mesmerized audiences with their astounding spectacle of movement and life like abilities. These masterpieces of engineering, "mechanical marvels, clockwork dreams" (Schaffer 2013), could move, play an instrument, write, even breathe, exactly like—and sometimes even better than—a human being. Today, the Android OS (Operating System), powering over a billion hand-held devices all over the world, astonishes with its memory, processing speed, and sheer computational power, all ungraspable by the human mind.

This chapter brings together these two types of androids: the eighteenth-century humanoid automata, and the contemporary Android-powered digital devices. The idea is that, although culturally and historically specific, these two types of androids have traits in common. Both eighteenth-century and contemporary androids are framed by and reflect ideas about the power of technology to enchant and delight, and to make us think. Both kinds of androids pose questions about what it means to be human in a world populated by machines that exceed human mental and physical capabilities. Mechanical or digital, both sorts of devices captivate with their capabilities, while prompting questions about the shifting boundary between the artificiality of life and the intelligence of machines.[1]

My investigation in this essay of the material and symbolic role played by androids in pre-industrial times can offer insights into how to rethink imaginatively our relationships with digital objects. This relationship is currently dominated by the twin technoscientific paradigms of dematerialization and perma-connectivity—the idea that devices require less and less material to operate, and the constant "online" status we now inhabit. We have come to expect (and demand) unlimited connectivity wherever and whenever; as digital devices and their components become increasingly miniaturized and more powerful, this connectivity takes place by largely invisible means. Our digital experience, mediated solely by omnipresent screens, seems to have dispensed with our perception of materiality in these experiences. The enchantment of our digital encounters, with flows of data appearing instantaneously as if by magic, is due to a great extent to our sense of the immateriality, invisibility and immediacy of these media.

To counteract this narrative, this essay locates "digital enchantment" within a history of the ways that technology produces "awe." This essay argues that both eighteenth-century and contemporary androids belong to a lineage of the "instruments of the imagination" (Hankins and Silverman 1995), an *imaginative*, yet *material* lineage of things that, by making us think, shapes who we are (Riskin 2003a). This gesture implies that there is nothing terribly new in the wonder that is inspired by our digital experiences. It imagines a *fil rouge*—a common thread—connecting the cams of the wondrous eighteenth-century androids to the codes of the Android phone. The eighteenth-century androids offered as enchanting an experience to their users as the twenty-first-century mix of technology and magic offers today.

Still, tempting as it might be to assert an unbroken lineage between Jacques de Vaucanson's androids[2]—to this day reputed the most astonishing automata ever created—and Android-run digital devices, we must be cautious.[3] The history of automata shows that our relationship with things that move and seem intelligent is more complicated and troubling than it appears to be. The lineage that I propose in this essay will reflect these complications.

Automata as eloquent metaphors

> All the questions that we ask now about computers, can it play chess, can it think independently, will it take over, were asked of mechanical automata. Gradually, however, clockwork suffered the fate of all technologies. Inspiring awe and fear when it was barely understood, then curiosity, it came gradually to seem trivial. (Hill 1992: 8)

Diderot's *Encyclopedie* (1751) defines *automaton* as a "device that moves by itself, or a machine that carries in itself the principle of its motion."[4] While this term refers to all sorts of moving machines, the word *android* is specific to humanoid automata: "an automaton in the figure of a human, which by means of certain well-arranged springs, etc., acts and performs other functions outwardly similar to those of a man" (Landes 2011: 50).

Automata are deemed crucial to the development of ideas about the relationship between human and machine—the way we think about the interaction between technology and us. Automata are eloquent metaphors for how changes instigated by technological innovations

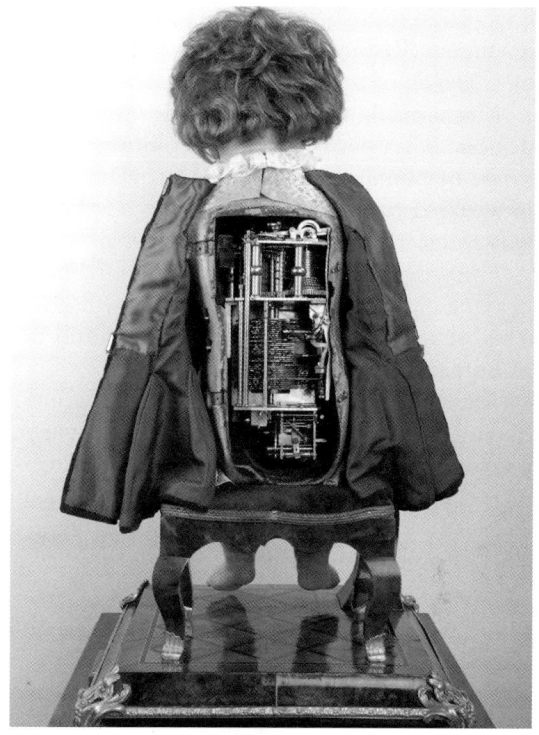
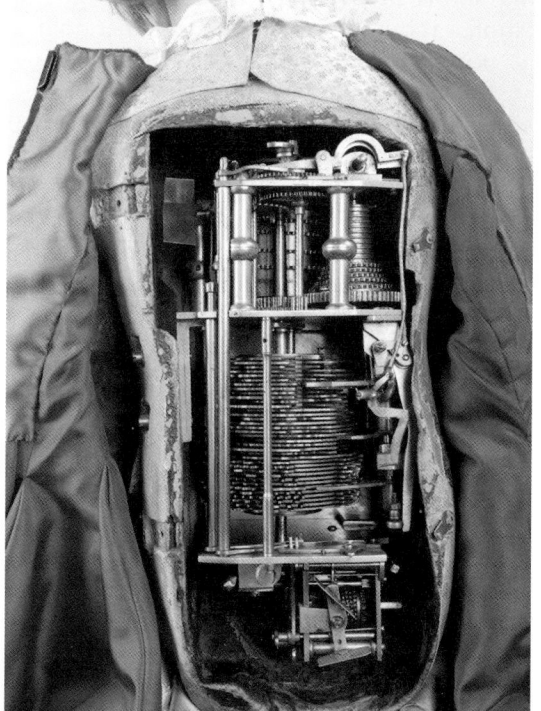
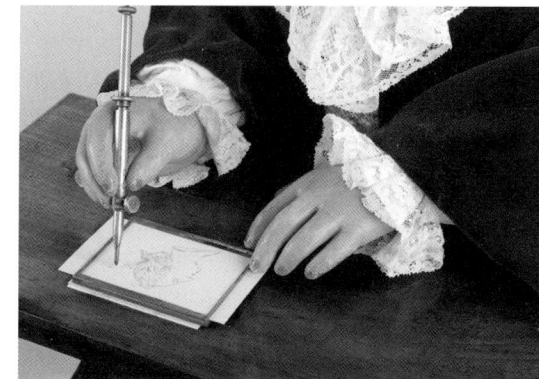

FIGURE 1.1 The Scribe, Pierre Jaquet-Droz's automaton (1721–90), 1770. Credits: Musee d'Art et d'Histoire, Neuchatel, Switzerland.

have continuously redesigned the sense of self in relation to, and often in opposition to, machines (Riskin 2003a, 2003b, 2010; Schaffer 2001). Automata are also "forerunners and figureheads of the modern, industrial machine age" (Voskuhl 2013: 2).

Mechanical androids are the ancestors of robots. They were extraordinary automatic devices. They moved with absolute grace, and they could perform with stunning accuracy a range of human behaviors. Jaquet-Droz's famous boy writer, built in the 1770s, which is still in working condition at the *Musee d'art et d'histoire* in Neuchâtel, Switzerland (Pointon 2009), was programmed to write messages up to forty characters.

Likewise, Jaquet-Droz's harpsichord player is a female android whose elegant playing and heaving chest simulating breathing and sighing, greatly impressed and troubled her audiences. This simulation of lifelike movement and human emotions cast doubts over the very meaning of humanity.

Androids were, indeed, a source of wonder and anxiety. As inanimate objects that appeared to move autonomously they charmed viewers with their skillful construction, but they also provoked unease. They were uncannily too similar to living creatures, as if their movements were the result of magical forces. Aptly, androids have been described as "symbols of both forward-looking technological rationality and ancient supernatural belief" (Tresch 2012: 174). This elusive mix of technology and magic seems remarkably applicable to the contemporary Android OS as well.

Automata as cybernetic constructions

Eighteenth-century androids occupied a threshold status in between the animate and the inanimate. Their existence provoked many questions about given ontological hierarchies, those that relate to existence—the living and the non-living, the human and the machine. Thus, these androids performed as entertainment, but they also performed as "arguments" (Shaffer 2001: 135). They were rhetorical devices that actively participated in the intellectual milieu in France and England, where the boundaries between life and non-life were discussed and experimented upon. Mechanicist philosophers such as Julien Offray de La Mettrie, for instance, thought that human beings are like machines. In *L'Homme-machine* (1748), La Mettrie declared that life itself was a mechanical and entirely reproducible affair. As the historian of automata Jessica Riskin points out, these philosophical arguments worked both ways: "If life was material, then matter was alive, and to see living creatures as machines was also to vivify machinery" (Riskin 2003a: 99). This notion of "vivified machines" seems entirely appropriate to describe the behaviors, expectations and narratives that circulate around our interactions with digital devices: objects to which we talk and which can talk back to us (Marenko 2014).

The philosophical debates about life and machines greatly influenced the design of Vaucanson's "cybernetic constructions" (Stafford 1994: 191). Vaucanson's *Flute Player* (1738), for instance, was the first automaton to actually play the instrument—versus the decorative flute-playing human figures that were often used to conceal music boxes. Air was blown through the *Flute Player's* lips, and to simulate life as much as possible, his fingers were covered in real skin. And yet, these moving machines were also artifices, designed to surprise, entertain and seduce by deception, like Vaucanson's celebrated *Defecating Duck*—a duck-machine that could ingest food and allegedly eliminate it as waste too (Riskin 2003b).

It is important to note that these constructions were not meant to represent life. Instead, they strived to *simulate* life by collapsing "the gap between animate and artificial machinery" (Riskin 2003a: 101). They held the promise that "organisms could become infinitely perfectible by blending muscle with metal" (Stafford 1994: 195): a sort of proto-cyborg. They made visible the quandary about where the machine ended and the living creature began (Riskin 2003b). They enacted the drama between thinking and not thinking, life and non-life (Pointon 2009). They were, in short, the embodiment of an exquisite contradiction: machines behaving like living creatures while simulating life as the antithesis of machines. *Siri*, the iPhone voice-activated operating system, represents this conundrum.[5]

The materiality of androids

A code is a series of activated mechanical gears, or a stack of punched cards circulating through a tape-reading machine, or a flow of light-pulses or bits in a transistor or on silicon. (Thacker 2004: xiii)

During the golden era of automata—between 1720 and 1780—the most talented clockmakers in pre-steam-power Europe used their skills to build androids. A mix of technologies went into making them: hydraulics and gravity, springs and pulleys, and cogs and very intricate systems of cams.

Cams are rotating pieces in larger mechanisms, usually wheels with eccentric and irregular shapes on an axis. Their function is to translate rotational movement into linear movement, and vice versa. Historian Simon Schaffer (2013) describes cams as a sort of "mechanical memory." As each cam moves, its shaped edge is read by other cams, and this is translated into movement. We should imagine a cam as a device that stores memory, with each groove and pattern in its edge creating a movement translated with perfect fidelity every time. Thus, cams are a technology that captures movement, records it as a specific shape (set of instructions) and activates it by a mechanical sequence.

Can we then, paraphrasing media theorist Eugene Thacker's epigraph at the beginning of this section, consider a stack of cams as a material version of an algorithm? Algorithms are recipes, or sets of basic instructions arranged in any desired sequence. Can we, based on this definition, also imagine a relationship between algorithms and magic? After all, a magic formula is nothing but a sequence of spells that is associated to a procedural sequence whose enunciation creates a full cognitive plan. Incantations are like algorithms. And vice versa. This should not be surprising, as magic and enchantment are deeply woven in the history of technology (Grafton 2002; Bredekamp 1995; Stafford 2001).

If we consider the materiality of these technologies, the transition from cams to punched cards to microprocessors is well documented (Stafford 2001; Schaffer 2013). What perhaps still deserves attention is the role played in the prehistory of computing by Vaucanson, the designer of sublime androids. Before turning to Vaucanson, however, the next section introduces two ideas that are key to my argument: "thick things" (Alder 2007) and the evolution of technical objects (Simondon 1980).

Matter and meaning: In the thick of it

Historian Ken Alder (2007) suggests that things are "thick" because of their complicated enmeshing of materiality and meanings.[6] The material world possesses a degree of opacity and recalcitrance that can be acknowledged only by assuming that things are always partial negotiations. "Thick" things are thus the material embodiment of multiple and divergent perspectives. They are the coordination of "the diverse sets of human agents who design, make, and use them" (Alder 2007: 82). Alder observes how "attention to the thickness of things can help break down distracting dichotomies like science/technology, idea/thing" (Alder 2007: 82).[7]

What is at stake here is how this commingling of disparate elements (idea/thing, material/digital) enables things to exist and to produce meanings. In the case of both sorts of androids that are examined here, the notion of "thick things" offers a perspective on how to chart their lineage across different historical times, while insisting on their disruptive material-symbolic presence. By taking both eighteenth-century and contemporary androids as "thick things," we focus on how they enmesh materiality and meanings. Only in this way can we capture their significance beyond the alleged division between materiality and immateriality.

The evolution of technical objects: "That which forces thought"

> There is no moment at which humanity comes to be contaminated by technical objects and practices—no fall into a world of things—because there can be no human without them. The history of the human animal—and indeed the history of culture—is thus necessarily the history of stuff that is, from the beginning, part and parcel of human life. Our embodied relations with things are not something that come to be "added to" human life. The human body and its capacities emerge as such in relation to a technicity that precedes and exceeds it; there is no body, no original body, no origin outside this relation; no thinking, no thought, no logos, without that which forces thought. (Braun and Whatmore 2010: xix)

French philosopher Gilbert Simondon's notion of evolution of technical objects rethinks the human–machine interaction in terms of an evolutionary continuum (Simondon 1980; Chabot 2013; Schmidgen 2012). Simondon tells us that objects are always the concrete expression of a spontaneous evolution, which depends neither on natural processes nor on human design. Rather, technical objects gain "an intermediate position between natural object and scientific representation" (Simondon 1980: 46). Moreover, far from evolving in isolation, technical objects are the result of a process in which internal parts converge and adapt "according to a principle of internal resonance" (1980: 13). This process (*concretization*) involves a convergence of functions by which the object acquires an internal coherence propelling it beyond the intention of its inventor. For instance, the migration of silicon transistors from computers into a number of objects to make them "smart" (mobile phones, cars, smoke detectors) promotes innovations that feed back to the original solutions. The result is that computers are also changing and evolving (Hayles 2012).

Even though they are designed and made by human beings, technical objects *have a life of their own* (Schmidgen 2012). They create webs of associations, surfacing as elements in cultural lineages that possess an imaginative life while being profoundly material.

The implications of Simondon's theory of technology are significant for two reasons. First, the genesis of technical objects—the development of common artifacts, sophisticated machines of wonder or digital devices from conception to maturity—is understood as fully integrated into culture. Simondon's theory of evolution does not position technical objects as an extension of a pre-existing body, but as fully inherent to human life (Braun and Whatmore 2010). The computers and smartphones that we use for work and leisure, for instance, should not be considered to be extensions of our bodies or memories. Instead, they are intrinsic constituents of who we are now, and who we may become in the future.

Humans are always already among machines. Likewise, technical objects are always already among, and coevolving with humans. This means that the boundary between natural and artificial, animate and inanimate becomes harder to locate. It also signals the impossibility of thinking of "technology" as something that humans invent, design and produce that is either completely separate from, or an extension of, themselves.

Second, Simondon's theory draws attention to the materiality of things, not as something passive and given, but as something that emerges from a process of co-evolution and co-creation. This prompts us to reflect on the embodied significance of technological apparata as diverse as cams, punch cards, and codes, and to map their material participation to different cognitive metaphors and cultural paradigms.

The material form and the proximity of our devices shape our ideas about technology as well as our notions of personhood. The eighteenth-century automata I discuss in this essay were developed during the Enlightenment—a period during which philosophers and scientists privileged reason over ideas that were grounded in tradition and faith. During the Enlightenment, the metaphor used to think about technological innovation was philosopher Rene Descartes' image of a clockwork universe—the idea that the whole universe, including the human body, works like a clock and, like a clock, depends solely on mechanical functioning. Technology was seen as an extension of nature. Today's pervasive computational metaphor—which is derived from machines whose performance is measured in processing speed and miniaturization—has become the byword for technology as well as the model that is used in the neurosciences and cognitive sciences to represent the human brain (Daugman 2001).

As we shape technology, technology shapes us.

From automata to looms, from cams to codes

Vaucanson's prodigious work was favoured by King Louis XV, who appointed him in 1741 to be the Royal Inspector of Silk Manufactures. Vaucanson took his skills, knowledge and expertise to the pre-industrial arena, and applied them to weaving technology. In 1747, he built an automatic programmable loom that operated via punched cards.

Refined by Joseph-Marie Jacquard half a century later (1801), this machine "would revolutionize weaving and in the twentieth century, would be used to input data into computers and store information in binary form" (Stafford 2001: 44).[8] Inspired by Vaucanson, Jacquard's automatic weaving machine worked by encoding the pattern in a specific arrangement of holes in a stack of punched cards. These cards work as "a *memory* that holds the pattern the loom will 'recall' and 'obey,' as a *blueprint* for how a piece of cloth is to be woven, and as a *program* that drives the loom" (Dasgupta 2014: 20).

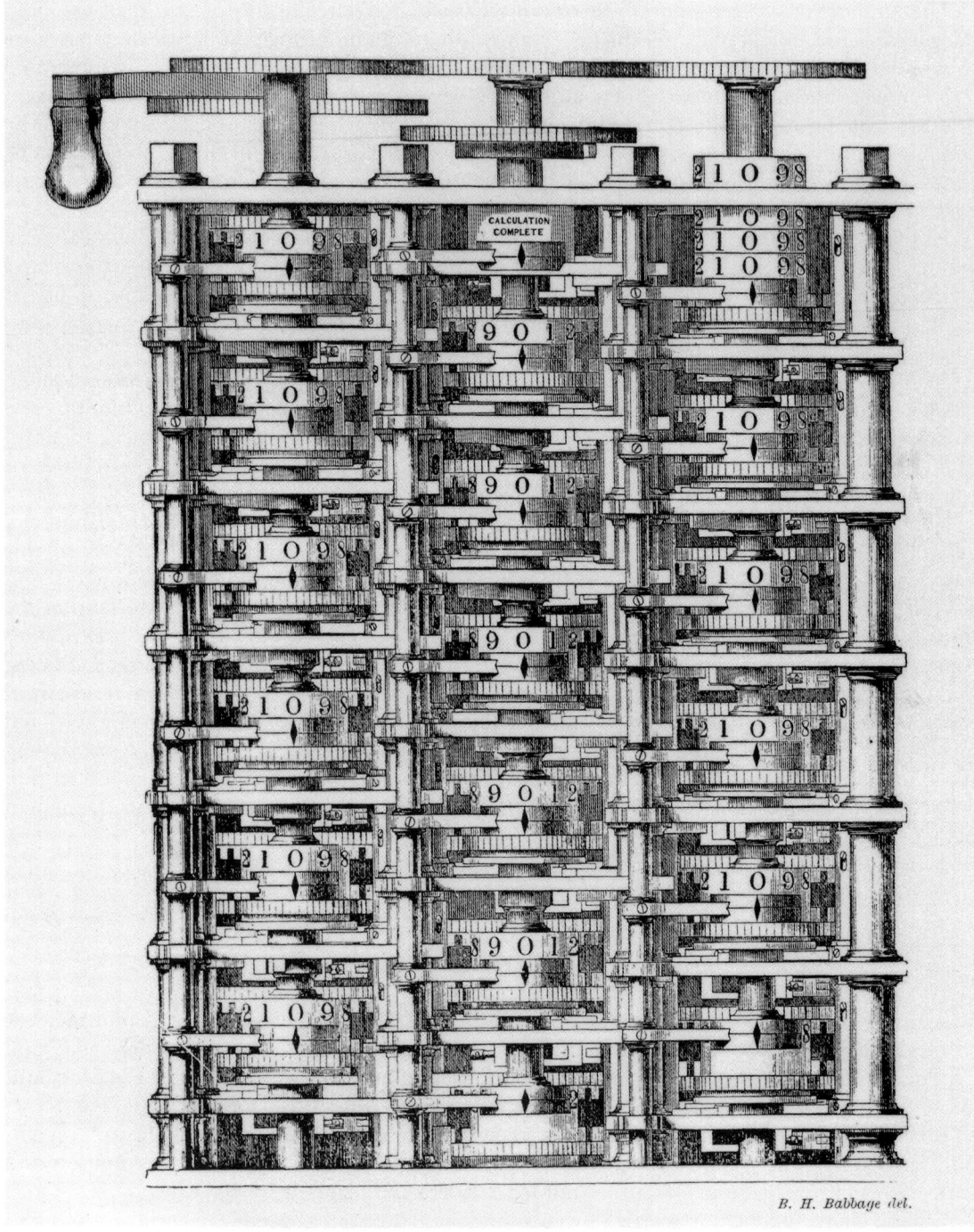

FIGURE 1.2 Difference Engine woodcut. Charles Babbage's Difference Engine No. 1, c. 1830s. Credits: Science Museum (London) / Science and Society Picture Library.

FIGURE 1.3 Difference Engine Cogs details. Demonstration model of Babbage's Difference Engine No. 1, nineteenth century. Credits: Science Museum (London) / Science & Society Picture Library.

It is remarkable that Vaucanson, the creator of both androids and automatic looms, had such a crucial role in the transition from the pre-industrial to the industrial era. What is even more so is that the punch card technology that he devised after working with cams later informed the first computational machine ever created, the Difference Engine by English scientist Charles Babbage. Astonishingly, this punch card technology remained in use until the 1960s when the IBM punch card systems were superseded by computers (Essinger 2004).

Babbage, the inventor of modern computers, was in equal measure fascinated by androids and by the Jacquard loom. Guests at Babbage's fashionable London soirées were entertained by a prototype of his automatic calculating machine and by an exquisite singing android (Schaffer 1994).[9] The coming together of these two automatic devices in the home of the inventor of modern computers is a testament to "the imaginative dimension in the advance of technology" (Pointon 2009: 228).

Babbage's great insight was to deploy the technology from Jacquard textile manufacture to design a universal computing machine that could perform without human intervention. He introduced the separation, familiar to us, between data processing ("mill") and data storage ("store") (Eames 1990).[10] He also figured out that changing the pattern of holes in the punched cards could alter the loom program—which was programming in its infancy. He understood that the same loom had "the capability for, potentially, an *infinity* of weaving patterns" (Dasgupta 2014: 21).

This is the key innovation in the Difference Engine. While the Jacquard loom works by analogy, the Difference Engine works by program. In the Jacquard loom, the loom can only weave the pattern corresponding to the holes in the pre-loaded punched cards, but there is no "accumulation" of information. In the Difference Engine, on the other hand, each calculation depends on previous results. Each numerical output is the input for the next step of the calculation" (Brennecke 2002).[11]

Babbage's machine therefore possessed features that are now associated with a modern computer; it was not just a mechanical processor. It was an instrument of the imagination. Its material form—a complicated system of springs and weights, gears and pulleys, wheels and chains, levers and barrels (Dasgupta 2014)—enabled the abstract reasoning necessary to propel technological evolution into the next stage of modern computing machines: the *Android* as we know it now.

Androids meet the Android OS

The imaginative lineage which I have charted in this essay is manifested in the name Google chose for its mobile Operating System: Android. This name, which is familiar to billions of users all over the world, harks back to automata, and suggests continuity with the history of human–machine interaction. Android is an "open-source software stack created for a wide array of devices with different form factors."[12] Different types of phones and tablets use this software resulting in a range of different graphical user interfaces (GUIs). "Built for you. Android keeps you connected to what matters," claims the tagline on Google's *Meet Android* website.[13] If we could imagine the Android meeting its eighteenth-century counterpart, as this essay proposes, we might at a first glance conclude that beyond the name little similarity exists. After all, the old android was a uniquely designed, tangible, anthropomorphic moving machine. The Android is a digital platform, intangible and invisible, that needs to be loaded onto standardized hardware—the ubiquitous smart devices with a uniform rectangular design that we know so well.

To capture their similarities, we need to unpack the tangible/intangible distinction as this fails to account for the materiality of digital media. The transition from mechanical to digital paradigms is marked by the contradictory "spectres of virtuality and dematerialization" (Gabrys 2011: 4). The result is that the materiality of our always-on status is seldom, if ever, acknowledged. The contradiction sociologist Jennifer Gabrys alludes to concerns dematerialization's double claim for invisibility and immediacy. This assumed invisibility and immediacy obscures the tangled, messy, material infrastructure upon which any digital performance depends: silicon, circuit boards, copper wires, optic fibers, cables, radio masts, servers' warehouses, minerals. Invisibility and intangibility do not mean absence of materiality. The trope of dematerialization is therefore problematic and misleading.

As historian of science Simon Schaffer reminds us when describing Babbage's automatic machines: "to make machines look intelligent it was necessary that the sources of their power, the labour force which surrounded and ran them, be rendered invisible" (Schaffer 1994: 204). This original displacement of the real labor behind machines is important in order to understand dematerialization.[14] As the smooth surfaces of our laptops and our smartphones seduce us into an exquisite experience of interaction and connectivity, they obfuscate the work and resources (both human and non-human: bodies, energies, materials, minerals, etc.) that go into producing such an experience. This has an effect at once enrapturing and spellbinding. Streams of data appear incessantly on our screens, as if the world was magically flowing towards us. It becomes easy, then, to grasp the intrinsic connection between technology and magic.

Technology is magic by other means

> Magical technology consists of representing the technical domain in enchanted form. (Gell 1992: 59)

Anthropologist Alfred Gell (1988) describes three different human technological capabilities: technology of production (concerning primary needs such as food, shelter, manufacture, and communication); technology of reproduction (concerning kinship and the social arrangements needed to ensure species reproduction); and technology of enchantment, strategies deployed to enchant and to various degrees convince, persuade, or manipulate others. Art, music, and rhetoric all belong to this technology, which concerns broadly the sphere of affects, passions, desire, fantasy, and wonder.

The connection between technology and magic is explicit. Magic is essentially a craft activity, whose goals are aligned with the goals of technology. Both aspire to change and control natural environment by artificial means.[15] This is why "magic haunts technical activity like a shadow" (Gell 1992: 59). Remarkably, Simondon makes a similar argument. Technicity, he argues, emerges from, and is the heir of, magic—together with religion (Simondon 2010: 118). It is impossible to understand technical objects if not in the context of "the entire genesis of the relations between man and the world," engendered from this "primitive magical unity" (Simondon 2010: 100).

If technology is "the pursuit of difficult to obtain objectives by roundabout means" (Gell 1988: 7), and magic is what "formalizes and codifies the structural features of technical activity, imposing on it a framework of organization which regulates each successive stage in a complex process" (1988: 8), then magic is "the ideal technology" (1988: 9), "the ideal means of technical production" (Gell 1992: 59). It can therefore be claimed that "technical innovations occur, not as a result of attempts to supply wants, but in the course of attempts to realize technical feats heretofore considered 'magical'" (Gell 1988: 8). Technology is, in other words, magic by other means.

Indeed, many scholars have articulated the link between the development of modern technoscience and the tradition of sixteenth-century natural magic (Hankins and Silverman 1995; Grafton 2002; Stafford 2001). Historian Anthony Grafton uses the expression "technological brand of magic" (2002: 18) to describe the work of military experts, clockwork makers, engineers, and architects—like Filippo Brunelleschi—who used innovations in fields as diverse as optics, hydraulics, pneumatics, and warfare as a kind of *technological spells* to harness and outdo the forces of nature and "to amaze and frighten their audiences" (2002: 24). Let us not forget that the Enlightenment, the era of the androids, was also the time when the inanimate forces of electricity, heat, steam, and gas were tamed and becoming alive (Tresch 2011).

In his erudite account of the *Kunstkammer*, art historian Horst Bredekamp (1995) emphasizes the presence of occult and magical tendencies in seventeenth-century mechanistic philosophies and their role in shaping attempts to synthesize life and generate autonomous movement. Automata were the most obvious expression of this yearning. The power of magic was elicited in order to do the impossible. An undercurrent of "mathematical" and "artificial magic" (Grafton 2002) clearly traverses Western history of technology. It is often overlooked, yet vividly present (Stafford 2001). Magic never really disappeared. It was "merely subsumed under new categories such as entertainment, technology, and natural science" (Hankins and Silverman 1995: 4). One of the reasons for its persistence was practicality:

> We tend not to think of magic as a practical art, certainly not in a utilitarian sense, but many of the goals of natural magic – creating realistic images where there is no substance, communicating instantly around the globe, imitating and preserving the human voice, revealing hidden sources of power, travelling under the sea, and flying through the air – are technologies we now take for granted. We no longer consider them magic, but in the seventeenth century they were. (Hankins and Silverman 1995: 5)

The persistence of magic is rooted in historically variable and materially diverse ecologies of objects. Whether machines of wonder or digital devices, they are all instruments of the imagination, able to enchant by movement, speed, instantaneous communication and, above all, by bestowing upon us what cannot be fully grasped, yet.

The imaginary meeting of androids evoked in this essay is an invitation to pay attention to the materiality of our digital encounters, even though unlike cams, codes cannot be touched. This meeting is not only to grasp better how digital devices work and how they came into being. It is a way to rethink them in a more imaginative way by positioning them within a wider cultural history of technologies of enchantment (Gell 1988, 1992). This imaginary meeting of androids casts a new light on today's digital enchantment.

Conclusion

The more impalpable and invisible the machines around us become, the more pressing is the urge to investigate the prehistory of our digital world. It is by looking into a past made of cogs and cams that we may find a way of unlocking some of the narratives shaping our experience of digital devices. Our permanent wired state is also the product of centuries of experiments, dreams and nightmares that are populated by machines that behave like humans. Today's complicated digital interactions, in which the boundaries between the artificial and the organic, and the real and the simulated, are blurred, should be sited within the lineage of human-machine interaction.

A kinship between the androids of the eighteenth century and today's Android emerges because of the name they share, but also because of the capacity of machines both to have lives of their own and to have impact on our lives. Both eighteenth-century and contemporary androids are "thick things" that embody the historically located form of a technology that continuously co-evolves with humans. Whether by mechanical or digital means—by cams or codes—they are both touch-points of the fluidity of the boundary between human and machine.

Eighteenth-century androids raised these philosophical questions through a spectacular enactment and simulation of life. The Android, on the other hand, is fast becoming a universal enabler. It does not simulate life. Instead, it is increasingly the optimized channel that makes life possible at all in our digital era. Both androids are designed objects whose roles go beyond spectacular entertainment (eighteenth-century androids) and data processing with instant connectivity (Android OS). Instead, both these objects work at redrawing imagined boundaries, and redefining what we take to be intelligence in an era of things that move.

Most important, this essay hints at the fact that the paradigm shift from mechanical to digital technologies is perhaps more seamless than we are led to believe. By dispelling the paradigm of dematerialization, we can recapture an originary magical union of human and machines. Sited within the history of "marvellous machines," our digital enchantment can be rethought imaginatively and grafted upon the undercurrents of magic that traverse Western history of technology. Magic never really disappeared. It morphed into the new categories of entertainment and technology and all their hybrid offspring that beckon to us from our screens.

If eighteenth-century androids were "philosophical animated experimental objects" (Landes 2011: 54) prompting questions about humanity, then today's Androids should be more than our indispensable connectivity devices. They too should be "philosophical animated experimental objects," inviting us to reflect on the dazzling forms that enchantment takes in our machine-inhabited world.

Notes

1. On automata and androids' role in defining technological paradigms and embodying critical interrogations about the human/machine relationship, see Schaffer 2001, Pointon 2009, Riskin 2003a, 2003b, 2007, 2010; Kang 2011; Landes 2011, 2007; Liu 2000; Reilly 2011; Voskuhl 2013. On the history of automata and androids, see Chapuis and Droz 1958.

2. Jacques de Vaucanson (1709–82) was a French inventor. He designed and built astonishingly complicated automata whose technological prowess has never been surpassed. They were so life-like that he was hailed as a modern Prometheus by philosophers La Mettrie and Voltaire (Cottom 1999: 56).

3. See Voskuhl (2013) for a critique of current literature that tends to modernize automata by assuming a direct link between them and contemporary technology. The risk is of overlooking the differences in the ever-shifting relationship between human and machines.

4. This definition contains some ambiguity: it is not entirely clear whether the spontaneous movement of the inanimate object is self-generated or merely *appears* to be so. Compare to the definition found, 250 years later, in Menzel and Aluisio (2000) where *automaton* is "a mechanism that is relatively self-operating, like a robot, and designed to follow automatically a predetermined sequence of operations, or respond to encoded instructions" (2000: 234), and android "a robot that approximates a human in physical appearance. A humanoid" (2000: 234).

5. Siri is an intelligent personal assistant that allows users to ask questions directly to their iPhone. The implications of a human chatting away with a machine are well captured by Spike Jonze's movie *Her* (2013), which tells the story of a man who not only chats with his voice-activated operating system, Samantha, but falls in love with "her."

6. In his afterword to the special issue of *Isis* on "Thick Things," Bruno Latour (2007) observes: "many descriptions of 'things' have nothing 'thingly' about them. They are simply 'objects'

7   This echoes Latour's concept of "hybrids," or Michel Serres's "quasi-objects"—things as the expression of entangled networks that cannot easily be pulled apart (Latour 1993), or occupying a position in between object and subject (Serres 1982). Latour (1993) offers some examples of these hybrid objects: "we find ourselves invaded by frozen embryos, expert systems, digital machines, sensor equipped robots, hybrid corn, data banks, psychotropic drugs, whales outfitted with radar sounding devices, gene synthesizers, audience analyzers, and so on [...] When none of these chimera can be properly on the object side [society] or on the subject side [nature], or even in between, something has to be done" (Latour 1993: 49–50). See also Henare, Holbraad, and Wastell (eds) 2007, for the proposal of "a methodology where the 'things' themselves may dictate a *plurality* of ontologies" (2007: 5).

Opening context (not numbered): mistaken for things. Hence the necessity of a new descriptive style that circumvents the limits of the materialist (in effect idealist) definition of material existence" (Latour 2007: 138).

8   See Riskin (2003b) for a detailed account of Vaucanson's preoccupation with issues of automation and life-simulation, and the application of his work from automata to automatic machinery. On his role in the transition to the industrial revolution see also Stafford (2001: 44).

9   Babbage saw this automaton, exhibited at Merlin's Museum, in Hanover Square, in 1783, as a child, and bought it thirty years later.

10 It is interesting to note that both words chosen by Babbage to define these two functions ("store" and "mill") come from the weaving industry.

11 In his classification of early programmable machines, computer scientist Andreas Brennecke (2002) uses the terms "analog" and "digital" to distinguish different forms of sequence control. Analog refers to a control sequence that is part of the construction of the machine. Control mechanisms are based on physical analogies. Digital refers to a control sequence based on abstract rules of algorithm—set of basic instruction arranged in any desired sequence. Brennecke notes that the generic term "program" can be used to describe a number of very different sequence controlled machines, from Heron of Alexandria's automata, early musical automata, Jacquard looms, sequence controlled calculating machines, and modern computers. See also Koetsier (2001).

12 From The Android Source Code, Google Inc., http://source.android.com/source/index.html (accessed June 21, 2014).

13 Google Inc., www.android.com (accessed June 21, 2014).

14 To consider here is also Marx's critique of capitalist production and objectification of the world of things, where the shift from artisan handcrafted production to serial machine production determines a shift in the social character of objects, from product to commodity. As a consequence of industrialization the connection between objects and world of things is interrupted. Objects lose their singularity, become all copies of a series, and, crucially, a gap is wedged between use value and exchange value.

15 On the general theory of magic, see anthropologist Bronislaw Malinowski (1992)

Bibliography

Alder, K. (2007), "Introduction. Focus: Thick Things," *Isis* 98: 80–3.
Braun, B. and S. J. Whatmore (eds) (2010), *Political Matter: Technoscience, Democracy and Public Life*, Minneapolis and London: University of Minnesota Press.
Bredekamp, H. (1995), *The Lure of Antiquity and the Cult of the Machine. The Kunstkammer and the Evolution of Nature, Art and Technology*, Princeton, NJ: Markus Wiener Publishers.
Brennecke, A. (2002), "A Classification Scheme for Program Controlled Calculators," in R. Rojas and U. Hashagen (eds), *The First Computers: History and Architectures*, Cambridge, MA: MIT Press.

Chabot, P. (2013), *The Philosophy of Simondon: Between Technology and Individuation*, London: Bloomsbury.
Chapuis, A. and E. Droz (1958), *Automata. A Historical and Technological study*, trans. Alec Reid, Neuchatel and London: Editions du Griffon.
Cottom, D. (1999), "The Work of Art in the Age of Mechanical Digestion," *Representations*, 66: 52–74.
Dasgupta, S. (2014), *It Began with Babbage. The Genesis of Computer Science*, Oxford: Oxford University Press.
Daugman, J. (2001), "Brain Metaphor and Brain Theory," in W. Bechtel, P. Mandik, J. Mundale, and R. Stufflebeam (eds), *Philosophy and the Neurosciences*, Oxford: Blackwell Publishers.
Eames, C. and R. Eames (1990), *A Computer Perspective. Background to the Computer Age*, Cambridge, MA, and London: Harvard University Press.
Essinger, J. (2004), *Jacquard's Web. How a Hand Loom Led to the Birth of the Information Age*, Oxford: Oxford University Press.
Gabrys, J. (2011), *Digital Rubbish. A Natural History of Electronics*, Ann Arbor, MI: University of Michigan Press.
Gell, A. (1988), "Technology and Magic," *Anthropology Today*, 4, 2: 6–9.
Gell, A. (1992), "The Technology of Enchantment and the Enchantment of Technology," in J. Coote and A. Shelton (eds), *Anthropology, Art and Aesthetics*, 4–66, Oxford: Clarendon.
Grafton, A. (2002), *Magic and Technology in Early Modern Europe*, Dibner Library Lecture, October 15, Smithsonian Institution Library.
Hankins, T. L. and R. J. Silverman (1995), *Instruments and the Imagination*, Princeton, NJ: Princeton University Press.
Henare, A., M. Holbraad, and S. Wastell (eds) (2007), *Thinking Through Things: Theorising Artefacts Ethnographically*, London: Routledge.
Hill, R. (1992), *Automata*, The Southbank Centre. Exhibition Catalogue.
Kang, M. (2011), *Sublime Dreams of Living Machines. The Automaton in the European Imagination*, Cambridge, MA, and London: Harvard University Press.
Koetsier, T. (2001), "On the Prehistory of Programmable Machines: Musical Automata, Looms, Calculators," *Mechanism and Machine Theory* 36: 589–603.
Landes, J. B. (2007), "The Anatomy of Artificial Life: An Eighteenth Century Perspective," in J. Riskin (ed.), *Genesis Redux. Essays in the History and Philosophy of Artificial Life*, 96–116, Chicago and London: University of Chicago Press.
Landes, J. B. (2011), "Vaucanson's Automata as Devices of Enlightenment," *Sjuttonhundratal Nordic Yearbook for Eighteenth-Century Studies* 8: 50–9.
Latour, B. (1993), *We Have Never Been Modern*, Hemel Hempstead: Harvester Wheatsheaf.
Latour, B. (2007), "Can We Get Our Materialism Back, Please?," *Isis*, 98: 138–42.
Liu. C. (2000), *Copying Machines. Taking Notes for the Automaton*, Minneapolis and London: University of Minnesota Press.
Malinowski, B. (1992), *Magic, Science and Religion, and Other Essays*, New York: Waveland Press.
Marenko, B. (2014), "Neo-Animism and Design. A New Paradigm in Object theory," *Design and Culture*, 6, 2: 219–42.
Menzel, P. and F. D'Aluisio (2000), *Robo Sapiens. Evolution of a New Species*, Cambridge, MA: MIT Press.
Pointon, M. (2009), *Brilliant Effect. A Cultural History of Gem Stones and Jewellery*, New Haven, CT, and London: Yale University Press.
Reilly, K. (2011), *Automata and Mimesis on the Stage of Theatre History*, Basingstoke: Palgrave Macmillan.
Riskin, J. (2003a), "Eighteenth Century Wetware," *Representations* 83: 97–125. Reprinted in B. Bensaude-Vincent and W. R. Newman (eds) (2007), *The Artificial and the Natural: An Evolving Polarity*, Cambridge, MA: MIT Press.

Riskin, J. (2003b), "The Defecating Duck, or, the Ambiguous Origins of Artificial Life," *Critical Inquiry* 29 (4): 599–633. Reprinted in B. Brown (ed.) (2004), *Things*, 99–133, Chicago and London: University of Chicago Press.

Riskin, J. (ed.) (2007), *Genesis Redux: Essays in the History and Philosophy of Artificial Life*, Chicago and London: University of Chicago Press.

Riskin, J. (2010), "Machines in the Garden," *Republics of Letters: A Journal for the Study of Knowledge, Politics, and the Arts* 1 (2): 16–43.

Schaffer, S. (2001), "Enlightened Automata," in *The Sciences in Enlightened Europe*, W. Clark, J. Golinksi, and S. Schaffer (eds), 126–65, Chicago and London: University of Chicago Press,.

Schaffer, S. (2013), *Mechanical Marvels, Clockwork Dreams*. Documentary BBC4.

Schaffer, S. (1994), "Babbage's Intelligence: Calculating Engines and the Factory System," *Critical Inquiry* 21 (1): 203–27.

Schmidgen, H. (2012), "Inside the Black Box: Simondon's Politics of Technology," *SubStance*, 41, 3, 129: 16–31.

Serres, M. (1982), *The Parasite*, Cambridge, MA: MIT Press.

Simondon, G. (1980), *On the Mode of Existence of Technical Objects*, London, ON: University of Western Ontario. Trans. Ninian Mellamphy (1958), Part 1 or. *Du mode d'existence des objets techniques* Méot; 2nd edn. (1989), Paris: Aubier.

Simondon, G. (2010), *On the Mode of Existence of Technical Objects*, London, ON: University of Western Ontario. Trans. Ninian Mellamphy (1958), Part 2 or. *Du mode d'existence des objets techniques* Méot; 2nd edn. (1989), Paris: Aubier.

Stafford, B. (1994), *Artful Science. Enlightenment Entertainment and the Eclipse of Visual Education*, Cambridge, MA: MIT Press.

Stafford, B. (2001), *Devices of Wonder: From the World in a Box to Images on a Screen*, Cambridge, MA: MIT Press.

Spufford, F. and J. Uglow (eds) (1996), *Cultural Babbage: Technology, Time and Invention*, London: Faber & Faber.

Thacker, E. (2004), "Foreword: Protocol Is as Protocol Does," in A. Galloway, *Protocol: How Control Exists After Decentralization*, xi–xxii, Cambridge, MA: MIT Press.

Tresch, J. (2011), "The Machine Awakens: The Science and Politics of the Fantastic Automaton," *French Historical Studies* 34: 87–123.

Tresch, J. (2012), *The Romantic Machine. Utopian Science and Technology after Napoleon*, Chicago and London: University of Chicago Press.

Voskuhl, A. (2013), *Androids in the Enlightenment. Mechanics, Artisans, and Culture of the Self*, Chicago and London: University of Chicago Press.

Wood, G. (2002), *Living Dolls*, London: Faber & Faber.

2

When objects fail

Unconcealing things in design writing and criticism

Peter Hall

Introduction

While most of us understand what is meant by an object—a teaspoon, hammer, cup, chair, or lamp—no one is quite sure what is meant by a thing. The word holds within it an "audacious ambiguity" (Brown 2001: 4), referring to not just a loss of words (Q: "where did you put the thing? A: "It's behind the thing in the thing"), but all the things (ideas, interests, materials, decisions) that come together to form the object—including the ones about which we do not know. Despite a longstanding philosophical discussion on the discrepancy between the object and the thing,[1] popular design discourse—in magazines, books, and exhibitions—is still in a state of denial. The currency of design discourse remains, for the most part, the photograph of the object frozen in time or exhibited in a gallery in eye-popping color on a white pedestal against a white background. Drawing terms from Brown and the philosophers Bruno Latour, Michel Serres, and Martin Heidegger, this essay argues that one way to put thing theory to use in design criticism is by analyzing objects that have failed. Whereas we tend to look *through* objects, a thing that has clearly failed us "can hardly function as a window" (Brown 2001: 4). Instead of starting the critical journey with pictures of successful objects on pedestals, why not begin with recognized failures, or look for the failures that the object supposedly fixes? When something fails, we want to know why, a question that immediately moves design criticism past its obsession with style, form, movements and biographies and into a mode of explication—literally unfolding or "unpleating" as Michel Serres has pointed out (Serres and Latour 1995: 65).

Since my own background is as a trade journalist and design magazine editor whose job was to perpetuate the idea that the latest designed object was interesting *because* it was new, my perspective for this essay comes from a back catalog of journalistic reporting. As every design writer secretly knows, as soon as an object ceases to be new, it resumes its dance with the spectre of failure. But while noble efforts have been made by design writers and editors to follow up on a story and investigate what happened to the "next big thing" one year later, this is not common practice in popular design journalism. The mechanisms of design news making today are, in fact, little different from those of the mid-twentieth century when consumerism was still untainted by a guilty conscience about environmental impact. The backstories of objects—how they came to be in their translation from idea to form—are commonly boiled down to a success narrative (for example, a designer's genius idea, a client's foresight in picking that designer, or the value of design to society in general). The new forms are photographed, and publicists are hired to dispatch photographs and press releases to time-pressed magazine editors and bloggers; writers attach texts to the images based on the press releases or interviews with the designers and their clients (who both inevitably recapitulate the standard success narratives); the story is published and the search resumes for new, fresh images. In the parade of objects and fanfare that stands in for design discourse, the thing is all but forgotten.

Explicating the image of the object

Explicating things first requires a little unpacking of the way we see objects. Seeing, as John Berger has argued repeatedly, is a culturally constructed activity, itself a product of distinctive lineages (Berger 1972). In that eye-popping photograph of a decontextualized designed object (or faux-contextualized amid spotless architecture and lithe, disinterested-looking models) is a hybrid of three big ideas: the Classical notion of the ideal form, the Cartesian subject separated from the object, and the adulation of the present.

The first idea, the Classical notion of the ideal form, lurks behind the entire representational apparatus of contemporary design. To expose the Classical underpinnings of the mode of representing designed objects we need look no further than the pivotal industrial design exhibition *Machine Art*, curated by Philip Johnson at the Museum of Modern Art in 1934, in collaboration with the museum's director Alfred H. Barr. In an audacious stroke, Johnson and Barr brought into the white-walled galleries of the young museum a collection of industrial parts, household and office equipment, furnishings, kitchenware, scientific instruments and laboratory glass, and porcelain wares. These were extracted from their indigenous habitats within manufacturing facilities, laboratories, machines, homes, retail outlets, and workplaces, and exhibited on shelves and pedestals, carefully juxtaposed to elicit their formal correspondences and contrasts. Johnson and Barr then framed the collection with a heavy dose of Platonic metaphysics. "The beauty of machine art is in part the abstract beauty of 'straight lines and circles' made into actual tangible 'surfaces and solids' by means of tools, 'lathes and rulers and squares,'" Barr wrote in the foreword to the *Machine Art* catalog, citing Plato's *Philebus* (Marshall 2012). The implication was clear: industrially made objects could be raised to the level of art objects, paving the way for design as an important new field of study in the arts. By recruiting Plato to the Modernist cause, Johnson established that the discourse of design would be primarily formal, the pursuit of "perfection of shape and rhythm, beauty of surface," and one premised on a firm distinction between objects and subjects. What Johnson perhaps did not anticipate was the extent to which his bold elevation of machine-made objects would provide the de facto visual mode for both exhibiting design—and selling it. One could thank *Machine Art*'s formal framing of design as the central method for almost every contemporary design show since: including the survey shows at the Cooper-Hewitt National Museum of Design, the

Red Dot Museum in Germany, and the London Design Museum; not to mention those more openly provocative shows like the *Art of the Motorcycle* exhibition at the Guggenheim Museum in New York. MoMA's own efforts to further the discussion around design by exploring new materials, methods of manufacture and modes of design exploration might all be viewed in terms of the shadow cast by *Machine Art*'s celebratory Machine Age zeal.

The second big idea, the Cartesian subject, the "I" that, in thinking supposedly proves its own existence (*cogito ergo sum*), remains stubbornly behind the scenes of the photograph of the designed object and its exhibition, separating the object from its viewer and its creator and allowing us to construct a discourse of desire: we desire the thing that is not us and we admire the creator of that thing. Against this position is the relational one of Latour and others, which can be summarized as "the view that a thing is defined solely by its effects and alliances rather than by a lonely inner kernel of essence" (Harman 2009: 75). This view does not privilege a human subject who relates and assembles the external world: all things, or "actors" have the power to relate and assemble. Against the Cartesian dualism implicit in the photographed artifact, then, is the realism of things that are made up of human and non-human assemblages: the hard metal elevator door that closes before you can dash inside, the tax forms that force one's previous year of existence into categories and boxes, the mobile phone that won't stop interrupting you. Latour's relational position is shared by many contemporary thinkers seeking to dissolve the subject–object divide: psychologists and philosophers seeking to establish

FIGURE 2.1 Installation view of the exhibition "Good Design." November 27, 1951–January 27, 1952, MoMA, New York. Photographic Archive. Photographer: George Barrows.

situated and embodied accounts of cognition,[2] Byzantine art historians struggling to make sense of a pre-modern world view of objects that refused to separate subject from object,[3] and hopeful design writers seeking to implicate us in our inventions and the effects of our inventions upon us.

The third big idea, the adulation of the present, lurks behind the implication that the objects photographed on pedestals are worthy of attention *because* they are the latest, the newest. This assumption drives the entire project of Modernity, with its notions of a rational break with the past and progress through science and technology. Serres aligns this tempocentrism with ancient diagrams that put Earth at the center of everything.

> Just as in space we situate ourselves at the center, or at the navel of the things in the universe, so for time, through progress, we never cease to be at the summit, on the cutting edge, at the state-of-the-art of development. (Serres and Latour 1995: 45)

The view that the latest is the greatest is the invisible guiding hand that puts objects on pedestals in museum galleries in an almost identical setting to that of the museum stores. Philip Johnson's counterpart at MoMA, Edgar Kaufmann, heir to the Kaufmann department store empire, had no qualms about moving Johnson's approach to objects into a commercial setting. For Kaufmann's *Good Design* shows, introduced to MoMA and the Merchandise Mart of Chicago in 1950, Plato was jettisoned in favor of "eye appeal" to guide in the jurors' selection of objects. This established, as Terence Riley and Edward Eigen put it in an essay about the program, "an equivalence between the good and the new" (Riley and Eigen 1994: 160). It provided evidence of Heidegger's argument (1977: 130) that *the world has become a picture* in the modern age. It cemented the importance of the image as the means by which product design is judged, prefacing Guy Debord's sardonic prophesy, "that which appears is good, that which is good appears" (Debord 1967: 3).

The legacy of modernity

How then, might we move design discourse beyond the slavish reification of the new, the fresh, and the present? How might we re-establish the relational nature of objects to their thingness? The reason that we need to do this should be perhaps first spelled out by taking a position drawn from Latour's arguments in *We Have Never Been Modern* (1993). Modernity, and our predominant way of thinking about the world for the last few hundred years (at least in the West since the Enlightenment), has done a great job of separating the human sphere from the non-human sphere. The soft sciences took care of the human sphere while the hard sciences got on with the serious business of explaining how the physical world works. But as Latour and others in the study of science and technology have shown, hard matters of fact are assembled, not discovered, and achieve their objectivity through the process of assembling alliances of human and non-human actors and translating their interests to strengthen the alliance. Latour's extensive work in this area follows the development of "black boxes," or "matters of fact" in science and industry, such as vaccines, the diesel engine, and DNA. The DNA example (detailed in Latour's book *Science in Action*) provides a useful example of how the early hypotheses of two researchers, James Watson and Francis Crick, in 1951 gained traction by bringing elements and evidence into alliance, from laws to metal pieces to rival theories, until their guesses became less contentious hypotheses and finally matters of fact. At this point the human role was purged or "purified" from the science: In Latour's terms *translation* was accompanied by *purification*: the general consensus moving from "Crick and Watson claim that DNA is a double helix" to "DNA is a double helix" (Latour 1987: 14).

This process seems commonsensical until we consider the consequences of the purification. Black boxes, from scientific truths to technological truths like automobiles, once purified of their human content, become uncontested and astonishingly powerful. This, in essence, is the ontological power of design—its ability to shape behavior and thought, and, as Tony Fry (2008: 26) argues, "obscure those agendas that, beyond the most immediate concerns, would make designers fully accountable for what design brings into being." A simple example is the automobile:

> One does not have to exercise too much brain power to decide how many of the creators of motor cars remotely considered its impact upon the world's climate, trauma medicine, wildlife, house design, urban form, cultural values, road construction, waste generation and so on. (Fry 1999: 90)

By purging the human sphere from the non-human sphere, we have ended up in a situation where we can somehow separate human behavior from the behavior of the world, and of things. This project has been underway at least since John Locke invoked the idea of nature as an infinite storehouse awaiting human exploitation (Markley 2012: 55). To illustrate the fallacy of this bifurcation, Latour adopts Serres's term "quasi-objects" to draw out the social nature of the (technological) object. A quasi-object, Serres explains, "traces or makes visible the relations that constitute the group through which it passes, like a token in a children's game" (Serres and Latour 1995: 161).

Serres's potent example of a quasi-object is the space shuttle Challenger, the explosion of which, in 1986, killed all seven crew members, and which he controversially aligns with the sacrifices of children to Baal in Carthage. Although we prefer to think of Challenger as an object of the world (a product of pure science and technology), it is simultaneously an object of society—one which transforms our rapport with things and our relations among ourselves. In ancient Carthage, children were reportedly lifted onto the arms of a giant statue of Baal, where they were roasted to death. The Challenger, argues Serres, allowed us to "assuage our unslakeable thirst for human sacrifice to the gods, whom we think we have forgotten" (Serres and Latour 1995: 160).

Whether we like it or not, Serres's argument provokes us to rethink the supposedly objective, scientific agenda of the space shuttle project, which even betrays its social objectives in its name, Challenger. His point is not to critique science but to draw comparisons in history through anachronistic leaps that reveal the cultural nature of science. He asks Latour:

> Don't you think that the Western nations explore space in order to demonstrate their power to the rest of the world, rather than for any useful reason? (Serres and Latour 1995: 140)

To put Serres's quasi-object to work at making relations visible, we must turn to Latour's discussion of another space shuttle disaster, the Columbia, which exploded on re-entry in February 2003 due to damage incurred during the launch, again killing all of its crew members. Latour focuses on a particular image of the debris after the explosion, laid out on a grid on the floor of a hangar at Kennedy Space Center, where NASA crash investigators tried to learn what caused the shuttle to break up. In this "exploded view" argues Latour, is the image of the thing, or in German, *Ding*, which originally designated a certain type of archaic assembly (Latour 2005: 22). Heidegger's translation of *Ding* as "gathering" is appropriated by Latour and company in the *Making Things Public* project to refer to technological objects when revealed in all their thingness (Latour 2005: 24).

In Heideggerian terms, the thingness of the object is brought to our attention when it breaks: the broken hammer brings our labor to a halt and makes us see it as a hammer for the first time (Harman 2005). It took the catastrophic failure of the shuttle, then, to remind us that a shiny object, or black box like the Columbia pictured on its launch pad, is a "lie" in its concealment of all the actors or interests that gathered together to form the space shuttle. The crash investigation drew the hundreds of "hitherto unknown" actors into the discussion, and as Latour argues in *Making Things Public*, revealed how the shuttle's complex technology "should have been drawn with the NASA bureaucracy inside of it" (Latour 2005: 24). The information design guru Edward Tufte has argued that Microsoft presentation software was in part to blame for the accident (Tufte 2006: 157–85). PowerPoint's "hyper-rational" hierarchy, according to Tufte, abbreviated and then de-prioritized or deleted important data that would have indicated to NASA that Boeing's test data was not optimistic, as NASA management officials assumed from the slides. Because of this PowerPoint-assisted misinterpretation of evidence, no action was taken and damage caused by the foam debris caused the shuttle to burn up on re-entry. Both the 2003 Columbia Accident Investigation Board report and the Final Report of the Return to Flight Task Group (2005) concurred that the endemic use of PowerPoint briefing slides instead of technical papers highlighted a problem with technical communication methods at NASA (Tufte 2006: 166). PowerPoint did not single-handedly cause the accident, but was one of many hundreds of actors gathered together in the quasi-object. As we trace the path back through the exploded parts, visible and invisible (e.g., NASA's organizational culture), light is shed on the agendas, alliances, and translations that took place in the making of the thing.

Method

How then, might we introduce the concept of the quasi-object into conventional design discourse? Latour's rules of method in the appendix of his 1987 book *Science in Action* provide some guidance. "We study science *in action* and not ready made science or technology … we either arrive before the facts and machines are blackboxed or we follow the controversies that reopen them" (Latour 1987: 258).

Latour provides an intriguing model of such a reopening with his analysis of Aramis, the "personal rapid transit system" developed and prototyped in France between 1964 and 1987, when it was scrapped. Its failure is an essential part of its appeal; the case is not closed. It is less an object than an event, a "quasi-object"—neither social relation or thing (Latour 1993: 372). Pictured in a Parisian workshop the year of its demise, Aramis bears Latour's caption of the light rail car as "suspended between heaven and earth" (Latour 1996: Fig. 16). Aramis cannot be narrativized as a black box because it was a known failure. It thus points toward the stories of its development.

The Aramis system aimed to blend the benefits of mass transit with those of point-to-point private car transportation. The point of the Aramis investigation is not to blame a single individual or even to identify a single reason why the project failed; and less still to come up with a grand narrative (e.g., the postmodern condition) to explain things away. Instead, the study is a close analysis of how the precarious network of alliances between actors—the engineers, the politicians, the coupling system, and the pilot vehicle—fell apart. Latour's fifth and seventh rules of method warn against prioritizing particular actors or human interests to settle a controversy; the third and fourth rules of method similarly warn against explaining the settling of a controversy in terms of society or nature. In other words, neither technical hitches, the French government, cultural expectations, nor political power mongering can be singled out to explain the failure of the project.

Patching up Concorde

To test Latour's relational method on typical design magazine fare, we can now turn to material unearthed for two journalistic articles written for *Metropolis* magazine. The first is my article on the Concorde supersonic airliner, which, in 2001, shortly before its retirement, was given a rather lavish $24 million makeover by British Airways, involving the design consultancies Factory and Conran & Partners. While the "hook" of my article was ostensibly the news of the redesign and relaunch, the controversy was Concorde's air-worthiness, its hitherto impeccable safety record now scarred by the crash six months earlier of Air France's Concorde flight AF4590, which led to the deaths of all 109 passengers and crew on board.

Post-crash, Concorde's quasi-object status was suddenly visible for the world to see: no longer a black box or shining image of mid-century super-modernity, Concorde was grounded pending safety checks. An old question resurfaced: was cutting transatlantic flight time by three hours for 100 wealthy passengers worth the environmental impact? Concorde's utopian image of postwar, pan-European collaboration and technological prowess (to rival that of the USA) had been punctured, just as the fuel tanks under its wings had been punctured by a blown-out tire that caused the catastrophic implosion during takeoff. Engineers patched up Concorde's fuel tanks with a Kevlar lining, adding unwanted weight to the delta-shaped wings, and British Airways' designers and PR people tried to patch up the image. But Concorde's semiotics could never be detached from its materiality. It emerged from a Modernist faith in the inexorable march of technological progress, progress that would allow us to conquer time and distance. But when it finally rolled into service in 1976 Concorde had cost $4 billion—four times more than promised—and attracted howls of protest about its noise and environmental impact. The 2001 patch up job was explained by BA and its designers in simultaneously material and semiotic terms, as an attempt to "bring the outside in"—recreate the iconic modernity of Concorde's shape on the inside. The entire renovation was couched in terms of illusion: giving the cramped 1960s interior the illusion of space, building a lightweight, carbon-fiber bucket seat that compensated passengers' claustrophobia with references to Formula One racing cars, and signifying the airline's achievement of Mach 1 with a lighting trick: a stream of blue light would wash down the cabin interior. But less than two years later, the patched up plane was retired for good, with BA citing rising maintenance costs, the crash, and low passenger numbers following the terrorist attacks of 2001. The thing never quite regained its object status.

A shiny chair in the ruins

To suggest that the object becomes a thing when it has failed is the main purpose of this article. But this does not quite equip us with the tools with which to critique the new (aka that-which-has-yet-to-fail), the stuff of popular design discourse. The second of my journalistic articles discussed here arguably illustrates how Latour's rule of method, to "arrive before the facts and machines are blackboxed or … follow the controversies that reopen them" can lead us beyond the object in question to the systemic failures that caused an organization to decide that a new object was needed in the first place. Published in *Metropolis* magazine, the article's "hook" was a new chair designed by IDEO for school classrooms (Hall 2010: 98–123). Launched by the furniture manufacturer Steelcase in 2010, the swiveling chair was designed to replace the aged "one-armed bandit" seen in lecture theaters around the world since the 1950s—a four-legged seat with an articulating writing surface that pivots up and across the student's lap. The new chair, named Node, was designed for a student in an *active* rather *passive* learning situation, and in which any number of activities could be happening: the student might be watching a teacher at the front of the room click through a series of slides, then turn to a neighboring student and discuss the question, then stand up and present the outcome of the discussion to

FIGURE 2.2 Node Chair. Image used with permission of Steelcase.

the class, then join a break-out group of ten students in the corner of the room. This series of activities is facilitated by Node in its design: the chair swivels, it has a double hinge mechanism that allows the work surface to pivot separately from the seat, allowing for easier egress. The student's movement around the room is made easier by the chairs being on wheels and the fact that the large backpacks that students typically bring to class can be tucked away on a large shelf underneath the chair. Other design characteristics speak to the hard knocks anticipated in the life of classroom furniture, and twenty-first-century body types: a flexible nylon seat accommodates a variety of sitting positions (always preferable to ergonomists and back specialists than a fixed position) and eliminates upholstery (expensive). The chair is also large, to accommodate the physiologies of the fast food generations. Node is, in fact, tested to support 2,500 pounds of static load, the equivalent of a 300-pound student flopping into the seat.

Rather than simply reinforce the manufacturer's sales pitch, however, Latour's rule of method invites us to follow the controversies. Outside of the constraints of a trade magazine beholden to advertiser budgets, we might consider the fate of the modern university in a market economy, and call to the witness stand Bill Readings to explain why the university is "in ruins" (Readings 1996). Broadly speaking, the education controversy surrounds Latour's process of purification. In place of a cross-disciplinary pursuit of understanding has come the blinkered pursuit of disciplinary expertise through purifying science and technology of their social content.

Node has taken on the Herculean task of promoting active, cross-disciplinary learning amid the "stack 'em deep and teach 'em cheap" trends in higher education. In its swiveling maneuverability, Node adapts the argument that students of the twenty-first century learn not by sitting and absorbing information but by finding things out for themselves, by *constructing* knowledge in social contexts. In its embrace of collaboration in the classroom, Node perhaps acknowledges that problems of the twenty-first century are inherently interdisciplinary. Climate change, population growth, globalization, and unequal distribution of resources are not problems that can be solved in the engineering school or the statistics department alone. But a chair alone cannot change the economics and culture of education in the university's ruins. Passive learning is cost-effective, and regardless of a teacher's intentions, we have a well-established "fill me with knowledge" consumerist-education culture, reinforced by the spaces themselves.

By prompting us to follow the controversy around the thing rather than remaining fixated on the shiny object, Latour's method leads us from the object to a failure that the object seeks to address. After following the "university-in-ruins" controversy, we might follow the tangled nest of short-term and long-term ethics around environmental impact, again a framework of great importance among the actors of the contract furniture industry. When, for example, is no chair better than manufacturing thousands of new "green" chairs?

Conclusion

I have argued here that the predominant tools of design criticism are too reductive and fixated on the present. In essence, this essay has sought to explicate Brown's observation that, "We begin to confront the thingness of objects when they stop working for us: when the drill breaks, when the car stalls, when the windows get filthy, when their flow within the circuits of production and distribution, consumption and exhibition, has been arrested, however momentarily" (Brown 2001: 4). When things stop working or before they start working, intentions, motives, and negotiations reveal themselves barefaced behind the objects and facts.

Elsewhere, I have made a case for replacing the usual fare of design museums with an exhibition of design failures (Hall 2011). This could be a crowd pleaser in the nostalgic sense, lining up the failures of the past (Sony's Betamax, Ford's Edsel, Microsoft's Bing?), and paving the way for positivist accounts of how failure analysis leads to greater understanding in the spirit of Henry Petroski. But at the heart of this argument is a more fundamental project to recognize the end of Modernity, and with it the end of the idea that social matters and science and technology matters are separate. The argument seeks to expose and undermine the conceit that the present manifestation of any object or technology is the best one.

Notes

1 For example, see G. Harman (2005).
2 See, for example, T. Ingold's account of wayfinding (2000), or A. Nöe's account of cognition (2012).
3 For example, see G. Peers (2013).

Bibliography

Berger, J. (1972), *Ways of Seeing*, London: BBC and Penguin Books.
Brown, B. (2001), "Thing Theory," *Critical Inquiry* 28 (1): 1–22.
Debord, G. (1967), *The Society of the Spectacle*, trans. Donald Nicholson Smith, Cambridge: Zone Books.
Fry, T. (1999), A *New Design Philosophy: An Introduction to Defuturing*, Sydney: University of New South Wales Press.
Fry, T. (2008), *Design Futuring: Sustainability, Ethics and New Practice*, London: Berg.
Fry, T. (2011), *Design as Politics*, Oxford and New York: Berg.
Hall, P. (2010), "Back to School," *Metropolis Magazine*: June, 98–123.
Hall, P. (2011), "The Uses of Failure," *Abitare*, 508.
Harman, G. (2005), "Heidegger on Objects and Things," in B. Latour and P. Weibel (eds), *Making Things Public: Atmospheres of Democracy*, Cambridge, MA, and London: MIT Press.
Harman, G. (2009), *Prince of Networks: Bruno Latour and Metaphysics*, Melbourne: Repress.
Heidegger, M. (1977), *The Question Concerning Technology, and Other Essays*, trans. W. Lovitt, New York: Garland Publishing.
Ingold, T. (2000), *Perception of the Environment: Essays on Livelihood, Dwelling, and Skill*, London and New York: Routledge.
Latour, B. (1987), *Science in Action: How to Follow Scientists and Engineers Through Society*, Cambridge: Harvard University Press.
Latour, B. (1993a), "Ethnography of a High-tech Case," *Technological Choices: Transformation in Material Cultures since the Neolithic*: 372–98.
Latour, B. (1993b), *We Have Never Been Modern*, trans. C. Porter, Cambridge: Harvard University Press.
Latour, B. (1996), *Aramis: Or the Love of Technology*, Cambridge: Harvard University Press.
Latour, B. (2005), "From Realpolitik to Dingpolitik, or How to Make Things Public," in B. Latour and P. Weibel (eds), *Making Things Public: Atmospheres of Democracy*, Cambridge, MA, and London: MIT Press.

Markley, R. (2012), "Time," in T. Cohen (ed.), *Telemorphosis: Theory in the Era of Climate Change*, Ann Arbor, MI: Open Humanities Press.
Marshall, J. (2012), *Machine Art*, Chicago: University of Chicago Press.
Nöe, A. (2012), *Varieties of Presence*, Cambridge: Harvard University Press.
Peers, G. (2013), *Byzantine Things in the World*, Houston: The Menil Collection.
Reading, B. (1996), *The University in Ruins*, Cambridge: Harvard University Press.
Riley, T., and E. Eigen (1995), "Between the Museum and the Marketplace: Selling Good Design," in Szarkowski, J. and J. Elderfield (eds), *The Museum of Modern Art at Mid-Century: At Home and Abroad (Studies in Modern Art)*, 4: 151–79.
Serres, M. and B. Latour (1995), *Conversations on Science, Culture, and Time: Studies in Literature and Science*, trans. R. Lapidus, Ann Arbor, MI: University of Michigan Press.
Tufte, E. (2006), "The Cognitive Style of PowerPoint," originally published in *Beautiful Evidence*, Cheshire: Graphic Press.

3

The practically living weight of convenient things

Cameron Tonkinwise

Prologue

Things have agency. They have the power to act, to do things, above and beyond mechanically reacting to what humans do to them. They can do things to people. They have certain powers over people.

This is the sort of theoretical thing literary types tend to say, the sort of thing that makes you want to bang on the inert table in front of you. But when someone says something counter-intuitive, it is best to give pause, to acknowledge, as Stanley Cavell puts it (1969), that that person is most likely not an idiot, but is trying to point out something that is not readily accepted, something concealed or denied by everyday experience. The person who says "things have agency" clearly knows that, at the moment, things are by definition inertly material, even when they are capable of independent mechanical movements or "machine learning." He or she is trying to challenge this very materialism. This is why provocations like this should not be too quickly judged as straightforward claims.

There are perhaps three other ways of understanding "things have agency":

1 It could just be *metaphorical*. "Imagine that things have agency, or think of the ways in which things appear to have agency." These "as if's" are explicit speculations—thought experiments that are very different from statements of fact. The outcome of thinking in these metaphors might be new ways of understanding things without entailing the factual claim that "all things have agency."

2 It could be meant *symmetrically*,[1] a claim that is as much about the notion of agency as about things. "If things have agency, then we need to change what we mean by 'agency'." Rather than being an inflation of the powers of things, the phrase instead intends to deflate "agency," or at least to transform it away from the sovereignty it suggests when the purview is only living things, especially humans.

3 It could be *anticipatory*, a placeholder for something we need but do not yet have. In this case, the phrase is saying something like, "things have qualities beyond those

attributed to inert things, qualities that are more like agency." The person who says "things have agency," is trying to insist that there appears to be something more to things than our current ways of talking about them allows. What that "more" entails can be somewhat captured by referring to it as "agency"; but we also need to understand "agency" differently as well. "Things have agency" is therefore the motivating brief for a research project.

In the following essay, I want to articulate this third version of "things have agency." I want to explore how we let things come to have agency. If I suspend disbelief in the patterns of light on the wall of cinema, for example, I will experience those images as people in a story—experiences that will have agency over my mood. I want to argue that the phrase, "things have agency" aims to elucidate a similar phenomenon; we let things have agency, but as a result, our subsequent experience of those things is of them having a certain type of agency. The phrase is phenomenological: "we (make ourselves come to) encounter things as agential."

To get to this sense of the agency of things however is difficult due to four further complications of the meanings of this phrase:

4. It should be understood *non-semiotically*. Part of what this phrase infers is decoupling of agency from capacities that are considered to be distinctly human, such as language. Agency is normally attributed to beings with the capacity to form intentions, and intentions depend on the ability to form representations of future states. In other words, agency is normally restricted to beings with semiotic capacities. To say, "things have agency" means that there is a kind of agency that entities without the capacity to form signs can have. What could be the agency of these more materialistic things?

5. It should refer to that subset of things called *artifacts*. In most cases, the phrase "things have agency" is not meant to apply to all things, to anything and everything. It ordinarily refers only to products, to artificial things that have been made by humans for human use. There are philosophies that insist on the agential nature of every thing, from rocks and rivers (Bennett 2010) to hyperobjects like climate change (Morton 2013), and even "fictional" things—Speculative Realism, for instance. And in these philosophies such things manifest agency toward each other irrespective of the presence of humans (Harman 2005). However, for our purposes "things have agency" is more the claim of sociologies of technology (Costall and Dreier 2006), anthropologies of material culture, whether archaeological (Malafouris 2013), or organizational (Leonardi et al. 2012).

6. It could refer to *multiple* things, or better, *networks* of things. Despite the plural, the phrase "things have agency" implies that each thing is distinctly an agent. Again, this derives from a more 'sovereign" sense of agency. But I want to argue that the plural should instead be understood to be how things come to have agency, as was just suggested by point 5. "Things together, constructed into constellations, come to have a forcefulness." Agency is built up or corralled by things acting in concert.

7. It should be *relational*. Agency suggests autonomy, but insofar as agency impacts other people and/or things, it implies, at another level perhaps, some kind of connection. There must be a medium in common through which the thing with agency interacts with the things—or, in our case, people—over which it has agency. As nineteenth-century German philosopher Georg Wilhelm Friedrich Hegel famously noted, the

Master is somewhat enslaved to what he or she has mastery over; or as yet another nineteenth-century German philosopher Friedrich Nietzsche deconstructed, the effect causes the cause to appear as a cause.² Thus, even though the phrase "things have agency" foregrounds the materiality of things, the context for the phrase is rather *sociomateriality*—the way in which the material is the social materialized, and the social only ever manifests in and as material things.

Given these complexities, I want to explore three related perspectives on the phrase "things have agency":

A) *Animating*: The motivations behind and processes by which designers make agential things
B) *Practicing*:³ The everyday activities that interconnect things in ways that give them agency
C) *Gravity*: Recharacterizing a) and b) using a more material metaphor in order to escape a language-dominated version of the agency of things

The person who has recently made the most noise about the agency of things is Bruno Latour. As a sociologist of the practice of science, Latour described the work that scientists required of things in their laboratories in the process of creating knowledge. This alerted Latour to the ways in which everyday life similarly relies on artifacts doing things for us, even helping us to lead more moral lives. The three perspectives on "the agency of things" that I will explore in this chapter, aim to supplement or translate aspects of Latour's ideas about the actions that things do for us. Latour's account of the forces that artifacts can exert mostly applies to things that are already made and operating in the world (Latour 1992). He has also provided descriptions of how technologies are developed through a process of linking components into systems or networks (Latour 1996). But there is a gap between the latter and the former that I will try to fill with respect to A) *Animating*: The motivations behind and process by which designers make agential things.

Latour is also a "frontiersman" on the topic of the agency of things, so, for the purposes of polemic, he is careful to avoid socialization, and especially psychologization, in his descriptions. It is researchers who are committed to Social Practice Theory who reconnect the networking of things that are involved in the development of technologies to more everyday experiences of convenience, comfort, and cleanliness (Shove 2003). Practice Theory is a form of sociology that takes the basic unit of society to be practices, that is, skilled but habitual activities that use networks of devices to accomplish certain qualities of life—e.g., showering, commuting, meal-preparing, etc. B) *Practicing*: The everyday activities that interconnect things in ways that give them agency. I will attempt to show how the agency of things lies with the affects that networked things generate; but again, with an emphasis on how things get enrolled into those networks.

Finally, Latour is very ambiguous with the metaphors structuring his account of thingly agency. Things are originally proposed as representing a "missing mass," a materiality with a social force. However, the vocabulary Latour develops with Madeleine Akrich to describe these forces is explicitly semiotic—that is to say, it emphasizes the role of signs, communications, and meanings: description, prescription, inscription, etc. (Akrich and Latour 1992). So C) *Gravity*: to escape a language-dominated version of the agency of things, I will try to reinstate a material version of the force of things that is more appropriate to how Animating and Practising happen.

Animating

Why do we humans make useful things?

When the things that are made prove useful, the answer seems obvious—things are made to make our lives easier; they increase the effectiveness and/or efficiency of being human. But the process of making itself is not inherently efficient. Imagine, for instance, being a hunter/gatherer with a tight energy budget: you must not expend more energy pursuing food than you can get from the food. In that case, what prompts the gamble to expend energy designing and then making a tool for pursuing food?[4] If the tool proves useful that will have been energy well spent, but there is no way to know this beforehand. This situation suggests that while an outcome of making useful things can be greater effectivity, this is not what motivates the making in the first place.

To put this another way, it is important not naturalize efficiency and/or effectivity with presumption that living inherently tends toward—even to the point of seeking to make—what is easiest and most convenient. Critics of capitalism worry when they hear industrial objectives for continuous productivity improvements cast as inevitabilities. What about all the seemingly unproductive activities, such as play, that most animals and humans, perform (Graeber 2014), or the pleasures we pursue that deliberately take time (Grosz 2011)—precisely the kinds of pursuits that we associate with creativity, and also making?

James Gibson, the ecological perception theorist whose notion of affordance has proved important for understanding how designs are useful, would argue that the question "why do we make useful things?" is ill-framed. It assumes that humans are distinct from their environments, separated from the things lying around that would make their survival easier. Gibson's ecological perception theory instead insists perception is interactional, that things are perceived always with respect to their usefulness. Humans perceive things-in-the-world not as abstract shapes that need decoding, but as potential "usables," as body-action-extensions that humans already imagine themselves deploying.

Here we have a first instance of agential things. To capture the interpenetration of humans and their environments, Gibson coins the term "affordance." It implies a symmetry of action; not only by the perceiving human but also by the perceived thing. Affordances manifest as things that are always already communicating to humans about their capacities. It is as if some thing nearby perceives my imagined action and calls out its capacity to help without my having to develop an abstract representation of it. I do not look for it; it suggests itself. This animism, if not anthropomorphism, seems necessary to explain how it is that humans find uses in things when they are not entirely sure what kind of thing it is that they might need to accomplish what they are doing.

As I will discuss in the final section, this things-calling-out-to-us version of affordances is still very communicative. While the relation between the subject perceiving and the perceived object is more symmetrical—the thing is an active participant in the process—there is still a gap between the two, a gap that still involves a kind of interpretation. Gibson's ecological perception theory tries to move away from this kind of representational decoding version of perception, and instead toward perception as a less mediated experience. In the *Gravity* section below, I aim to describe perceiving useful things more in terms of "attraction" than communication—the pushing or pulling force that affordances have.

While Gibson's account explains how humans (and animals) come to use things as tools in the moment of undertaking an act like food gathering, almost without thinking, his notion of affordances does not yet explain more considered acts of making, like design. What motivates humans to spend time speculating about possibly useful new things to make?

To my mind, one of the only answers lies in the work of Elaine Scarry. Perhaps best characterized as a Philosopher of Literature (and consequently a progenitor of thing theory), Scarry closes her giant text, *The Body in Pain* (1985), with an account of artifact creation. The book commences with an examination of torture and the way torturers "unmake" the world of those they torture, breaking them down to access information. Scarry's analysis turns on the fact that much torture involves the use of domestic tools. This prompts the final chapter in the book in which Scarry looks at the reverse process of "making"—why and how do humans make domestic worlds filled with everyday tools?

Making, according to Scarry, is motivated by the desire to animate the world to human needs, to make our material environments more humane, as if filled with human capacities for empathy. As I cradle a partner in pain, I imagine a materialized cradler, a chair that can relieve my partner's weight more permanently. I make the world afford this weight relief:

> The chair is therefore the materialized structure of a perception; it is sentient awareness materialized into a freestanding design. If one pictures the person in *the action* of making a chair—standing in one place, moving away, coming back, lifting then letting fall his arm, kneeling then standing, kneeling, half-kneeling, stooping, looking, extending his arm, pulling it back—and if one pictures all these actions as occurring without a tool or block of wood before him, that is, if one pictures only the man and his embodied actions, what one at that moment has before one is *not* the *act of perception* (his seeing of another's discomfort and wishing it gone) but *the structure of the act of perception visibly enacted*. What was originally an invisible aspect of consciousness (compassion) has now been translated into the realm of visible but disappearing action. The interior moment of perceiving has been translated into a willed series of successive actions, as if it were a dance, a dance entitled "body weight begone."
>
> If, now, the tool is placed back in his hand and the wood placed beneath that tool, a second translation occurs, for the action, direction and pressure of his dance move down across the tool and are recorded in the surface of the wood ... from disappearing action to an enduring material form. Thus in work, a perception is danced; in the chair, a danced-perception is sculpted. (Scarry 1985: 290–1)

Scarry's description explicitly reaches beyond metaphor. Things are made to "know" things about the humans they are designed to serve. A chair is the materialization of knowledge about the pain associated with carrying bodily weight continuously; and the form of the chair is materialized knowledge of human anatomy. Making a chair involves converging these two pieces of knowledge into an object that actively affords the weight removal through sitting. When someone makes an artifact, they are trying to make the world more animate to human needs, more sensitive to human feelings. They are replacing a brutish natural world indifferent to humans with one that has been designed to care for humans. Talk of the made thing "knowing" fits with how we evaluate made things, judging the limits of their knowledge—that certain chairs do not know that humans are becoming more obese and so risk collapse, or that some humans like to rock on the back two legs of a chair:

> The chair must "know" about the problem of weight; the lightbulb must "know" about the problem of seeing at night. But it here becomes noticeable that artifacts must know a

great deal more about their human maker than the particular needs they accommodate ... A stepladder, for example, not only "knows" (incorporates into its design the knowledge that) human beings are shorter than they often need to be, but also "knows" that human beings tend to overstep themselves when lost in trying to be taller than they are: the top step may bear the words, "Do not step onto this step" (i.e., "I know that you will fall, even if you do not know that at this moment"). An object must be *self*-aware: its design must ... anticipate how it will be used (and even how it might be oddly used). (Scarry 1985: 302–3)

When Latour describes thing agency, he makes use of the fact that a compressed-air door-closing device is named after the doorman whose activities it replicates and so makes redundant. In the article, "A sociology of a door-closer,"[5] Latour's intention is to describe the anthropomorphic manner in which things function, not how they are made. Scarry's account shows that Latour's anthropomorphism is also an accurate account of how the making of such devices happens, with designers imagining how to make a mechanism that embodies "human smarts." Things have agency because making is making things have agency; that is why they were made in the first place, to make the world more (re)active toward humans.

Arguing that things are made animate by designers might seem to be a way of denying that those things are in fact animate; while they are made to act in ways that seem animate, agency appears to lie ultimately with the designer. However, Scarry very carefully describes how making is always a two-stage process: Making-Up and Making-Real (Scarry 1985: 313; Scarry 1992). New things are invented or "made-up"; they are imagined, but even when they are built they remain the products of someone's imagination; they bear the signature of their makers. But a subsequent stage in their becoming-real involves the denial of their ever having-been-made in the first place. Marxists call this reification, the way in which products are alienated from the workers who created them so that they can circulate as unencumbered commodities. Once a thing is animated into active service by a designer, it is able to function as designed long after its maker, as well as the person for whom it might have originally been made, are dead. Things continue to act in the real world independent of their having-been-once-made(-up).

If we recall Gibson now, we can see that "making real" is also the moment at which affordances materialize in artifacts: the intent of the designer transfers over to the thing itself, which now actively offers its capacities to anyone who perceives it. These offers are ever-present rather than dependent on our conscious intentions as makers or users. In other words, we take thing agency for granted as the background to all that we do. Scarry finds evidence for this idea in the strange reflex we have to "punish" objects that fail us, as if we are surprised when things suddenly appear before us as dumb and fallibly made:

The ongoing, day-to-day norm is that an object is mimetic of sentient awareness: the chair routinely relieves the problem of weight. Should the object prove insufficiently mimetic of awareness, insufficiently capable of accommodating the problem of weight (i.e., if the chair is uncomfortable—an animistic phrase we use to mean if "the person is uncomfortable in the chair"), the object will be discarded or set aside ... [should] the legs of the chair suddenly break beneath the weight of the person and he is hurt ... the chair's object-stupidity strikes all who witness its collapse as a surprise, an outrage ... In fact, it is crucial to notice that if the person now picks up a fragment of that object and hurls it against the wall (as though it could be made to feel the hurt in just inflicted), the person is actually continuing to act out of the context of the normal situation (in which the chair indeed has the mimetic attributes of sentient awareness) rather than out of the immediate moment (in which the chair has just exposed its object-obliviousness). (Scarry 1985: 295–6)

Far from animism being the exceptional make-believe practice of children and "savages," Scarry indicates that it is a necessary norm for everyday life. It is the agency of made-up-then-real things that makes living less of a pain.

Practicing

The poetic force of Scarry's argument depends in part on the fact that it centers on emotive examples of strong pain: pregnancy, the death of a child, a headache, pinching your finger in a door. Her argument is made more plausible by the fact that making is explained as a drastic response to situations that clearly call out for a response. The time and energy to make up new things seems appropriate to such directly empathic situations. But most of the things we make use of in our everyday lives ameliorate only the most minor of annoyances. The base rim of a coffee cup might have a small gap in it, for example, to ensure that any water that might pool after dishwashing can leak away, just in case that tiny amount of water falls on you as you turn the cup over to put it back in the cupboard. This is far from the kind of emotion that Scarry imagined drives makers.

Scarry's account needs supplementing with Thomas Tierney's *Genealogy of Technical Culture*, which centers on *The Value of Convenience* (1993). It seems obvious that technologies are designed to enhance convenience, but, as with claims about the inherent value of efficiency, we should still wonder why and how. Tierney's involved argument ties together religion, technology, and attitudes toward life and death. Because Western religions prize the afterlife above all else, secularization seems to reverse this, revalorizing mortal life. Tierney disputes this by showing how technological innovations are attempts to overcome the imperfections involved in living. In Tierney's version of the technological imaginary, all pains, from the serious ones that Scarry places at the basis of her animistic analysis to the minor ones that indents in the base of coffee cups correct, are equivalents; even death is just another pain that technology wants to overcome. Modern technology is less about meeting biological demands, for survival for example, than it is about overcoming limits, liberating us from embodied encumbrances.

For the purposes of this chapter, I want to reverse Tierney's argument somewhat in order to explain better how made-up things get realized as useful agents. I want to suggest that the making-real process happens as the construction of convenience; or more precisely that convenience is created by ceding agency to things, letting made-up things carry out activities for us.

Tierney reminds us that in the ascetic traditions of many religions and even in secular philosophies (for example, the "work ethic") people often choose ways of living that seem inconvenient. This suggests that convenience is relativistic construct. A car is convenient to own, but the cost of the car is inconvenient, and the latter may cause car-share systems to appear more convenient even though the use process involves more time and is less immediate. Convenience is then better thought of as a settled pattern of use; it is a result rather than a cause. The term convenience itself refers to things coming together (*con-venire*). This may be physical collocation, as when a modern bourgeois house is said to contain "conveniences." But this coming together is also what happens when things are enlisted as parts of a routine. When a set of things can be used habitually, without deliberation, those things feel convenient. There is nothing inherently convenient about a washing machine; it becomes a convenience once it is part of the only-ever semi-conscious activity of laundering.

I am referencing Social Practice Theory here (Schatzki et al. 2001), and particularly Elizabeth Shove's account of assemblages of devices, skills, and meanings into practices of convenience, comfort, and cleanliness (Shove et al. 2012). What is convenient is what lies close at hand and can be taken up semi-automatically as part of an established practice. This then is how made-up things become made-real; as components in a system, but one in which those components, those things, act in ways that allow me to proceed without thinking about them. In a convenient practice, I am collaborating with things with agency, rather than consciously using inert things; and their agency derives from their being enlisted into a regularized practice, a place and rhythm in which they come alive and do their part.

When you perform an everyday practice, it is as if everything needed is acting in concert, appropriately offering itself at the right time for the completion of the task. The way your conduct happens assumes that all the things involved are reliably there for you, as if sensing where you are in the practice. To describe some thing as convenient implies that it has a kind of networked agency which comes from, but is more than, its being close by at hand. Convenient things serve the practices they enable as active participants.

To put it the other way around, the agency of things is made real by their enrollment in practices. Their agency is never sovereign, but relational, sustained by the other things they collaborate with, and by the humans conducting the practice. This means that the agency of things is never instantaneous. Things must be trained into their role as actors (Ilmonen 2004). They are made to linkup with other things in cascading affordances that over time blackbox how they act. They are rehearsed into the practice until they no longer need support but can be relied on "to do their bit."

And, obversely, people are also "configured" by those rehearsed networks of things into the role of users (Woolgar 1990). They learn to act in ways that respond to the emerging agency of things, doing as things say. A designed artifact can only do what it does when interacted with in the right way—you must press the right button to start it; clapping or shouting will not work. The agency of that designed artifact arises out of this well-practised relation(ship).

Gravity

I think evidence for this relation between the agency of things and convenience lies in the fact that convenience, though a relativistic cultural construct, has force once it is located in a collection of things. We moderns find ourselves drawn to what is convenient. Things that offer convenient ways of doing things are not neutral tools, but attractors. This force that they exert on us is not irresistible; we can always choose to do what requires more effort. But my point here is that that choice is one we experience as an act of resistance; to exercise our agency, we must actively defy the way convenient things draw us to them. By contrast, doing what is convenient is more like giving in, or giving over to, ceding our agency to things.

So far, I have mostly been using communicative metaphors to capture this animistic force of things: things "call out" to us about what they afford; things are "conscripted" into performative "roles;" users are "configured" to do what things "say." These are misleading characterizations that provoke defensive reaction—"you cannot mean that things express intentions." To some extent, I agree; these phrases do not do justice to the very material nature of this agency. We need a different metaphor for elaborating the convenient agency of things.

Latour's most strident argument for recognition of thingly agency is: "Where are the Missing Masses?" Latour describes debates in cosmology that assert that there is not enough visible mass in the universe to hold it together. Astrophysicists must posit an invisible form of "dark matter" to explain the amount of gravity needed to sustain the universe's structure. He uses this to argue by analogy that there is not enough 'sociality" to stop our societies falling apart; there must be something else sustaining the social, and for Latour that is literally some "things," material things to which humans delegate morality so that "society can be made durable." At this point, the analogy has done its work and he does not dwell on this way of understanding things as socially gravitational. But I believe the analogy can do more work.

When Jaap Jelsma (2006) takes up Latour's ideas of "things scripting users" to understand how designers can steer people toward more sustainable futures, he enlists a diagram from Conrad Waddington's paper (1977) on chreods in evolutionary biology. That diagram was already being used by sociologists to explain the "path dependent" evolution of certain technologies. Jelsma recontextualizes that diagram as an account of a person navigating domestic device ecologies. The visual argument is that designs that make certain actions more convenient act like gradients to a rolling ball; the ball can be pushed back up hill, but "going with the flow" downhill is more likely. The diagram becomes an illustration of the agency of things, with convenience portrayed as a gravitational pull. It is weak force that can act at a distance. It is less a communication, requiring mindful decoding, than a more immediate thing–body attraction, a physically material power.

Latour says as much in his "Missing Masses" article, when discussing cascading affordances that chunk distinct actions into the one activity:

> most of the effect finally ascribed to [these devices] depends on lines of other setups being aligned ... This gradient of aligned setups that endow actors with the pre-inscribed competences to find its users is very much like Waddington's "chreod" ... The result of such an alignment of setups is to decrease the number of occasions in which words are used; most of the actions are silent, familiar, incorporated (in human and nonhuman bodies). (Latour 1992: 240)

And Peter-Paul Verbeek and Peter Kockelkoren make a similar observation when describing how human-technology relations stabilize:

> We thus need a new concept to clarify the relation between people and products if we want to take products seriously *as* things. Such a concept can be found in Don Ihde's work *Technology and the Lifeworld*. He develops a perspective on technology that does justice to both the mediated character of people's relation to reality and the "own weight" of technical artifacts ... "Once technologies have received a (relative) identity," according to Ihde, "*within that relation* they nevertheless can have an own weight." Ihde calls this "own weight" *technological intentionality*. With this concept, he wants to indicate that technologies-in-use are no neutral objects, but that they themselves co-shape the use that is being made of them. Practices around technologies cannot be entirely reduced to human intentions ... In all of these instances, no obligation is involved, but rather inclination: technologies invite certain ways of dealing with them ... The concept of "technological intentionality"

thus makes visible nonlingual aspects of the relation between people and things. It does not reduce artifacts to "signs" or "intentions of designers" but indicates the way in which they are present and help to shape their environment *as things*. (Verbeek and Kockelkoren 1998: 36–7)

Verbeek and Kockelkoren's article, "The Things that Matter," has the same ambitions for a post-semiotic account of the thing agency as I have pursued here. To this end, they test the limits of this gravitational metaphor, exploring the extent to which the correlation between microwaves and divorce in households can be interpreted as causation—insofar as the device makes more convenient individual rescheduling of meals by allowing reheating, disrupting practices of family gathering around just-now-prepared meals. This is clearly not a case of things scripting social relations. But there does appear to be a force at work, forces that can be resisted, but forces that we can also conveniently "make real."

Practically living weight

"Things have agency" is therefore not a straight claim that things are willfully alive. It is a strategic claim that draws attention to the forces that things can exert. It says that things are practically living—by which I mean both that they are almost alive, and that they come to life as part of practices. Things exert a force that feels like a gravitational weight when they are networked into the practices of everyday life. Made up fictions about things having agency become conveniently real, in ways that words do not have the weight to effectively convey.

From the outset, I pointed out that the claim "things have agency" should be understood in an *anticipatory* way, as a brief. I have tried to argue that making things have agency is precisely the brief of design. Designers feel for humans struggling against the indifferent material world. So they make things that make the world more alive to human needs. But those designed things can only do what they have been designed to do in concert with humans. Things need humans to interact with them in particular ways so that they can appropriately proffer their services. So designers design things in ways that afford particular kinds of uses, and users learn to make habitual those kinds of interactions with things. The result is a convenient practice, a routinized coming together of people and things.

In that performed ensemble, things feel like they have agency; they do what is needed, playing their part, without the user having to think about it. It is as if humans can be more thing-like, less consciously active in steering this or that practice, because things have been allowed to become more human, as per their design. Everyday life, moving from practice to practice, can then feel like a series of looping orbits as we are pulled to swing first around this convenience, and then around that convenience, and then around another. Each of these practices is nevertheless no mere dead weight, but an active force, with its own quality. Some practices are short and fast, others longer, more involved, sometimes not even smooth. We live each day alongside all these other practically living things, pushing and pulling to occupy our time more or less conveniently.

Notes

1 I use the term "symmetry" to refer to the way the phrase "things have agency" might be trying to say as much about agency as about things. I have chosen this descriptor for the phrase's bi-directionality so as to reference a contentious principle of Bruno Latour's philosophy which he has since recanted. In his chapter on "Objects too have Agency" (2005), Latour clarifies that, "To be symmetric, for us, simply means *not* to impose *a priori* some spurious *asymmetry* among human intentional action and a material world of causal relations" (76).

2 "The disappearance of agency in the so called 'materialist world view' is a stunning invention, especially since it is contradicted every step of the way by the odd resistance of reality; every consequence adds slightly to a cause. Thus, it has to have some sort of agency. There is a supplement, a gap between the two. If not, there would be no possible way of discriminating causes from consequences" (Latour 2010: 482).

3 This now archaic spelling is intentional to foreground the process by which devices are enlisted into a habitualized activity—through practise (rehearsal), things become animated components of an everyday practice (routine).

4 Luis Fernández-Galiano recalls Reyner Banham's fable of the origin of architecture lying in the moment that someone decides to build a house out of wood rather than just burn the wood for warmth (2000: 6).

5 An earlier version of the essay "Where are the Missing Masses" (Latour 1992) was published by Latour under the deliberately North American pseudonym Jim Johnson (1988) with the title "Mixing Human and Nonhuman Together: The Sociology of a Door-Closer."

Bibliography

Akrich, M. and B. Latour (1992), "A Summary of a Convenient Vocabulary for the Semiotic of Human and Nonhuman Assemblies," in W. Bijker and J. Law (eds), *Shaping Technology / Building Society: Studies in Sociotechnical Change*, Cambridge, MA: MIT Press.

Bennett, J. (2010), *Vibrant Matter: A Political Ecology of Things*, Durham: Duke University Press.

Cavell, S. (1969), "Knowing and Acknowledging," in *Must We Mean What We Say?*, Cambridge: Cambridge University Press.

Costall, A. and O. Dreier (eds) (2006), *Doing Things with Things*, Burlington, VT: Ashgate.

Edwards, D., M. Ashmore, and J. Potter (1995), "Death and Furniture: the Rhetoric, Politics and Theology of Bottom Line Arguments against Relativism," *History of the Human Sciences* 8 (2).

Fernández-Galiano, L. (2000), *Fire and Memory: On Architecture and Energy*, Cambridge, MA: MIT Press.

Graeber, D. (2014) "What's the Point if We Can't Have Fun?," *The Baffler*, 24.

Grosz, E. (2011), *Becoming Undone: Darwinian Reflections on Life, Politics and Art*, Durham: Duke University Press.

Harman, G. (2005), *Guerrilla Metaphysics: Phenomenology and the Carpentry of Things*, Peru, IL: Open Court.

Ilmonen, K. (2004), "The Use of and Commitment to Goods," *Journal of Consumer Culture* 27 (4).

Jelsma, J. (2003), "Innovating for Sustainability: Involving Users, Politics and Technology," *Innovation* 16 (2).

Johnson, J. (1988), "Mixing Human and Nonhuman Together: The Sociology of a Door-Closer," *Social Problems* 35 (3).

Latour, B. (1992), "Where are the Missing Masses? The Sociology of a Few Mundane Artefacts," in

W. Bijker and J. Law (eds), *Shaping Technology / Building Society: Studies in Sociotechnical Change*, Cambridge, MA: MIT Press.

Latour, B. (1996), *Aramis: For the Love of Technology*, Cambridge, MA: Harvard University Press.

Latour, B. (2005), *Reassembling the Social: An Introduction to Actor-Network Theory*, New York: Oxford University Press.

Latour, B. (2010), "An Attempt at a 'Compositionist Manifesto," *New Literary History* 41 (3): 471–90.

Leonardi, P., B. Nardi, and J. Kallinikos (eds) (2012), *Materiality and Organizing: Social Interaction in a Technological World*, Oxford: Oxford University Press.

Malafouris, L. (2013), *How Things Shape the Mind*, Cambridge, MA: MIT.

Morton, T. (2013), *Hyperobjects: Philosophy and Ecology at the End of the World*, Minneapolis: University of Minnesota Press.

Scarry, E. (1985), *The Body in Pain: The Making and Unmaking of the World*, London: Oxford University Press.

Scarry, E. (1992), "The Made-Up and the Made-Real," *Yale Journal of Criticism* 5 (2): 239–49.

Schatzki, T., K. Knorr-Cetina, and E. von Savigny (eds) (2001), *The Practice Turn in Contemporary Theory*, London: Routledge.

Shove, E. (2003), *Comfort, Cleanliness and Convenience: The Social Organization of Normality*, Oxford: Berg.

Shove, E., M. Pantzar, and M. Watson (2012), *The Dynamics of Social Practice: Everyday Life and How it Changes*, London: Sage.

Tierney, T. (1993), *The Value of Convenience: A Genealogy of Technical Culture*, Albany: State University of New York Press.

Verbeek, P. and P. Kockelkoren (1998), "The Things that Matter," *Design Issues* 14 (3).

Waddington, C. (1977), "Stabilisation in Systems: Chreods and Epigenetic Landscapes," *Futures* 9 (2): 139–46.

Woolgar, S. (1990), "Configuring the User: The Case of Usability Trials," *The Sociological Review*, 38 (S1): 58–99.

4

Big things

The vibrant culture of boomboxes

Prasad Boradkar and Lyle Owerko

In Spike Lee's legendary film *Do the Right Thing*, we see Radio Raheem walking down a Brooklyn street with an enormous, black-and-chrome boombox in his hands, playing Public Enemy's "Fight the Power," when the sound starts to falter and eventually stops (see Plate 1). He fiddles with the buttons on the box and realizes that the batteries have run down. Raheem walks into a convenience store and asks for "twenty D Energizers." The shopkeeper, who apparently does not hear him right, asks a couple of times if he wants C-size batteries. Raheem, annoyed and incredulous that he would buy anything smaller than D-size, shouts back "D motherfucker D." A heated exchange ensues, the shopkeeper puts the batteries in a bag, Raheem checks to ensure there are indeed twenty of the right size, and leaves the store.

Part of the appeal of Raheem's boombox, a Clairtone 7985/Tecsonic Promax Super Jumbo J–1, was the fact that it needed ten of those large batteries to power up. Twenty-five pounds in weight, 31-inches long and 16½-inches high, this massive music player was an imposing slab of audio technology. It boasted a highly glossy black and chrome body, 8-inch woofers, mid-range speakers and tweeters, dual cassette decks, a ten-band equalizer, and a series of flashing lights that pulsated with the beats. This boombox was loud, not only in the sound it produced, but also in its visual presence.

We, the authors of this visual essay, have a special interest in the materiality and cultural import of these devices: one of us, Lyle Owerko, is an avid collector and photographer of boomboxes, while the other, Prasad Boradkar, studies and writes about music technologies. And, in this chapter, we present boomboxes as things that possess vibrant power, as devices that had the capability to gather people as a community, but also to give individuals a sense of empowerment. This capability can be described as the agentic power of boomboxes, and it can be attributed, at least partially, to their designs. They were often very large, shiny objects with chrome-plated buttons and flashing lights, and they were outfitted with massive speakers that could create ear-splitting sound. They were instruments of visual and audio power that appeared on record covers, in music videos, and in films as material icons of a generation.

The boombox as a phenomenon

While the origins of the term "boombox" are not known with any certainty, audio and electronics stores apparently began using it in the United States in marketing and advertising in the early to mid-1980s.

> The emergence of cassettes and FM radio demanded a new generation of equipment that was both portable and able to reproduce music in high quality stereo. These needs combined with a growing cultural fascination with consumer electronics in general to create a market for a new product: a combined radio and cassette player that was high-quality, high-powered, stereophonic, and portable. (Schloss and Boyer 2014: 401)

Boomboxes were reasonably priced and therefore affordable to inner city youth. Most of them had an AM/FM radio, two cassette players to dub tapes, two or more large speakers for volume, battery and AC capability, and several auxiliary connections to plug in other equipment like microphones or turntables. All these design features made it possible for people to make mixtapes, breakdance in the streets, and broadcast music in public spaces, and they made boomboxes iconic products of a generation.

The JVC RC–M90 boombox, shown in Plate 2, for example, is a benchmark piece of electronics—it is well balanced in size, shape, and audio output, and was a highpoint of the boombox era, both in quality and craftsmanship. It was not flashy, but was one of the loudest boomboxes around; it was the one used by hip-hop artist LL Cool J on the cover of his album *Radio*. This was the first long-playing record released by the label Def Jam, and is often considered to be one of the first hip-hop albums as well. "My radio, believe me, I like it loud, I'm the man with a box that can rock the crowd, walkin' down the street, to the hardcore beat, while my JVC vibrates the concrete" are the opening lyrics of the song "I Can't Live Without My Radio" on this album. The reference to the power of the boombox in its loudness and its ability to shake the ground are evident in the words. LL Cool J creates an urban scene opening with "street" and "concrete," describing further in the song how he plays "even on the subway," as he "drive[s] up to the ave," and when he "walk[s] down the block." He also highlights the materiality of the boombox in calling attention to the "woofers," "tweeters," "wires," "cassette," and the "power meter." The song has four verses, and each ends with the refrain "I'm the leader of the show, keepin' you on the go, but I know I can't live without my radio." These lines deftly capture the spirit of the times, offering insights into how essential these boomboxes were for music culture of the 1980s.

Does size matter?

Boomboxes can be described, in Jane Bennett's terms, as "vibrant matter" (2010). In developing the notion of "vibrant materiality," she suggests that things are not inert, passive, or dead as they are often made out to be; instead, they have a vitality and a liveliness that gives them agency, action, and independence. It is as if they have a life of their own, irrespective of humans. Boomboxes were vibrant in all senses of the word. Their rectangular, hard-edged bodies were adorned with steel and aluminum face-plates, banks of dials, buttons, knobs and switches, and rows of LEDs programmed to pulsate with sound. Many of these boomboxes were aggressive in appearance, and even when silent, their imposing bodies commanded attention. Like "magnets," they attracted urban youth to parks and street corners to gather around them. The larger they were, the more monumental was their presence in people's lives and in the city. And once the play button was pressed, and the speakers came to life, it was as if a boombox was releasing its pent-up audio power and discharging a torrent of sound out into the world. Designed to attract attention, these devices clearly possessed and exercised power.

"Thing-power gestures toward the strange ability of ordinary, man-made items to exceed their status as objects and to manifest traces of independence or aliveness, constituting the outside of our own experience" (Bennett 2010: xvi). And their power, their agency, is transferred to humans, too. When Radio Raheem encounters Stevie and a group of young Puerto Rican men playing their own boombox in the street, a battle of loudness ensues. Stevie turns up the volume on his boombox, and Raheem responds by doing the same on his Promax Super Jumbo J–1. The (thingly) power of the Promax drowns out Stevie's Latin music and he turns it down in an act of submission.

So, size does matter: It exaggerated everything the boombox could do. Not only did size give the boomboxes significant visual and material presence, but it also created room for larger speakers and a whole new range of features. Therefore, larger boomboxes could be a lot louder, and could be outfitted with additional functions that transformed these devices into portable recording studios. Introduced in 1984, and weighing in at 26 lbs. without batteries, the Sharp GF–777 (see Plate 3), was one of the heaviest and largest boomboxes ever made. Its body, at 29-inch long, 15-inch high and 6-inch deep, had enough space on it to have two 6.5-inch super woofers, two 6.5-inch woofers, and two 2-inch horn tweeters that could pump out 90-watts of peak music power output (PMPO). With dubbing switches and indicators, input jacks for microphones, ability to record from radio and turntables, separate base controls for the super woofers, loudness switches, and echo control, aspiring DJs and MCs could set up these boomboxes anywhere for a party. These features attracted audiences; people gathered around them.

Design and technology

Boombox manufacturers, such as Clairtone, Sony, Panasonic, Lasonic, Marantz, and others produced a staggering variety of boxes in an assortment of styles, sizes, and colors, and with a variety of features, in order both to feed and capitalize on this culture. The designers and manufacturers clearly recognized the value of the material presence of the boomboxes on the streets. In addition, the cultural power of the boombox as a thing was reflected in movies and the content of the songs. The scenes we describe above from *Do the Right Thing* demonstrate that the forms, textures, shapes, and features of boomboxes were expressions of power and community—power of music, power of youth, and power of street culture—all expressed through the physical, tangible, material thing.

One such shiny chrome boombox with a "sci-fi" aesthetic was the 36-inch long and 16-inch high Conion CF–100 (see Plate 4). This boombox had one unique feature that no other device did—two cassette decks that were stacked one above the other. The top deck was a horizontal slot where the cassette would be inserted through a spring-loaded door, while the bottom deck was in the standard position. The two 8-inch woofers, two 4-inch mid-range speakers, and two 2-inch tweeters gave this device the ability to generate sound across a wide range of frequencies.

Other features included a series of dials, toggle switches, two analog VU (Volume Unit) meters, LED meters, and a blue station display panel. In addition, it was outfitted with motion-detector, anti-theft technology that was fabled to set off a deafening alarm if the box was moved. This was essentially a state-of-the-art (at the time) sound system, and the device was used by many major artists when rap was crossing over into mainstream music.

These boomboxes and their thingly attributes—those aspects of their being that made them meaningful—such as big power, enormous sizes, shiny chrome surfaces, large dials and buttons, big speakers, and flashing lights—left an impression not only on the young men and women who carried them, but also on the audiences. If thing-power is "the curious ability of inanimate things to animate, act, to produce effects dramatic and subtle" (Bennett 2010: 6), boombox-power animated individuals and groups of people. These devices exercised their agency and power on young men like Radio Raheem who carried them around everywhere they went. This flashy CF–100 certainly mobilized a following. "I have to agree with everyone that the Conion C100 is almost every collectors dream machine," says a member of the popular website boomboxery.com in a post from 2010.

Gathering things and bodies

"Each object gathers around itself a different assembly of relevant parties" (Latour 2005: 14). The portability of the boomboxes encouraged shared moments of music consumption in highly public spaces in the city—in parks, parking lots, and street corners. Young men and women congregated around these portable devices, drawn to their material, auditory, and visual power. In other words, the material forms and functions—the design features of the boomboxes—brought people together, often in impromptu gatherings in the city. Interestingly, the role of a physical object as an agent in gathering people together has a history in the discussion of the meaning of the word "thing." In his seminal essay, "What is a Thing?," philosopher Martin Heidegger discusses the origin of the word thing (*Ding* in Old German), and suggests that it refers to gatherings; it denotes anything that is a "matter of pertinence," and a "matter for discourse" (1971: 172). "To be sure, the Old German word *thing* means a gathering, and specifically a gathering to deliberate on a matter under discussion, a contested matter" (Heidegger 1971: 172). In other words, things are political gatherings.

As a thing that had the power to assemble young people to own, reformulate, and contest public spaces, the boombox, too, can be described as being political. "Both the recording function and the portability of the boombox enabled its ubiquitous presence at gatherings of activists, enabling music to function as a resource for the forging of political community" (Von Eschen 2016: 195). Initially, the boombox was identified with certain segments of urban society, primarily African American and Hispanic youth, as a tool of disruption and subcultural identity, garnering epithetic nicknames like "ghetto-blaster" and "jambox." But as more people began to embrace these gargantuan, chrome-plated electronic gadgets, an intensely public form of portable entertainment and personal expression was born. Debates and discussions accompanied boombox gatherings. In *Do the Right Thing*, Radio Raheem listens to the song "Fight the Power" by Public Enemy over and over again. The lyrics "freedom or death" and "fight the powers that be" establish that this song, Radio Raheem, and the young men and women in the film, are rebellious and anti-establishment. By its capacity to bring youth to assemble in public spaces and through the music they played, the boombox took on the meanings of *Ding*.

From public to private music consumption

The boombox was a portable audio device, but its use was highly public and communal rather than individual and private; it gathered people around itself. It was designed to be played publicly; it was designed to be loud. However, over time, cities started issuing noise ordinances in reaction to complaints about the volumes of the boomboxes. The device was seen as disruptive and uncivil. "The sphere of the ghetto blaster is public; the psychological imperatives at work are sociability (the kindest reading) and a desire to dominate and make oneself heard or one's presence known (the least kind reading)" (Berger 1992: 83). Boomboxes can be understood in two distinct ways—as social magnets that encouraged people to gather around them, but also as antisocial devices that allowed individuals to flaunt dominance and disturb others.

The Walkman, on the other hand, an audio player which was introduced by Sony in 1979, was a private device to be listened to on headphones by individuals rather than groups. Today's MP3 players (like the iPod) are also individual listening devices. "If ghetto blaster users are anomic, and disregard the rules of conduct and codes of civility relating to being quiet in public places, Walkman users are alienated and antisocial. Walkman users do not bother people the way ghetto blaster users do, but they do something even worse—they reject them" (Berger 1992: 83–4).

Portable audio devices, like many other products of digital technology, have gotten more individualized and significantly smaller over time. Their sleek touch-screen designs with interface-based virtual controls have moved far from the large, dial-studded boomboxes we have seen here. Music players are slipped clandestinely into pockets today, rather than being carried brazenly on shoulders. They are silent and invisible. Boomboxes too have become silent and invisible: they are no longer seen on streets, but rather in collectors' homes, in books, and on websites, as imposing ghosts of an era bygone.

Bibliography

Berger, A. (1992), *Reading Matter: Multidisciplinary Perspectives on Material Culture*, New Brunswick, NJ: Transaction Publishers.
Bennett, J. (2010), *Vibrant Matter: A Political Ecology of Things*, Durham: Duke University Press.
Clarke, J. (2003), "The Creation of Style," in S. Hall and T. Jefferson (eds), *Resistance Through Rituals: Youth Subcultures in Post-war Britain*, London: Routledge.
Heidegger, M. (1971), *Poetry, Language, Thought*, New York: Harper & Row Publishers.
Latour, B. (2005), "From Realpolitik to Dingpolitik," in B. Latour and P. Weibel (eds), *Making Things Public: Atmospheres of Democracy*, ZKM Publishing/MIT Press Books.
Schloss, J. and B. Boyer (2014), "Urban Echoes: The Boombox and Sonic Mobility in the 1980s," in Sumanth Gopinath and Jason Stanyek (eds), *The Oxford Handbook of Mobile Music Studies*, Vol. 1, Oxford: Oxford University Press.
Taylor, T. (2001), *Strange Sounds: Music, Technology and Culture*, London: Routledge.
Von Eschen, P. (2016), "Di Eagle and Di Bear: Who Gets to Tell the Story of the Cold War," in R. Radano and T. Olaniyan, *Audible Empire: Music, Global Politics, Critique*, Durham: Duke University Press.

Website

Boomboxery.com
http://boomboxery.com/forum/index.php/topic/7055-vintage-conion-cf-100/ (accessed April 10, 2016).

5

Theorizing the *hari kuyō*

The ritual disposal of needles in early modern Japan

Christine M. E. Guth

When Bill Brown analyzes how the thingness of material objects is apprehended, he does so from a modern Western perspective that takes for granted the ontological distinction between subject and object, human and non-human (Brown 2001: 1). Brown is not explicit about what distinguishes thingness, characterizing it as the often unnamed, unrecognized constituent of a physical form that may become apparent through failure. As he writes, "We begin to confront the thingness of objects when they stop working for us: when the drill breaks, when the car stalls, when the windows get filthy, when their flow within the circuits of production and distribution, consumption and exhibition, has been arrested, however momentarily" (Brown 2001: 4).

This experience, however, does not acknowledge that in certain non-Western cultures and contexts, the relationships between people and physical objects may be understood in ways that call for an interpretive framework quite different from his own. In Japan, for instance, the moment when a tool ceases to work may draw attention not to those qualities that separate and distinguish it from its user, but rather to the animistic qualities that liken it to him or her. In this interconnected world, objects are recognized as having a lifetime in one form that comes to an end when they wear out or break, but it is only one of many lives; through transubstantiation, even after having outlived their practical function, they may continue to "work" in other forms. *Tsukumogamiki*, a well-known Japanese tale, for instance, warns of the dangers of carelessly discarding the affordances of daily life such as umbrellas and cooking pots because these have the potential to assume potentially harmful forms (Reider 2005).

This outlook follows from the syncretic Shinto-Buddhist belief system that holds the boundaries between humans, plants, animals, and things to be fluid, with all inexorably caught up in an endless cycle of birth, death, and rebirth. Plants and grasses, for example, are sentient beings with the potential for enlightenment; humans can be reborn as animals and vice versa in an endless karmic cycle; and material things are endowed animistic agency that enables them to act both in concert with and in opposition to human intentionality (Lafleur 1989; Pflugfelder and Walker 2005; Rambelli 2007). This ascription of animistic power to the natural and manufactured world has had a profound and enduring influence in Japanese cultural formations, including attitudes toward technology. Anthropologist Anne Allison, for instance, has linked these values and beliefs to what she calls the "techno-animism" of contemporary popular culture products, asserting that "this is more than an aesthetic proclivity, a tendency to see the world as animated by a variety of beings, both worldly and unworldly, that are complex (interchangeable) and not graspable by so-called rational (or visible) means alone" (Allison 2004: 12).

Given this intrinsic strain of theory in Japanese culture, in which things share the social spaces and potentialities of sentient beings, it could be argued that the answer to Brown's rhetorical question whether "we really need anything like thing theory" cannot be a simple yes or no (Brown 2001: 1). While thing theory may not be as applicable in non-Western cultures, this does not necessarily mean that that all critical theory should be rejected. Recognizing the danger of interpretations that are inappropriate to early modern Japan, this essay takes the position that the critical distance provided by theorized analysis can extend cultural analyses that emerge from existing studies.

The blurring of the boundaries between human and non-human that is fundamental to Actor Network Theory (ANT) is particularly useful in this respect. Latour offers a critique of subject–object dichotomies, because "the subject-object dichotomy distributed activity and passivity in such a way that whatever was taken by one was lost to the other," further arguing "that their human-non-human does not involve a tug-of war between two opposite forces. On the contrary, the more activity there is from one, the more activity there is from the other" (Latour 1999: 147). In an actor network, human and non-human act upon other objects and subjects and processes to create a circularity of mutually constitutive actions (Latour 2005). Although ANT seeks to transcend the distinction between subject and object, human and non-human, the agency attributed to objects is not grounded in animism, but in their physical structure and design. It is through these material qualities that Latour understands technologies so mundane as to be almost invisible such as seatbelts, automatic door closers, or keys not as passively caught up in social relations, but as active producers of them (Latour 1992). Likewise, as will be argued here, in the context of Japan, the seemingly trivial needle is a dynamic material technology that has implications whose full import may be understood by considering it as part of a complex socio-technical network that includes its ritual disposal.

Taking as its point of departure a moment that Brown has characterized as "failure," this essay asks why the seemingly mundane, worn and broken needle was singled out for special recognition in the form of a ritual still held annually at temples and shrines on either December 8 or February 8, in various parts of Japan. In the *hari kuyō*, commonly but misleadingly characterized in English as a funeral or memorial for needles, women lay to rest in soft beds of tofu the worn or broken needles that have served them over the past year. As it is practiced today, participants are primarily elderly seamstresses and the decorative pins and needles they discard ritually are not necessarily worn or broken, transforming the *hari kuyō* into a performance that makes women custodians of professional and national traditions for touristic consumption.[1] However, historically grounded interpretation informed by ANT can help to illuminate the logic of this enduring practice.

The term *kuyō* is a translation of the Sanskrit *puja*, an activity involving prayer, worship and offerings, and in Japan these take many forms. For manufactured things, *kuyō* is performed chiefly with tools recognized as having special animistic power because they extend human capabilities. These include, most notably, carpentry tools, calligraphy brushes and needles (Rambelli 2007: 172–210). Because the *hari kuyō* is the earliest documented instance of such ritual disposal, there is considerable scholarly literature about it, especially as it developed at the Kada Awashima Shrine in Wakayama, where the practice is thought to have originated in the early Edo period (1603–1867) (Kretschmer 2000; Rambelli 2007; Yanagita 1951: 482; Yanase 1998: 1021–4). As the practice has undergone considerable change since that time, it has assumed diverse regional variations, leaving no consensus in its interpretation (Rambelli 2007: 220–5). Most historians of religion, anthropologists, and folklorists have focused on the needle's metaphorical value at the expense its materiality. It is not treated as a thing with a distinctive volumetric shape and tactility: that it is tiny, long, slender, sharply pointed, made of molten metal, and with an eye to carry thread are significant details of its physical and design presence that are generally overlooked. Even historian of religion Fabio Rambelli, in his richly textured exploration of the material as a site of social and religious communication and exchange, a study to which I am much indebted, has failed to do justice to the technological complexity of the needle's manufacture, the full range of its uses in early modern culture, or the relationship between its making, uses, and disposal.

In this essay, I present the needle as a dynamic material instrument that exists in the world, bound up in a network of interactions that includes its materials, processes of manufacture, uses, and disposal, as well as the discourses of which they are a part. In other words, I take into account its status as both a technology and a design object. In the absence of actual needles from the early modern era, I offer close readings of representations in popular encyclopedias to provide insights into their material meanings in the context of the times. To be sure, these visual resources cannot hope to address all the ways that needles figured in the lives of their makers and users, but they can shed light on why these tiny, seemingly prosaic tools became sites of special meaning in the Japanese object world.

Representing needles

The agency of needles resonated throughout Japanese society in early modern times. Needles served, for instance, for acupuncture, for sewing tatami, and for commercial embroidery, but they had particular significance in the domestic sphere since a married woman's duties involved making clothing and other articles for herself and her family. The fabrications created and maintained by the movements of the needle defined female identity both individually and collectively. Despite their socio-cultural and economic importance, however, these instruments were not the subjects of pictorial representation in their own right before the seventeenth century.

Commercially published, illustrated reference books that may be loosely classified as encyclopedias helped to shape the discourse through which the needle's network of purposes and expectations was established. By the eighteenth century such books, whose contents were understood to be part of "civilized knowledge," were essential household items (Berry 2006: 328). Literacy levels were high in Japan and these informative and inexpensive publications catered to a wide social spectrum of both male and female readers. By defining how the *hari*, needle, comes into being, and acts as it does with people, encyclopedias served as both products and producers of commonplace understandings of this instrument.

Jinrin kinmō zui (Illustrated encyclopedia of humanity) and *Wakan sanzai zue* (Sino-Japanese encyclopedia) feature illustrations of *hari* in a variety of shapes and sizes adapted to suit their specific functions (Asakura 1998b: 200, 201; Terajima 1992: 15). These include acupuncture needles, clock needles, and sewing needles. *Joyō jinrin kinmō zui* (an illustrated encyclopedia for women) features the sewing needle as a gender-specific affordance that is part of a larger network of things (Asakura 1998a: 46). Despite this typological diversity, *hari* was commonly understood to refer primarily to needles as instruments of female domesticity, a prescriptive representation of gender that masked the reality that male craft professionals also depended on them for their livelihoods. In other words, even without will or devoid of intention, the needle participates in a network of actions with consequences for other objects and subjects.

These representations portray needles as articles of everyday life that could be readily purchased by consumers of various socio-economic backgrounds. They were among the commodities that became ubiquitous and pervasive across society as a result of the surge in artisanal production following the long peace after the unification of the country. Their appearance in print culture also made needles a part of an expanding classificatory discourse involving technology, people, and things that belong to multiple and mutually reinforcing categories: professional instruments, gendered possessions, artisanal products, and gifts.

Making needles

In *The Social Life of Things*, Appadurai suggests that "we have to follow the things themselves, for their meanings are inscribed in their forms, their uses, their trajectories. It is only through the analysis of these trajectories that we can interpret the human transactions and calculations that enliven things" (Appadurai 1986: 5). These trajectories, or biographies, may be described as journeys of objects from their initial conceptualization in the minds of designers and makers to their final disposal. The journeys of these needles start with the craftsmen involved in their production. Unfortunately, in spite of their long history in Japan, there is no extended written or visual evidence of their manufacture before the seventeenth century, although there was already a well-established genre of painted portrayals of craftsmen. Why this profession eluded representation before this time may have to do with the fact that, owing to the sourcing and forging of the iron used in their manufacture, the needle wires were made at some distance from the metropolitan centers where artists and publishers were active, and the finished needles were sold by itinerants with a reputation for dishonesty (Saikaku 1959, 46). The *harisuri*, needle sharpener, and *nuiharishi*, embroidery needle maker, included among pictures of craftsmen in *Jinrin kinmō zui* may be among the earliest representations of this profession. The former, depicted on the right, is in the act of examining a newly sharpened acupuncture needle. The embroidery needle maker on the left admiring his handiwork, sits surrounded by the wires, hammers, and other tools used for making needles, as well as an array of finished ones. The curtained workshop and formal dress of the former and partially unclothed figure and undefined outdoor setting of the latter speak to status distinctions within these professions. Hierarchy among makers depended not only on skill but also on product differentiation, and more prestige was attached to acupuncture than to sewing needles.

The appearance of needle makers among the multitude of professionals depicted in *Jinrin kinmō zui*, as well as the list of the names and addresses of shops selling their products, may be taken as signs of the consolidation of this specialist domain of production within the metropolitan centers of Kyoto, Osaka, and Edo. It also speaks to the needle not as a scarce and precious thing, but as a commodity that was integrated into a flourishing market economy.[2]

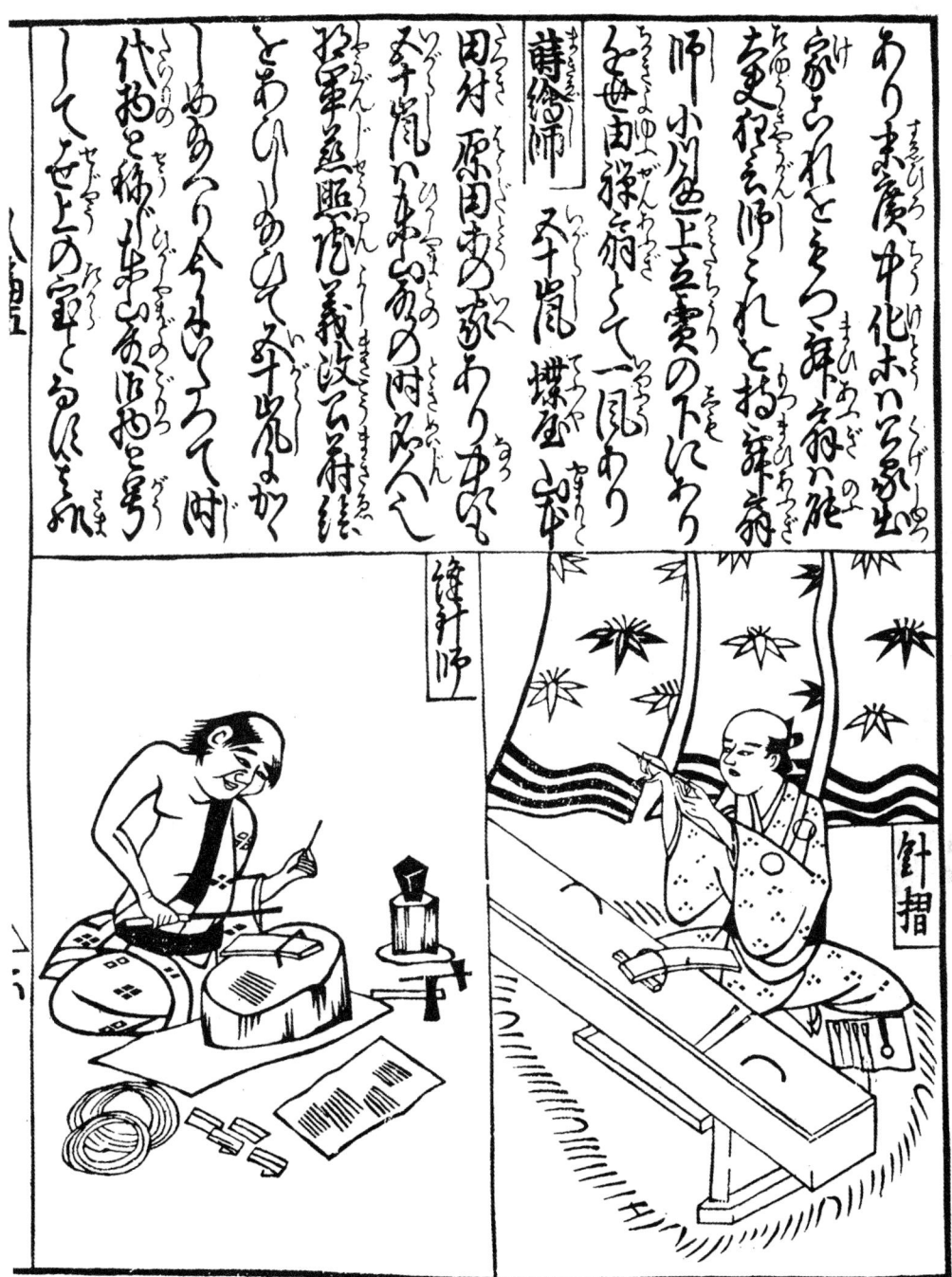

FIGURE 5.1 Needle makers from *Jinrin kinmō zui*. After *Kinmō zui shūsei*, vol. 13, p. 201. Image used with permission of Ozorasha.

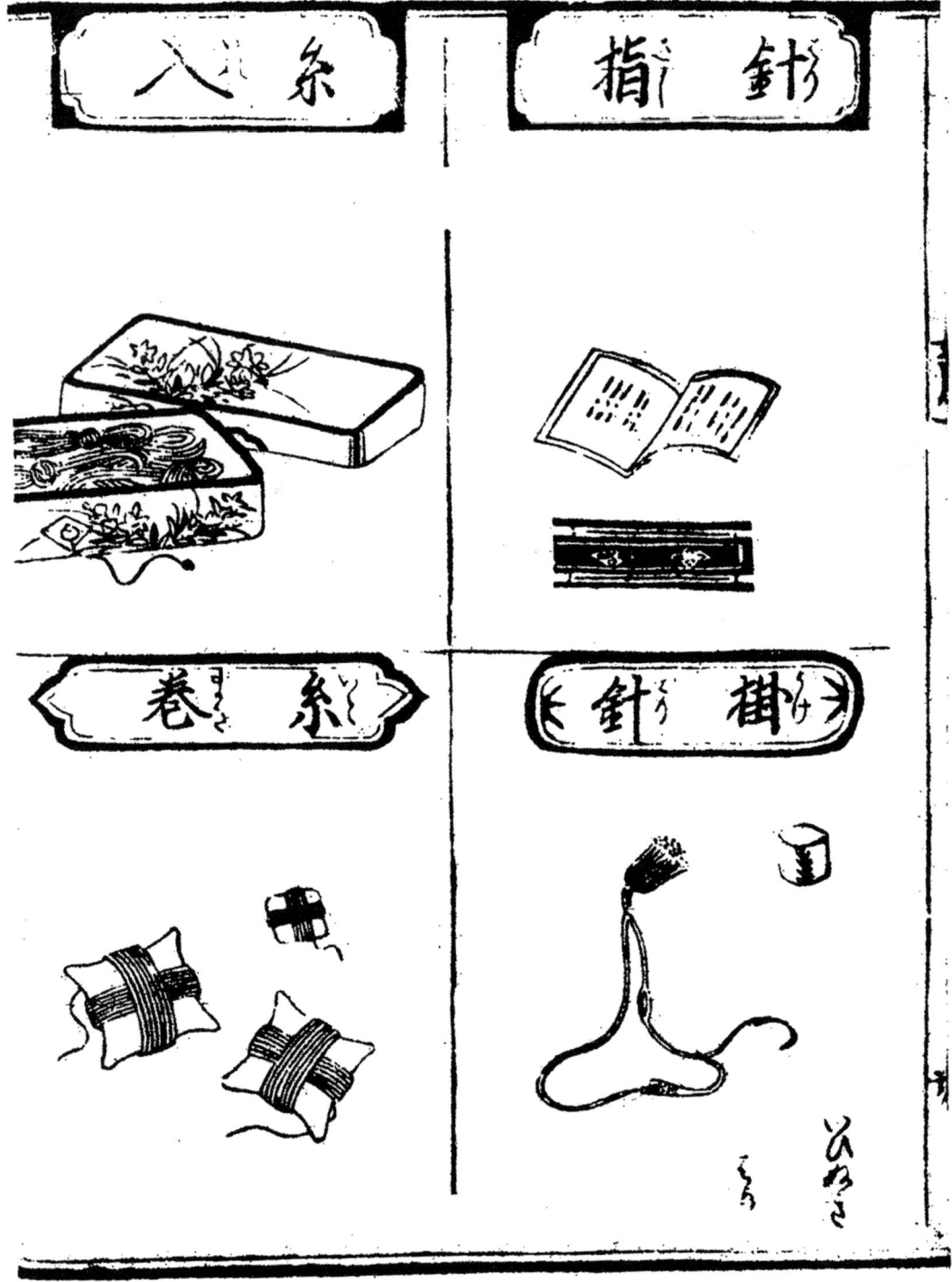

FIGURE 5.2 Sewing equipment from *Joyō jinrin kinmō zui*. After *Kinmō zui shūsei*, vol. 10, p. 46. Image used with permission of Ozorasha.

Latour's notion of "retrofitting" in the constitution of knowledge demonstrates how both absence and presence are constituents of an actor network. Needle makers didn't suddenly appear on the scene; they had existed before, but new conditions brought them into view through their representation, and this in turn produced new perceptions of them. Facts, as Latour argues, have historicity, and merely by their passing, they set up new relationships that have the power to influence human understanding (Latour 1999).

Like most other professionals, needle makers were organized into workshops structured hierarchically along familial lines with the tacit knowledge required for needle making transmitted from master to disciple. They are portrayed here alongside such artisans as lacquerers, fan makers, and picture mounters, who were already part of the pictorial canon, as well as specialists in luxury articles fashioned from exotic ivory and shagreen (Ono 1978). In this way, the identity and stature of the needle maker is once again reordered discursively by his reciprocal relationship to other professionals.

Both of these illustrations focus on the finished tools, leaving the manifold, complex technologies involved in their production a mystery. The accompanying text, however, refers to needle making as having been introduced from China. The *Tiangong kaiwu* (Exploitation of the works of nature), a seventeenth-century Chinese publication reprinted in Japan, helps to visualize the complex manufacturing process also likely to have also been used in Japan (Sung 1966; Schafer 2011; Yabuuchi, 1953). The printing of this book in China, its export to Japan, and its republication and circulation by local booksellers is part of the extended network that makes possible the coming into being of the needle. The more specialized nature of this book, with its focus on technologies including dyeing, ceramics, and metallurgy, however, would have given it a more limited circulation than the general encyclopedia mentioned above.

Needle making is included in the *Tiangong kaiwu* (Tenkō kaibutsu in Japanese) in a section on forging, along with farm implements, carpentry tools, and anchors, and is accompanied by two full-page illustrations.

The text explains how the forged iron, which may come from articles that have been melted down (Sung 1966: 189), is hammered into slender strips then pulled through a drawplate to reduce the width and extend the length to the desired size; how the eye is formed with a bow drill and the exterior smoothed; and finally, how the needles are tempered by being placed in a pot heated over a slow fire (Sung 1966: 196–7). The drawplate, file, bow drill, and other instruments conspicuously depicted here dramatize the needle's dependence on other technologies for its own existence.

The representational objectives of the classification of craftsmen in *Jinrin kinmō zui* are multiple, but one clear message is the celebration of the power of making. Iron was indispensable for the manufacture of the tools of agriculture, cooking, and warfare. Smelting, forging, and casting, moreover, required highly specialized knowledge of the properties of substances and their potential for modification. Yet even this was not sufficient to guarantee successful production; metallurgy was often accompanied by prayers and offerings to the deities identified as special protectors or even founders of the profession. The successful manufacture of a needle, no less than that of a sword or other status object, had to be performed in accordance with specific ritual procedures involving the transmutation of natural substances.[3] Indeed, it might be argued that because of its small scale, which concentrated the agency of molten metal, ritual was all the more important in the manufacture of these sewing implements. By the same token, needle making could be understood as an act of creation entailing more than manual labor and those who had the skills to carry out this activity as possessing special powers.

FIGURE 5.3 Preliminary steps in needle making from *Tiankong kaiwu*. After E-Tu Zen Sun, tr. T'ien-kung k'ai-wu: Chinese Technology in the Seventeenth Century, p. 188.

Using needles

Constituents of what Japanese historian Mary Elizabeth Berry has called the "library of public information," encyclopedias do not simply represent, but also produce an understanding of the subject or activity depicted (Berry 2006: 15). As key mediators of knowledge transmission, visual and verbal definitions in encyclopedia placed constraints on some activities and behaviors while making possible, encouraging, or demanding others. An illustration in *Joyō Jinrin kinmō zui* devoted to articles used by women helps to visualize the economy of things that defined female identity in the early modern era. This publication tells women how to behave in the social world, reminding them that material things, not human agency alone, shape domestic space. In explaining the agency of things, Brown offers the example of the Russian Constructivists, who "sought to recognize objects as participants in the reshaping of the world", and things as "equals, comrades" (Brown 2001: 10). The *Joyō Jinrin kinmō zui* presented and categorized culturally significant articles, making clear how these material things increasingly objectified everyday life in the early modern era. For the most part, the pictures represent commodities, such as lacquer shelves, writing and clothing boxes, and cosmetic cases that would have figured in the dowries of elite women. The publication was written, however, with the authorial and ideological purpose of prescribing the behavior of women of all classes.

Needles were among the commodified articles whose availability across classes in the early modern era refashioned domestic space.

While the illustrations discussed above gave primacy to maker over object, in Figure 5.4 the visual narrative depends explicitly on the needle as a part of a "system of objects" (Baudrillard 1996). The picture on the upper right tells us that needles were purchased in quantity and wrapped for safety and convenience in paper packets; the image beneath it depicts a hook to pull out stitches threaded onto a special holder to avoid becoming lost; on the upper left, a decorated lacquer box holding thread lies open for inspection; beneath it, thread is neatly wound around a paper support. These orderly representations speak to the way that the domestic economy of things, human action, and social structures are inextricably bound up with one another.

The emphasis on this equipment also attests to the moral and social weight of home sewing for married women, themes that are elaborated in other forms of print culture, including a plethora of woodblock prints depicting women sewing while children look on. A didactic print in captioned wisdom (*chi*), forming part of a set of pictures tellingly titled *Mirror of Eternal Feminine Virtue* (*Teisō chiyo kagami* 1843) makes this message explicit.[4] The recollections of a woman named Ushigome Chie, although considerably later in date, further underscore the ideological implications of sewing:

> in the provinces, until that time [1910–20s], the idea remained widespread that skill in sewing determined a person's value as a woman. I was bad at sewing and calligraphy as a child, and was scolded at home "You're not a girl." This was not simply a judgment on skill in sewing, but a view of education that believed morality was nurtured through mastery of the techniques of what one might call the Way of Sewing. (Gordon 2012: 80)

By her reference to "The Way of Sewing," Ushigome implies that this activity assumed a ritual dimension akin to that of other professions and activities ranging from carpentry and calligraphy to the tea ceremony to which the honorific word "way" (*michi* or *dō*) was also appended.

FIGURE 5.4 Final steps in needle making from *Tiankong kaiwu*. After E-Tu Zen Sun, tr. T'ien-kung k'ai-wu: Chinese Technology in the Seventeenth Century, p. 193.

The *Joyō jinrin kinmō zui's* prescriptive and taxonomic nature precludes descriptions of the needle's agency to create drudgery, companionship, or complex physiological sensations, but these tacit phenomena must all be included in the network of which it was a part. Sewing is an embodied occupation, and to achieve competence the appropriate positioning of the body and movements of the hand had to be learned through repeated practice. Any motion, if repeated sufficiently, becomes second nature and it is possible that women may not have been conscious of the habitual movements through which they became one with the needle. Even as needles and the skills associated with them materialized and secured gender, status and life-stage roles within familial relationships, they also provided opportunities for sociability with other women. In addition, as the product of an activity invested with morally prescriptive values, needlework provided an outlet for creative talents that allowed women to draw attention to themselves in a socially affirmative way.

Sewing, however, is a practice that is dichotomously empowering: women use needles in a proprietary way, controlling their movements to achieve their desired objective, but needles control them as well by routinizing the practice of everyday life. This refers to the "reciprocity of agency" between human and non-human actors, foregrounding the process by which "people and things configure each other" (Boradkar 2010: 4–5). If on the one hand, a needle's breakage was emblematic of the repetition and even drudgery associated with its obligatory daily use, on the other, as a tool invested with biographical significance its loss also had deep emotional resonance.

Disposal of needles

Brown suggests that breakage may be required to awaken our consciousness to the specificity that defines the "thingness" of material forms. But this user-centric perspective does not extend to a consideration of other phenomenological implications of wear on an object. The disposal of needles ritualized in the *hari kuyō* serves as a reminder that when a technology can no longer carry out its work as intended, it may demand our attention by requiring proper disposal so that it will not cause harm. Just as today many homes and hospitals have special containers for the safe disposal of hypodermic and other needles, so too Japanese temples have long had specially demarcated stone lanterns, boxes, or even trees where needles could be deposited (Kreshmer 2000: 387–8). In the karmically interconnected Buddhist worldview, care of objects must extend beyond their working life. Because needles are animate objects that have the potential to be reborn in other forms, their "demise" needs to be treated especially carefully, in a way that acknowledges and honors their social lives. A proper *kuyō* mediates the smooth passage from one state to another, while its neglect may result in the deceased assuming a malevolent form in its next incarnation. Disposal by gifting to a temple is therefore a practical safeguard as well as an honorific act that assists the needle's transition from the realm of the commodity to that of the sacred, and thus potentially to buddhahood. Gifting a needle to a temple also enhances the donor's welfare in both a material and a spiritual way because prayers and offerings to a temple or shrine and the deities within them, engender Buddhist merit and other social benefits such as good health.

Returning again to the *Jinrin kinmō zui*, we may gain further insights into the ritual ecology of which these tiny tools were a part in the *hari kuyō's* earliest manifestations. Two illustrations that appear in a section of the publication devoted to the activities of itinerant monks and

FIGURE 5.5 Itinerant monks with portable shrines collecting offerings to forge a bell from *Jinrin kinmō zui*.

nuns relate to this practice. One depicts the itinerant monks from the Kada Awashima Shrine who traveled around the country carrying portable shrines bearing images of deities to whom prayers and offerings were made for safe childbirth and protection from diseases (Asakura 1998b: 301). There is no reference to a connection with needles, however, only to the human means by which the Awashima cult spread around the country. The reference to the *hari kuyō* appears in another illustration a few pages earlier that is reproduced here. It shows two apparently separate, but I would argue, interconnected activities.

On the right, a monk solicits donations for the making of a new temple bell, and on the left, another monk collects donations of small metal articles including mirrors, fishhooks, and needles. The cartouche above the collection box identifies this activity as *hari kuyō*, and the text explains that this ritual originated during the lifetime of the ninth-century monk Dengyō Daishi when needles were buried in mounds around Kyoto to protect the city. The reference to the burial of needles notwithstanding, it would seem that the rationale for pairing these scenes is that the metal items collected under the banner of the *hari kuyō* also served the purpose of making a new bell. This potentially conflicting conflation speaks to Latour's insistence on the significance of both intended and unintended agency in the constitution of a network.

Religious institutions in Japan have long engaged in a ritual economy of recycling involving materials of many kinds. Female garments made of silk brocade gifted to temples after their owner's deaths were often cut up and refashioned into altar clothes or even, in defiance of their vows of poverty, into patchwork monastic robes (Milhaupt 2004). Some temples are also known to have collected old printed books and paper, which were then ritually purified in a *kuyō* ceremony before being dissolved in water to make the pulp for new paper (Rambelli 2007: 248–50). Articles made of metal, however, were especially sought after since demand for iron often outstripped supply owing to the Edo period's vibrant consumer economy. Consequently, it was common practice for old and broken implements to be melted down for both secular and sacred reuse. The degree to which this was true is clear from the memoirs of the scholar Fukuzawa Yukichi. When he traveled in 1860 as a member of his country's first diplomatic mission to the United States, he was surprised by the great waste of old tins and broken tools. As he observed in his autobiography, this was remarkable because in Japan, "after a fire there would be hundreds of poor people swarming in the ruined district looking for nails in the charred wood, so valuable was metal in Japan" (Fukuzawa 1948: 128). Thus it would appear that the *hari kuyō*, in its early forms at least, intersected with other practices involving the sacralization of things through their donation to temples and shrines where they could be recycled for other religious purposes.

Why, among the many things that might be donated to temples and shrines, were needles singled out for special recognition at the Kada Awashima Shrine? The institutionalization of the *hari kuyō* in this particular locale was mutually constituted by women's devotions there to deities associated with easy childbirth and female health and the physical shape and creative powers of the needle, features that lent themselves to multiple metaphorical readings. While specifics vary, narratives linking needles, women and childbirth have been extremely common since the medieval era. The needle figured as protagonist, for instance, in the tenth-century *Utsubo Monogatari* (*Tale of the Cavern*), where a dream involving a hawk bearing needle and thread is an auspicious sign that an impoverished woman will give birth to a son fathered by a nobleman. (*Tale of the Cavern* 1984: 24). Popular oral variations of the ascription of phallic powers to the needle in circulation in the Edo period are likely to have informed the veneration of the deities of the Awashima Shrine in the form of offerings of needles.

This symbolism is easily understood in the context of needlework, a gendered practice that entails the physical interaction between a slender, hard pointed instrument and another softer, more pliant material. The needle's facility to pass both in and out of narrow spaces lent itself to identification with both phallic penetration and with the newborn's passage through the birth canal. These associations with movement, transformation, and liminality are all rooted in experience acquired through the female body. With its alternating movements of pressure and release, grasping and manipulating, even caressing, sewing is analogous to our most basic visceral engagements with the world. Just as needles and women constituted one-another physically through sewing, needles constituted women metaphorically through their association with childbearing. As the above account suggests, the *hari kuyō* is best understood as an assemblage made up of many practices rather than a single homogenous and immutable ritual. That needles were the first manufactured objects to be honored by *kuyō* must take into consideration the complex network of beliefs and practices associated with the special material and manner of their manufacture as well as their size and shape, all of which were intrinsic to their animistic status. First, as noted above, the ability to work with molten metal, modifying its structure and properties by smelting, hammering, and casting was ascribed ritual properties that were transferred to the finished objects. Second, precisely because of their small size, needles were recognized as an extraordinary technology because of their capacity to fashion bigger things that bind society together both literally and metaphorically. Third, the donation of worn or broken needles enabled women, even women of the most modest means, the agency to participate meaningfully in ritual life, and in so doing to enhance their personal and familial wellbeing.

Conclusion

Thing theory implies an ahistorical universality about the nature of subject object relations that does not do justice to highly variable local contingencies. ANT may also lack a degree of geographical or cultural situatedness. Nevertheless, ANT may be used to isolate and identify the far-reaching and enduring material and technological agents, and the specific beliefs, norms, and practices that comprise the dynamic aggregate that is the *hari kuyō*. By drawing out the circuitry of the needle's components, making, and discursive meanings, ANT allows for both registration of the needle's complex relationships and the disclosure of "the sociology of mundane things."

Acknowledgments

Special thanks to Simona Valeriani and Suchitra Balasubrahmanyan for their helpful discussions in the course of the preparation of this paper and, especially, to Leslie Atzmon and Prasad Boradkar for their robust comments on its early drafts.

Notes

1. For images of the ritual as it is practiced today, see http://stitchtress.com/2010/02/08/hari-kuyo (accessed September 30, 2013).
2. Misubariya, one of the needle makers mentioned in the *Jinrin kinmō zui*, continues to hand make steel needles and sell them from its shop in Kyoto. See www.misuyabari.jp (accessed April 24, 2013).
3. For an example of this, see the illustration in Tachibana Minko's 1784 *Saiga shokunin burui* (Polychrome pictures of craftsmen), where the rice straw rope and paper hangings that are Shinto markers of sacred space ritualize the forging of a sword. See http://collections.vam.ac.uk/item/O93059/saiga-shokunin-burui-book-tachibana-minko/ (accessed November 21, 2013).
4. For reproduction see http://www.kuniyoshiproject.com/Mirror%20of%20Etermal%20Feminine%20Virtue%20(R61).htm (accessed May 26, 2013).

Bibliography

Allison, A. (2006), *Millennial Monsters: Japanese Toys and the Global Imagination*, Berkeley, London, and Los Angeles: University of California Press.
Appadurai, A. (1999), *The Social Life of Things*. Cambridge: Cambridge University Press.
Asakura, H. (1990), *Jinrin Kinmō Zui (Illustrated Encyclopedia of Humanity)*, Tokyo: Heibonsha.
Asakura, H. (1999a), *Kinmō zui shūsei*, Vol. 10, *Joyō Jinrin kinmō zui (Illustrated Encyclopedia of Humanity for Women)*, Tokyo: Ozorasha.
Asakura, H. (1998b), *Kinmō zui shūsei*, Vol. 13, *Jinrin kinmō zui (Illustrated Encyclopedia of Humanity)*, Tokyo: Ozorasha.
Baudrillard, J. (1996), *They System of Objects*, London: Verso.
Berry, M. E. (2006), *Japan in Print: Information and Nation in the Early Modern Period*, Berkeley, London, and Los Angeles: University of California Press.
Boradkar, P. (2010), *Designing Things: A Critical Introduction to the Culture of Objects*, London: Berg.
Brown, B. (2001), "Thing Theory," *Critical Inquiry* 28 (1): 1–22.
Dainihon hyakka jiten (Encylopedia Japonica) (1967), 18 vols, Tokyo: Shogakkan.
Fukuzawa, Y. (1948), *The Autobiography of Fukuzawa Yukichi*, trans. K. Eiichi, Tokyo: Hokuseido.
Gordon, A. (2012), *Fabricating Consumers: The Sewing Machine in Modern Japan*, Berkeley, London, and Los Angeles: University of California Press.
Kretschmer, A. (2000), "Mortuary Rites of Inanimate Objects: The Case of Hari Kuyo," *Japanese Journal of Religious Studies* 27 (3–4): 379–404.
Lafleur, W. (1989), "Saigyo and the Buddhist Value of Nature," in J. Baird Callicott and R. T. Ames, *Nature in Asian Traditions of Thought: Essays in Environmental Philosophy*, 183–209, Albany: State University of New York Press.
Latour, B. (1992), "Where are the Missing Masses? The Sociology of a Few Mundane Artifacts," in W. E. Bijker, E Wiebe, and J. Law, *Shaping Technology/Building Society: Studies in Sociotechnical Change*, 225–58, Cambridge, MA, and London: MIT Press, 1992.
Latour, B. (1999), *Pandora's Hope: Essays on the Reality of Science Studies*, Cambridge, MA: Harvard University Press.
Latour, B. (2005), *Reassembling the Social: An Introduction to Actor-Network-Theory*, Oxford: Oxford University Press.
Milhaupt, T. S. (2004), "The Four-Hundred-Year Life of Tsujigahana Textile: From Secular Garment to Museum Artifact," in *Moving Objects: Time, Space, and Context*, 47–56, Tokyo: National Research Institute for Cultural Properties.

Ono, T. (1978), *Shokunin Machigeinin Monomorai Zue (Artisans, Street Entertainers, Social Life Pictorial)*, Tokyo: Tenbōsha.

Pflugfelder, G. M., and B. L. Walker (2011), *JAPANimals: History and Culture in Japan's Animal Life*, Ann Arbor, MI: University of Michigan Center for Japanese Studies.

Rambelli, F. (2007), *Buddhist Materiality: A Cultural History of Objects in Japanese Buddhism*, Stanford: Stanford University Press.

Reider, N. T. (2005), "Animating Objects: Tsukumogami Ki and the Medieval Illustration of Shingon Truth," *Asian Folklore Studies*, 64: 207–31.

Saikaku, I. (1959), *The Japanese Family Storehouse or The Millionaires' Gospel: Modernised Nippon Eitaigura or Daifuku Shin Chōja Kyō*, trans. G. W. Sargent, Cambridge: Cambridge University Press.

Schafer, D. (2011), *The Crafting of the 10,000 Things: Knowledge and Technology in Seventeenth-Century China*, Chicago: University of Chicago Press.

Sung, Y-H. (1999), *T'ien-k'ung K'ai-wu: Chinese Technology in the Seventeenth Century (Exploitation of the Works of Nature)*, trans. E. Zen Sun, London and University Park: Pennsylvania State University Press.

Terajima, Ryoan and Isao Shimada (1992), *Wakan Sanai Zue (Sino-Japanese Encyclopedia)*, Tokyo: Heibonsha.

Uraki, J. (1984), *The Tale of the Cavern (Utsuho Monogatari)*, trans. Z. Uraki, Tokyo: Shinozaki Shorin.

Yabuuchi, Kiyoshi (1953), *Tenkō Kaibutsu No Kenkyū*, Tokyo: Kōseisha Kōseika.

Yanagita, Kunio (1951), *Minzokugaku Jiten (Encyclopedia of Folklore)*, Tokyo: Tokyodo.

Yanase, Kazuo (1998), *Shaji Engi No Kenkyū (Studies in the Origin of Temples and Shrines)*, Tokyo: Benseisha.

PLATE 1 The Promax Boombox from the set of the film *Do the Right Thing*. Image courtesy of Bonhams.

PLATE 2 The JVC RC-M90 Boombox which appeared on the cover of "Radio" by LL Cool J. Image courtesy Lyle Owerko.

PLATE 3 The Sharp GF-777 Boombox. Image courtesy Lyle Owerko.

PLATE 4 The Conion CF-100 Boombox. Image courtesy Lyle Owerko.

PLATE 5 Sheinart's (family-owned women's clothing store near Atwater Market, Montréal). Sign installed 1995; removed in 2013 with closure of store. Welded stainless steel; "bastard" script lettering. With thanks to Mr. Bernie Sheinart. Photo: Raphaëlle Garcia for the MSP.

PLATE 6 La Belle Province Meat Co. (Boulevard St. Laurent, Montréal). Handpainted on galvanized sheet metal with a wood frame. Late 1960s; discovered in situ in 2013. With thanks to: Mme. Léa Better. Photo: Raphaëlle Garcia for the MSP.

PLATE 7 Librarie Guérin (Bookstore, Rue St-Denis, Montréal). Panned acrylic with fluorescent interior lighting. Installed 1973; removed in 2014 with closure of store. With thanks to M. Claude Legault (LIDEC inc.). Photo: Raphaëlle Garcia for the MSP.

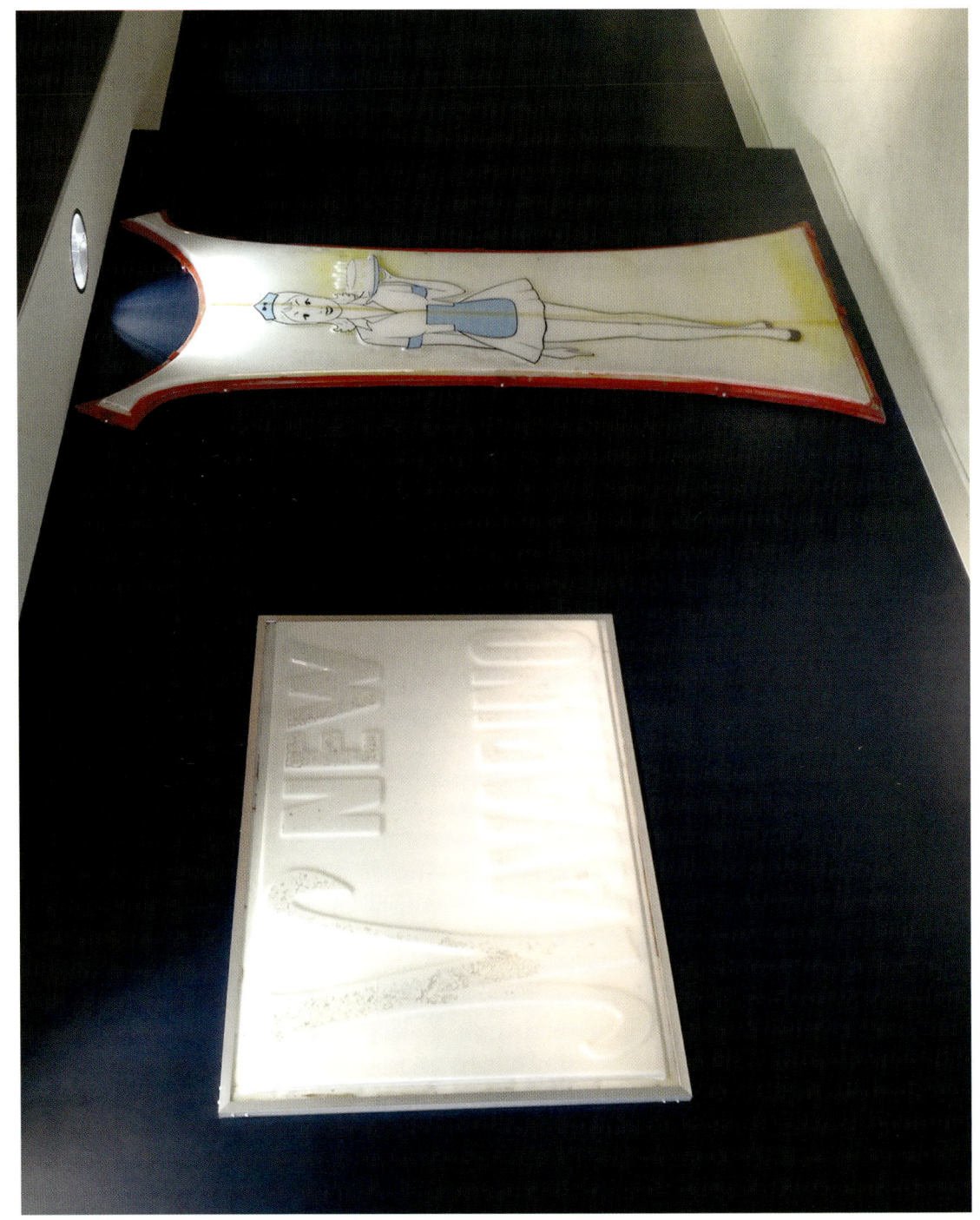

PLATE 8 Café Navarino (Avenue du Parc, Montréal). Panned acrylic with fluorescent interior lighting. Installed 1969; removed in 2010 during renovations. With thanks to Mr. Peter Tsatoumas. Photo: Raphaëlle Garcia for the MSP.

PLATE 9 *Tambat Ali* in Pune, India. Image courtesy Prasad Boradkar.

PLATE 10 Craftsman Shantaram Ambre hammering copper products in *Tambat Ali*. Image courtesy of the author.

PLATE 11 Hammertone texture on a utensil. Image courtesy Prasad Boradkar.

PLATE 12 Finished copper vessels with the hammertone texture, designed by Rashmi Ranade, stored on a shelf in the factory of Bhalchandra Kadu. Image courtesy Prasad Boradkar.

PLATE 13 Learning the hammertone technique from craftsmen Shantaram Ambre (center) and Ganesh Lanjrekar (right). Image courtesy artist and workshop owner Bhalchandra Kadu.

PLATE 14 Copper sheets in Bhalchandra Kadu's factory in *Tambat Ali*. Image courtesy Prasad Boradkar.

PLATE 15 Specialized hammers for *matharkam* in Bhalchandra Kadu's factory in *Tambat Ali*. Image courtesy Prasad Boradkar.

PLATE 16 The Water Bearer, designed by Rashmi Ranade. Image courtesy Studio Coppre.

PLATE 17 The cup in one of its primary shapes during the manufacturing process. Product designed by Rashmi Ranade. Image courtesy Studio Coppre.

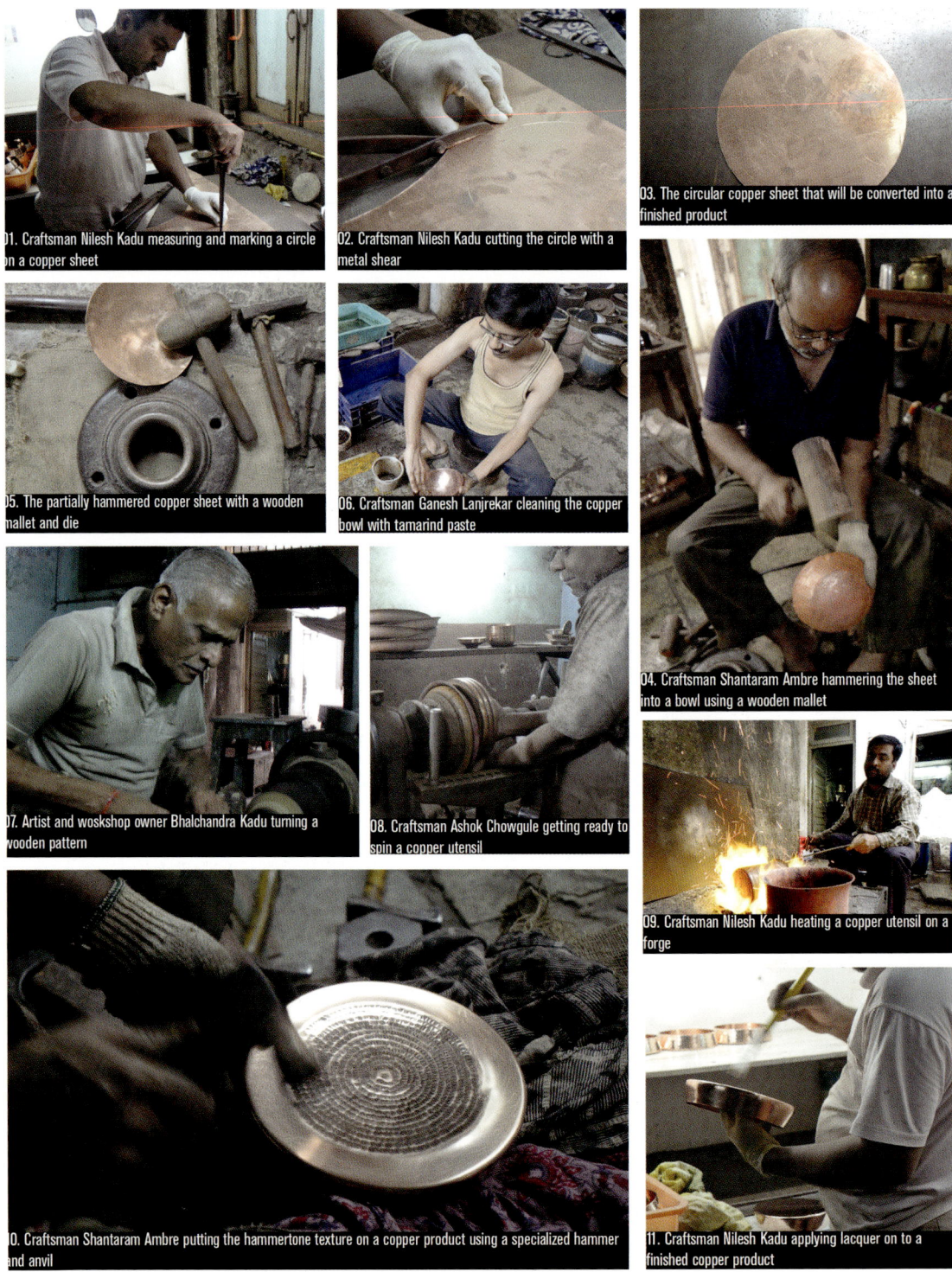

PLATE 18 The process of creating hammered copper artifacts. Image courtesy Prasad Boradkar.

6

Nothingness in April Greiman's *Does It Make Sense?*

Elizabeth Guffey

For more than thirty years, April Greiman's poster *Does It Make Sense?* has been a staple of graphic design history, thematizing subjectivity and expressing, as one scholar recalls, a "break with the norms of good practice" (Robertson 2013: 123). Alternately hailed, as another observer puts it, "as a radical advance in the art of poster design and condemned as pornographic, self-indulgent and inappropriate" (Whiteson 1988), Greiman's poster is both manual and manifesto. And yet, for all its significance, the design remains little studied, under-interpreted, and perhaps worst of all, poorly reproduced. For these reasons, the poster's allusive title, *Does It Make Sense?*, may be widely known, but its implications and sub-texts sometimes confused. The phrase "Sleep in Nothingness" is boldly printed along the poster's lower margin and might arguably be presented as a subtitle. And yet it's frequently overlooked and often simply cropped out of many reprints. Nevertheless, Greiman's phrasing is fundamental to her

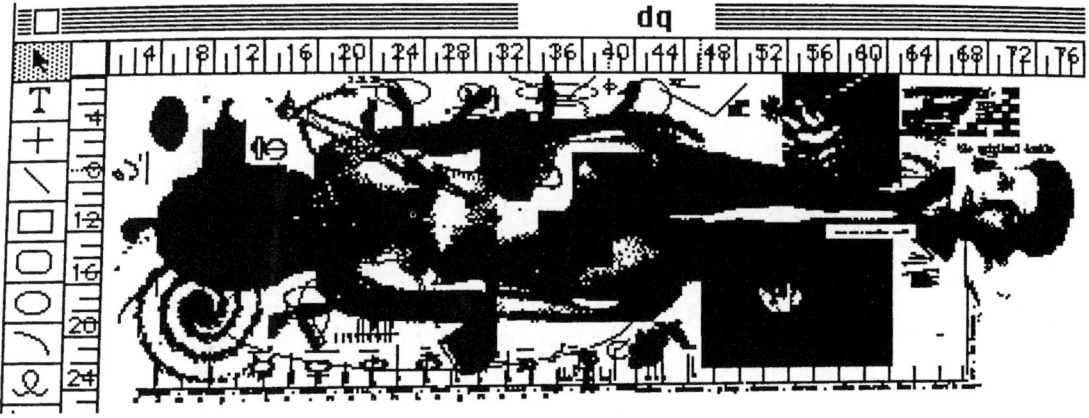

FIGURE 6.1 April Greiman, *Does It Make Sense?*, 1986. Courtesy of artist.

larger purpose. I want here to discuss these missing meanings and how they relate to Greiman's quick recognition that the computer was more than a simple tool; but most of all, I also want to explore how Greiman uses the overlooked phrase "sleep in nothingness," or as I'd rather put it, "no-thingness," to describe the immaterial realm.

Greiman's poster marks an alluring moment in digital making. Commissioned for issue number 133, 1986, of the venerable journal *Design Quarterly* (DQ 133), *Does It Make Sense?* was launched two short years after Apple produced the Macintosh computer; its graphical user interface, ultra-flexible mouse, color monitor, and other features were utterly new, and Greiman was one of the first designers to intuit their powerful implications for making. Unfolded to its fullest extent, the poster introduces us to Greiman herself, offering a nude self-portrait of the designer. She surrounds herself with a rich array of collaged images, ranging from simple Stone Age pictographs to a photograph of the earth seen from the moon. Bits of text appear to float across the images, cryptically whispering phrases like "live where you can" and "the spiritual double." The poster's text also describes scales of measure, recording for instance a range of meteorological conditions; a timeline runs on one edge, referencing a broad history of science and technology including the big bang and the industrial revolution. Printed in a monochrome blue ink and marking visible pixels, the poster's style insistently reminds us that it is a product of early desktop publishing. As images overlap and in some cases obscure one another, Greiman's title appears on the poster as spewed and garbled data: "doesitmakesense?" The question, posed by the Austrian mathematician and philosopher Ludwig Wittgenstein, is philosophical. Buried deep in the poster's text, Greiman answers the philosopher's question with his simple rejoinder: "Ifyougiveitasense,itmakessense." The title has guided a generation of viewers to see the poster as a probe of the limits of sense and nonsense, but also resembles the garbled printouts of early computers.

But I want to probe deeper in this essay, exploring the poster and its relation to a broader interest in material culture and the near simultaneous publication of Arjun Appadurai's ground-breaking volume, *The Social Life of Things*. The result of consultation between anthropologists and historians on the subject of commodities, Appadurai's edited volume signals a renewed interest in the "turn toward things." He does not foreground technological change, nor does he probe the distinction between "sense" and "nonsense." Nevertheless, Appadurai and his colleagues lay a foundation for further investigations of materiality and dematerialization. Following the 1986 publication of *The Social Life of Things*, a number of scholars pushed Appadurai's ideas further, even going so far as to ask us to revel in the sheer physicality of things. The literary scholar Bill Brown argued that such study could be "something warm. . . that relieves us from the chill" of theorization (Brown 2001: 1). In his 2001 essay, "Thing Theory," Brown looks to things to provide a different form of "sense." Material reality, he argues, can provide "something concrete that relieves us from unnecessary abstraction" (ibid.). In 1986, the year that Appadurai published his volume and Greiman's poster was issued, the nascent power of the computer was only beginning to be understood. I don't mean to imply that Greiman was reading thing theory or even Appadurai when she began her iconic poster. Instead, I want to historically situate Greiman's work, that is to connect it to the groundswell of interest in material culture that began in the mid 1980s and continues to this day. To do this, I argue, Greiman turns to an unconventional but richly diverse iconography, drawing from Apple's digital tools, marketing and user manuals, as well as a broader cultural reading of contemporary technoscience.

Why go to all this effort? Greiman's poster is prescient in bringing up a series of questions about computers and knowledge that continue to this day. She pioneered a way of thinking that is so normal to us today that we often forget how new it is. The relationship between the digital realm and the analog world continues to be ill explored. Working at the moment when these questions were quite new, Greiman broke with traditional analogue design but also introduced thingness (and no-thingness) as a key metaphor.

And so I want to outline briefly the ideas of both Appadurai and Brown, and also place them within their broader historical contexts. This largely academic discourse, I point out, ran parallel to a pressing and practical discussion of thingness that haunted makers and users of the earliest personal computers in the mid-1980s; at Apple computers itself, software developers and technology writers were also grappling with a series of ideas that seemed to cross the line between the material and immaterial. Examined against this background, Greiman's poster *Does It Make Sense?* explores thingness and no-thingness in several ways. In the introductory chapter to *The Social Life of Things*, Appadurai suggests that we should "approach commodities as things in a certain situation, a situation that can characterize many different kinds of things, at different points in their social lives" (1986: 13). The emergence of new digital technology, the nascent relationship between the physical thing and the digital thing, the screen and the printed page all provide different situations for Greiman to explore the nature of thingness. First, I draw our attention to the format of the poster itself, describing it as a thing. But then the imagery inscribed on the poster also represents things. Greiman turns to things to describe a series of abstract ideas as well. After describing Greiman's poster and imagery, I will turn back to Apple's struggles with conceptualizing and communicating the power of the digital to its early users, and the way in which they used things to do this. Greiman covers similar territory, introducing the notion of "no-thingness," that is a space lacking three-dimensional, physically realized things, as distinct from "nothingness," a state of emptiness or void. Similarly, "no-things" describe a state of immateriality like images seen on a computer screen, while things are tangible and material. In the final analysis, Greiman is enchanted and beguiled by states of "thingness" and "no-thingness," and invites us to experience the latter as a liberating form.

The turn toward things

If a turning point in attitudes to thingness occurred in the 1980s, this change can be seen in the landmark publication of Arjun Appadurai's *The Social Life of Things*. The volume asks us to reconsider the physical world, specifically the presence of things. The transformations in thought that characterize this period are charted in the volume, which draws from talks held at the University of Pennsylvania in the early 1980s. Here ideas of materialism were treated as a radical new force. In history to date, the term materialism was largely enlisted in Marxist theory in the name of taming capitalism and helping us understand how markets value people and the products of their labor. The latter become "commodities." Building on his own volume's subtitle, "commodities in cultural perspective," Appadurai argues that "commodities can provisionally be defined as objects of economic value" (1986: 3). A turning point in Western attitudes toward value, Appadurai argues, occurs in the work of the early twentieth century sociologist and philosopher Georg Simmel. Here, Appadurai observes, value is an abstract entity. It is "never an inherent property of objects, but is a judgment made about them" (ibid.). Discussions of the circulation of medieval relics, perceptions of authenticity in evaluating Oriental rugs, and patterns of consumption in central India are all part of Appadurai's volume;

in each case, "value" is inevitably revealed as, in Appadurai's words, "something separate, ever changing, and ultimately immaterial" (1986: 56).

The rug from Central Asia would seem to have little in common with Steve Jobs' Macintosh or April Greiman's *Does It Make Sense?*, and Appadurai's "turn toward things" does not foreground technological change. But Appadurai argues for a fuller understanding of a globalizing economy; his ideas are best understood in a changing world in which cars were made in Nagoya and sold in Des Moines and Hamburg. Appadurai suggests that value is variable depending on context. Although this very sober view does not foreground technological change, the ideas that characterize *The Social Life of Things* provide theoretical scaffolding for other scholars to push his ideas into the digital age.

Writing on the cusp of the twenty-first century, the literary scholar Bill Brown has urged us to build on Appadurai's seminal ideas and think in terms of a broader "thing theory" (Brown 2001). Brown takes up Appadurai's call to "follow the things themselves." Assuming that nothing is too mean or trivial, Brown argues that any thing is significant, as long as it is part of "the human production of materiality as such" (Brown 2001: 7). We have taken up a series of "habits," Brown says, that prevents us from thinking about the material things that surround us, even if they are as mundane as a plate glass window. In all, he asserts, we need a "new materialism that takes objects for granted only in order to grant them their potency" (ibid.).

This glimpse into the restless worlds of literary and anthropological theory might seem remote from the experience of mid-1980s' technologists, but in fact it curiously parallels questions being addressed in very practical terms in Silicon Valley and by early adopters, like Greiman, of home computers. Ideas of things and the "no-things" of the digital world were increasingly used to describe the power of the computer itself. Even at Apple, home of the new consumer friendly computers, a similar set of questions was being asked.

Apple's things and no-thingness

In 1986, few artists or designers were using the Macintosh in their practice. Even fewer were considering making, and the material presence of computer-made things. Indeed, some forty years after the computer was introduced to home users, it is hard to remember just how novel these machines were. With the Macintosh, Apple was selling a new keyboard, monitor, motherboard, and mouse. But these new things are less significant than the functions that they could perform. And early developers struggled to make sense of the new technologies for first-time users, many of whom were being asked to recalibrate their understanding of basic concepts like things and space.

At Apple, the company's technical manuals help us recall how conceptually new the Macintosh programs were and at the same time explicitly explain the simplest of procedures. Reading their 1984 user guide today is a study in technical ignorance. The first Macintosh user's guide ranges from the mundanely material ("before you start, make sure you plug your Macintosh into a grounded outlet and attach the keyboard and mouse to the main unit") to the outdated ("Most computer screens look like the departing flight schedule at a busy airport, but the Macintosh screen looks like a light gray desktop" (Apple 1984: 9–12).

The manual is written in measured, reassuring tones. It begins by assuring readers that "you don't need to know anything about Macintosh or any other computers to use this manual. And you won't have to keep learning new ways of doing things. One you've mastered a few new techniques, you'll use them whenever you use your Macintosh" (Apple 1984: 5). In order to explain procedures concretely, Apple's technical writers use analogies from the material world. For example, Apple's user guide described the computer's Finder as being "like a central hallway in the Macintosh house. It manages moving from one application to another like rooms in the house ... it's also like a front door—the way you enter the Macintosh house" (Apple 1984: 104).

But one of the first problems they dealt with was explaining to users how to understand the "no-things" of digital technology; the Macintosh was revolutionary in the way it made easier working with data that was intangible. Grappling with the new Graphic User Interface (GUI), Apple's designers also guided new users through an unlikely assortment of visual analogies from the real or material world by introducing a series of images. Of course, the Macintosh computer presented "icons" that were based on everyday things, for example trashcans, magnifying glasses, and other common household objects. It urged makers to use "tools," for example scissors and rulers, to measure and manipulate data in cyberspace.

Seen from within this context, in a world in which computers were beginning to dematerialize common objects within the real world, Appadurai's thing theory gains resonance. Indeed, this allows us too to follow Appadurai's injunction "to follow the things themselves, for their meanings are inscribed in their forms, their uses, their trajectories" (Appadurai 1986: 5). Neither anthropologist nor literary theorist, in her own way Greiman uses *Does It Make Sense?* to reconceptualize "thingness," through the poster's format and imagery. Above all, if we want to understand her work, we must understand it as a thing.

The poster as thing

Shortly after *Does It Make Sense?* was published, April Greiman was interviewed by the Los Angeles based designer Archie Boston. In the 1987 session, Greiman ruminates on design training, questions of quality, and evaluates her current work. With excited enthusiasm, she also uses the interview to introduce her latest project. Above all, she takes great pains to emphasize that the poster was carefully designed not as a crudely flat and bloodless form, but as a three-dimensional thing. Although little noted today, Greiman points out that her design must be pulled from a carefully designed, die-cut slipcase and is then meant to be unfolded. In the taped interview, Greiman demonstrates for Boston by deftly taking the poster out of its slipcase folder, then rather emphatically standing the slipcase upright on her desk. Reflecting further on the poster's title, she observes, "the sense it has for *me* is that it is new and yet old ... I mean it's printed, it's separated, it's very traditional in one way... on the other hand, it's a magazine which is a poster which is an object which is ... crazy." Greiman then announces that "this is the first time that *Design Quarterly*, or any magazine, would come out like a poster ... that's why we're wondering if it really does make sense."

This sense-making has largely been interpreted in terms of the poster's imagery. But returning to Appadurai and applying his thinking to Greiman's work more broadly, I want to tie its "sense" to an exploration of the poster's format; if Appadurai asked us to "follow the things themselves" by observing what he calls "things-in-motion," he suggested going right to the source (1986: 5). Quite literally, *Does It Make Sense?* was designed with circulation in mind. In truth, it is not a poster at all, but rather a special issue of the Walker Art Center's publication *Design Quarterly*. Commissioned by Mildred Freidman, head of the museum's design

 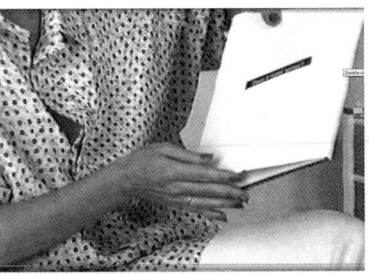 

FIGURE 6.2 April Greiman interview with Archie Boston, stills from 20 Outstanding Graphic Designers in Los Angeles, 1986. Courtesy of Archie Boston.

department and editor of the journal, it was published as a special issue; Greiman's poster is, in fact, published not as a thirty-two-page book, like earlier issues, but rather as a single piece of paper. That said, it also served as the venerable journal's issue 133 and the sheet was, in fact, printed on both sides. Moreover, the back or verso is densely printed in color, including a series of photographs, descriptive texts, and dedications, as well as an obligatory preface or introduction by Friedman. Neither fully a journal nor a poster, the sheet may be folded up and fitted snugly into the specially designed slipcase; thus, for practical purposes it functioned like a book. Indeed, the slipcase was essential as it allowed the poster to be addressed and mailed through the US postal system; the slipcase's firm wrapping also gave the sheet a spine, allowing it to be placed on the shelves of subscribers' libraries. Following Appadurai's suggestion, however, we must also think of the poster as something designed for movement; we might even trace the circulation as a magazine, tracing its restless movement through the systems for pickup and delivery in the mail, and its arrival in homes and libraries world-wide, as well as its subsequent history in various collections. But here, I want to concentrate on the poster's format and its sheer physicality in a different manner.

In the 1987 interview, Greiman's question "does it make sense?" is not theoretical. She poses the query directly to Archie Boston; but she is speaking not in relation to its content, but rather its unusual physical format. Setting it on a table she turns to the camera and asks, does a book as a poster, slipcase and all, make sense? Its three-dimensional presence—its thingness—is indeed an elegant solution to the physical demands of a poster/book. Wrapping around the poster, the die-cut case made good sense practically; and yet within design histories the slipcase is ignored. Furthermore, the poster is often treated as if it were a painting or Old Master print, that is, meant to lie flat and printed only on one side; the way it is mostly known today, laid out and photographed flat, then endlessly reproduced in books and online, it loses something palpable. Of course, on some level all paper posters are things. However thin the sheet of paper, it remains three-dimensional, if only for a fraction of a millimeter; a piece of paper always has depth.

To this end, as she ably demonstrates in the 1987 interview, Greiman is thinking of the poster in a new way. *Does It Make Sense?* is inscribed with a plan of action: it is meant to be folded and unfolded. Along with its slipcase, the entire 6 x 2 poster is conceived as one piece. To access the poster, the viewer must unfold the slipcase first; doing so is like unraveling a carefully designed package. As each fold is uncreased and opened, we learn more and more about Greiman's project. The exterior of the slipcase is boldly printed with the phrase "Does it make sense?" Once the first flap of the slipcase is lifted, Wittgenstein's rejoinder "If you give

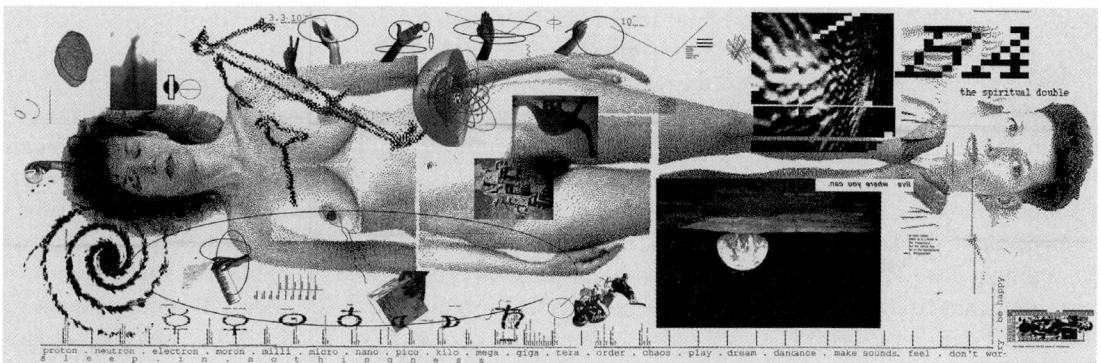

FIGURE 6.3 April Greiman, *Does It Make Sense?* (Det), 1986. Courtesy of artist.

it a sense, it makes sense" appears immediately below. But this action is only a prelude to the poster itself.

Opening the poster up, the *Design Quarterly* reader is forced to carefully unfold the work, seeing bits and pieces in a gradual act of unveiling. As Greiman introduces the poster to Archie Boston, she confidently moves through a series of individual panels. As it is unfolded, we encounter a series of separate parts, each inscribed with various words and images. The printed words "the spiritual double" and "don't worry, be happy," as well as the MIT press copyright, all unfold before us. As the unfolding process continues, piece by piece the visual display is revealed; face, hands, the brontosaurus, all whirl by us, providing multiple glimpses of the entire composition. Composed using the "tiling" method so that it could be printed on her Image Writer II dot-matrix printer, the first draft of the poster was printed on individual letter-sized pages. Each piece was assembled by the printer for the final photography, resulting in the final 76 by 26-inch poster. The blocky, fragmentary aspect of this process requires a high degree of reader participation; one must be careful in unfurling such a large-scale work. And yet, as complex as this process may be, at the end of the day, both slipcase and poster are things, carrying this discourse into the imagery imprinted on them.

Greiman's no-thingness

The poster format of *Does It Make Sense?* may play with our expectations, but its physical presence only scratches the surface of the project's meaning. Once the poster is spread out, on its front we encounter a series of things, some obviously useful, or important, or universal, and some not. A swift glance at the poster's imagery, for example, its photograph of an exploding supernova, the television screen shot of a brontosaurus, and an illustration of a human brain, all reveal Greiman's almost whimsical fascination with science and technology. Others, for instance the timeline that runs down one side of the poster, and fragments of information like "3.3×10^2 m/s, the speed of sound in air," are potentially valuable. Still others, like a hand holding a crystal ball, an oversized detail of Greiman's lips, and a blow-up of ancient pictographs, hold a more mysterious purpose. Visual emphasis is placed on the designer's body, which runs from end to end. But other objects, symbols, and images, whirl, hover, and float about, seemingly eclectically arrayed. How does one organize all these observations? How might one decide which phenomena are most important? Is any of it frivolous? And finally, how does one make sense of all these things?

As with its curious format, to understand the poster's imagery I want to return to ideas of thingness and nothingness as key metaphors. If Greiman's ranging visual references are varied, so too are the intellectual associations that swirl around the notion of nothingness. It might call to mind the Buddhist notion of *sunyata*, that is, emptiness, or ideas explored in conceptual art, for example Yves Klein's aesthetic of *le vide*, or the void. Furthermore, the root of the word *sunyata* is in the Indo-Aryan languages Pali and Sanskrit. In these languages, *shunya* refers to the number zero, which can also refer to emptiness. Because in the digital world zeros and ones are significant, they might serve as corollaries to no-thingness and thingness.[1] But here I want to examine Greiman's term by exploring things and no-thingness as part of the knowable world. We are surrounded by things: nothingness is emptiness.

There is a blankness to the space that Greiman's body inhabits, and we may call this a state of nothingness. Here, nothingness displays no ground, no landscape, no horizon, no sky. There is no shading to suggest a consistent light source. But this seeming void is not a vacuum. Not only does Greiman's sleeping body appear to hover in this emptiness, but she is surrounded by a series of representations of things. Entangled and enmeshed around her body, these seem to overlap and even obscure the self-image. The background of the poster is a void, the space of nothingness.

A poster depicting things

With *Does It Make Sense?*, we may be confronted with a kind of empty background, but the picture plane itself is filled with images of a phantasmagoria of natural phenomena and human inventions. The poster is filled with things. A series of hands appear around the designer's body, while a human brain appears to hover to her left. Imagery from the late twentieth century, including a photograph of an astronaut floating in space, coexists with a prehistoric stone axe. But the poster also depicts things too complex or distant to see with the naked eye. A representation of the galaxy spirals next to Greiman's head while a cut-away drawing demonstrates Rutherford's model of the atom. It hovers over her belly, while the photograph of an exploding supernova is imposed over her leg. Once again, the poster provides us with glimpses, in this case featuring fragments of a broader history of science and technology.

To take this idea further, Greiman mixes these representations of things with symbols and measured rules. Impossible to see before us, in the real world, she uses drawn symbols and graphs to describe complex ideas. Along one edge of the poster lie a series of symbols resembling the schematics typically found on weather maps or plotted meteorological reports. Greiman's accompanying text purports to identify these symbols by labeling them with terms of weather conditions like "snow," "heavy rain" and "foggy." These symbols appear along a second system of information, in this case a timeline measuring key moments in the history of technology, including the 1876 introduction of the telephone and the 1962 launch of the Telstar satellite. Like other timelines, it is distinguished by a series of lines used to measure and demarcate the passing of time itself. A third register of information emanates from the historical timeline's straight-edged rule; here a separate system of measures runs down the opposite side of the ruler. But there, instead of noting dates and historical events, the ruler is used to note gradations of scientific measure. And so, the words "proton," "neutron," "electron," etc., are noted.[2]

But again, these measures and forms of information are all abstractions; that is, none of these historical or scientific measures exist as three-dimensional "things" in our world. And yet, in the empty space represented in the poster, the words, symbols and registers representing abstract ideas seem every bit as real as the photographs of material things. The imagined timeline, weather symbols, and other abstractions depicted on this poster jostle and vie for space with the photographs of three-dimensional stuff. The measured timeline, for example, that runs along one side of the poster overlaps part of the spiraling galaxy, which itself overlaps Greiman's head, and so on and on.

It makes little difference whether they exist as objects in the real world. Indeed, abstract thinking is hard to convey and grasp. Through human history, we have used things to embody thought. In Western art history, lilies are used to represent purity, while books often stand in for learning. Indeed, we have developed systematizing constructs like timelines and graphs to represent and explain information. Unsurprisingly, then, Greiman uses things to tell stories, in this case about the history of technology and advent of the computer.

Of course, in books, posters, and other media, abstract representations have long shared pictorial space with reproductions of real things. Yet, here significance must be given not just to the things represented on the poster, but the way in which they were assembled, and how this feeds on and amplifies the poster's imagery. In the seemingly empty space of nothingness, Greiman's things do not flit about in a gadfly manner. Following a form of internal orderliness, each thing is woven into the very fabric of the composition. Key to understanding this order, we must observe two organizing milestones: the timeline and Greiman's own body. Each runs parallel to the picture plane. Images, texts, formulae and symbols all align either horizontally or vertically around these two hallmarks. Diagonals are almost non-existent; within the seeming randomness, each part of the poster aligns to a carefully formed grid. And yet this internal orderliness also suggests a deeper exploration into the nature of the Macintosh computer and its software.

Pushing pixels in nothingness

Midway through her 1987 interview with Archie Boston, Greiman does something unusual with her poster; gradually, in the midst of shuffling paper, unfolding some parts, and then re-creasing others, she essentially unfurls then refolds the entire poster back up in an entirely different way. But when she holds the reconfigured poster up for the camera, she reveals a diminutive screenshot of the poster, as seen in Apple's original MacDraw program. Easily overlooked, this tiny image is secreted in one corner; like the answer key to yesterday's newspaper crossword puzzle, the screenshot is hidden in plain sight.

Greiman's emphasis on the screenshot directs our attention to the very software she was using. Working with a program similar to Apple's MacPaint, engineer Mark Cutter developed software based on LisaDraw, originally designed for the company's earlier Lisa computer. The adapted MacDraw program allowed users to work with things, or rather electronic representations of things. Moreover, these digital no-things can be subjected to processes and actions usually reserved for things being handled in the three-dimensional world. Greiman's fascination with new digital practices introduces another process driven register of meaning for this poster.

Understood in this way, it's clear that this small corner of the poster registers a crucial explanation of the larger poster and the power of the computer used to make it. Greiman has, for example, digitized and blown up some of her images so large that they break into a pixilated haze; the photograph of her body and the hieroglyphic drawings on the poster, for instance, are so enlarged that they resemble a scrim of squarish dots. The screenshot printed on the poster and shown to Boston not only reveals Greiman's poster—as it looked on her screen—but also specifically alludes to Apple's innovative What You See Is What You Get (WYSIWYG) and Graphic User Interface (GUI); thus the screenshot stands in for a broader process of working in the virtual dematerialized realm. More specifically, it highlights and attempts to explain the ability to, as Macintosh engineer Andy Hertzfeld puts it, "push pixels around" (Hertzfeld 2005: 99).

Today, the very notion of "pushing pixels" may seem confusing; after all, the verb "pushing" implies that real things are being shoved, thrust, and otherwise set in motion. In art theory and practice, "pushing paint" around had, by the 1970s, become an overused phrase. Most often it describes the physical manipulation of the medium, often practiced for the sheer joy of the act itself.[3] Artists who push paint revel in the materiality of what they are doing. But, Hertzfeld's curious phrase is helpful when applied to Apple's consumer-friendly break-through with the Macintosh. To engineers like Hertzfeld and users like Greiman, the computer's new interface seemed to extend the forms and physicality of the real world into the ethereal realm of the digital. This realization tempted the curiosity of Greiman, who quickly realized that, digitized and appearing on the screen of the Macintosh, imagery can appear three-dimensional; furthermore, these digital no-things could even be subjected to actions that mimic the three dimensional actions in the material world.

Of course, the Macintosh's operating system was first conceived for the earlier Lisa computer; both moved away from the dots, spaces, backslashes, and other elements that made up DOS, the incommodious operating system that dominated personal computers to-date. By creating a graphical interface, Apple's engineers tried to normalize otherwise complex actions and conceits; moreover, the GUI made abstract functions comprehensible to engineers, technology writers, and users alike. As theorist Johanna Drucker notes, "We look at interface as a thing, a representation of computational processes that make it convenient for us to interact with what is "really" happening" (Drucker 2014: 138). Thus, the Macintosh's basic operations were displayed as a "toolbox" filled with menus and scrolls, not hammers and nails; its tools were specific to functions needed when dealing with information, not carpentry. More to the point, it helped engineers and users alike to expand the limits of what they believed a computer could do.

Greiman's tiny, printed screenshot unlocks for us the power of the Macintosh's GUI. We see precisely what she saw on the screen, roughed out in areas of light and dark. It reveals not just the configuration of the image being worked on, in this case the poster design, but also the surrounding screen. Thus we see both the poster's final composition, but also the program's vector based drawing tools and rulers. Here, all is laid bare. Many of these toolbar symbols, for example the + sign for enlargements or the oval for cutting, are recognizable as Macintosh tools still used today.

But the screenshot also reveals the source of Greiman's gridded order. Two sides of her screen were lined with the software program's own rulers. These rulers were not part of the poster's final composition. Indeed, Apple's "what you see is what you get" principle only applies to the image seen within these measured software borders. But, realizing this, Greiman echoes them in the poster's final composition. That is, they are mimicked on the timeline that runs down the side of the poster itself; thus we realize that the composition of the larger 2 x 6-inch poster is also aping the software toolbars used to format and manipulate the digitized no-things that Greiman saw on the MacDraw screen.

But it soon becomes clear that the poster also echoes various actions performed on the computer with its powerful graphic user interface. "Scrolling" on-screen, for example, allowed a user to sort through a document that is too big to take in as a whole. The first Macintosh user guide describes this process: "most of the time, a window on the desktop can't show you the entire directory or document all at once, even when you've made the window very large. There's often more information than can fit in the window at one time" (Apple 1984: 26). The guide presents a line drawing of a scroll, noting "the scroll bars in an active window let you move what's in the window so you can see more of it" (1984: 27). As we watch Greiman unfurl *Does It Make Sense*, its slow process of revelation also recalls the manner in which a small computer screen forces us to see only small snatches of a larger composition. The scrolling mechanism was reinforced by the dot matrix printer, which was fed long rolls of paper that were fed through the machine in order to be printed. Better than verbal instructions, unfolding the poster helps us experience an unfolding mechanism similar to Apple's rectangular windows. One can store up snippets of information as the poster is unfolded. As she methodically labors to unfurl the paper poster, this real-world scrolling action is hardly seamless; unlike the fluid, continuous line-by-line or window-by-window scrolling described in the Macintosh manual, the paper poster must constantly be straightened, readjusted, and carefully unfolded so there are no creases or tears.

The seamless power of this virtual making process is also reflected in her digitized body image which surrounds Greiman with a series of octopus-like arms. Writing shortly after the poster was completed, she emphasized the way in which these hands were produced, stressing that she wanted them rendered for utmost clarity, but also in contrast to the rest of her pixilated body. But why emphasize them so? The hands surrounding Greiman hold a variety of tools, many capable of mark-making of the stretch of human history. And indeed, they include a sharpened stone blade fine enough to cut hair but strong enough to mix and apply ochre. Also featured is a spray can (a favorite tool of street artists working in the early 1980s). But she also features a more traditional mark-making device, including to her left a hand holding a pencil or stylus. Each of these tools is inscribed with a potential action, indicated on the poster by strong, clear lines formed in circles, ellipses, arcs and lines. These map potential movement, but they also recall the shapes of the "new" mark making "tools" of the digital age. Some hands carry tools, others appear empty, extending an open palm poised for movement; these tool-less hands are also marked by implied circles and ovals of action every bit as distinctive as hands holding actual tools. A series of lines have been drawn, overlaying the forms and implying the tracing movements of hands; these follow the new mark-making patterns of the digital realm, the (here invisible) mouse. As Greiman would later describe of the computer, "what is great about this tool—all the real activity is invisible" (Farrelly and Greiman 1998: 13).

The dematerialization paradox

Of course, if Greiman believed that the computer could render all the "real activity" of making invisible, it was because she was dematerializing things. That is, to make this poster, she took photographs or videos of very real things around her. Or she used photographs and video made by others. By digitizing her images, of course, she was then able to manipulate them with software. But also, as these things entered a state of blips and electronic pulses, they lost their physical form. They were reduced to a series of ones and zeros, transformed into digital code.

Greiman herself alludes to this process on the poster itself; when printed, the poster's principle figures appear as a delicate haze of enlarged, pixilated imagery. The scrim of squarish dots gives us the impression that solid things, for instance the moon, earth and Greiman's own body, were breaking down before our eyes. But they also remind us that this isn't a real person, only a representation of one. We can see something similar happen with Apple's user friendly GUI. Its "tools" and "toolbars" are digital and exist only within the computer's ether. Of course, as Drucker has observed, any conception of "interface as *thing* (italics hers)" is ultimately an "illusion" (Drucker 2011: 12).

Keeping this curious effect in mind, I want to go back to Appadurai's notion of things in motion as well as Brown's thing theory and what he calls the "dematerialization hypothesis." Returning to Appadurai then, we recall that "value" is inevitably "something separate, ever changing, and ultimately immaterial" (1986: 56). Updating Appadurai's suggestion some fifteen years later, Brown took stock of a world in which information is no longer kept in dusty archives and quiet libraries, but has been translated into electronic information immediately available on gently humming screens. Things like pens and pencils, paper and books have become digitized, their functions translated into code. But in some quarters such change has been greeted with shocked alarm; looking back on his earliest work on thing theory, Brown has updated his ideas, noting more recently the emergence of what he has called "the dematerialization hypothesis" (Brown 2010: 51). This, Brown says, is a nagging fear that the world around us is disappearing into a series of digital blips. Archaeologist Colin Renfrew has given voice to this worry, declaring that "physical palpable material reality ... disappearing, leaving nothing but the smile on the face of the Cheshire Cat" (Renfrew 2003: 185–6).

For his part, Brown sees thing theory as a bulwark against such fears. Indeed, he argues that philosophers have worried about the dematerialization of stuff at least since the great German theorist Immanuel Kant. He observes, "the grand sociological accounts of modernity—by Emile Durkheim, Max Weber, and George Simmel—all consider the increase in abstraction to be a chief characteristic of the modernizing world" (Brown 2010: 52). Calling this a "dematerialization hypothesis" (Brown 2010: 51), Brown argues that such assumptions are "hasty." Instead, he notes an especially marked ambivalence towards more recent forms of media, including photography, stereoscopes, and film; "new media," he argues, "always seem to provoke this old melodrama" (Brown 2010: 53). But also, he insists, there is no ignoring "the materiality of something (be it the stone on which you stubbed your toe or the handle you're about to grab within an immersive VR system)" (Brown 2010: 52). In fact, he insists, materiality is anything but "besieged." For all the talk about digitization, the material world continues to exist.

In the long run, Greiman's poster reinforces Brown's position; it may have been made in dematerializing code, but the poster continues to be mounted on walls, or folded up and stored on a shelf. It can be taken out of its slipcase, picked up and held. It continues to exist as a thing. Moreover, it is also best understood in person. Not only are the specially designed slipcases not reproduced with it, but its key subtitle, "sleep in nothingness," is often cropped out of reproductions. Indeed, the very question it poses, "does it make sense?," is best understood in the poster's material presence. Confronted with the physical object, its basic query, *Does it Make Sense?*, becomes more than a rhetorical question. In any format, the poster should be a pivotal marker for histories of the digital, but seen in person, it is clear that it also bridges a key moment in our understanding of materiality and the immaterial. Read appropriately, as an early attempt to understand things, and the concept of digital "no-thingness." No matter how it is seen, Greiman's poster continues to make good sense. The real question is how can it be understood so it makes the best sense?

Notes

1   I am grateful to Prasad Boradkar for bringing this to my attention.

2   As her interpretation of a ruler spreads across the poster, Greiman mixes scientific terms like "neutron" and "electron" with gloriously absurd notations, like "moron," and lighthearted commands such as "dance" and "make noise."

3   See, for example, Robert Irwin's description of painting practice in Lawrence Weschler and Robert Irwin's *Seeing is Forgetting the Name of the Thing One Sees: A Life of Contemporary Artist Robert Irwin* (Berkeley: University of California Press, 1982), 54.

Bibliography

Appadurai, A. (ed.) (1986), *The Social Life of Things: Commodities in Cultural Perspective*, Cambridge: Cambridge University Press.
Apple Computers (1984), *Macintosh User Guide*, Cupertino: Apple Computers.
Brown, B. (2001), "Thing Theory," *Critical Inquiry*, 28 (1): 1–22.
Brown, B. (2010), "*Materiality*," in W. J. T. Mitchell and M. B. N. Hansen (eds), *Critical Terms for Media Studies*, 49–63, Chicago: University of Chicago Press.
Drucker, J. (2011), "Humanities Approaches to Interface Theory," *Culture Machine* 12: 1–20.
Drucker, J. (2014), *Graphesis: Visual Forms of Knowledge Production*, Cambridge: Harvard University Press.
Eskilson, S. (2012), *Graphic Design: A New History*, London: Yale University Press.
Farrelly, L. and A. Greiman (1998), *April Greiman: Floating Ideas into Time and Space*, New York: Watson Guptill.
Greiman, A. (1987), "Interview with Archie Boston," *20 Outstanding Los Angeles Designers*, DVD.
Greiman, A. (1990), *Hybrid Imagery: The Fusion of Technology and Graphic Design*, New York: Watson Guptill.
Greiman, A. (2010), "Interview with Louise Paradis," *Typografische Monatsblätter*, http://www.tm-research-archive.ch/interviews/april-greiman/ (accessed February 12, 2013).
Gomez-Palacio, B. and A. Vit (2008), "The Visual Perils of Graphic Design History," Underconsideration http://www.underconsideration.com/speakup/archives/005595.html (accessed March 3, 2013).
Guffey, E. (2014), *Posters: A Global History*, London: Reaktion.
Heller, S. and L. Fili (2006), *Stylepedia: A Guide to Graphic Design Mannerisms, Quirks, and Conceits*, San Francisco: Chronicle.
Hertzfeld, A. (2005), *Revolution in the Valley*, Sebastopol: O'Reilly.
Johnson, S. (2011), "Marrying Tech and Art," *Wall Street Journal*, August, 27, 2011 http://online.wsj.com/news/articles/SB10001424053111904875404576532342684923826 (accessed February 2, 2013).
Poynor, R. (2003), *No More Rules: Graphic Design and Postmodernism*, London: Yale University Press.
Renfrew, C. (2003), *Figuring It Out: What Are We? Where Do We Come From? The Parallel Visions of Artists and Archaeologists*, London: Thames & Hudson.
Robertson, F. (2013), *Print Culture: From Steam Press to Ebook*, New York: Routledge.
Smith, J. (2009), "Design discussions: April Greiman on technology," *idsgn*, np. http://idsgn.org/posts/design-discussions-april-greiman-on-technology/ (accessed on January 12, 2013).
Whiteson, L. (1988), "A Designing Woman With Radical Ideas," *Los Angeles Times*, October 9, 1988.

7

Making things, things

Nina Rappaport

Introduction

We are surrounded by things that are made, in turn, by other things. This making encompasses a complex network that includes, among other things, tools, machines, drawings, and factory spaces that come together in a range of specialized processes and sometimes ad hoc methods. Although ubiquitous, the general public does not focus on how things come to be what they are. The thing's early life is rarely revealed unless one ventures on a behind-the-scenes factory tour in which processes of weaving, piecing, molding, welding, and assembling things into other things are made visible. The transition from an object to a thing is cultural and depends on the relationship between the human and the thing: when objects are made into things (designed and produced) they become *some*thing with specific cultural meaning; they emerge from a process during which they build exchange value, enter the market and achieve commodity status. As Bill Brown writes, "the story of objects asserting themselves as things … is the story of a changed relation to the human subject and thus the story of how the thing really names less an object than a particular subject-object relation" (Brown 2001: 5). In this essay, I argue that the way things were manufactured in the pre-industrial era had far-reaching personal and cultural value. That value has been diminished by global manufacturing practices today, leading to a disconnect between processes by which things enter our lives and us. With more decentralized manufacturing, an increased role for the worker participating in the design-to-production process, localized production returning to western cities, and small-scale manufacturing through new technologies such as 3-D printing, however, making practices are changing. It is critical to analyze questions about the values of making today.

    Mass production is still the dominant paradigm by which consumer goods are manufactured today. But when a product is manufactured in subcontracted factories in China, for instance, there is a separation between the designer and the production process due to distance. And though designers may visit factories to understand the production process in conjunction with the manufacturer, the distance can diminish the quality of the goods (Midler 2009). The value of making things in advanced Western capitalist societies has been lost in what I call "process removal"; that is, the process of making is hidden in the generic global factory.[1] Making things is sequestered from public view. The person working in a factory manufacturing goods is not only invisible to designers but also to consumers, who might have never seen the inside of a factory. Often consumers do not have any knowledge of the effort, time, and process involved in making something. However, practices of making are taking on new significance with more people moving toward craft and maker culture in neo-cottage industries.[2] The production of goods today unfolds under a variety of circumstances involving individual craftspeople and multinational corporations, garages, and factories, as one-offs and in high volumes. To understand these diverse approaches—from that of the craft worker to the factory worker and the engagement of the industrial designer—a few theoretical concepts are folded into this discussion. In the realm of the most engaged industrial designers and manufacturers, the necessary collaborative process elides with Bruno Latour's Actor Network Theory (ANT). In factory production, ANT plays out as orchestration among designers, production engineers, workers, and machines—human and non-human "actants" involved in processes of making. Production also relies on interaction and feedback among all of these actants. This essay juxtaposes the making of things in factory production with the role of the factory worker as someone who is engaged in the design of a product that can be seen as parallel to craft production. Looking beyond established protocols for production in the common top-down manufacturing process, I ask: how does the individual factory worker impact the making of a thing? What is the value of his or her contribution, and how does it shape the thing itself? The production process and the required actions of a worker upon an object to make it a thing reveal cultural constructs, despite the fact that making is largely invisible as, in Brown's terms, the object transitions to thingness.

Homo faber

Philosophers Hannah Arendt and Henri Bergson expressed an interest in why we make things; they recognized the human drive and the concept of *homo faber*—man who makes. Indeed, Bergson defines intelligence as the "faculty to create artificial objects, in particular tools to make tools, and to indefinitely variate its makings" (Bergson 1911). In the 1970s, the Czech philosopher Vilém Flusser too described humankind as *homo faber*—man who makes—rather than *homo sapiens*—man who knows—because as "true" men and women we form societies and make things in production centers called factories. According to Flusser, in a particular era "[e]verything about the knowledge, politics, art and religion of society at that time can be discovered by studying the organizations of potteries and the articles produced in them" (Flusser 1993: 43). In other words, the study of designed artifacts in the form of archaeological remains is a way to gain insight into cultures of the past. Flusser also argues that, whereas the privileged classes produce art, we actually learn more by investigating workshops and guilds because that is where everyday people work. He suggests if we want to understand the past and present, or to anticipate the future, we need to ask questions about where and how things are, or were made.

Historically, people made things at home. Making by hand imbued the thing made with a specific cultural and artistic quality of the time, place, and style in which it was made. The conceiver, maker, and user/consumer were typically one and the same. Places of work expanded from the home, into the cottage industries of the Middle Ages, and then were organized into workshops. According to historian Fernand Braudel, these workshops—the artisanal work of bakers, distillers, and locksmiths—were still the center of the family craftwork that continued

FIGURE 7.1 Bicycle Manufacturer, 1880. Oxford Science Archive, Heritage-Images.

through the mid-nineteenth century (Braudel 1979: 298). He points out that the clustering for shared resources fed into a network of workers for whom trial by error and experimentation led to new discoveries and new inventions (Braudel 1979: 344). In the nineteenth century, Russian economist Peter Kropotkin wrote about the making of hair combs, in Oyonnax, France, where the 200-year-old profession expanded with the use of celluloid and the introduction of electricity in the home-based workshops led them to gradually become larger enterprises (Kropotkin 1912: 168). However, when production moved out of the home, that physical distance also separated the thing from its making. The idea of homemade became valued when things were rarely made in the home, as making transitioned from home to mass-production and in many ways the product quality diminished.

Value has been placed on inventive handcrafted skills in all eras. Art historian George Kubler recognized the difference between and interaction among craft techniques and artistic invention noting that:

> among craftsmen a technical innovation can often become the point of departure for a new sequence where all the elements of the tradition are revised in the light of the possibilities open to view by the innovation. An example is the displacement of black-figure vase painting near the end of the sixth century B.C. by red-figured technique. One sequence may yield to another when an item in the composition of the original sequence in significantly altered ... The point is that the formal sequence always corresponds to a distinct conception of a potential series of changes (Kubler 1962: 48).

Kubler emphasized that craft education contains repetitious actions, and that artists must depend on the instruments of the craft, or the tools necessary in the making of that thing. Once this process is mastered then craftspeople can produce innovative new solutions. The ownership of a technique, or of a new solution, for a production method typically includes the craftsman as part of a new methodology.

Manufacturing moved from handmade products created in home workshops to mass-produced goods built in factories in late nineteenth-century industrial cities such as Manchester, England. Marx and Engels observed that the commoditization of goods and mass production often entirely stripped public awareness of the production process for factory-made items from the product (Marx 1906: 197–221). The move from baking bread in the home where it was a daily activity, to an urban factory owned by a company, diminished bread's quality and freshness and transformed baking into a large-scale business, capitalizing on new production machinery. For clothing, the shift from a custom or self-made item to one that was ready-made by garment manufacturers and sold in the new department stores, changed the status of the worker to an unaccounted for participant in the process.[3]

Marx defines *commodities* as manufactured goods with capitalist modes of production in his seminal work, *Capital* (*Das Kapital* 1906). His insight identified the value of labor in both the making of the tools in shaping the product and the monetary value of that product beyond the value placed on it in the market because of demand. For Marx, the means of manufacturing added value to a product because the worker was part of the financial equation of production through *labor-power*. In this process, workers themselves become commodities engaging both their brains and physical actions in making products, for the marketplace.

The social life of things

In assessing material culture as *The Social Life of Things*, anthropologist Arjun Appardurai examines, "the circulation of things themselves, for their meanings are inscribed in their forms, their uses, their trajectories" (Appadurai 1986: 5). He focuses on the biography of things and asks, "What sort of an exchange is commodity exchange?" Appadurai argues that: "*The commodity situation in the social life of any 'thing' can be defined as the situation in which its exchangeability (past, present, or future) for some other thing is its socially relevant feature*" (original emphasis) (Appadurai 1986: 13). Things evolve, according to Appadurai, so that at some stages they are not commodities, and at others they are given value by each culture or person as they are made and used in specific contexts. Appadurai also recognizes that a commodity of *context* refers to the social arenas within or between cultural units that reinforce its commoditization (Appadurai 1986: 15). Extrapolating this context to that of workers, his theory would enhance their role, and thus the value of the object. For him, a commodity is something that at a certain phase in the life of the object, in a particular context, and considering certain cultural and temporal aspects, meets the requirements of what he calls "commodity candidacy." This candidacy emerges when a culture accepts a thing and exchanges it in the marketplace (Appadurai 1986: 16).

Marx, on the other hand, recognized that the skills required to manufacture a commodity are part of its "life history." Appadurai argues that a new product "has had the least opportunity to accumulate an idiosyncratic biography or enjoy a peculiar career" (Appadurai 1986: 16). He does not discuss the production process as integral to the commodity in the same way that Marx does by linking labor-value to products (Appadurai 1986: 42). In this essay, I emphasize that production and labor are just as critical to the life of the object and to its value as its entry into the market. A thing and its thingness have more intrinsic value when we know who makes it and how it is made, because it unites the design, the process, and the evolution of the object, giving it authenticity.

In discussing the connection between producer and consumer, Appadurai stresses that: "As technology changes, the reproduction of the product on a mass basis becomes possible and the dialogue between the consumer and the producer is more direct" (Appadurai 1986: 44). I contend that, while today it is easier to customize or choose a product online, the gap between producer and consumer now is greater still than it was around the first industrial revolution. Consumers rarely have any connection to producers. This is true, in part, because making something has become so complex that its network evolves longer and longer supply chains of outsourced production to subcontracted factories. These subcontractors make different products under one roof. In fact, it is often ignored that the same factory will commonly make products for many different brands. For example, Yue Yuen Holding makes sneakers for Nike, Adidas, and Reebok (*Newsweek* 2014). Making is no longer visible and the supply chain is a distant and secretive process. Marx also had an acute understanding of the estrangement process between workers, things, and consumers.[4] He claimed that as the institutional and spatial journeys of commodities grow more complex—and the alienation of producers, traders, and consumers from one another increases—culturally formed mythologies about commodity flow are likely to emerge. These are "mythologies by traders, consumers alienated from production, and workers, who are divorced from the distribution and consumption logics of the commodities they produce" (Appadurai 1986: 48). Thus, removing the intellectual or physical connection between a worker and production detracts from the labor-power that is invested into the thing, and a product is only considered to be a marketable thing—a commodity. The worker, the tools and the manufacturing process transform the thing into a commodity with value. The worker steps away from the product once it is made, and that is when the consumer then picks it up and engages with it as a commodity.

Instead, what I propose—after reflecting on the thoughts of Apparadurai, Latour, and Marx—is the need for the acknowledgment of workers' innovations on the production line. Often, in today's factories, the individual worker's contributions to the process on the factory floor are ignored. These sorts of worker innovations enhance a thing's value because of better quality, closer attention, and an authenticity now valued by the consumer; they occur in the gaps between the original design, the manufacturing process, and a product's circulation in society. This value might not be one that is readily visible by the public, as noted previously, or even have a value that is perceived by the general public. But in the range of the design of things, this value is significant because of additional worker input into the object as creative labor-power. As commodities, the labor-value then enhances the cultural and economic value of the thing.

In "Thing Theory," Bill Brown emphasizes that things are general and specific, that they take on meaning beyond what they are as representatives of cultures. Brown also writes of the individual subject who places significance on a thing after it is made (Brown 2001: 8). But the collaborative process of making provides a different orientation and significance. Clearly, things have value when they are in people's lives and embedded in cultural systems, but that does not mean things do not have meaning when they are on the assembly line prior to entering the social world. The object made from labor has increased value on account of the labor that is expended in its making.

Heterogenous invention—ANT

That the making of a thing expands beyond its conception fits Latour's Actor Network Theory.[5] Those who act upon the object (the "actants"), in response to feedback from the object, interact in a hybrid manner across disciplines in the making of things. Latour's heterogeneous network of factory production—the raw materials, the machinery that the operators use, and the supply chain: the entire production process—deals with objects as they are being made and transformed into things. Designers don't work alone: they collaborate with factory workers and manufacturers who produce what they have conceived. The workers utilize various areas of expertise that then become a part of what they are making. The networked manufacturing process—from the initial design concept to the marketplace (and also including the consumer and how that thing then becomes part of material culture)—is defined via ANT. In *Science in Action*, Latour offers examples of factory-sited actor networks (Latour 1987: 122). These networks involve both people and inventions, such as Eastman and the Kodak camera; or Diesel and the Diesel engine; and Bell and the Bell telephone. Latour elaborates the ways that these inventions were transformed into objects and sold to the public (which is part of the chain of actions and reactions), and the human network alliances, including the object actant and its random or intuitive connections that influenced the product's success. The connections and interactions Latour describes allow for indeterminacy as well as for an unpredictable potential for change. Kodak was Eastman's dream for a mass market for photography, but realizing it involved an entire company making a product through many trials and errors. This is precisely where factory workers, laborers, or operators play a role as actants: they contribute to the common goal of making the thing inclusive in the overall network.

Alienation

Factory work has been specialized since Adam Smith's eighteenth-century analysis of pin workers. In the mid-eighteenth century, Smith noted that each worker had a specific, repetitive task to perform. In 1911, during the days of the Gilbreths and Taylor's Scientific Management for efficient modes production, error was to be eliminated and speed was to be increased in manufacturing. Frederick Taylor developed methods for workers to be more efficient rather than to follow rules of thumb. The Gilbreths photographed and evaluated workers' movements; these evaluations were used to recommend timesaving methods. Together these analyses and methods led to rational factory production in the Western world. The skilled worker wasn't asked to make a product better, only to make it more efficiently. Thus, the assembly line process was established, a process that transformed factory workers into "cogs in a wheel." This structure continues in many factories, including those of the corporation Foxconn, in which the workers do not know that the electronic parts they are independently assembling ultimately become an iPad (Zhang 2012). Workers in these factories have no control over the objects they are making because they are simply making a component rather than a thing; they are making something that they never see; they are making a product they may not be able to afford to buy. These workers are alienated from their work, using Marx's terminology, and this alienation is so severe in many global factories that workers have committed suicide (Chan and Pun 2010). We must ask: how can the value of people who are working in factories be revalued in the production process?

From design to making

In contemporary Western factory production, it is not only workers who are alienated. Consumers are also alienated, distanced from the making of things since we have removed production not only from daily life, but also from the local surroundings. The Industrial Revolution moved the production process away from home to city factories; digital processes that are linked to globalization have removed the process from locally based production, or "process removal." In many Western cultures the things we buy are no longer made where we live. Consumers have no connection to production because factories have been removed from the urban core, and are sequestered from daily life. Removing factories from local spaces also means that we don't see materials enter or leave the factory. Things appear in our everyday lives without our knowledge of the processes by which they come into being. Globalized manufacturing also tends to raise questions about inequality often because of reduced oversight on labor conditions, factory safety, fair wages, etc. A jeweler can design a ring, set the specifications, and send details digitally to a company in Taiwan, where it is made in a factory by a worker who does not have any connection to the designer or her creative process. This sort of mass-production exists in stark contrast to that of a designer collaborating with a metal worker in close proximity in a craft-like process, for example, in New York's Diamond District. The thing being made is in a direct relation with action and reaction between design, hand, and material so that the process is less opaque both physically and ethically.

Designing and production are codependent processes, even if the agents are not one and the same. Two methods are enhanced by this codependency: in factories workers redesign products as they are reconfigured for assembly lines, and in neo-cottage industries "makers" and DIY enthusiasts are reimagining standardized mass production. In these situations, the manufacturing method is incorporated into envisioning the thing in precisely the same way that an architect works with a carpenter to make refinements to a design. In the more direct design-build process, the designer actually has the opportunity to understand production processes and to invent and build simultaneously. In a kind of rebellion against immaterial labor (that of virtual products and information jobs) that has been catalyzed by internationalization and digital design, and in contrast to process removal, there is a new interest in crafts, the Etsy marketplace, and other personal or collaborative ways of working directly with other actants. In these situations, the person making is often the person designing and selling, and this person is making something directly. This is especially true with the advent of 3-D tabletop printers as well as crowd-sourced funding that encourages neo-cottage industries.

On the factory floor

Using these new collaborative processes, factory workers contribute to improving the product on the factory floor—to either fit the production process at hand, or to invent new methods, as products are designed. Changes are made by production managers or by industrial engineers, but these changes can be handled by skilled workers who are involved in production improvement. As with pre-industrial-revolution craftsmen, unexpected developments that spur invention are more likely to occur.

In older production models, industrial engineers were tasked with the job of organizing the production line and planning the factory layouts, improving timetables, filling in spreadsheets, controlling production; i.e., they were not involved in making the product. Collaboration between inventor and product in an actor-network can be seen in examples from Albert Pope, who in the late nineteenth century found a more efficient way to produce bicycles in his Connecticut sewing machine factory using drop forging, a method for iron production that he applied to bike manufacturing. Or in Henry Ford's collaboration in 1912 with engineer Charles E. Sorensen. Together they made iterative adjustments to the meatpacking disassembly process and can packing assembly line that led to the development of the continuous moving production line, and thus mass production.

In the twenty-first century, the manufacturing process is again becoming collaborative and more localized. In the mid-twentieth century, computer technologies encouraged a fascination with the machine and anything automated and laborsaving. Company owners would usually not go to the factory floor, and changes would be made in the engineers' offices to be sent down to the operators to implement. But in the 1960s, with Toyota's concepts for Just-in-Time and Lean Manufacturing, a combination of machine-driven methods and worker feedback produced better results. Using the Kaizen system with electronic Andon boards mounted above the production line, feedback loops signal a product's status on the assembly line, so that the workers can respond in a responsive actor-network. Cellular manufacturing, in contrast to linear production, became prominent by making a product in one area, or cell, of the factory. Groups of workers completed all the stages of product in a more flexible process than the one seen in assembly line work. In addition, "continuous improvement" became a standard way to include the operators (or workers) in the process. In the mid-twentieth century, workers optimized production by giving their opinions on how something should be done, often

FIGURE 7.2 Oyonnax, France, steam-power building. Photograph by Nina Rappaport, 2015.

together with engineers on the floor. This collaboration provides workers with more authority and control, reestablishing pride in their work.

The design of the factory in the post-Fordist era is also implicated in the organization of work on the factory floor, where companies integrate the production organization, offices and R&D with the manufacturing floor. Instead of a physical hierarchy with the shop supervisor and engineer in the mezzanine office looking down at the workers who complete repetitive motions and have no control of their work, engineers and supervisors work side-by-side. This proximity is visible both physically and organizationally in the Skoda factory that was designed by Henn Architects in 2006. In this factory, manufacturing moves along a central spine within pods. The pods are office nodes with movable wall panels, and tables serve as workstations for the auto mechanics and engineers to collaborate and resolve production issues.

Flusser projected that "The factory of the future will certainly be much more flexible than that of today and it will, without a doubt, revolutionize the relationship between man and tools … The factory of the future will … [be] a place in which the creative possibilities of *homo faber* can be realized" (Flusser 1993: 50). Combining technology and intellect, he envisioned the factory as a place of education and hands-on work. Flusser presaged the "third" industrial revolution, a conglomeration of new technologies, collaborative intellectual production, and shared skilled work.

Toward a theory of making things

Many designers have increased their involvement with production, bridging the divide between designing and making. New York-based industrial designer Rama Chorpash emphasizes that he "is constantly engaging with the workers on the factory floor. But you have to get into the factory to begin with. Factories don't often allow designers to visit because it is secretive and they might not want to reveal things like the fact that they have second suppliers in their supply chain, or where the raw materials come from."[6] For his wire potato masher project, Chorpash turned to a Brooklyn factory that made wire spring products and convinced them to take on his concept. He produced CAD sketches and a prototype and the production engineer, who was a second-generation spring bender, was enthusiastic. Chorpash observed that the will to take on a product and to figure out how to make it became a sense of pride for all involved. For a furniture design project, a factory in Brazil resolved his design with mechanical drawings, but they did so in their own way. It was not a standard with which Chorpash was familiar. He learned that their perspective was called *mandeta*, which means "the way" in Portuguese. They made the furniture the way they knew they could and his design was successfully produced. In his project *Err*, artist Jeremy Hutchinson plays games with factory workers, trying to see if they are aware of what they are making. He provided designs for objects that are not working functional things, but were defective on purpose: odd soccer balls with the colors in the wrong places, for example, or shoes with the heels put on backward. The workers didn't want to make products with built-in intentional mistakes, and couldn't understand why someone would want a defective product. Hutchinson thus played up the disconnect between worker and product as the workers became engaged in his dialogue.

During a Long Island City, New York piano factory's "continuous improvement" process, industrial engineers routinely bring in a group of workers for discussions of issues and opportunities. In almost every discussion, a union operator adds a suggestion for a quality or

FIGURE 7.3 Spiraloop designed by Rama Chorpash.

efficiency improvement that is implemented into the permanent process. In one recent program in production, for example, an operator involved in installing a piece of hardware onto a piano noticed regular errors. The operator suggested that, since the location of the hardware always was the same, they could create a fixture that would regularize the process and increase accuracy. This simple solution was adopted, and it ultimately led to a faster install time and a reduced defect rate. This case study demonstrates the importance of the responsive solutions that include employees.[7]

Another factory, where workers once made steam irons for the garment industry, and which now makes steam machines, also focuses on continuous improvement with the factory-line employees. In this steam machine factory, workers had to reach over the conveyor line to drag a steel box across the rubber belt at each station. The exposed edge of the box would get caught on the line and this slowed down the process. A worker on the production line suggested setting

FIGURE 7.4 Worker at Steinway Piano, Astoria, Queens. Photograph by Nina Rappaport.

up a bridge with a nylon sheet that was spaced above the belt, so that when the box came by, workers could tip it. This change eliminated wear and tear on the line, back strain, and worker injury. The company decided to have their supplier flat-pack the metal box and shipped flat with perforated edges to be then folded in the steam machine factory. This change reduced the lead-time, conserved materials, and took away the need to overstock supplies. The change also reduced shipping costs, which helped the company's bottom line—but it also imbued workers with pride because they were involved in the decision.

There are numerous questions to be asked such as: Why don't most workers receive recognition for the production of things? What happens if the design that is produced for an object is improved by the fabricator? What if the prototype is not the same as the original thing? Can a thing created by a designer still be what it was intended to be if the manufacturing process changes it? How does a worker gain agency in the actor-network? How does the worker play a part in the evolution of the thing as it becomes a commodity (as defined by Marx) and culturally meaningful (as spelled out by Appadurai)? Kubler emphasized that "the history of things is intended to reunite ideas and objects under the rubric of visual forms … all materials worked on by human hands under the guidance of connected ideas developed in temporal sequence." What he calls, "a shape of time" is a "visible portrait of the collective identity, whether tribe, class or nation, comes into being. This self-image reflected in things is a guide and a point of reference to the group for the future, and it eventually becomes the portrait given to posterity" (Kubler 1962: 9).

What will *homo faber* be in the future archaeology of our factories and workplaces; how will we see the maker's personal imprint in what is being made? If labor value is situated in the maker whose role is merged with that of the designer, then designing and making take on some of the character of handworkers in cottage industries. The workers' input is both a commodity with increased labor-value, but it is also a representation of a new ethical consciousness of where things come from and where they go in a new circular supply chain.

Notes

1. Marx discussed related ideas in the late 1880s.
2. See Richard Sennett, Chris Anderson, and Kevin Kelly who write about the new "maker" culture and craft.
3. Things are commodities in Marx's terms that have value beyond their own intrinsic essence; where value is placed on them by their circulation in society and through the supply and demand of goods and their invisible imbedded politics.
4. "The alienation of the worker in his product means not only that his labor becomes an object, an external existence, but that it exists outside him, independently, as something alien to him, and that it becomes a power of its own confronting him" (Marx 1968: 72)
5. See, in general, B. Latour (1987), *Science in Action*, Cambridge, MA: Harvard University Press.
6. Conversation between the author and Rama Chorpash, June 2014.
7. Conversation between author and production engineer at Steinway & Sons factory, June 2014.

Bibliography

Appadurai, A. (1986), "Introduction: Commodities and the Politics of Value," in Arjun Appadurai (ed.), *The Social Life of Things*, Cambridge: Cambridge University Press.
Bergson, H. (1911), *Creative Evolution*, trans. A. Mitchell, New York: Henry Holt and Company.
Braudel, F. (1979), *The Wheels of Commerce, Civilization and Capitalism, 15th–18th Century*, Volume 2, New York: Harper & Row.
Brown, B. (2001), "Thing Theory," *Critical Inquiry* 28 (1): 1–22.
Chan, J. and N. Pun (2010), "Suicide as Protest for the New Generation of Chinese Migrant Workers: Foxconn, Global Capital, and the State," *The Asia-Pacific Journal* http://japanfocus.org/-jenny-chan/3408/article.html (accessed October 29, 2015).
Conversation between the author and Rama Chorpash, June 2014.
Conversation between author and production engineer at Steinway & Sons factory, June 2014.
Flusser, V. (1999), "The Factory," in *The Status of Things, A Small Philosophy of Design*, London: Reaktion Books. Originally published as (1993) "Die Fabrik," *Vom Stand der Dinge*, Carl Hanser Berlag.
Kropotkin, P. (1912), *Fields, Factories and Workshops*, reprint, New York: G. P. Putnam's Sons, 1898.
Kubler, G. (1962), *The Shape of Time*, New Haven: Yale University Press.
Latour, B. (1987), *Science in Action*, Cambridge, MA: Harvard University Press.
Marx, K. (1987), *Economic and Philosophic Manuscripts of 1844, in the Marx-Engels Reader*, Edited by Robert C. Tucker, second edition, New York: W. W. Norton & Company, 72.
Marx, K. and F. Engels (eds) (1906), Part III of *Capital*, 197–221, New York: Modern Library.
Midler, P. (2009), *Poorly Made in China*, New Jersey: Wiley.
"Thousands Strike at Chinese Factory," *Newsweek,* April 21, 2014.
Zhang, C. (2012), "Apple Manufacturing Plant Workers Complain of Long Hours, Militant Culture," *CNN News Report*, February 6 www.cnn.com/2012/02/06/world/asia/china-apple-foxconn-worker (accessed October 29, 2015).

8

Distributing stresses

The development and use of the Eames Dining Chair Metal (DCM)

Michael J. Golec

Introduction

Programs of action. Patterns of transmission. Survivals. Distributing stresses. A consideration of thing effects—in *media res*—as media in action. In this chapter, I outline an alliance between plywood sculpture, plywood splints, and plywood chairs—between aesthetics, medics, and therapeutics—where affordances proliferated into instances of assistance.[1] In order to accomplish such a weighty task, I take the ubiquitous 1946 Dining Chair Metal, or DCM, by American designer Charles Eames as a focal point in a program of media/material action and distribution: wood-devices-made-for-caring-for-the-injured to wood-devices-made-for-sitting-and-caring.[2]

The sculpting of laminated plywood forms, the wartime technological advances in orthopedic care, and the design of chairs were enmeshed in composite form in many of the seats supporting the post-World War II American body. Each form received data (meaning or content) from the preceding form, not merely in terms of its significance but in its material, concrete form. Plywood forms informed splints, which, in turn, informed seats.

The DCM, to a fair extent, remained *splintish* since it took up the care for the post war body and psyche. Indeed, the DCM did not completely obsolesce the splint (nor the plywood sculpture, for that matter). In fact, one of the chair's component parts intensified *splintishness* and the care for the postwar sitter. Among all the talk of plywood bending and molding were shock mounts: little rubber disks that were Cyclewelded to plywood and metal. The rubber shock mounts transmitted caregiving from splints to chairs: things that made things right. Shock mounts assembled humans and non-humans. They gathered stresses, taking them on to mediate between wood and body.

This chapter considers the transformational effects of things—media in action, transmissions, and survivals—as they generate new conditions of environmental service and of life.

FIGURE 8.1 Charles Eames, "Chair," United States Patent Number 150,685 (1947–8).

Throughout this text I use "media in action" to underscore characteristics of things in between things, and to consider important distinctions that matter in terms of what some*thing* does in relation to another *thing*. The chapter extends the technological alliance between splints and chairs—between medics and design—as the two exist as the products of a method of making laminated seating and rubber shock mounts, but also as products of an attunement to wartime and post-war therapeutics.[3] I will focus on splints, chairs, and molded plywood, and more specifically on shock-mounts because those thick rubber disks attached to chairs gathered all the attention from critics at the time, especially when American curator and designer Elliot Noyes commented on the splints and chairs both distributing stresses (Noyes 1946: 44). Indeed, by 1946, when the DCM and DCW (Dining Chair Wood) chairs were exhibited at the Museum of Modern Art (MoMA), bentwood was already a familiar medium and hardly worth noting at this late stage in the development of seating technologies. The innovation in these chairs lay elsewhere. The addition of the rubber shock mounts to a system of sitting—to bent metal and laminated plywood—assisted the postwar body in contending with the challenges of the "condition of public helplessness" (McLuhan 1995 [1951]: 21) deeply felt in the post-World War II age of "the lonely crowd" (Riesman 1969) and "the organization man" (Whyte 1956). This chapter will follow things in action, mediations, connections, distributions, and redistributions from splints, to bodies, to shock mounts, to chairs, and from aesthetics to medics to therapeutics as design for living.

In taking up "media in action" as a method of thinking about things, I want to confront what material culture studies has long taken for granted: that things (or objects) are encoded with meaning and significance such that they embody human mental structures and patterns of belief (Prown 1982); that things illuminate spheres of human interaction (Appadurai 1988; Miller 1987, 2010); and that things constitute the "missing masses" in the production of the social (Latour 1992, 2005; Shanks 1998).[4] In all three of the above instances, and to various degrees, things, as much as humans, play roles—embodying, illuminating, and appearing—in the making of the social. The ability to think about the social role of things as they mingle with their human counterparts is most evident in Actor Network Theory (ANT), and especially in the work of French sociologist of science and philosopher Bruno Latour, where associations, relations, transfers, and translations proliferate construct symmetrical social relations between humans and non-humans. For Latour and ANT, symmetries balance the social so that non-human things can take their place among human things (and *vice versa*). Latour and ANT have exerted pressure on material culture studies to take on analytic and descriptive work by tracing the place taking of things *and/or* things taking place within networks. In this way, ANT foments more accurate accounts of the missing masses of material artifacts.

In what follows, I argue, in reference to the place taking of things, that meaning and significance are not merely in things as material artifacts—as in Prown's "mind in matter"—but that networks of relationships between humans and things are saturated with meaning and significance.[5] Rubber disks, laminated wood, metal spindles, and humans are all equal things under the socio-technical organization of sitting in postwar United States.

Equivalency for the sake of leveling out everything under the sun so that everything is the same, however, is not an admirable goal per se. There must be something other than sameness at stake in the constitution of human thing and non-human thing symmetries. While the socio-technical organization of sitting, indeed, might force uniformity (as demonstrated in the multiple photographs of Charles Eames in his DCM), links must be made in order to constitute the assemblage of mid-century modern seating and mid-century humans as equal. In the case of DCM and distributed stresses, each link in the distribution of things provided an opportunity to register an intensification at the joint, as it were. Joints connect, but they do so with varying degrees of integrity (as any sailor with an injured limb bound in an Eames splint could attest to). For the purposes of this chapter, the patent drawings of the DCM and the "shock-mount" are preferable to the photographic depictions of the same objects. The patent drawings point to the chair's "ontography," which Ian Bogost defines as the "revelation of object relationships," in ways that photographic reproductions do not (Bogost 2012: 58).[6] The patent drawings embody the epistemology of the diagram, and thereby clarify the complex physical system of the chair, but also gesture toward the repleteness of the chair's network of relations. As diagrams, the patent drawings inscribe (describe) connections which defeat the illusions of wholeness or unity often rendered in photographic representations of Eames objects. As Bogost defines his use of the term, "ontography can take the form of a compendium, a record of things juxtaposed to demonstrate their overlap and imply interaction through collocation" (Bogost 2012: 38). It is the side-by-sidedness of the patent drawings (how things fit together) that is suggestive of the connections I seek to draw with this chapter.

In general, and following Latour, some connections are stronger than others, hence the greater potential for intensification. Sturdy bonds result in heightened intensifications. According to Latour, strong and weak connections exist within networks. Strong connections are present where human and non-human "mediators," to use Latour's term, establish associations in the designing of assemblages (Latour 1993: 78).[7] Strong connections produce "well-formed" assemblages, which can be observed and are traceable (Latour 2005: 30–6). From Latour's perspective, it is important to note that the associations that constitute a "well-formed" assemblage exist independent of direct observation and analysis, and that this independence is what makes them strong. In other words, the connections that forge collectives among the things I discuss in this essay are not the product of my analysis but exist irrespective of my mapping. It is possible, perhaps necessary, to push even further on these points—assembly, joinery, connectivity—to follow something of French philosopher Gilles Deleuze in Latour's ANT.[8] That is to say, where we find interconnections—media in action—we likewise find intensifications of meaning and significance.[9]

Medics

In December 1941, Charles and Ray Eames invited Dr. Wendell Scott to their apartment in Westwood. Scott was an acquaintance of Charles from his St. Louis days, and he had arranged to meet the couple on his visit to Los Angeles. Ray and Charles had recently moved into architect Richard Neutra's 1937 Strathmore Apartments. Just married and relocated from Cranbrook Academy of Art in Michigan to Los Angeles, the Eameses occupied themselves at night with the problem of manufacturing low-cost laminated plywood. Much of their nighttime experimentation on plywood, however, resulted in the making of compound-curved plywood sculptures. On his visit to the improvised workshop at the Strathmore, Scott confronted a variety of falling and cresting shapes, plywood veneer spans, and plies on top of plies. He stepped right into the messy process, disturbing the homeostatic environment of the newly wed's apartment and its inhabitants of humans, sculptures, chair seats and backs, and sundry tools. He entered into an environment saturated with agency and interconnectivity, one where he could socialize as much with his hosts as with their objects. Mediators everywhere, Scott, a thing himself, stood as a catalyst for the formation of a network—a system of distribution, of transmission, and of transposition.

A year prior to Scott's visit, Charles and Ray, in collaboration with architect and designer Eero Saarinen, submitted designs to MoMA's "Organic Furniture Competition." They took first prize in both of the two main categories. The competition stipulated that the winner's submissions were to be manufactured and sold to the public at a reasonable cost. Unfortunately, the engineers at the Haskelite Manufacturing Corporation could not figure out how to mass-produce economically the Eames/Saarinen organic chair. While bent wood furniture was hardly a radical manufacturing proposition, the organic chair was a complex affair. Some plywood shells were made according to the designers' specifications, but the molds were costly and produced inconsistent results, requiring additional hand finishing work. The competition chairs were never mass-produced; hence Scott's observance of the continuation of the earlier Michigan experiments in California. Within the space of cast-off plyformed seats, Scott intensified connections.

Scott's appearance in their Los Angeles apartment motivated Ray and Charles to rededicate their experiments to a different sort of organicism—the mending of damaged bodies. A medical doctor with military experience, Scott informed the couple of recent problems with the US military Medical Corps use of metal leg splints in the field. While providing ambulatory aid to wounded soldiers and sailors, the metal leg splints that were used in the field provided insufficient support, restraint, and comfort for the injured party. In a moment of empathic feeling-into the prosthetic possibility set off by undulating laminated plywood, Scott was struck with an idea for a hybrid design: the adaptation of the chair and sculpture manufacturing process to the production of wood laminated splints for the military (Kirkham 1998: 212–13). Surprisingly, scooped seats to ease backs and nestle behinds, and biomorphic sculptures to test formal and material standards, evoked a technological response to wartime injury, as if images of broken limbs and body hugging encasements could be derived from the modest forms exhibited in the Neutra apartment building.

It would take close to six months for the Eameses to realize a new program of action—a shift from wood-devices-made-for-sitting-and/or-viewing to wood-devices-made-for-caring-for-the-injured—from chairs and sculpture to splints.[10] It is difficult to know for certain what role Scott's suggestion played in the transformation from experiments with laminated plywood chairs and sculptures to the mass-production of leg splints (and, for a short period, arm splints, litter prototypes, horizontal and vertical aircraft stabilizers, and glider sections).[11]

Aesthetics

To what extent do objects aid humans, even if they have nothing of the character of helping and are themselves standoffish, as *might* be the case with artworks? This question bears on the role of the sculptural plyforms displayed in the Eames' apartment. While the production of the US Navy splints was crucial to the development of the DCM, a good deal of emphasis has been laid on the sculpture work that transpired while experimenting with plyformed seats. To some extent the emphasis on sculpture has been to raise Ray's avant-garde pedigree and to secure her "aesthetic brilliance" in the face of Charles' overwhelming "technical achievement" (Giovanni 1997: 47).[12] There is good reason to offer this revision, since so much of the Eames collective enterprise was consistently attributed to the male half of the partnership. The inequity is best exemplified in the *New Furniture Designed by Charles Eames* at MoMA (not new furniture designed by Charles and Ray Eames) in March 1946, and scholars have made efforts to reclaim Ray's influence on the plywood furniture exhibited in the museum. Design historian Esther McCoy first observed the collaborative significance of Ray's art training, identifying Ray's involvement in the Eames and Saarinen submissions to the *Organic Design* show (McCoy 1975: 21). Pat Kirkham completes the narrative of influence when she asserts, "the final form of the famous DCM chair owes a great deal to [Ray's] interest in abstract art" (Kirkham 1995: 80).

Under these descriptions, the sculptural forms are indexes, stand-ins, or exemplars of Ray's avant-garde pedigree and her aesthetic acumen. The reinsertion of Ray into the history of the early development of the Eames chairs should result in an instance of aesthetic innovation trumping technical progress. More often than not Charles admitted to Ray's contribution to their partnership as having to do with "the consistency of structure," which he viewed as much aesthetic as technical (quoted in Kirkham 1995: 82). Consistency of structure meant, for Charles, something made well—as in *techné*—and intelligible or sensible—as in aesthetic. Speaking of the DCM, Charles explained, "One of the things *we* had committed ourselves to was trying to do a chair with a hard surface that was as comfortable as it could be in relation to the human body and also that would be self-explanatory as you looked at it—no mysteries, so that the techniques of how it was made would be part of its aesthetics" (quoted in Gingrich 1977: 328).[13] And, yet, consistency of structure had an additional meaning within the context of a program of action: wood-devices-made-for-the-distribution-of-the-sensible.

In what French philosopher Jacques Rancière refers to as a "distribution of the sensible," Ray escalated the proliferation of connections within the space of cast-off plyformed seats and shapes. Sculpture connected to splint and chair. And Scott further multiplied connections. Stressing different attitudes and/or approaches, aesthetics in the case of the former and medics in the case of the latter, Ray Eames and Scott redistributed the senses so that the plyforms could be thought otherwise. They were mediating things amongst the piles of structural lumber, the hammer, the saw, the bicycle pump, and the "Kazam" machine—a molding machine on which they carried out their experiments.[14] A sculpture story converged with a splint story, and the distribution of pleasure translated (transformed) into the distribution of care. In this sense, prosthetics like aesthetics presumes that humans are deficient, and that we cannot do without the splint or the sculpture. Humans need the support of things—both art and medical apparatus. So, what was held tight in the contours of plywood's sculptural form? Bum legs or refined tastes? Sculpture might distribute care in the configuration of, what Rancière identifies in the aesthetic regime as, "what can be seen and what can be thought, [as] certain forms of inhabiting the material world" (Ranciére 2009: 91). As the "distribution of the sensible," the aesthetic regime constitutes a shared material-thing world, a *common sense* that is activated by working with the objects of everyday life (Rancière 2006: 9–19). After all, didn't Scott see pain and its relief in the swooping curves of laminated plywood—the objects more commonly referred to as sculpture? The plywood splint forms were hardly meant to result in pleasure, but in lessening pain they must have assuaged some displeasure from the war-torn body.

Bentwood, bent metal, and bent backs were instances of the distribution of the sensible, standing as an instance of the logic of postwar common sense. The pliability of wood and tubular metal, thanks to the application of the "shock mount," were equal to the pliability of the human body. The former assisted the latter toward compliance to a culture of efficiency. Relations—'the connections, the connections, the connections," as Charles once stuttered—were crucial to the DCM enterprise. Therefore, the human connected to the technical artifact—chair to body—constituted the prosthetics and aesthetics of Eames design. Distributions and redistributions require mediators (or instances of non-humans taking over for humans, as in media in action)—splints and chairs, for example. Wood-devices-made-for-the-distribution-of-the-sensible were translated into wood-devices-made-for-sitting-caring-and-distributing-stresses.

Stresses

An unidentified clipping in the exhibition files for the *New Furniture Designed by Charles Eames* show at MoMA reads: "Marge Harris, who is a great big beautiful blonde show girl in Billy Rose's Diamond Horseshoe, sat down in one of the new chairs being shown at the Museum of Modern Art, and a startled expression came over her face. 'My goodness,' she said, 'it feels like I'm sitting in somebody's hands.'" The same file contains a press release for the exhibition that stated, "Seats and backs are joined to chair frames by rubber mounts which absorb shocks and distribute stresses, a technique long used in mounting engines. This provides resilience and flexibility, permitting the chair to yield to changes of sitting position." A short article, entitled "Shock-Proof Furniture," in *Architectural Forum,* stated, "Eames' big new idea is the precision-engineered joint—the first flexible joint ever applied to furniture construction" (1946: 10). Sitting in somebody's hands. Absorbing shocks. Not just comfort, but assurance. Not just aesthetics, but technical innovation. The MoMA exhibition even featured a demonstration of energy transfer throughout the chair. These brief and randomly chosen texts responded to an inscription of a program of action. Like the traction splints before it, the DCM, with its shock-mount technology, relieved the pressure of, what, in reference to the Eames exhibition, the *Post* called, "a mobile world." Where the shock-mount helped to distribute the weight of the human body it also redistributed the care-giving program of the wartime splints. In short, the shock-mount settled the jangled nerves of its human sitter.

The shock-mount first appeared in the early proposals for the *Organic Furniture Competition*. The shock-mount was a thick rubber disk that joined the wood and metal chair parts. Ideally, the goal was to not use bolts to connect any parts, and this was the case for the DCW. Borrowing a technique used during the war known as Cycleweld, the process used an electronic instrument that transmitted heat by radio wave directly to a resin, which bonded wood, rubber, and metal parts to each other. The end result was a combination of joinery and pliancy that dispersed pressure over the entire area of the mount rather than concentrating the entire load at a single point. In the case of the DCM, Cycleweld and self-locking aircraft bolts resulted in a precise fitting that was both strong and durable.

Shock-mounts were intensifications, turning resiliency and toughness to the care of the body. Their location revealed an Archimedean point where a simple operation (such as allowing movement) was used for great effect—to absorb postwar agitation. Also, shock-mounts encouraged collectives in the formation of heterogeneous assemblies of actants—an ANT term meaning human and non-human actors in a network—in which humans and non-humans combined energies to gain control and influence. A crowd converged at the point indicated by the little rubber disk: Saarinen took hold of the shock-mounts, designer Harry Bertoia grabbed for the bent metal armature, Ray took possession of the contoured laminated plywood seat and back, and Charles, well, he went for it all. The inverse was also the case: shock-mounts took hold of Saarinen, Bertoia, bent metal, Ray, plywood, Charles, and his rear-end. The shock-mount pried open the black box of the collective, both in terms of the studio and in terms of so-called modern existence.

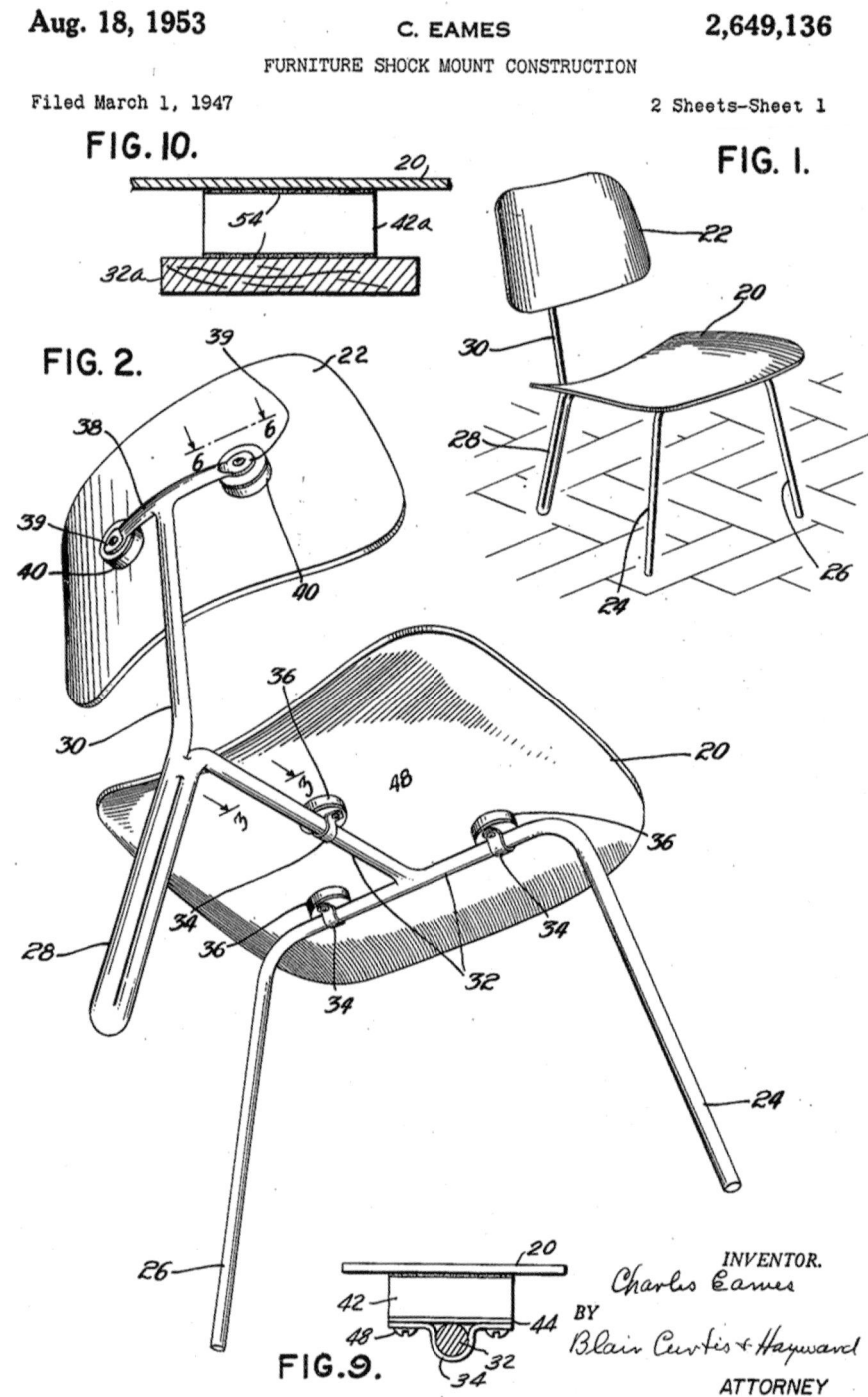

FIGURE 8.2 Charles Eames, "Furniture Shock Mount Construction," United States Patent Number 2,649,136 (1947–53).

At the interface where wood-joins-rubber-joins-metal, the tolerances, measurements, and precision that were typically required of engines shifted to the normalizing and comforting actions of the DCM. The shock-mount helped to stabilize high-performance humans who were revved up by postwar politics, economics, and culture. As a Herman Miller brochure that featured Eames chairs described this redistribution: "Modern furniture is an effort to bring superior performance into another area; and, psychological factors aside, it might be described as nothing more than an attempt to bring certain apparatus into line with what has been happening in almost every other area of modern existence" (Nelson 1949: 7). We should wonder why the brochure wants to set aside "psychological factors." It would seem impossible to align a "certain apparatus" with "modern existence" without an acknowledgment of the status of the modern psyche (Gafijczuk 2001: 447).

When referring to the compromised position of designers in the post war era, the sociologist C. Wright Mills considered designers to exist as mechanisms of control—things in the middle. Designers occupied "the observation posts, the interpretations centers, the presentation depots" that constituted the "cultural apparatus." In other words, these mechanisms of control were, for Mills, the forces that organized the sensations and perceptions of a public. For Mills, the cultural apparatus was a "put-together contraption," an amalgam of economic, political, and social actants that managed the postwar threat of the banality of day-in-day-out middle-class, corporate, and suburban existence (Mills 1972: 376). Or was it that aligning "certain apparatus [...] with what has been happening" functioned both to discipline the public, as Mills worried, and to displace its collective anxiety by externalizing (one might say, *thinging*) it in a chair. The point of convergence and explosion that I remarked on above—the crowding of humans and non-humans at the point of greatest stress—registered an aesthetic, affective character that was both the result of anxiety and its potential overcoming. The shock-mount *prosteticized* postwar experience and defense against the shocks of modern life.

The DCM and its rubber shock mounts both absorbed the energies of the cultural apparatus and intensified the shocks by making material the post-World War II discourse on modern alienation. Why else was there an emphasis on these seemingly inconsequential details? Because the flexibility and comfort the rubber discs provided were also technological remedies for what Sigmund Freud argued is a loss of happiness, which is "the price we pay for our advance in civilization [...]," and what philosopher Herbert Marcuse observed of a repressive society where "individual happiness and productive development are in contradiction" (Freud 2010: 131; Marcuse 1955: 223). The postwar human subject was susceptible to a nagging malaise when faced with the relentless contradiction of individuality and conformity. This phenomenon is best expressed in sociologist David Riesman's *The Lonely Crowd*, and historian Daniel Boorstin's "extravagant expectations" (Boorstin 1964). How could anyone really have fathomed the prospects of attaining individual happiness while having to conform to social norms at every turn? In this version of a postwar era of contradiction, the aspirations of the "organization man" whose willing acquiescence to team work was to attain individual happiness through total assimilation. The psychological toll that resulted from giving in to what journalist William Whyte identified as the "dehumanized collective" was effectively measured in John Updike's *Rabbit Run* (1960) and Richard Yates' *Revolutionary Road* (1961). In both instances of alienation, the external directedness (or "other directed," as Riesman diagnosed) of postwar identity—the striving for acceptance in a culture of conformity—threatened to undo the tidiness of suburban life. And nowhere was the twilight of inward directed identity—the confidence in the self as autonomous and not in need of public acceptance—best examined than in poet Allen Ginsberg's *Howl*, where those who survived were mere contortions of modern civilization:

> burned alive in their innocent flannel suits on Madison Avenue amid blasts of leaden verse & the tanked-up clatter of the iron regiments of fashion & the nitroglycerine shrieks of the fairies of advertising & the mustard gas of sinister intelligent editors, or were run down by the drunken taxicabs of Absolute Reality [...] and who were given instead the concrete void of insulin Metrazol electricity hydrotherapy psychotherapy occupational therapy pingpong & amnesia [...]. (Ginsberg 1956: 16, 18)

The DCM met damaged psyches just as the previous wartime splints met damaged limbs. Where previous iterations of bent wood, bent metal and bent backs were instances of the distribution of the sensible, standing as a logic of prewar common sense, the DCM lent itself to psychosomatic re-calibrations. Its contours and shock absorbing rubber mounts cradled an already *bent* postwar posture.

Externalization

The connections, the connections, the connections. "Welded rubber connections" (Caplan 1976: 20). "Ariel amongst the synthetic resins" (Caplan 1976: 25). Things—media in action. Metal to rubber, rubber to wood, wood to spine. Just as the splint was entrusted to assist in the healing of damaged human limbs, so, too, was the DCM entrusted to assist in the dampening of human aspiration and in the soothing or damaged human nerves. Mid-century Americans had externalized (*technologized*) their defenses in things. Human traumatic excitation was absorbed by the inorganic, exterior, and posterior of Eames' rubber shock-mount.[15] The result was a greater and more intensified distribution of care from the organic human nervous system to the inorganic synthetic rubber pressure point of the DCM.

Both splints and chairs assisted humans where mere defenses were inadequate. Just as the splint worked as an orthopedic technology to provide traction for and to immobilize bones, so too did the chair aid weary bones of sitters. The splint and the chair were both meant for broken bodies, both meeting humans at times when and where they hurt most. Yet, whereas the splint managed isolated fractures, the DCM managed the unmanageable circumstances of postwar expectations and normative ideologies. If one wondered where he or she fit, the DCM provided—however temporary—a place of comfort and conformity. With the introduction of the DCM, a conscious program of action—wood-devices-made-for-caring-for-the-injured—shifted to an unconscious program of action—wood-rubber-metal-devices-made-for-the-alienated.

Medics and design. Splints and shock-mounts. Interfaces. An account of the logic of the DCM's connectivity—its distributions and redistributions—refocuses attention on the shock-mount. It is here that transitions occurred and where assistance exerted an enormous effort balanced by a small effort—alienation and existential angst balanced by serenity. The shock-mount on the DCM was an entry point. It embodied technological and physiological inscriptions—programs—that transmitted what could or should be inscribed in users. The DCM was a reliable form of assistance, of aid, of sympathy. "It feels like I'm sitting in somebody's hands."

Notes

1 On the play of multiplicity and discreteness of things as both relate to allure and affordance, see Boetzkes (2014: 269–89).

2 On programs of action and the programming of automatic doors, see Latour 1992: 237–9.

3 Gafijczuk observes the relation of bent-wood furniture, psychology, and cultural history in-fin-de-siècle Vienna, specifically on the intersection of the Thonet bent-wood chair and psychoanalysis. The implication is that both, while developed separately, were the product of a shared habit of mind, or habitus. See Gafijczuk 2009. My argument differs from Gafijczuk where I focus on the transfer of the therapeutic from splint to chair, and where the former survived in the latter.

4 For the purposes of this chapter, I use "thing" and "object" in their colloquial senses.

5 For an excellent summary of this issue as it relates to techniques, see Lemonnier (1993: 6–27).

6 As Bogost explains, "ontography" was first introduced in Dilillo's *White Noise* (1985) and later taken up by Graham Harman, who explains that the term addresses the limited dynamic of relations between objects (Bogost 2012: 36).

7 "A mediator ... is an original event and creates what it translates as well as the entities between which it plays the mediating role" (Latour 1993: 78).

8 As Latour admits, "Of course, Deleuze is in my bones ..." See interview with Latour, http://figureground.org/interview-with-bruno-latour/ (accessed May 5, 2014). Also, when considering alternative names for Actor Network Theory, he offers "actant-rhyzome sociology" as an option (Latour 2005: 9).

9 My use of the term "significance" implies something of the affective character of connection and intensification. How is it that one takes a thing as significant such that feelings are attuned to things? See Thrift (2008).

10 In November 1942 the U.S. Navy ordered 5,000 splints and the Eameses, along with John Entenza, founded Plyformed Wood Company, moving their impromptu production facility to 10946 Santa Monica Boulevard. Work on the Navy splints would continue throughout 1943 with production moving to 555 Rose Avenue in Venice and with a influx of much needed cash from the Detroit based Evans Products Company. In July of that year, the company became the Molded Plywood Division, a West Coast subsidiary of Evans Product Company. Charles became the Director of Research and Development. By the end of the war, the Eameses, Entenza, Herbert Matter, Harry Bertoia, and Gregory Ain, along with production workers, had produced 150,000 splints. Toward the end of wartime production, the Molded Plywood Division moved to 901 Washington Boulevard in Venice; the space would eventually convert into the Eameses' design office (Neuhart 1989: 29–35).

11 In *Design Meets Disability*, Graham Pullin states, "It was the particular constraints of the US Navy brief that led the Eameses to Develop their own technology for forming plywood in complex curvature" (Pullin 2009: xiii).

12 Also, for an more in-depth discussion of the merits of Ray's avant-garde practices, specifically as they influenced the design of interiors, see Havenhand (2006).

13 The emphasis is mine.

14 According to Charles' February 1946 patent application, the "Kazam Machine" consisted of a bicycle pump that was attached to a pressure chamber, which consisted of a die-bed, a bladder, and a die member. The pump worked to fill the bladder air at about 30 pounds per square inch. With constant pressure and application of thermal controlled heat, the compression chamber allowed the wood blanks to press against and conform to the die. Later, the pump was transferred to more efficient machines that formed wood under pressure to achieve the desired curves. In the most explicit indication of its importance, the Library of Congress installed the so called "Kazam!" with

its bicycle pump outside the entrance to the "The Work of Charles and Ray Eames: A Legacy of Invention" exhibition in 1999. Library of Congress "Bulletin." www.loc.gov/loc/lcib/9905/eames.html (accessed October 26, 2010).

15 This passage is greatly influenced by Wolfgang Schivelbusch's "Stimulus Shield: or, the Industrialized Consciousness" (Schivelbusch 1986: 159–70).

Bibliography

Appadurai, A. (1986), *The Social Life of Things: Commodities in Cultural Perspective*, Cambridge and New York: Cambridge University Press.

Boetzkes, A. (2014), "Interpretation and the Affordance of Things," in A. Boetzkes and A. Vinegar (eds), *Heidegger and the Work of Art History*, Farnham: Ashgate.

Bogost, I. (2012), *Alien Phenomenology, Or, What It's like to Be a Thing*, Minneapolis: University of Minnesota Press.

Boorstin, D. J. (1964), *The Image: A Guide to Pseudo-Events in America*, New York: Harper & Row.

Callon, M. (1991), "Techno-Economic Networks and Irreversibility," in J. Law (ed.), *A Sociology of Monsters: Essays on Power, Technology, and Domination*, London and New York: Routledge.

Caplan, R., J. Neuhart, and M. Neuhart (1976), *Connections: The Work of Charles and Ray Eames*, Los Angeles: Frederick S. Wright Art Gallery, U.C.L.A.

Freud, S. (2010), *Civilization and Its Discontents*, New York: Norton.

Gafijczuk, D. (2009), "Bending Modernity: Chairs, Psychoanalysis and the Rest of Culture," *Journal of Historical Sociology* 22 (4) (December): 447–75.

Gingrich, O. (1997), "A Conversation with Charles Eames," *The American Scholar* 29: 326–37.

Ginsberg, A. (1956), *Howl, and Other Poems*, San Francisco, City Lights.

Giovannini, J. (1997), "The Office of Charles Eames and Ray Kaiser," in D Albrecht (ed.), *The Work of Charles and Ray Eames* (ed. Donald Albrecht), New York: Abrams.

Havenhand, L. (2006), "American Abstract Art and the Interior Design of Ray and Charles Eames," *Journal of Interior Design* 31: 29–42.

Kirkham, P. (1995), *Charles and Ray Eames: Designers of the Twentieth Century*, Cambridge, MA: MIT Press.

Latour, B. (1992), "Where Are the Missing Masses: Sociology of a Few Mundane Artefacts," in W. E. Bijker and J. Law (eds), *Shaping Technology/building Society: Studies in Sociotechnical Change*, Cambridge, MA: MIT Press.

Latour, B. (1993), *We Have Never Been Modern*, Cambridge, MA: Harvard University Press.

Latour, B. (2005), *Reassembling the Social: An Introduction to Actor-Network-Theory*, Oxford and New York: Oxford University Press.

Lemonnier, P. (1993), "Introduction," in P. Lemonnier (ed.), *Technological Choices: Transformation in Material Cultures since the Neolithic*, London and New York: Routledge.

Marcuse, H. (1955), *Eros and Civilization: a Philosophical Inquiry into Freud*, Boston: Beacon Press.

McCoy, E. (1975), "Charles and Ray Eames," *Design Quarterly* 98/99: 20–9.

McLuhan, M. (1995), "The Mechanical Bride," in E. McLuhan and F. Zingrone (eds), *Essential McLuhan*, New York, NY: Basic Books.

Miller, D. (1987), "The Humility of Objects," in *Material Culture and Mass Consumption*, Oxford and York, New York: Blackwell.

Miller, D. (2010), *Stuff*, Cambridge: Polity Press.

Mills, C. W. (1972), "Man in the Middle: The Designer," in I. Horowitz (ed.), *Power, Politics, and People: The Collected Essays of C. Wright Mills*, London: Oxford University Press.

Nelson, G. (1949), *The Herman Miller Collection: Furniture Designed by George Nelson, Charles Eames, Isamu Noguchi and Paul Laszlo*, Zeeland: Herman Miller, Inc.

Neuhart, J., M. Neuhart, and R. Eames (1989), *Eames Design: The Work of the Office of Charles and Ray Eames*, New York: H. N. Abrams.
Noyes, E. (1956), "Charles Eames," *Arts & Architecture* (September): 26–45.
Prown, J. D. (1982), "Mind in Matter: An Introduction to Material Culture Theory and Method," *Winterthur Portfolio* 17: 1–19.
Pullin, G. (2009), *Design Meets Disability*, Cambridge, MA: MIT Press.
Rancière, J. (2006), *The Politics of Aesthetics: The Distribution of the Sensible*, London and New York: Continuum.
Rancière, J. (2009), *The Future of the Image*, London and New York: Verso.
Reisman, D., N. Glazer, and R. Denney (1969), *The Lonely Crowd: A Study of the Changing American Character*, New Haven: Yale University Press.
Schivelbusch, W. (1986), *The Railway Journey: The Industrialization of Time and Space in the 19th Century*, Berkeley, CA: University of California Press.
Shanks, M. (1998), "The Life of an Artifact in an Interpretive Archaeology," *Fennoscandia Archaeologia* XV: 15–30.
Thrift, N. (2008), *Non-Representational Theory: Space, Politics, Affect*, London and New York: Routledge.
Updike, J. (1960), *Rabbit, Run*, New York, Knopf.
Whyte, W. H. (1956), *The Organization Man*. New York, Simon and Schuster.
Yates, R. (1961), *Revolutionary Road*, Boston: Little, Brown.

9

What design tells us about objects and things

Giorgio De Michelis

Introduction

If we assume that the terms "object" and "thing" correspond to two different perspectives on the entities we experience around us, i.e., that they are not just synonymous, then a question emerges about their mutual relationship: What distinguishes objects from things and how do they relate to each other? Let me try to refine this distinction by considering things to be "real" entities and objects to be partial or limited models. I will use the term "entity" to refer to a broad category that includes both objects and things within its purview. Objects characterize the way we associate with entities; they include the set of possible interactions that we can have with entities and the mechanisms with which we familiarize ourselves with them. When we put a letter in a mailbox, the mailbox is the object we use for sending letters, and we are confident that it will do its job: the postal service will take our letter from the mailbox and help it reach its destination. The very same mailbox is a thing if we consider it beyond its functional role; but this is all that we can say about a thing. If things are real entities, then we cannot describe them, since describing them, in some sense, objectifies them. In this situation, why should we bother with things? Or, in Bill Brown's words: "Why not let things alone? (Brown 2001: 1). When we interact with an entity, its thingness disappears and we encounter the object.

On the other hand, if we take into consideration the entity we have objectified as a mailbox, we discover that this process of objectification does not capture its essential nature at all. Things cannot be described; we can only conjecture about and experiment with them. For human beings, then, objects and things are mutually exclusive ways to approach entities: when we consider objects, things disappear; and, viceversa, when we consider things, objects disappear. This description is not fully convincing, however, since it does not allow us to investigate what binds things and objects. This characterization of things and objects limits their relationship to a set of complementary roles, and it does not acknowledge or permit the possibility of distance, tension or intersection between them. Additionally, this characterization fails to take into account the thingness of objects or the objectness of things (an important consideration that is less frequently considered in the literature). We cannot resolve this deadlock without taking one step back to examine more precisely what we do when we objectify a thing.

Design can offer a unique and constructive viewpoint about the thing/object problem since incipient design deals with the experience of a thing that does not yet exist. Design allows us to look predominantly and deeply at objects while leaving things in the background. As A. Telier has observed in *Design Things* (2011: 51–78), design practice, in essence, consists of the development of a design object as a means for creating the design thing that will be delivered at the end of the process. The design object can be envisioned as an evolving web of things created, imported or modified by designers.

During the design process, designers outline in provisional, incomplete and contradictory ways what is being designed. They do this through implicit or explicit inscriptions—i.e., by associating written or unwritten shared "tags" with the things they import or create. These "tags" label things, indicating their relationships with other things that constitute the design object. When designing a building, for example, the architects draw on paper; they develop geometric representations of different views of the building using CAD; they build 3-D models of the building or of its parts; they collect samples of the materials that will be used in different parts of the building. These practices and the products they generate are related to each other and/or to the building to be designed by explicit or implicit tags, indicating, for each new thing, how it contributes to the characterization of the building. We can say that all of these things, with their mutual relationships, constitute the design object.

Things and objects revisited

In his seminal work on the philosophy of things, Martin Heidegger (1971) explains "*Ding*" (thing) as the governing assembly in ancient Germanic societies, comprised of the free men of the community and presided over by speakers fluent in the law. At these assemblies or "things," disputes were solved and political decisions were made. This original linguistic "thing," from the pre-Christian culture of Scandinavia and North Germanic languages, provided a means to assemble and share "matters of concern" with the community. As French sociologist and anthropologist Bruno Latour explains in "Why has Critique Run out of Steam? From Matters of Fact to Matters of Concern," "a thing is, in one sense, an object out there and, in another sense, an *issue* very much *in* there, at any rate, a *gathering* ... the same word *thing* designates matters of fact and matters of concern" (Latour 2004: 233). Even today, things contribute to creating the landscape in which we assemble with other human beings. As Heidegger explains, "thinging" gathers human beings, prompting things to play a central role in the common experience of community (Heidegger 1971: 176).

In order to seek clarity regarding objects and things, it is of paramount importance to progress from a structural static view in which things and objects are fixed in a precise moment as if they had an existence per se, to embracing a process dynamic view in which things and objects are considered in their evolution. The latter approach will lead us to devote attention to the process through which we create objects from entities, i.e., objectification.[1] In this context, we can associate "objectification"—the reduction of an entity to some predefined scope—with the terms "appropriation" and/or "domestication" in order to emphasize how objectification shapes the <subject–object> (or human–object) relationship. Appropriation underscores the idea that objectifying an entity means getting control of it, reducing the entity to the actions and interactions it makes possible. Domestication, the never complete reduction of wild entities, in which the irreducibility of the objectified thing is better captured, lightens the learning process that allows us to discover the object embodied within the entity.

In this essay, I will demonstrate that objectification is an inherently social process situated within a dynamic actor network in which material and semiotic actors create meaning.² In some sense, an object is a partial, intentional view of the actor network in which it is situated. In order to understand this approach, we first need to understand how things and objects emerge in human experience.

More on objects and things

The word "thing," as established earlier, has evolved from a Nordic and Germanic term meaning ancient assemblies that dealt with "matters of concern" to a community to a term meaning an object or "an entity of matter." There is a *fil rouge*—a guiding thread—that connects an assembly (thing) and entities (things): entities are the matters of concern for assemblies; in some sense entities (things) are the *raison d'être* for an assembly (thing). The strict coupling between an assembly and the entities it uses for decision-making explains why both may be called things. A shared concern may relate to the scarcity of a thing, or with its deterioration, or with it becoming (temporarily) useless or even cumbersome, or with it becoming obsolete or dysfunctional. These changes in things can lead to disagreements among the assembly members. What emerges in these situations is the social dimension of things; such encounters between human beings manifest the irreducible aspects of things: it's within social experience of things that human beings discover their irreducibility.

Concerns that arise among people are generally demanding and frequently unpleasant (even in the cases where there are positive expectations of things, the latter seem to require constant attention and elicit, at least, a sense of anxiety and/or of fatigue). And finding solutions requires governance and the process of grappling with things by "domesticating" them (as with wild animals).

"Light domestication" occurs when we share concerns within the community; light domestication involves the concerns that other people share with us, and the ways that sharing these concerns alleviates our stress and anxiety. What I term "heavy domestication" is instead related to the process of annihilating concerns. Issues disappear when things cease to be matters of concern and we agree on what they may do, or for what they may be used. Generally, and in all cases meriting our attention, heavy domestication is temporary since new concerns arise and reveal the irreducibility of things.

In principle, contending with a thing has the goal of "domesticating" it in order to dissolve the concerns it generates. Objectifying is an essential component of what assemblies do with things; and assemblies are aware of the contingent nature and the limits of domestication. Even when domesticated, things require attention. Thus, objectification is mainly the characterization of an entity in functional terms—i.e., with respect to its potential for action and interaction. In order to objectify a thing, the person creates a <subject–object> (human–object) relationship with that thing. As a natural consequence, objectifying things characterizes the way human beings interact with them and describes what they can do with them.

My account of how assemblies objectify things seems contradictory to the assertion that assemblies have things as matters of concern. But this is only an ostensible contradiction; assemblies are constituted for dealing with things, and the participants instinctively understand that any objectification does not dissolve the thingness of entities. Rather, these participants appreciate at some level that they must continually reenact the objectification process. Assembly members understand instinctively that objectification is necessarily partial and limited. If a river crosses its territory, for example, the assembly decides the rules to be followed for navigating and/or fishing on the river, what will be done to protect the houses from flooding, who will be in charge of responding to flooding, and so on, so that the daily life of the community can proceed in an orderly fashion. But the assembly members are aware that the status quo is continually changing, that they are not capable of dealing with every event. The assembly members realize that new actions, rules and role definitions may be necessary, and therefore the river remains a matter of concern even if the assembly is continually domesticating it. Even when they are objectified, things remain things!

The difference between a thing and an object starts emerging in the decision-making space of the assembly, and the process expedites the objectification of things. Further, the assembly's legitimacy results from its ability to re-activate the mechanism of objectification on a continual basis. Returning to the river example, the authority of the assembly is recognized by the community to the extent that decisions about dealing with the situation can domesticate the river. The members of a community expect that the assembly governing them is able to objectify things, enabling them to perform effectively and live safely. As Harrison and Dourish (1996) have explained: while a space is populated by things, a place is populated by objects.

The puzzle is now clear: we seem unable to pin down the thingness of objects (Brown 2001: 4), as well as the objectness of things (this question seems to me less considered in the literature). As anticipated in the Introduction, we cannot resolve this deadlock without taking one step back to examine more precisely what we do when we objectify a thing. In other words, if things are the entities we recognize for their irreducibility by objectification, then what constitutes objects? Are things and objects in actuality the very same entities perceived from different viewpoints? And, if this is so, what does objectification mean and how do human beings perform it? If objectification is a purely mental process, then how can people share objects? At this point, it appears clear that in order to illustrate objects, we cannot rely solely upon the points of view of the people carrying out the objectification. Rather, we need to look to the specifics of the practice of objectification and not rely only on its sense, or on the outcomes it produces. Design can provide some helpful mechanisms for scrutinizing objectification.

Design objects and design things

As I suggested earlier, design is primarily an experience of a thing that does not yet exist. Design practice always entails defining the qualities and features of a yet-to-exist artifact that will be delivered at the end of a process (the design thing). In design, therefore, as in any other experience of something that does not yet exist—for example, in cooking—the object of design comes before the thing of design (the design outcome). However, in the experience of existing things, objectification follows the encounter with the thing (Stein 1927: 44).

In fact, when the thing of design is delivered and its stakeholders begin to use it, the story changes and designers are no longer at the center of the scene. The new story becomes the users' experience of an existing thing: their encounter with the thing and the objectification that follows. Design is successful when stakeholders discover in the design thing the qualities that designers introduce into their design objects. The clear-cut separation between design and the users' encounter with it, however, allows stakeholders to experience the design thing without it being subordinated to the designers' intention.

What are design objects? How do designers create them? Irrespective of what is being designed—a house, a chair, a software program, a machine—design practice involves designers gathering a variety of items such as sheets of paper, photographs, videos, three-dimensional models, sample materials, digital files. Designers may then modify these items, inscribe them in explicit and/or implicit ways with words or drawings, or delete or store them. The richness and diversity of the things populating designers' studios changes with different types of design, but design processes always evolve, populating the studio with things. The things gathered in an assembly during the design process constitute the design object.

I would like to comment briefly about designers inscribing—explicitly and/or implicitly—the things they gather while designing. Things constituting the object of design are not gathered for their intrinsic qualities. Rather, they give sense to the design process, contributing to the thing that the designer aims to create. The piece of marble is not just a sample of material; it is the surface of the third floor that is shown in several handmade and CAD drawings. The arc drawn on a sheet of paper is not just a geometric shape; it is the form of the main door of the south façade that is visible also in the 3-D model of the building and in other drawings. The photograph of a landscape is not just an image of an outdoor scene; it shows the natural environment in which the new building will be placed.

The attributes that characterize all of the gathered things and link them to each other can be either written (inscribed) explicitly on them (as in a caption on the drawing of the arc, a post-it on the piece of marble) or shared by the designers without any explicit notes. This has important implications in our discourse: first, the links connecting the gathered things shape the object of design as a "web of things," detailing the qualities the design thing should have if and when it will be delivered; second, taking full account of the implicit inscriptions requires designers themselves to be included in the object of design, making it an "actor network" as described in Actor Network Theory (ANT) (Law 1999).

The design object is continually changing during the design process: new things are added, new links are traced, old things or old links are modified or deleted. In this dynamic process, the things that constitute the object of design, together with their inscriptions, cannot remain fully aligned with each other. Consider, for example, the difference between a building as it is represented in a handmade draft by the chief architect, and its geometrical representations made by means of a CAD system. Or imagine that one of the architects changes the shape of a window on the south façade, and modifies the drawing accordingly. This change will misalign the drawing with respect to any other thing representing the south façade. Consider also the drawings prepared for the construction workers that detail the practical problems needed to modify the exact dimensions of a wall in order to fit the new window. As designers re-align interventions (e.g., by reproducing changes in all representations and models of the building), the new changes or new details create new misalignments. The persistence of misalignments does not allow us to consider any representation to be a partial view of the building: the design object is necessarily affected by inconsistencies and partialities. Misalignments among the constituents of the object of design are the natural derivatives of the design process: whatever designers do introduces something new, and its novelty may either delineate what was not yet specified or modify a previous specification. The moves that realign what was misaligned in the design object are generally unable to eliminate all misalignments. This happens because design is a highly concurrent process with multiple actors, and designers are not, often, fully aware of ongoing or recent misalignments.

Design is a process in which misalignments clear and indicate space for innovation, and realignment creates order. The process proceeds well if misalignment and realignment are in balance. Misalignment must be part of the process, but realignment must hold misalignment in check in order to avoid the disintegration of the design object.

The design object, therefore, is intrinsically complex: it combines high multiplicity with high variance. Even if the design object responds to a demand of determinacy (insuring the outcome of the design process, the design thing, is able to respond to the aims of its designers), both its aims and its outcomes are not precisely determined.

This observation tells us that we are misled in opposing the transition of rational, well-defined objects to complex, irreducible things. The object of design is not a consistent, rational account of the functions and features of the design thing. Rather, it is an evolving web of things that characterizes the design thing in incomplete and contradictory ways. That it is cumbersome, if not impossible, to reduce the design object to a pre-defined scope should not be considered a limitation. Instead, it adds value to the design process. The collective construction of a design object by a design team, in conjunction with its stakeholders, is an inherently complex process. Through its elaborate web of things, a complex design object allows designers and stakeholders to participate in the richness of the design thing to be delivered.

Objects and actor networks

When a subject (human) enters into a relationship with an existing thing, the object emerges. This process is the same but upside-down for design objects: design creates an evolving web of things that reflects the way the design thing will be used, the functions it will accomplish, and the emotions it will elicit. This web reveals the images its constituents evoke, the stories they tell, and the diverse views any stakeholder may have on it.

The irreducibility of the thing emerges from its being a "matter of concern" that is open to new revelations. The complexity of the object has a social nature: it reflects the diversity, needs, desires, cultures and emotions of the people interacting with it.

Objectification, as a domestication and appropriation process, is not about reifying things. Rather, it reflects the irreducible complexity intrinsic to things into the evident multiplicity of the subjects involved with them. Inner complexity reflects outer complexity, or better yet, we can access the complexity of things only through the complexity of the social processes that objectify them. Reductionism is not implicit in domestication and/or objectification. The social dimension of our linguistic experience and of our knowledge creation processes seem to indicate that the reduction of things to objects embodies the same nature as the reduction of most social complexity. In both cases, in fact, the disappearance of social diversity is required.

Objectification begins when things become matters of concern for the community of stakeholders, i.e., when people are recognized as members of an actor network. The process through which the relationship of a thing with the other actors of the network develops is consubstantial with the process through which the human beings who are part of the network appropriate it. In fact, the actor network itself participates in the appropriation. In some sense, objectification is the local, internal viewpoint of human actors about the network of which they are a part. While an external observer sees an assembly making decisions about things, any member of the assembly participates in its discussion, looking for the most effective domestication of those things.

In the dialectics between things and objects, the discovery of the irreducibility of things is not a form of reaction to their objectification; rather it is the natural counterpart to their incompleteness and inconsistency. We objectify because this is the only way we have to contend with a matter of concern, but while we do it we discover that there is a thing behind the object. Going back to the river example, the rules for boating and fishing were set with the assumption that the number of potential requestors was below one hundred. When the number of people wanting to boat or fish grows beyond a thousand, the rules become ineffective and there are inevitable conflicts among people. The river becomes a matter of concern again for the assembly. In order to decide the new rules, the assembly needs to go back to the river as a thing in order to discover in it aspects that previous objectification hadn't taken into consideration.

If we consider objectification to be a reification (or concretization) of a thing, we also reify our experience of that thing because we do not see the irreducibility that objects manifest in their evolution. It is misleading to consider the struggle to capture things through objects as an attempt to reduce things to something with a fixed sense in our life; rather, it reflects the imperfect coupling between the thing and its evolving social appropriation. Being cognizant of this is the first step for being a "reflective designer" (Schön 1984), i.e., a designer who reflects on his or her practice, who carries out what Donald Schön terms "reflection in action."[3]

In an actor network, the irreducibility of things is coupled with the social complexity of objects. It is, in fact, what exceeds objectification in entities that allows their thingness to emerge. At the same time, being irreducible, things create the space for diversity in objectification processes. This observation reveals a surprising perspective: thingness does not emerge in opposition to objectness; rather, objects and things emerge together and we cannot look at either of them without giving a sidelong glance at the other.[4] In some sense, we can discern thingness as we discover the complexity of objects—thingness causes the complexity of objects.

Apollo 13 revisited

Let me use this proposed conceptual framework to interpret the most dramatic moment of the movie *Apollo 13*. This compelling scene occurs when the group on Earth tries to solve an issue with the Odyssey module by using square filters in the Aquarius's round receptacles. The team on Earth solves the problem as follows: first they recreate on Earth the "actor network" inhabiting the two modules in space. The Earth team includes all of the human and non-human actors in its reproduction of the modules: every actor is considered not for its role in the modules (as an object), but for its potential with respect to the problem to be solved (as a thing). The Earth team discovers a handbook on Odyssey with a rigid square cardboard cover into which a round hole can be made that could connect the round receptacle with the square filter. The Earth team explains this repair process to the crew of Apollo 13. Thus, even if no member of the team is classified as a maintenance worker for the filters, and the designated handbook is not classified as maintenance information, together they are capable of both making the round hole in the cover, and using it to connect the round receptacle to the square filter.

In *Apollo 13*, the interplay between objects and things becomes clear because the Earth team considers the shuttle in space along with its human and non-human actors to be a "matter of concern," while the crew of Apollo 13 seems unable to break out of the role it plays. We can say that the crewmembers in space are not able to "see a thing" in the handbook, or see the potential of its rigid cover.

Conclusion

In this essay, I characterized objectification as the process through which human beings appropriate and domesticate things. Making reference to A. Telier's book *Design Things* (2011: 51–78), I defined the object of design as the web of inscribed things that designers gather during the design process, distinguishing the object from the design thing they deliver at its completion. I also observed that the object of design constitutes, together with the designers and the stakeholders, an actor network (Law 1999). Finally, I argued that objectification should neither be considered a reification of things, nor an opposition between things and objects since accessing things is inseparable from objectifying them, and vice versa. When we objectify an entity, its thingness emerges through the ambiguities, inconsistencies, and incomplete specifications of the object we create. The thing, as the very same entity is, in summary, not "catchable": we recognize it when we discover its irreducibility by objectification.

The emergence of the things behind objects is intrinsically social, confirming the intuition of Bruno Latour that "things do not exist without being full of people" (2000: 10). The discrepancies, misunderstandings, and conflicts that can occur while trying to share an object appear in a completely different light when they are interpreted as signals of the emergence of a thing beneath the object that seemed, for a while, to be at hand. Instead of establishing a contraposition among stakeholders, "thinging" opens to the stakeholders new possibilities to be investigated and discussed. "Making things public," as the title of the exposition curated by Latour and Weibel at ZKM in Karlsruhe (2005) claims, is the only way to avoid ideological conflicts and to make democracy work.

Breakdowns[5] that emerge from an object's functions often induce stakeholders to look beyond the object's surfaces to find the resources needed to overcome the crisis, allowing them glimpse the thing hidden behind. The shift between objects and things plays a principal role in many innovations.

Returning to design, our characterization of the <object–thing> couple has two important implications: first, it means that the object of design is not a rational specification of what the thing we are designing should be, but instead it is an anticipation of the richness that the design thing should exhibit to its stakeholders. The design object tries to anticipate the experiences stakeholders will have with the thing, the emotions the thing will raise (today, design is only possible from a phenomenological stance; De Michelis 2008). Second, the participatory design practices of "drawing things together" (Telier 2012), within which stakeholders and designers collaborate in the design process, despite their differences of interests, cultures and viewpoints, are enriched by the perspective we have proposed. Stakeholders cease to be either those who inform designers about what they want, or those who relay the context for which they design. Rather, they are involved in a process in which new possibilities are imagined and framed, discovering in the things behind the objects with which they are familiar the resources for inventing new ways of acting and interacting. This process begins during design itself and, if the design thing allows and supports it, continues when the design thing is used.

In this way, in fact, we can observe how, without any confusion of roles, all the stakeholders contribute to the construction of the design object, adding new things and/or new inscriptions to it.

Acknowledgments

I am the only one responsible for what is written above, but I must thank several people with whom I have discussed the ideas in this essay: Thomas Binder, Pelle Ehn, Giulio Jacucci, Per Linde and Ina Wagner, with whom, under the pseudonym of A. Telier, I wrote *Design Things* (2011); the editors of this book, Leslie Atzmon and Prasad Boradkar, whose reading of the first version of the paper helped me to improve its clarity; and Deborah Koshinsky, who gave a sound English form to its final version.

Notes

1. Objectification has different meanings in different contexts (objectification of a woman, objectification of a concept, etc.). In this essay, I use "objectification" to indicate the process through which we create objects from entities.
2. Actor networks are "collectives of humans and non-humans" (Latour 2009) as presented in Actor Network Theory (ANT; Law 1999). ANT is an approach to social theory and social research that was originated by Bruno Latour, Michel Callon, and John Law in the field of science studies.
3. "Reflection in action […] is closely tied to the experience of surprise. Sometimes, we think about what we are doing in the midst of performing an act. When performance leads to surprise—pleasant or unpleasant—the designer may respond by reflection in action: by thinking about what she is doing while doing it, in such a way as to influence further doing. For example, when talented jazz musicians improvise together, they listen to one another and to themselves. Within the structure of the piece and a familiar harmonic scheme, they think-or perhaps feel-what they are doing. While in the process, they evolve their way of doing it. The players keep on playing while, on occasion, noting and responding to the surprises produced by other players" (Bennett, Schön 1996:173).
4. The Italian philosopher Alfonso Maurizio Iacono has discussed this problem in depth in his studies on "the tail of the eye" (Iacono 2010).
5. There is an immense literature on 'breakdowns'. Let me quote for its extensive attention on them and for the impact it had on my research, the book of T. Winograd and F. Flores (1986), "Understanding Computers and Cognition."

Bibliography

Bennett, J. and D. Schön (1996), "Reflective Conversations with Materials," in T. Winograd (ed.), *Bringing Design to Software*, 172–83, New York: ACM Press, 1996.
Brown, B. (2001), "Thing Theory," *Critical Inquiry* 28 (1): 1–22.
De Michelis, G. (2008), "The Phenomenological Stance of the Designer," in T. Binder, J. Loewgren, and L. Malmborg (eds), *(Re)searching the Digital Bauhaus*, 145–62, Berlin: Springer.
Harrison, S. and P. Dourish (1996), "Re-place-ing Space: The Role of Place and Space in Collaborative Systems," in *Proceedings of the 1996 ACM Conference on Computer Supported Cooperative Work*, 67–76, New York: ACM Press.
Heidegger, M. (1971), "The Thing," in *Poetry, Language, Thought*, 174–82, New York: Harper & Row.
Iacono, A. M. (2010), *L'illusione e il sostituto. Reprodurre, imitare, rappresentare*, Milano: Bruno Mondadori.

Latour, B. (2000), "The Berlin Key or How to do Words with Things," in P. Graves-Brown (ed.), *Matter, Materiality, and Modern Culture*, 10–21, London: Routledge.
Latour, B. (2004), *Politics of Nature*, Cambridge, MA: Harvard University Press.
Latour, B. (2004), "Why has Critique Run out of Steam? From Matters of Fact to Matters of Concern," *Critical Inquiry* 30 (2): 225–48.
Latour, B. (2009), "A Collective of Humans and Nonhumans: Following Daedalus's Labyrinth," in D. M. Kaplan (ed.), *Readings in the Philosophy of Technology*, 158–68, Lanham: Rowman & Littlefield.
Latour, B. and P. Weibel (2005), *Making Things Public: Atmospheres of Democracy*, Cambridge, MA, and London: MIT Press.
Law, J. (1999), "After ANT: Complexity, Naming, and Topology," in J. Law and J. Hassard (eds), *Actor Network Theory and After*, 1–14, Oxford: Blackwell.
Schön, D. (1984), *The Reflective Practitioner*, New York: Basic Books.
Telier, A. et al. (2011), *Design Things*, Cambridge, MA, and London: MIT Press.
Telier, A. et al. (2012), "Drawing Things Together," *Interactions* 19 (2): 34–7.
Winograd, T. and F. Flores (1986), *Understanding Computers and Cognition*, Norwood: Ablex.

10

The modern American telephone as a contested technological thing, 1920–39

Jan Hadlaw

> "*What would happen, I wonder, if we tried to talk about the object of science and technology, the Gegenstand, as if it had the rich and complicated qualities of the celebrated Thing?*"
>
> LATOUR 2004: 233

In his essay "The Matter of Materialism," Bill Brown (2013: 60–77) recounts the historian C. L. R. James' description of being "knocked silly" during his visit to the Science Museum, in London, in 1932, by the sight of a racing airplane capable of traveling "at a speed of 407 miles an hour," and his amazement at how "what has been built solely for utility turns out to be so beautiful." Brown suggests that the significance of the airplane for James had less to do with its aesthetic appeal than with how it served for him "as an allegorical object [standing in] for those opportunities presented by the twentieth century, and those denied." In recognizing "the role of the inanimate object within culture, as culture, and as a means for apprehending culture," Brown proposes, "James [found] a *thing* to think with [emphasis added]. Similarly, the historian of communications James Carey (1992: 186), when commenting on the wide-ranging effects of telegraphy on modern life, has argued that the telegraph should be viewed not only as "a new tool of commerce but also a *thing* to think with, an agency for the alteration of ideas [emphasis added]."

It is worth noting that the objects of both James' and Carey's attention were technological artifacts. A technological object has a peculiar status in the material world, understood alternately, or in some cases simultaneously, as a research object, a scientific instrument, a utility, and a commodity. In both popular and theoretical senses, then, there are tensions between these different ways of thinking about or imagining an object, and each conception also tends to call forth groups that identify with or privilege one or another of these meanings. The elevated status of objects-as-scientific-instruments can too often act to dissuade scholars interested in technological objects from thinking and talking about them as "mere things." However, as both Brown and Carey suggest above, technological objects can and often do serve as useful things-for-thinking.

How do (technological) objects become "things?" Brown (2001: 4) suggests that we "confront the thingness of objects when they stop working for us: when the drill breaks, when the car stalls, when the windows get filthy, when their flow within the circuits of production and distribution, consumption and exhibition, has been arrested, however momentarily." Objects become things for us when we can no longer ignore them, when they challenge or defy our expectations, but also when ambiguity over their practical or symbolic uses arises. Brown writes that "[the] story of objects asserting themselves as things, then, is the story of a changed relation to the human subject"—not so much a change in the materiality or the utility of the object, but rather a change in the perception of its value (2001: 4).

Bruno Latour (2004: 234–5), too, identifies failure as the condition for "the metamorphosis of an object into a thing." Taking the US space shuttle Columbia disaster in 2003 as a tragic case in point, he writes that at the moment of its disintegration on re-entry into the earth's atmosphere, that scientific object, a "taken-for-granted, matter-of-factual projectile" was instantly transformed into "a sudden shower of debris," a broken thing. For Latour as well, the transformation of objects into things is not only a physical event; it also involves a change in the relationship we have with them. So when the shuttle, which had performed dependably and unremarkably for twenty-seven missions, suddenly broke apart during the return from its twenty-eighth, scattering fragments over several states, it transformed from being a matter of fact into "a matter of great concern"—the focus of attention, alarm, and interest.

Both Brown's (2001) and Latour's (2004) examples refer to physical breakdowns that result in a loss of object's integrity, capability, or functionality, but they also suggest that objects can stop working in other ways. In the case of technological objects, it is important to recognize that they are not just connected to technical networks (such as communications or electrical networks), but that they are also connected to social and cultural networks of value and meaning, which often manifest as matters of fashion, display, style, taste, aesthetics, or status. They can function, or fail to function, in one context as well as the other. To put this another way, a telephone can become a thing when it falls off of a desk or succumbs to mechanical fatigue and ceases to function; likewise a telephone can also become a thing when it falls out of fashion or succumbs to aesthetic fatigue, in which case its social and cultural meaning and usefulness break down.

Objects become things for us when they fail, when their usefulness is disrupted, when they cease to function as we expect but also when their meaning exceeds their materiality, when they provoke concern and attention. Things are therefore actors—they perform in practical and symbolic ways, they are "lively." Pointing to Arjun Appadurai's observation that "it is things-in-motion that illuminate their human and social context," Brown (2001: 7) suggests that by turning our attention to the work that things perform, rather than what they are, we can begin to make sense of how things "organize our private and public affection"—and I would argue, our private and public antipathy or ambivalence—in specific temporal and spatial contexts. The idea of things-in-motion allows us to consider how the same technological object can be perceived in any number of different ways, as any number of different *things*—including as research object, scientific instrument, utility, and commodity. Different groups and different circumstances tend to privilege one or some meanings over others and, indeed, Igor Kopytoff (1986: 90) writes that "an eventful biography of a thing [is] the story of the various singularizations of it, of classifications and reclassifications in an uncertain world of categories whose importance shifts with every minor change in context."

In the narrative that follows I explore how a technological object came to mean very different things—or perhaps even more accurately, *be* a very different thing—to different groups. This chapter examines the dispute between America's Bell Telephone Company and its early residential telephone subscribers over the design of the telephone and takes up the modern telephone as a useful "thing" for thinking about contested notions of technology, design, modern identity, and progress in the United States during the early decades of the twentieth century.[1] By considering how different groups—including electrical engineers, manufacturers, designers, and residential subscribers—imagined the telephone's practical and symbolic uses, it offers insight into how technological things mediated human relations and acted as potent signifiers of identity, status, and group membership. It is also suggestive of how human relations mediated technological things, and how the meaning of things is invariably to be found in the relationships that arise through and around them.[2]

By the beginning of the twentieth century, a new professional middle class had emerged as American businesses grew into regional and national enterprises. This new middle class was both a product of, and a market for, the material and technological innovations of the era. A new faith in science and innovation, industrialization, mass production, and new forms of communication acted to reorganize social relations and transform both the material values and conditions of American society. The new social fluidity of American society gave rise to what cultural historian Warren Susman (1984: 184–8) called a "self-conscious search" for ways to express the new experiences of everyday life in meaningful ways. In the search for a new cultural identity that reflected the conditions of social existence, "the words "modern" and "streamlined" [came to be] used not only in reference to design of particular objects but also to a quality of living, a lifestyle."

In the early decades of the twentieth century, electric technologies like the telephone, radio, and phonograph were transforming the spatial and temporal coordinates of everyday life. The new middle class identified with these products of the modern age and, through them, was inspired to imagine new ways of being and living. Encouraged by advertisers to think about the furnishings and appliances in their homes as "outward and visible signs of an inward and spiritual grace," home décor took on new significance.[3] Technological goods—electric lamps, phonographs, radios, and especially, telephones—were embraced as symbols of a modern sensibility.

By the end of World War I, America's new middle class was responsible for a marked upswing in the number of requests received by Bell for residential telephone service. A telephone in the home was a practical convenience. It allowed householders to live their lives in the new "modern tempo" by calling in orders to merchants, planning activities and social events, and staying in touch with friends and family. As the cost of telephone service was not insignificant, a residential telephone also served to identify the class status of its owner. While members of the middle class were eager to acquire the telephone for both its practical utility and the social prestige it conferred, the machine-like appearance of Bell's candlestick telephone was at odds with their desire that the things in their homes reflect their taste and refinement. Increasingly, their applications for telephone service to Bell included a request for a "French phone."

What was commonly called the French phone was a handset telephone with the receiver and transmitter both located in the handle. Introduced in France in 1882, it became popular throughout Europe by the early 1900s. American travelers visiting the continent occasionally brought French phones back home to the United States, as did some American soldiers returning after World War I. In the early 1920s, the French phone began to appear in Hollywood films and magazine pictorials as a signifier of sophistication and refinement. Movies and magazines were growing in popularity as leisure time activities for the middle class, especially middle-class women. Magazines were particularly popular for the advice they offered middle-class

FIGURE 10.1 AT&T Candlestick Telephone, 1910. Courtesy of AT&T Archives and History Center.

homemakers on home décor and the management of the modern household. In its December 1923 issue, the style-conscious *House & Garden* magazine cast a critical eye on Bell's candlestick telephone: "It is a curious fact that the telephone, probably the most indispensable of all our modern luxuries, has been allowed to retain its original unprepossessing aspect. Even when painted to harmonize with the surroundings, it strikes a discordant note by the very ungainliness of its lines which no amount of painting and decorating can transform." The author concluded by advising: "There is only one thing to do with the telephone—conceal it."[4] Quite simply, the idea of the telephone had changed, but the telephone artifact, the telephone-thing had not.

What members of the discerning middle class wanted was not to hide the telephone but to display it prominently. As mass-production made more and more goods available, design became a way to distinguish one manufacturer's product from another's, and consumers quickly became accustomed to choosing between goods on the basis of their appearance. Many of Bell's middle-class subscribers failed to understand why the French telephone they saw in movies and magazines could not be installed in their homes. They had come to see a telephone as one among an ensemble of things in their homes that gave material expression to their taste and class position. Latour (2008: 4) writes that when objects are seen to be either well or poorly designed, they draw our attention and cease to be matters of fact, appearing instead as matters of concern, or "things." As the article in *House & Garden* made clear, the candlestick telephone had become a matter of concern (as well as some irritation) for Bell's middle-class subscribers. For them, the candlestick telephone was "broken" because it did not function as a signifier of their taste and refinement.

Bell's first reaction was to ignore its subscribers' requests. There are many reasons that might explain why Bell was initially unconcerned. Bell's monopoly status allowed it to remain insulated from—and to some degree dismissive of—public opinion, and as a result it badly underestimated the growing importance of the consumer in America's transformed economy.[5] But perhaps the more significant influence was the "ideology of systems engineering" that informed Bell's research culture and corporate identity (Galambos 1992: 108). In 1907, after a decade of problems with the technical quality of its telephones that had tarnished its reputation with both subscribers and federal regulators, Bell radically rearranged its corporate structure and research goals. Rather than continuing to compete with regional independent telephone companies for subscribers, Bell focused on building a national long distance network. This objective established scientific research and engineering as the core of Bell's activities. Given this context, Bell's engineers and managers simply didn't see the telephone as a consumer good and certainly not as a decorative accouterment for the home. So while subscribers might have seen the candlestick telephone as "broken," Bell certainly did not. The telephone that so roused the ire of Bell's more fashion-minded subscribers was the product of a research and engineering culture that saw the telephone artifact as merely one component of many that made up a large technological system.

Since Bell leased rather than sold its telephones to subscribers, it (not incorrectly) considered the telephone to be its property. From Bell's point of view, there was no reason to introduce a new telephone model and every reason not to. A new telephone would make its stock obsolete and create supply problems. Manufacturing a new model of telephone would also require a sizable capital investment that would delay the completion of Bell's national network. In very simple terms, Bell misjudged the importance of the telephone's appearance to its residential subscribers because from its perspective, its appearance was not a matter of concern at all; it was the telephone's function that mattered.

And yet as much as Bell dismissed subscribers' concerns over the design of the candlestick telephone, I suggest that its appearance was likely an important factor in Bell's reluctance to comply with its subscribers' desires. While the candlestick telephone has been (and continues to be) held up as an exemplar of purely functional design, there is no such thing as a "neutral" or non-signifying artifact. The candlestick's sober machinic appearance spoke to the seriousness of technological innovation and likely appealed to the sensibilities of Bell employees. For them, the telephone was a scientific instrument, a technical device, but one component of the many that made up the Bell telephone network. One might argue that Bell employees—its engineers and managers, linesmen and operators—were also part of that network—flesh-and-blood components as important to the working of the telephone system as cables, switches, and transmitters. Projecting on the candlestick telephone a seriousness of intent and purpose strengthened their own identity as scientists and technologists, as experts and professionals. Carolyn Marvin (1988: 61–2) points out that among the professional societies in the engineering fraternity, electrical engineering was the last to develop a coherent set of qualifications by which to define itself. Ambiguities over their social and professional status made the electrical engineers eager to have the legitimacy and significance of their work recognized. Indeed, it can be argued that the candlestick telephone had come to symbolize the Bell Company itself and embody its ideal of scientific rationality. In its institutional advertising between 1908 and 1912, the candlestick telephone quite literally "stood in" for Bell and often took its place among the scientific innovations of the day.[6] In this way, for the engineers at Bell, the efficient, scientific candlestick telephone was also a thing-to-think-with that confirmed their identity as professionals and experts.

While for Bell engineers, the telephone was a scientific instrument and a technical device, independent telephone manufacturers who produced telephones for small regional telephone companies had no difficulty also seeing the telephone as a commodity and they were receptive

THE EFFICIENT MINUTE

We have speeded up our ships and railways; we have made rapid transit more and more rapid; we have developed a mile a minute in the air and much faster in an automobile.

But the Bell Telephone is quickest of all. It is *instantaneous.* No weeks or days or minutes wasted in waiting for somebody to go and come; no waiting for an answer.

It is the most effective agency for making minutes more useful, more efficient.

In almost every field of work men are accomplishing more in less time with the Bell Telephone than they could without it. They can talk with more people, near and far; they can keep the run of more details; they can buy or sell more goods, and to better advantage; they can be active in more affairs.

The Bell Telephone has placed a new and higher value upon the minute—for everybody. It has done this by means of One Policy, One System, and Universal Service.

Bell Long Distance Telephone service not only gives an added value to a man's minutes—it accomplishes business results which would be absolutely impossible without it. Every Bell Telephone is the Center of the System.

AMERICAN TELEPHONE AND TELEGRAPH COMPANY
AND ASSOCIATED COMPANIES

FIGURE 10.2 "The Efficient Minute." AT&T advertising proof, 1910. N. W. Ayer Advertising Agency Record, Archives Center, National Museum of American History, Smithsonian Institution.

to using style as a selling point. Kellogg introduced a handset telephone—the Grab-a-phone—as early as 1905. By the mid-1910s, other American manufacturers were producing versions of the French phone, including Magnavox and De Veau. By the 1920s, several models of handsets were available and some manufacturers began to experiment with different finishes and colors. The Kellogg Grab-a-phone was made in a variety of finishes including a black handset with chrome detailing, a copper model with chrome and brass details; a removable base-cover in embossed antique brass was also available (Donner 1993: 14). In 1926, the More-Tel Corporation's "French Phone" was available in nickel, brass, bronze, and gold- and silver-plate; and in 1929, the American Electric Company advertised its Monophone in eight distinctly fashionable colors, including mahogany, Chinese red, orchid, and Nile green.[7]

Independent telephone manufacturers advertised their handsets as the solution to the middle class desire to reconcile technology and taste, often contrasting their stylish telephones with Bell's "ungainly" candlestick. The headline of a 1928 advertisement for the Monophone asked bluntly: "Why Should a Telephone Be Ugly?" Another ad for the same phone directly appealed to the aspirations and apprehensions of middle-class subscribers, promising that "the graceful form and attractive appearance of this modern telephone instrument make it of definite value to the tasteful furnishing of any room. It is a decorative asset, rather than a liability."[8] An ad for the Mor-Tel French Phone clearly identified the candlestick telephone as a matter of concern for "[t]hose who take pride in the appearance of their home and office, shun to every degree possible, the too evident present day influence of standardization" and asked: "Do you enjoy in your home, the phone that is used in every factory, garage and store?"[9] While early ads by all manufacturers promoted handset telephones for use in both home and office settings, increasingly they began to focus on the telephone's residential uses and directed their appeals to women as the managers of the modern middle-class home and guardians of its values. "When Mrs. Marshall Uses the Telephone" declared one such ad featuring an illustration of a well-dressed woman at ease in an elegantly appointed drawing room, "she demands beauty as well as efficiency."[10] Much like the interior design pages of the era's popular magazines, these ads portrayed the telephone, and more specifically the French phone, as a decorative element in the modern home.

Determined subscribers dealt with Bell's refusal to offer a handset telephone by purchasing handsets made by other manufacturers and illicitly connecting them to the Bell network. Ironically, by doing so, subscribers actually did "break" their telephones—or more accurately, significantly lowered the quality of signal transmission. Because most independent manufacturers made telephones intended for use in regional rather than national systems, they often had lower technical tolerances than Bell's instruments and, when connected to the Bell system, provided less than dependable service. Bell ran warnings in local newspapers advising their subscribers that connecting "foreign" telephones was in violation of their contract and that any unlicensed instruments would be disconnected. However subscribers who had purchased fashionable telephones were undeterred and kept using their handsets despite Bell's threats.[11] Instead of heeding Bell's warning, they blamed Bell for providing poor quality service as well as for failing to offer a fashionable telephone. Bell was ultimately forced to acknowledge its subscribers' demands or lose their business to competitors willing to give them what they desired. The candlestick telephone, or perhaps more accurately, the question of telephone design had finally become a matter of significant concern to Bell.

Bell engineers were not unfamiliar with the design of the French phone. They had experimented with various handset designs as early as 1890, but all work on handset telephones had stopped in 1907. Bell's reluctance to design and manufacture a handset telephone was due in

FIGURE 10.3 "When Mrs. Marshall Uses the Telephone ..." advertisement, 1928. *Telephony*, Vol. 94 No. 17 (28 April 1928).

large part to the failure of these earlier attempts. Putting both the transmitter and the receiver in a single unit created problems with signal efficiency and sound clarity because the transmitter acted to amplify speech. With the transmitter and the receiver in close proximity, the vibrations between them caused the handset to "howl" and overpower voice transmission. Reducing the transmitter amplification would diminish howling, and this was the strategy employed by European and independent US telephone companies as their handsets were used mostly for short-distance calling. However, since reducing the level of amplification also weakened the signal emitted by the transmitter, this solution was incompatible with American geography and the terms of Bell's monopoly status. In order to win its national monopoly, Bell had convinced federal regulators that it alone could provide the high quality instruments and reasonably priced service required for long distance communication. Inferior or unreliable transmission threatened to erode not only Bell's reputation but also its plans for a continental long distance network. On the other hand, delaying the release of its handset telephone could only further provoke many of its residential subscribers.

By the fall of 1926, Bell had produced a handset that was less susceptible to howl but not all transmission problems were solved. Concerned over the inroads made by the independent manufacturers, Bell made the decision to release a small number of experimental handsets in January 1927, with the precaution that they be provided only to the most demanding subscribers and their availability not be advertised.[12] It was a decision Bell soon came to regret. Nearly one-third of the handsets released in 1928 were withdrawn from service by June of that year.[13] Compounding the problem was demand for the French phone, which continued to rise despite the lack of promotion. While Bell had anticipated some technical problems, it was completely unprepared for the overwhelmingly negative response to the design of its first handset telephone. In its attempt to address the concerns of subscribers over the appearance of the telephone, Bell found itself with a handset telephone that was now perceived as "broken" by both its subscribers and its engineers, a failure in both aesthetic and technical senses.

Bell engineers had scrutinized every conceivable technical detail of the handset—going so far as to take "4,000 measurements of head dimensions" to insure optimal spacing and position of the receiver and transmitter on the handle—and yet they ignored what mattered most to the public: the telephone's appearance.[14] To make its handsets, Bell engineers had simply shortened the shaft of the candlestick base and fitted it with a cast aluminum cradle-style hook switch. Bell subscribers who had been eagerly awaiting the opportunity to install a fashionable telephone compared it unfavorably to the models of other manufacturers. One disenchanted subscriber wrote:

> Our office has recently installed a French-style of telephone made by your Company [placing] the order without looking at the design. [...] in my opinion the real French type telephone is attractive in design, whereas the [telephone] furnished by the [Bell] Telephone Company strikes me as being "something awful."[15]

It may be difficult to understand how Bell engineers gave the appearance of the handset telephone such short shrift—especially as it was precisely the appearance of the telephone that was a matter of concern for subscribers—but it is perhaps less bewildering if one remembers that Bell did not consider the candlestick telephone to be "broken" in any sense. What subscribers saw as the candlestick's "ungainly" form was, for Bell engineers, the embodiment of their expertise. It is perhaps notable that the chief engineer who halted Bell's research on the handset in 1907, was Bell's vice president in 1927 when the "awful" looking French phone was released. I suspect that it was not, as Bell historian John Brooks (1975: 130) suggests, that

FIGURE 10.4 Bell's WE "200 Series" telephone, 1928. Courtesy of AT&T Archives and History Center.

FIGURE 10.5 Telephones designed for Bell's 1929 design competition by (clockwise starting at top left) Lucian Bernhardt, Gustav Jenson, Réne Clarke, and John Vassos. Courtesy of AT&T Archives and History Center.

"[he] just didn't like French phones," but rather that the technical rationalism that informed his views and those of the engineers charged with the development of the telephone simply did not include "style" as an element of what they considered a scientific undertaking. In their view, the appearance of the candlestick telephone—or any telephone—simply was, and should be, a matter of fact. The strategies of system engineering that organized Bell's research, production, and distribution efforts embraced a notion of progress based on technological advancement. Bell's demanding middle-class subscribers, on the other hand, saw progress embodied in ideas of self-improvement and refinement, and in the objects they chose as reflections of their taste and social status.

The determination of middle-class subscribers finally resulted in Bell's somewhat reluctant acknowledgment that "the modern trend is toward a more pleasing appearance of utilitarian things."[16] In 1929, Bell decided to hold a design contest to create a new modern telephone in keeping with the desires of its subscribers. Four well-respected artists—John Vassos, Réne Clark, Gustav Jenson, and Lucian Bernhard—were invited to take part in the competition.[17] As the consulting artists began to work on their designs with Bell engineers, it quickly became clear that each group imagined the telephone in radically different ways. Like most designers working at this time, Vassos, Clark, Jenson, and Bernhard had little experience with the design of technological devices. Accustomed to designing fashionable consumer goods, they approached the design of the telephone from the same perspective. Employing art nouveau and art deco motifs, the telephones they designed were highly idiosyncratic and featured beveled edges, fanciful cradle lugs, and other decorative details. In the analysis that accompanied his submissions, Vassos explained that his goal was to make the telephone "an interesting object from a sculptural point of view." His declaration that "[t]he telephone should not be classed in the minds of the public as a mechanical device but rather as a desk accessory" could not have been more expressive of the sentiments of Bell's subscribers and more out of step with the sensibilities of the Bell engineers.[18]

The report on the artists' models prepared by Bell's apparatus development engineer D. H. King indicated that their designs were fraught with problems that would be difficult and costly to resolve. King's list of flaws included fragility of parts, details which would cause finishing problems, high cost of making and maintaining the molds for some of the more decorative housings, and in one case, inadequate space allowance in the body of the phone to accommodate technical apparatus. While ostensibly limiting his analysis to the mechanical aspects of the telephone designs, King's remarks actually focused a great deal on questions of telephone maintenance and care—with which subscribers were clearly not to be trusted. He objected to one of Vassos' more elaborate designs on the grounds that "[i]t offers too many places for the collection of dust and dirt." King was equally critical of Bernhard's design which included a groove to accommodate a pen or pencil: "what apparently was intended as a feature [...] may prove to be a serious maintenance nuisance as it probably will invite subconscious defacing of the mounting surfaces while the subscriber is writing." While initially impressed with Jenson's more restrained design, he ultimately rejected it as well because its novel handset support would require completely redesigning the switchhook mechanism. King concluded his report with the withering observation that the designs exhibited "very little consideration from the practical or manufacturing viewpoint."[19]

King's report can be read as an account of what engineers viewed as a failed attempt at redesigning the telephone. It unequivocally confirmed Bell's position that aesthetics and engineering were incompatible. In February 1930, it was decided that two engineers would be assigned to work on the design of the new telephone, with a consulting designer to "aid and inspire" them. No doubt Bell's 1928 French phone fiasco was responsible for the suggestion that "an advisory committee consisting of an architect, a master designer, and an interior decorator" assess the engineers' designs before taking any decisions to move forward with production.[20] Bell's engineer-designers immediately discarded the consulting artists' designs.[21] That year they redesigned the offending French phone, replacing its round base with one that was elliptically shaped. *Bell Laboratories Record* featured the new design in its October 1931 issue, noting that the telephone's new contours were based on Euclid's Golden Section, "the empirical rule for achieving beautiful proportions" and "a fundamental principle underlying all creations of beauty" (Dilts 1931: 97). Perhaps not surprisingly, Bell engineers found their solution to the dilemma of their French phone's appearance in a mathematical formula—it would be science and not fashion that would dictate their design of the modern telephone.

FIGURE 10.6   Bell's WE "200 Series" telephone with elliptical base and dial, 1930. Courtesy of AT&T Archives and History Center.

In 1934, Bell engineers developed a new direct-action transmitter that solved the problems of output efficiency that plagued the French phone and was economical to manufacture. That same year, Bell hired industrial designer Henry Dreyfuss to design a telephone to replace the troublesome French phone and to finally put an end to the contest over the "appearance" of the telephone.[22] Interestingly, Dreyfuss' first submissions were in keeping with the fashionable models proposed by Vassos, Clark, Jenson, and Bernhard. He suggested a streamlined design and recommended that Bell offer the telephone in a range of fashionable colors. Dreyfuss' proposals quickly met the same end as those of the industrial designers who preceded him and his contribution was largely restricted to giving form to the ideas of Bell engineers. The resulting No. 302 phone was a model of functional design and it went into production in 1937.[23]

During this period, independent manufacturers in the US continued to experiment with both the materials and appearance of the telephone. In 1933, Kellogg introduced the Masterphone 900—a non-dial combined set telephone with a Bakelite housing—and in 1935, the Masterphone 925, a dial version. Sometimes called the "ash tray phones," with their quintessentially art-deco styling, they approached John Vassos' ideal of a telephone with the styling of a desk accessory rather than a mechanical device. Stromberg-Carlson's first combined telephone, the stylish No. 1212 was introduced in 1936 and it, too, featured a Bakelite housing.

It was not long before the telephone's "art-deco period of great diversity" ended (Meyer 1995: 117). By 1940, Bell's No. 302 became the standard for all telephone design. Stromberg-Carlson replaced the fashionable No. 1212 with the No. 1222, which was very similar to Bell's No. 302 including its die-cast zinc housing, and the shape of the Kellogg Masterphone began to shift perceptibly towards Bell's model as well. In the mid-1930s, Bell subsumed telephone design under the purview of "human factors research," which studied how people used the telephone in order to insure that it was used in ways that did not conflict with Bell's objectives. Design became a means by which Bell engineers were able to standardize not only telephone apparatus and components, but more significantly, the use of the telephone by subscribers. The 1949 press release announcing Bell's new No. 500 telephone left little doubt as to the supremacy of engineering over design: "The appearance of the set was designed by Bell Telephone Laboratories' engineers working with Henry Dreyfuss, one of the country's leading exponents of functional design."[24]

FIGURE 10.7 Bell's WE #302 introduced in 1939. It was a "combined set" with the ringer integrated into the telephone housing. Courtesy of AT&T Archives and History Center.

Studies of the telephone have typically focused on its functions as a communication and technological system. However, the contested meaning of the modern American telephone in the first decades of the twentieth century serves to remind us that the telephone was also a thing that mediated human relations and embodied myriad social, symbolic and instructive meanings. As Bill Brown (2010: 191) has argued, "human subjects depend on inanimate objects to establish their sense of identity" and we can see this was true for each of the groups involved in the contest over the design of the modern telephone. For Bell's middle-class residential subscribers, the failure of the candlestick telephone had nothing to do with the telephone's technical aspects, and everything to do with their perception that its material form was at odds with the meanings they assigned to it. Likewise, the modern-ness they projected onto the French phone was the modern-ness—the sense of distinction, sophistication, uniqueness—they experienced when they gazed upon images of the French phone in advertisements, magazines, and the movies. Although the design of the telephone seemed to be of little importance to Bell's managers and engineers, their attachment to what they perceived as the candlestick telephone's serious and utilitarian appearance suggests otherwise. The candlestick telephone's use as the corporate symbol in Bell's institutional advertising campaigns between 1908 and 1912 suggests that Bell saw the candlestick as the thing that most eloquently embodied the company's identity and ethos of engineering.

Latour (2008: 4) writes that, "[t]o think of artifacts in terms of design means conceiving of them [...] more and more as "things"[...] as complex assemblies of contradictory issues." Viewed in this way, the design of the telephone can be understood as a site of negotiation over the *meaning* of the modern telephone, what it communicated, about whom, and to whom.

Notes

1. The American Bell Telephone Company was incorporated in 1880. Bell acquired Western Electric Manufacturing Company (WE) in 1882 and licensed it as the sole producer of Bell telephones and equipment. In 1900, American Bell Telephone Company was re-structured and renamed American Telephone and Telegraph (AT&T). The term "Bell System" was introduced in 1908 to describe the

AT&T network. In 1925, WE Research Laboratories and the AT&T Engineering Department were consolidated and renamed Bell Telephone Laboratories. In this article, I refer to all the various divisions and subsidiaries that made up the Bell System simply as "Bell."

2   The telephone-as-object has received relatively little scholarly attention despite its ubiquitous presence in North American homes for most of the twentieth century. Writing about the invention of the telephone in the United States in the 1870s, W. Bernard Carlson observed that most historical accounts of technological developments have failed to present technological developments as both material and political. He suggested that historians of technology had been "reluctant to investigate the interplay between technological design and political ideology," while "nontechnological historians" tended to concentrate on "the discourse of ideas and fail to look at what happens when ideas are manifest in material objects." W. Bernard Carlson, "The Telephone as a Political Instrument: Gardiner Hubbard and the Formation of the Middle Class in America, 1875–1880", in M. T. Allen and G. Hecht (eds), *Technologies of Power: Essays in Honor of Thomas Parke Hughes and Agatha Chipley Hughes* (Cambridge: MIT Press, 2001), 26–7.

3   Roland Marchand notes that this description was used in a promotional booklet produced by the Henri, Hurst and McDonald agency for a bathroom fixture manufacturer. It also appeared in an ad for the company's products in Printer's Ink, July 28, 1927, 30–1. It was used by A. W. Page, AT&T's vice president of publicity and public relations, in a speech at the AT&T General Sales Conference in 1929. Marchand suggests that Page used the phrase before 1927 and attributes this quote to him. Roland Marchand, *Advertising the American Dream* (Berkeley: University of California Press, 126). For use of quote by Page see A. W. Page, "Coordination of Sales and Advertising Activities," Speech at the General Sales Conference, January–February 1929. File 140 10 01, Box 2034, Talks and Papers—A. W. Page, Corporate Collection, AT&T Archives.

4   "Concealing the Unsightly Telephone," *House & Garden*, December 1923, 65.

5   "We have had enough experience with the public to know just how fickle they might be." F. M. Jewett (Bell Laboratories President) to B. Gherardi (AT&T Vice President and Chief Engineer), memorandum, April 10, 1928. Box 73, Series 7: Apparatus and Systems, F. B. Jewett Collection, AT&T Archives.

6   "The Efficient Minute." AT&T advertising proof, 1910. File 1, Box 21, Series 1, N. W. Ayer Advertising Agency Records, Archives Center, National Museum of American History, Behring Center, Smithsonian Institution.

7   Mor-Tel Corporation, "The 'French Phone'," in *American Perfumer & Essential Oil Review*, September 1926: 84–5; American Electric Company, "Now in Color, the Monophone," in *Telephony*, June 15, 1929 (n.p.).

8   Strowger Automatic, "Why Should a Telephone Be Ugly?" *Telephony*, May 5, 1928: 28–9; "Reflecting the Modern Trend," February 23, 1928: 30–1.

9   Mor-Tel Corporation, "The 'French Phone'," in *American Perfumer & Essential Oil Review*, September 1926: 84–5.

10 Strowger Automatic, "When Mrs. Marshall Uses the Telephone …" *Telephony*, April 28, 1928 (n.p.).

11 The *New York Times*, March 1, 1927.

12 B. Gherardi, letter, May 4, 1926.

13 F. B. Jewett, memorandum, July 13, 1928. Box 73, Series 7: Apparatus and Systems, F. B. Jewett Collection, AT&T Archives.

14 M. D. Fagan notes that this research "was one of the early applications of anthropomorphic measurements in industry and one of the first applications of 'human factors' studies in the Bell

System." M. D. Fagen, ed., *A History of Engineering and Science in the Bell System: The Early Years (1875–1925)*, 146.

15 C. M. Owens (Bell subscriber), letter, January 24, 1927, AT&T Archives.
16 William Fondiller, Bell Lab's assistant director of apparatus development, speaking at the American Management Association convention in 1929 cited in M. Heymann, "It's Still a Phone—But What a Phone!", *Indiana Bell Highlights* 24, 1973.
17 Correspondence with Consulting Artists, 1929. File "Correspondence with Outside Consulting Artists," Case 35585, Vol. A, AT&T Archives.
18 Ibid.
19 D. H. King, "Report on Artists' Models." Box 2, Case 34648, AT&T Corporate Collection, AT&T Archives.
20 R. L. Jones, "Proposal to Strike Advisory Committee." File "Correspondence with Outside Consulting Artists," Case 35585, Vol. A, AT&T Archives.
21 See "The First Meeting of the Advisory Committee," June 17, 1930. File "Correspondence with Outside Consulting Artists–U 169 S8," Case 35585, Vol. A, AT&T Archives.
22 On Jewett's impatience with the dilemma of "appearance," see F. B. Jewett to E. S. Bloom, May 28, 1935. File 08 04 03, H. P. Charlesworth Collection, AT&T Archives.
23 While Bell prized innovation in the field of engineering, it clearly did not value originality in design. The similarity of Dreyfuss' No. 302 to Jean Heiberg's 1930 telephone design for Sweden's L. M. Ericsson Company was remarkable. See Kathryn B. Hiesinger and George H. Marcus, *Landmarks of Twentieth-Century Design: An Illustrated Handbook* (New York: Abbeville Press, 1993), 121. Dreyfuss's biographer, Russell Flinchum notes that "the fact that the No. 302 as it first appeared was available only with a die-cast metal base while the Hieberg design was produced in Bakelite plastic from its inception is a gauge of the relative conservatism of [Bell] engineers." Russell Flinchum, *Henry Dreyfuss, Industrial Designer: The Man in the Brown Suit* (New York: Rizzoli Publications, 1997), 97.
24 AT&T Public Relations Department, "500-Type Set Takes a Bow on National TV Program," February 1, 1955. File: 500 Set, Bell Canada Historical Archive.

Bibliography

Brown, B. (2001), "Thing Theory," *Critical Inquiry* 28 (1): 1–22.
Brown, B. (2010), "Objects, Others, and Us (The Refabrication of Things)," *Critical Inquiry* 36 (2): 183–217.
Brown, B. (2013), "The Matter of Materialism: Literary Mediations," in T. Bennett and P. Joyce (eds), *Material Powers: Cultural Studies, History and the Material Turn*, 60–78, London: Routledge.
Carey, J. W. (1992), *Communication As Culture: Essays on Media and Society*, London: Routledge.
Donner, K. E. (1993), *Telephone Collecting: Seven Decades of Design*, Atglen, PA: Schiffer Publishing.
Galambos, L. (1992), "Theodore N. Vail and the Role of Innovation in the Modern Bell System," *Business History Review* 66 (1): 95–126.
Kopytoff, I. (1986), "The Cultural Biography of Things: Commoditization as Process," in A. Appadurai (ed.), *The Social Life of Things: Commodities in Cultural Perspective*, 64–94, Cambridge: Cambridge University Press.
Latour, B. (2004), "Why Has Critique Run Out of Steam? From Matters of Fact to Matters of Concern," *Critical Inquiry* 30 (2): 225–48.
Latour, B. (2008), "A Cautious Prometheus? A Few Steps Toward a Philosophy of Design." Keynote

lecture, Networks of Design Conference, Design History Society, Falmouth, Cornwall, September 3, 2008. http://www.brunolatour.fr/sites/default/files/112-DESIGN-CORNWALL-GB.pdf (accessed January 14, 2014).

Marvin, C. (1988), *When Old Technologies Were New*, Oxford: Oxford University Press.

Meyer, R. O. (1995), *Old-Time Telephones!*, New York: McGraw-Hill.

Susman, W. I. (1984), *Culture as History: The Transformation of American Society in the Twentieth Century*, New York: Pantheon.

11

Memory, materiality, and the Montreal Signs Project

Matt Soar

In the basement of the Communication Studies and Journalism (CJ) building, on Concordia University's Loyola campus, is a popular undergraduate study-space known colloquially as the Monsieur Hot Dog lounge. There is no fast food here, or franchises of any description. Just a lurid red-and-yellow sign that hung for decades outside a poutine joint on the Eastern edge of the campus. It's about five feet square, made from panned acrylic, and, like several other signs in the MSP collection, was one of a pair, originally mounted back-to-back on a metal frame and illuminated from within. Today's students may not remember this classic local "resto," but the sign serves as a handy reference point when looking for somewhere to hang between classes—or for locating the adjacent washrooms. The West End franchise of Monsieur Hot Dog is, however, a fond memory among the alums of Loyola College— which amalgamated with the downtown Sir George Williams University in 1974 to become Concordia.

The Montreal Signs Project is an ever-expanding collection of old commercial signs from all over this unique island city. As of Summer 2015, there are twelve signs on display, representing some of the most enduring local instances of postwar entrepreneurship in retail and food: bicycles, women's clothing, a butcher's, a deli, a bookstore, a café, etc. As the project's founder and director, I often say that it isn't really about signs at all: as the Monsieur Hot Dog sign suggests, it's a gentle provocation: a set of *aides-mémoires,* often evoking surprising cultural associations.

Within sight of the Hot Dog lounge is a cinderblock wall carrying an open-channel metal sign from the Monkland Tavern in NDG (a neighborhood that takes its name from Notre-Dame-de-Grâce, the parish church). The 14ft-long sign is a relic from the 1950s, when Montreal bars were usually just for men; imagine hockey on the TV, and the reassuring neon message "*verres stérilisés*" glowing in the front window. In 1995, it became an upscale restaurant, maintaining the original name and its twin signs; one in English (*Tavern*), one in French (*Taverne*). It was only in 2005 that, due to a complaint received by the Office québécois de la langue française, the owners were obliged to remove the English version. (Law 101, a legacy of Quebec's Quiet Revolution, stipulates that all commercial signs must be in French—unless they're brand names—and that versions in English, or any other language, cannot be as prominent.) The sign's neon is long gone, but the "bastard" lettering (i.e., not based on a specific typeface) has a delightful, looping rhythm, with a distinctive, swooping crossbar on the "T."

What we've collected so far are not the generic, mass-produced signs of mega-banks or supermarket chains, but unique, complex things (Brown 2000), being, all at once: discarded junk; commercial detritus; exemplars of fading, or lost artisanal practices; lightning rods for the personal and collective memories of particular street corners, or entire neighborhoods. Visitors sometimes take the trouble to examine the signs more closely, but many, having given them a cursory glance, will then turn their backs and offer a cherished anecdote about a childhood memory, or their student days, or historical family connections.

On the top floor of the CJ building is a long corridor stretching westward from the central elevators, past more offices and classrooms, ending at a modest faculty lounge. This entire corridor is dominated by seven huge letters from the late 1950s, spaced along a specially built plinth. Spelling "WARSHAW," each letter is a spot-welded, galvanized metal box with a red plastic fascia, measuring about 5ft high by 1ft deep. Anyone over the age of eighteen who has lived on the Plateau (a hip, formerly working-class, residential neighborhood to the East of Mont Royal, the geological landmark that gives the city its name) remembers Warshaw's. But they probably don't know that the "H," while identical to the rest in material terms, is an interloper. Run by the Levy family, from 1935 until the early 2000s, this eclectic supermarket was a fixture on boulevard Saint-Laurent, otherwise known as The Main. Mrs. Levy, the family matriarch, attended the opening of the MSP in 2010. Surrounded by four generations of her family, she recounted that her own father, an illiterate Polish immigrant, had been approached by a sign painter who offered to paint her father's name on his store window for $5. Unable to spell his own surname, he suggested writing *Warsaw*, his former home. Unwittingly, the painter added an "h"—exactly as he'd just heard it spoken by the owner. Five dollars being five dollars, the name stuck.

Aside from their capacity to spark highly particular, even peculiar, memories, the old signs in the MSP collection also testify to the continually changing technologies of signmaking. They remind us of the anonymous, artisanal labor that went into their design and fabrication. When the first five signs were being repaired under the watchful eye of Bill Kovacevic, a veteran sign designer, he had to keep reminding the guys working on the job to use *old* methods and *old* materials, even though newer, better techniques were to hand.

Thirty miles northwest of the city is the Montréal-Mirabel International Airport. Its defining feature was the passenger terminal, a minimalist smoked-glass box designed by Papineau-Gérin-Lajoie. Opened in 1975, just ahead of the Olympics, the airport never met expectations in terms of passenger numbers. Walking around the deserted terminal in July 2014 was an eerie experience, a factor exploited very effectively by the makers of *Warm Bodies*, a lighthearted zombie flick filmed there in 2011. The wayfinding system is typical for the period: suspended or wall-mounted panels in bright yellow, with black Helvetica Bold. Most of it is applied poorly, however, and the accompanying pictograms lack conviction and consistency. Four months later, the MSP took delivery of three signs, including a splendid "split-flap" display: a highly distinctive electro-mechanical flight indicator, designed and built at the Solari factory in Udine, Italy. In terms of design quality, the Solari board is head-and-shoulders above everything else in the terminal: a black fascia with tumbling white letters, surrounded by a bulbous yellow frame. With the display removed from the terminal, and demolition imminent (as is often the case with salvaged signs), we would do well to reflect on the malleability of meaning, depending on time and place: the sign as concept, then manufactured object; cargo; beacon of technological novelty; banal messenger; dusty boondoggle; stored, mute artifact. (With luck and effort, it will find renewed purpose at the MSP as a Wi-Fi-enabled medium for curt, poetic ponderings.)

While the MSP runs on a shoestring budget, can't offer money for acquisitions, and never promises anything so grand as "restoration" or "preservation," there are far worse potential fates for the city's commercial detritus. Indeed, most of it has been casually destroyed over time anyway: look at an old National Film Board documentary about life in the city in years gone by, and the main thoroughfares are absolutely awash in neon marquees—all of it now long gone. A project of this kind is therefore as much about absence (Bille et al. 2010), or *lack*, as it is about messy, hard-edged physical presence. And all of the old signs testify, if only mutely, to the ways in which the meanings of things are always contextual rather than intrinsic (see for example: Boradkar 2012; Cut Rate Collective 2009; Straw 2000).

References

See plate section, images 5–8.

Acknowledgments

With thanks to Leslie Atzmon and Prasad Boradkar for the invitation and editorial advice. The Montreal Signs Project http://signs.concordia.ca is supported through the ongoing interest and efforts of individuals such as: Dr. Peter Morden, former Associate Dean of Academic Facilities, Faculty of Arts & Science, Concordia University; Ms. Nancy Marrelli, Archivist Emerita, Concordia University; and, Mr. Bill Kovacevic, Pattison Sign Group.

Bibliography

Bille, M., F. Hastrup and T. Flohr Sørensen (eds) (2010), *An Anthropology of Absence: Materializations of Transcendence and Loss*, New York: Springer.

Boradkar, P. (2012), "Rediscovering Value: The Second Lives of Secondhand Goods," *Design & Culture*, 4(2): 221–6.

Brown, B. (2001), "Thing Theory," *Critical Inquiry* 28 (1): 1–22.

Cut Rate Collective (2009), *Used/Goods* [exhibition catalogue], Montreal: Cut Rate Collective.

Soar, M. (2007), *Almost Architecture: A Film about Highrise Signs in Montréal* [interactive documentary], http://www.almostarchitecture.com

Soar, M. (2009), "Research in Brief: Hypercommercialism: On the Streets, in the Movies," *Canadian Journal of Communication*, 34: 283–9.

Soar, M. (2010) (ed.), "Signs and the City," *Design and Culture* 2 (2): 131–235.

Soar, M. (2013), "Raconter des histoires avec le Projet d'enseignes de Montréal," *L'Enseigne* 24 (4): 12–14 [trade journal of the AQIE: Association Québécoise de l'Industrie de l'Enseigne].

Straw, W. (2000), "Exhausted Commodities: The Material Culture of Music," *Canadian Journal of Communication* 25 (1): 1–8.

12

Connecting things

Broadening design to include systems, platforms, and product-service ecologies

Hugh Dubberly

Traditionally, design practice and design education have focused on giving form to physical *things*—apparel, buildings, messages, tools, and vehicles—the artifacts that constitute *material culture*. These artifacts are also the material of the traditional design disciplines—apparel design, architecture, graphic design, product design, and transportation design.

Recently, the field of cultural studies has turned much of its attention to physical *things*—not just how they are used, but also how they are designed, produced, and distributed. Somewhat paradoxically, just as the field of cultural studies is making its *material turn*, design practice is making a turn of its own—an *immaterial turn*—focusing less on physical things and more on connections between them. Increasingly, design practice is concerned with nodes *and links*—networks, systems, and communities of systems. These new concerns have given rise to new disciplines—business design, interaction design, service design, social innovation design, and trans-disciplinary design.

Design practice is not so much *turning away from things* as it is *connecting things*. Three main types of connections are involved. 1) Organizations are finding that opportunities for creating new value lie primarily in connecting products to services and experiences. 2) Design discourse increasingly recognizes that things are connected to ideas; that artifacts are tied to use, meaning, and context; and that design practice is bound up in language and conversation. And 3) new technologies are connecting things to data networks and complex systems that analyze the data, learn from it, and act on what they learn. The process of *connecting things* has already begun to broaden design practice from its traditional focus on stand-alone products to also include systems, platforms, and product-service ecologies.

From scarcity to commodity

For most of history, people made *things* by hand, one at a time, for themselves or their neighbors. They fit *the-thing-they-were-making* to a particular purpose, within a particular context, using materials and tools ready-at-hand. And because *making-things-by-hand* takes a great deal of time, for most of history, for most people, *things* were scarce and expensive. People had to work hard to gather materials and make what they needed to survive. (For many people, that is still true. Whether we can extend the economy of abundance to everyone is unclear. Even less clear is whether the earth can sustain the attempt.)

As production increased, an individual *thing* could be replaced by another *thing* that was almost the same. Substitution became possible. As *things* became interchangeable, they lost some of their particularity. They became less attached to particular people and particular places. They became not *things-in-their-own-right* but rather examples of a *class-of-things*. They became less individually recognizable, less special, and less valuable. A long and accelerating process unfolded. As trade developed, specialization became possible, and standardization followed. Standardization can increase efficiency, reduce cost, and create competitive advantage. Eventually, craftsmen who had designed *as* they made a particular thing, for a particular person, turned to producing many copies of the "same" thing, for "the market"—they began to manufacture. That shift separated *planning-for-making* from *making itself*. And design emerged as a "profession."[1]

Harnessing waterpower and then steam power dramatically increased the speed of *the-making-of-things*; it turned craft-production into mass-production, and brought about the industrial revolution. The industrial revolution led to unprecedented rates of production, turning more and more *things* into *commodities*—things that are essentially the same and differ only on price.

At first, when a new *thing* is manufactured, it's relatively rare, it commands a relatively high price and thus manufacturers are able to make a profit easily. This situation often tempts other manufacturers to begin making the "same" things, increasing quantities available for purchase. With more goods available, competition increases, and prices fall. Continuing to manufacture more of the "same" things becomes a losing proposition, and in order to survive, businesses have to look elsewhere to find value and difference.

Many sectors have gone through this process. Personal computers are a classic example. In 1981, IBM offered its first PC for $1,565 (more than $4,000 in 2015 dollars), featuring a 4.77 MHz processor, 16 KB of RAM, and no hard disk. Its PC line earned billions of dollars and became the industry standard. Nevertheless, twenty-four years later, IBM recognized it could no longer compete and sold its PC business to Lenovo. Today, Lenovo offers a $99 PC featuring a 1.33 GHz processor, 2 GB of RAM, and a 32 GB hard disk[2]—nearly 300 times faster, with 125,000 times more RAM, and the added benefit of a hard disk, for about 6 percent of the cost of the original IBM PC (less than 3 percent when adjusted for inflation). That's a once scarce thing becoming a commodity.

When products become commodities, manufacturers look for ways to differentiate them—ways to make them unique again. For a time, quality materials, quality manufacturing, and quality product design offered differentiation. As competitors begin to match quality, businesses must look elsewhere for differentiation and value.

From products to services

In 1998, Pine and Gilmore described the "experience economy." For example, raw coffee beans are a commodity worth only a penny or two per cup of brewed coffee. Roasting and grinding the beans creates a *product* worth $0.05 to $0.25 per brewed cup. Converting coffee beans from a *product* to a *service*—brewing and serving a cup of coffee at a diner—increases the value to $0.75 to $1.50. And wrapping a cup of coffee in a Starbucks *experience*—treating oneself to something special—increases the value to $2.00 to $5.00.[3]

As the economy has moved from manufacturing to services, products have not disappeared. Instead, services have become a way to deliver products, in part because services are a way to differentiate products and increase their value. GE, for example, builds jet engines *and* sells aircraft "up-time"—leases for engines and their maintenance that guarantee uninterrupted service. Auto industry experts report that almost 25 percent of new cars are leased.[4] Personal computer software used to be sold in *shrink-wrapped* boxes, but now boxed software is rare. Increasingly, software applications are *leased* (by Adobe, Autodesk, Microsoft, and many others) rather than sold.

Former *Wired* editor Kevin Kelly puts it well:

> commercial products are best treated as though they were services. It's not what you sell a customer; it's what you do for them. It's not what something is; it's what it's connected to, what it does. Flow becomes more important than resources. Behavior counts.[5]

Complex hybrids are forming. Services are delivering hardware; hardware is connecting to applications; and applications are connecting to each other—all at increasing speed—giving rise to what John Rheinfrank and Jodi Forlizzi have termed "product-service ecologies." Forlizzi writes, "networks of products, services, technology, people, and collective and collaborative interaction are generating value for the populations they serve."[6] For example, unlike Samsung MP3 players, iPod was not a stand-alone product; it was an integrated system of hardware, software, networked applications, and *content*—a dynamic *product-service ecology*. Apple has cautiously opened its ecology to others, teaming with Nike to extend the iPod system—and more recently publishing its HealthKit, HomeKit, and ResearchKit APIs (Application Programming Interfaces), enabling broader access and turning smartphones into hubs of body-area networks and home-management networks.

Amazon's Kindle-Reader-Whispernet-Store system is another *product-service ecology*. At the launch of a new Kindle Fire, Amazon CEO Jeff Bezos said, "I think of [the Kindle] as a service. Part of [it] is of course the hardware, but really, it's the software, the content, it's the seamless integration of those things."[7]

Systems thinking is not new to business. Kodak created an early product-service ecology, offering cameras, film, and processing services. Mass production has long included assembly lines, supply chains, distribution networks, and inventory management systems. Infrastructure—physical networks, such as canals, roads, and telephone lines—have been vital to economic growth.

The idea that utility arises through connections may be applied not only to the special class of things that are systems and infrastructure but also to all human-made *things*. Several critics have suggested that *things* exist within a complex social-technical-linguistic matrix (a web of relationships connecting people, things, and ideas). For example, Humberto Maturana and

Francisco Varela developed the theory of autopoiesis (literally "self-making"—the processes through which living systems create and maintain themselves), later with Niklas Luhman and others extending the idea to social systems. And Michael Callon, Bruno Latour, and John Law proposed Actor Network Theory (ANT), a method in which artifacts are described as participants in social and semiotic systems.

Archeologist Ian Hodder uses the term "entangled" in describing relationships between humans and their things. And in exploring these relationships, he discusses Heidegger's notion of "assembly" or "gathering," made famous through the example of a simple *thing*—a jug. Hodder explains:

> for Heidegger there is an aspect of the jug that is not captured by describing it as an entity or an object. The jug takes what is poured into it, and then pours the liquid out. The water and wine come from a rock spring or from the grape growing in the earth. The pouring out can quench thirst for humans or be a libation to the gods. So the jug connects humans, gods, earth and sky. It is this 'gathering' that makes the jug a thing. Heidegger refers to Old High German in which a thing means a gathering to deliberate on a matter under discussion. The jug, as thing, gathers together for a moment humans, gods, earth and sky.[8]

Product-service ecologies, like Heidegger's jug, gather together people, smart devices, software applications, and human services. These gatherings must be designed. In 1969, cybernetician Gordon Pask noted that a

> building cannot be viewed simply in isolation ... structures make sense as parts of larger systems that include human components and the architect is primarily concerned with these larger systems; they (not just the bricks and mortar part) are what the architect designs.[9]

Systems of manufacture and infrastructure have been explicitly designed, refined, and iterated. For a few designers, systems and infrastructure have always been *things-to-be-designed*—the material of design. Systems and networks can be treated as *sets-of-elements* and as *wholes*—just as stand-alone products are often both *collections-of-components* and *wholes*. A pot, lid, handle, whistle, and spout, for example, comprise a teapot, which we tend to see as a *whole*, until one of the parts breaks, thrusting *itself* into our view. This notion applies to systems of manufacture and infrastructure as well. ANT describes the process of parts forming wholes as *punctualization* and the process of wholes decomposing into parts as *depunctualization*. Indeed, mediating *between* the parts and whole—and the whole and the larger systems in which it is enmeshed—is a key element of what designers have always done.

Until recently, however, the vast majority of designers did not explicitly design systems. That situation began to change with the advent of the internet, which is making stand-alone products less and less viable. Oracle product manager Tim Misner argues that, "All products want to be web-sites." That is, they want to be systems for collecting information. And soon, most web-based applications will be connected.[10]

From increasing power to adding information

In the mid-nineteenth century, Western economies shifted from an agricultural basis (using human and animal power) to a manufacturing basis (using the power of falling water or steam). Adding power to *things* increased their value. A lot. As electric power emerged, motors were incorporated into many *things*, creating "powered" devices—air conditioners, cameras, electric toothbrushes, vacuum cleaners, and washing machines, for example.

In the late twentieth century, Western economies began to shift from products to services and from manufacturing work to knowledge work—to an *information economy*. In part, adding information to *things* meant incorporating microprocessors—the chips at the core of personal computers—creating "smart" devices. For example, the average car includes at least thirty microprocessors; some luxury cars include as many as 100.[11] Most new devices that include a motor are now likely to include a microprocessor—air conditioners, cameras, robot vacuum cleaners, smart toothbrushes, and washing machines, for example.

The move from industrial economy to information economy might appear to be a sequence—an evolution. Former *Wired* editor Kevin Kelly points out, however, that the industrial revolution "was not a preliminary primitive stage required for the hatching of the more sophisticated information revolution." The industrial revolution could not have moved forward without harnessing information to regulate manufacturing devices. Almost from the beginning, James Watt applied the fly-ball governor to regulate steam pressure in his engines and avoid explosions. Kelly adds, "The difference between a car and an exploding can of gasoline is that the car's information—its design—tames the brute energy of the gas."[12] Kelly's observation is important. Designing is not only *making things*. Designing is *adding information to things*. Designing is building-in what we have learned. In other words, designing is learning—a series of experiments, a trial-and-error process directed toward a goal, a *first-order* feedback loop.[13]

Many designers describe a four-step process: 1) analyzing the current situation; 2) framing the situation and representing it in a model; 3) reconfiguring the model to improve the situation; and 4) realizing the model in a tangible form—making something. This four-step process corresponds with organizational learning expert Ikujiro Nonaka's iterative model of "knowledge creation"—known as SECI—1) Socialization or "empathizing" (moving from tacit to tacit); 2) Externalization or "articulating" (moving from tacit to explicit); 3) Combination or "connecting" (moving from explicit to explicit); and 4) Internalization or "embodying" (moving from explicit back to tacit). The parallels between these models suggest that designing is creating knowledge and that design organizations are learning organizations.[14]

Chris Argyris, Stafford Beer, Peter Senge, and others describe organizations as systems that learn. Learning systems are *second order*; they don't merely achieve a pre-set goal, they also discover their own goals through conversations. When learning systems interact, they have "conversations" during which they learn from one another. Philosopher Donald Schön has described design as "a conversation with materials" and "a conversation with situations."[15] Architect Ranulph Glanville has described design as "conversation for action."[16]

The "conversations" that designers have help them learn—whether that means solving problems or facilitating agreement on goals—and then designers embody what they've learned in *things* they make. They connect ideas and *things*. That is, they *add information to things*.

The process of learning—of adding information to things—can be seen in the evolution of a product. Consider an example from the healthcare industry. The difference between a poison and an antidote is information. A drug is not merely a *molecular entity*; a drug is chemistry *plus* knowledge-in-action. In order to bring a drug to market, a producer must document its effectiveness and safety, indications and contra-indications, and potential interactions and other risks. This knowledge must be made explicit in a series of regulated documents—filings, package inserts, product data sheets, instructions for use, and packaging. In addition, the producer must have processes for ensuring quality components and quality manufacturing, and the producer must also have knowledge about stability of the compound and how it needs to be controlled during delivery.

New products rarely exist in isolation. Making a drug usable for patients often requires development of multiple *connected* systems:

- Systems for funding research and development, creating and protecting intellectual property, and rewarding investment
- The drug–knowledge–package system
- Compound sourcing, manufacturing, and distribution systems
- Drug delivery devices
- Systems for educating physicians and patients
- Systems for helping patients integrate the drug into their lives
- Insurance and government payment systems
- Government regulatory systems and professional association practices

Adding code to smart devices is another way to *add information*. Less obvious is that mechanical devices include code of their own—the gears in a mechanical watch are a sort of program, a pre-defined process. Even less obvious, the product's form and material represent accumulated knowledge—that is, *added information*. The product's very presence in the market likewise attests to knowledge learned—and *information added* to the network of systems in which any modern product is enmeshed.

From form giving to design thinking

For most of the twentieth century, design practice focused on artifacts—on *giving form to things*. Psychologist and designer Steve Wilcox tells of his first job at the venerable Herbst Lazar agency. His design team went to Ford to visit an engineering team; the person ushering them in opened the door and shouted, "The skinners are here."[17] "Skin" referred to the outside of the product—the surface that encloses it. In 2000, Apple CEO Steve Jobs challenged this view of design.

> In most people's vocabularies, design means veneer. It's interior decorating. It's the fabric of the curtains and the sofa. But to me, nothing could be further from the meaning of design. Design is the fundamental soul of a man-made creation that ends up expressing itself in successive outer layers of the product or service.[18]

Steve Jobs transformed popular perception of design. He connected design with cutting-edge technology and with serious business. He demonstrated that good design could make money. He saved Apple from bankruptcy and went on to create a series of iconic products—and the world's most valuable company.

The business world noticed. Apple became an exemplar—an "existence proof" that design could make a difference in business. Apple's success opened the door for *design thinking*—repositioning design from a service that delivered renderings to a business consulting practice that promised innovation. Bruce Nussbaum beat the drums at *Business Week*. IDEO demonstrated the idea on ABC's *Nightline*. Design thinking became so fashionable that the *Harvard Business Review* ran cover stories. Dean Roger Martin even re-organized the University of Toronto's Rotman School of Business around design thinking.

In a sense, design "dematerialized." Practice moved, to an extent, from *making things* to *making money* (an abstraction) or at least from *making things* to *creating value* (another abstraction). Practice likewise shifted focus from drawing things to discovering insights and turning them into innovations, and from *form giving* to *design thinking*.

This "dematerialization" process didn't happen overnight; it had been underway for a long time. Challenges to the frame of design as solely about *giving form to things* began to emerge in the late 1950s. The design school Hochschule für Gestaltung (HfG), Ulm, introduced students to semiotics and cybernetics. The design methods movement (a direct predecessor of the design thinking movement) focused on frameworks and processes. Political economist and computer scientist Herbert Simon described designing as a process that plays a role in all the professions. In the 1960s and 1970s, Scandinavian trade unions helped introduce participatory design.[19] Horst Rittel framed designing as building arguments. Later, Richard Buchanan, building on the work of Richard McKeon, framed designing as a form of rhetoric. Victor Papanek raised questions about "the moral responsibilities of the designer" and the problems of "shrouds ... appearance design, styling, or design 'cosmetics'."[20] Buckminster Fuller proposed "the comprehensive designer" as "an emerging synthesis of artist, inventor, mechanic, objective economist and evolutionary strategist."[21] Lucy Suchman, Rick Robinson, and others introduced ethnography to design practice. Robert Venturi and others prodded architects to consider context, meaning, and the vernacular. And Klaus Krippendorff, Michael McCoy, and others prodded designers to consider "product semantics."

Design work for the military, particularly on controls for jet aircraft, led to the study of human factors and ergonomics. It also led to the involvement of scientists in discourses about design. Psychologist James J. Gibson introduced the idea of affordances—"what [an environment] *offers* the animal, what it *provides* or *furnishes*."[22] Cognitive scientist Donald Norman brought Gibson's idea of affordances to the attention of designers, "Affordances provide strong clues to the operation of things. Plates are for pushing. Knobs are for turning. Slots are for inserting things into. Balls are for bouncing. When affordances are taken advantage of, the user knows what to do just by looking: no picture, label, or instruction is required."[23] Contemporary European philosophers, such as Asle Kiran and Peter-Paul Verbeek, have also begun to discuss affordances. They note that "what Heidegger calls the items' 'specific thingly character,' [is] a concept that roughly corresponds to affordance."[24]

Over the last fifty years, these ideas have entered design discourse, and some have seeped into design practice and design education. The contemporary mania for design thinking has also begun to bring these ideas to business. In the process, the designer's role has expanded from simply *making what's requested* to *participating in discussions about what should be made*. At a recent AIGA conference, the head of design for a large corporation lamented, "The worst part about my job is the politics." Yet, the designer's job *is*, in large part, politics. Design that matters has always been about coming to consensus on what matters—what we wish to conserve—and that's an essentially political question.

From applications to platforms

While commodification is bad news for the sector in which it occurs; it can be good news for other sectors. Google, for example, benefitted enormously from the commodification of the PC sector. Early internet services deployed large, expensive, special-purpose servers to handle high volumes of traffic. In 1999, Netscape (at the time by far the world's largest internet service) ran on just fifteen very large servers from Sun Microsystems (then the leading supplier of web servers). Just a few years later, Google took a very different tack, employing huge numbers of cheap personal computers. During "the internet bust" of 2000 Google quietly snapped up PCs from failed start-ups, paying pennies on the dollar and amassing a huge network.[25] Analysts estimate that Google's platform includes more than two million machines, and it continues to grow.[26]

Google's massive platform was a competitive advantage. Early in Google's development, its product managers and engineers were able to rely on Google's platform to quickly add capacity and launch new products almost overnight. Competitors like Apple, Microsoft, and Yahoo were slow to catch on to this change and what it meant.

Early on, Amazon founder Jeff Bezos recognized the need to take a connected systems approach to Amazon's internal applications. Former Amazon software architect Steve Yegge points out that:

> Amazon transformed internally into a service-oriented architecture ... SOA-driven design enables Platforms. Bezos realized long before the vast majority of Amazonians that Amazon needs to be a platform ... an extensible, programmable ... repurposable computing platform.[27]

Amazon's platform eventually became a product—Amazon Web Services (AWS). AWS runs many start-ups and several large, commercial services, including Airbnb, Flipboard, Netflix, Pinterest, and Redit. (What's more: some of the services running on AWS are themselves platforms. For example, Pinterest is a platform for sharing photos and other content.) Amazon's stock price has recently shot up as investors have begun to see the value of the AWS platform. According to Yegge, "A product is useless without a platform, or more precisely and accurately, a platform-less product will always be replaced by an equivalent platform-ized product."[28] Netscape founder and VC fund manager Marc Andreessen defines a *platform* as "a system that can be programmed and therefore customized by outside developers—users—and in that way, adapted to countless needs and niches that the platform's original developers could not have possibly contemplated, much less had time to accommodate."[29]

Smartphones are a classic example of platforms; Apple and other manufacturers leave a "space" in which third parties can build and sell add-ons—"apps." (The device maker is the first party; the device buyer is the second party; and app developers are the third parties.)

Platforms create value by creating opportunities for others to create value. Adding users makes the platform more attractive to developers. More developers mean more "apps." More apps mean more users, which makes the platform more attractive to developers. Each new user can make the platform more useful to all users. For example, Facebook becomes more interesting as more of your friends join.

What platforms really do is create frameworks for cooperation, and in so doing, they speed-up evolution.

From transactions to relationships

As *things* become more *connected*, they (and the systems in which they are enmeshed) are making it possible for producers and consumers to become more *connected*. Isolated transactions are giving way to on-going relationships. Even the formerly sharp line between producing and consuming is blurring.

In the *thing-focused* world of stand-alone products, the distinction between producer and consumer was clear, bridged only by a brief transaction—*the sale* of a thing. Both parties knew where they stood and stayed on their side.

In the emerging connected world of product-service ecologies, the distinction between producer and consumer is less clear. Services are co-created at the point of delivery; by definition, services require interaction between provider and user, often over an extended period. Thus, recognizing customers—remembering who they are, past interactions with them, and what they value—is becoming essential to organizations, just as it always has been essential for people to cooperate.

Once customers are recognized, relationships become possible. Organizations start to refer to customers as *members*. At first, this may be mostly aspiration. But the potential exists for membership to grow into a reality—for organizations to engage their members deeply in all aspects of their work. Engaging members—creating spaces in which relationships can grow—becomes a design task, a *thing* to be designed. These things are sometimes called engagement platforms; more generally, they are platforms for cooperation.

Organizations have always been subject to pressure from consumers. Recently, however, some are inverting this relationship, turning their organizations into platforms *through which* members can engage each other and sometimes work together for social change. The company Patagonia has explicitly embraced these transformations. Patagonia began by designing things, developing a new outlook on climbing gear and outdoor clothing. As the company grew, founder Yvon Chouinard became concerned about his suppliers' material sourcing and labor practices. He has worked to reform Patagonia's systems for qualifying vendors—and the vendors' systems. He's also shared what he's learned, and worked to reform the apparel industry, developing partnerships, associations, and training and certification programs. Patagonia has also taken strong positions on environmental issues and enlisted the support of its customers.[30] More recently, Patagonia has sought to engage its customers through on-line and mobile membership programs, repair services, corporate philanthropy, and sharing stories; some of its programs even encourage members to buy fewer products.

The larger context

The Economist forecasts that by 2020, more than fifty billion devices will connect to the internet.[31] That's quite a gathering of things, people, and information. It will change the economy and social structures, and it will transform design practice.

Recently, MIT Media Lab Director Joi Ito summed up how design is changing:

> Design has also evolved from the design of objects both physical and immaterial, to the design of systems, to the design of complex adaptive systems. This evolution is shifting the

role of designers; they are no longer the central planner, but rather participants within the systems they exist in. This is a fundamental shift—one that requires a new set of values.[32]

The fundamental shift that Ito mentions extends beyond designing; it is part of a larger cultural shift, from the Age of Enlightenment to "the Age of Entanglement" (as Thinking Machines co-founder Danny Hillis calls it).[33] Like the paradigm shift from the medieval, mystical view of the world to the rational Enlightenment view, this new paradigm is a fundamental change in how we explain the world. The Enlightenment replaced "unseen spirit forces" as explanation with "empirical evidence" as explanation—"A" causes "B", and "B" causes "C". The framework of "direct causality" has been spectacularly successful in improving the human condition, but it tends to view parts of the world in isolation, rather than taking a whole systems view. And over the last century, methods that rely on controlling single variables have run into challenges, as the leading edge of technology moves increasingly to complex, multivariate problems.

As linguist George Lakoff notes, in some ways, the frame of "direct causality" may hold us back and even create problems, for example, ignoring "externalities" such as those that stem from burning carbon-based fuels. The emerging frames of the Age of Entanglement embrace more complex notions of causality, such as cell signaling pathways, quorum sensing, and networks of feedback loops. "A" causes not only "B" but also a cascade of other effects, some of which loop back to cause "A"—what Lakoff calls "systemic causality."[34]

Designing systems, platforms, and product-service ecologies requires us to "connect things"—to think and act in terms of whole systems. Likewise, the problems that really matter—the many wicked problems society faces—require us all to "gather together" and connect people and things, ideas and artifacts, products and services, hardware and software, and thinking and doing. They require us to design relationships—and to design platforms in which others can design relationships.

Notes

1. Christopher Alexander (1964), *Notes in the Synthesis of Form*, Cambridge, MA: Harvard University Press.
2. Lenovo website http://shop.lenovo.com/us/en/desktops/#facet-1=1 (accessed December 27, 2015).
3. B. Joseph Pine and J. H. Gilmore (1998), "Welcome to the Experience Economy," *Harvard Business Review*, July–August. https://hbr.org/1998/07/welcome-to-the-experience-economy (accessed April 16, 2016).
4. *Edmunds, 2013 Car Shopping Trends Report*, PDF http://static.ed.edmunds-media.com/unversioned/img/industry-center/car-shopping-trends/QuarterlyReport_FINAL2.pdf (accessed April 16, 2016).
5. Kevin Kelly (1994), *Out of Control: The New Biology of Machines, Social Systems, and the Economic World*, 27, Reading, MA: Addison-Wesley.
6. Jodi Forlizzi, unpublished manuscript, via personal correspondence with the author.
7. "Amazon's Tablet Leads to Its Store," *The New York Times*, September 28, 2011, B1.
8. Ian Hodder (2012), *Entangled: An Archaeology of the Relationships between Humans and Things*, 7, Hoboken, NJ: John Wiley & Sons.
9. Gordon Pask (1969), "The Architectural Relevance of Cybernetics," *Architectural Design*, 494.

10   Tim Misner (2009), "Building Support for Use-Based Design into Hardware Products," *Interactions*, ACM 16 (5), September + October.

11   Jim Motavalli, "The Dozens of Computers That Make Modern Cars Go (and Stop)" *New York Times,* February 4, 2010. http://www.nytimes.com/2010/02/05/technology/05electronics.html (accessed April 16, 2016).

12   Kevin Kelly (1994), *Out of Control: The New Biology of Machines, Social Systems, and the Economic World,* 115, Reading, MA: Addison-Wesley.

13   Horst Rittel (2010), *The Universe of Design* (a series of lectures given at UC Berkeley in 1963, reprinted by Routledge.

14   Hugh Dubberly and Shelley Evenson (2011), "Design as Learning—or 'Knowledge Creation'—the SECI Model," *Interactions*, ACM 18 (1), January + February.

15   Donald Schön (1982), *The Reflective Practitioner: How Professionals Think in Action*, New York: Basic Books.

16   Hugh Dubberly and Paul Pangaro (2015), "Cybernetics and Design: Conversations for Action," *Cybernetics & Human Knowing* 22 (2–3): 73–82.

17   Personal conversation between the author and Steve Wilcox, July 10, 2015.

18   Steve Jobs (2000), "Apple's One-Dollar-a-Year Man," *Fortune*, January 24. http://archive.fortune.com/magazines/fortune/fortune_archive/2000/01/24/272277/index.htm (accessed April 16, 2016).

19   Liz Sanders (2008), "An Evolving Map of Design Practice and Design Research," *ACM Interactions* 15 (6), November + December.

20   Victor Papanek (1971), *Design for the Real World: Human Ecology and Social Change,* 41, New York: Pantheon.

21   Buckminster Fuller (1969), *Ideas and Integrities: A Spontaneous Autobiographical Disclosure*, New York: Macmillan.

22   James J. Gibson (1971), "The Theory of Affordances," *The Ecological Approach to Visual Perception,* Chapter 8, New York: Psychology Press.

23   Donald A. Norman (1988), The Psychology of Everyday Things, 9, New York: Basic Books.

24   Asle H. Kiran and Peter-Paul Verbeek (2010), "Trusting Our Selves to Technology", *Knowledge, Technology & Policy* 23: 409–27.

25   Personal conversation between the author and an early Google executive.

26   James Pearn calculated that Google would have more than 2,375,000 servers by early 2013. By now the number could be substantially higher https://plus.google.com/+JamesPearn/posts/VaQu9sNxJuY (accessed April 16, 2016).

27   Yegge, Steve, "Google Platform Rant," https://plus.google.com/+RipRowan/posts/eVeouesvaVX (accessed April 16, 2016).

28   Ibid.

29   Marc Andreessen, "The Three Kinds of Platform You Meet On The Internet," (personal blog post, September 16, 2007) http://pmarchive.com/three_kinds_of_platforms_you_meet_on_the_internet.html (accessed April 16, 2016).

30   Yvon Chouinard and Vincent Stanley (2012), *The Responsible Company,* Ventura: Patagonia Books.

31   "Home, Hacked Home: The Perils of Connected Devices," *The Economist*, July 12, 2014 http://www.economist.com/news/special-report/21606420-perils-connected-devices-home-hacked-home (accessed April 16, 2016).

32 Joi Ito, "Design and Science," http://www.pubpub.org/pub/designandscience (accessed January 31, 2016).
33 Danny Hillis (2010), "The Age of Digital Entanglement," *Scientific American;* September, 303 (3): 93.
34 George Lakoff, "Why Trump?" March 2, 2016 https://georgelakoff.com/2016/03/02/why-trump/#more-4935 (accessed on April 9, 2016).

Bibliography

Alexander, C. (1964), *Notes in the Synthesis of Form*, Cambridge, MA: Harvard University Press.
Andreessen, M. (2007), "The Three Kinds of Platform You Meet on the Internet," personal blog post, September 16, 2007 http://pmarchive.com/three_kinds_of_platforms_you_meet_on_the_internet.html (accessed April 16, 2016).
Chouinard, Y. and V. Stanley (2012), *The Responsible Company*, Ventura: Patagonia Books.
Dubberly, H. and S. Evenson (2011), "Design as Learning—or 'Knowledge Creation'—the SECI Model," *Interactions* 18 (1): 75–9.
Dubberly, H. and P. Pangaro (2015), "Cybernetics and Design: Conversations for Action," *Cybernetics & Human Knowing* 22 (2–3): 73–82.
"Home, Hacked Home: The Perils of Connected Devices," *The Economist*, July 12, 2014 http://www.economist.com/news/special-report/21606420-perils-connected-devices-home-hacked-home (accessed April 16, 2016).
Edmunds, 2013 Car Shopping Trends Report http://static.ed.edmunds-media.com/unversioned/img/industry-center/car-shopping-trends/QuarterlyReport_FINAL2.pdf (accessed April 16, 2016).
Forlizzi, J. (2011), "Amazon's Tablet Leads to Its Store," *New York Times*, September 28, B1.
Fuller, B. (1969), *Ideas and Integrities: A Spontaneous Autobiographical Disclosure*, New York: Macmillan.
Gibson, J. J. (1971), "The Theory of Affordances," in *The Ecological Approach to Visual Perception*, New York: Psychology Press.
Hillis, D. (2010), "The Age of Digital Entanglement," *Scientific American* 303 (3) (September): 93.
Hodder, I. (2012), *Entangled: An archaeology of the Relationships between Humans and Things*, New York: Wiley.
Ito, J. "Design and Science" http://www.pubpub.org/pub/designandscience (accessed January 31, 2016).
Jobs, S., "Apple's One-Dollar-a-Year Man," *Fortune*, January 24, 2000 http://archive.fortune.com/magazines/fortune/fortune_archive/2000/01/24/272277/index.htm (accessed April 16, 2016).
Kelly, K. (1994), *Out of Control: The New Biology of Machines, Social Systems, and the Economic World*, Reading, MA: Addison-Wesley.
Kiran, A. H. and P-P. Verbeek (2010), "Trusting Our Selves to Technology", *Knowledge, Technology & Policy* 23: 409–27.
Lakoff, G., "Why Trump?" March 2, 2016. https://georgelakoff.com/2016/03/02/why-trump/#more-4935 (accessed on April 9, 2016).
Lenovo website http://shop.lenovo.com/us/en/desktops/#facet-1=1 (accessed December 27, 2015).
Misner, T. (2009), "Building Support for Use-Based Design into Hardware Products," *Interactions* 16 (5): 58–64.
Motavalli, J. (2010), "The Dozens of Computers That Make Modern Cars Go (and Stop)" *New York Times*, February 4 http://www.nytimes.com/2010/02/05/technology/05electronics.html (accessed April 16, 2016).
Norman, D. A. (1988), *The Psychology of Everyday Things*, New York: Basic Books.
Pask, G. (1969), "The Architectural Relevance of Cybernetics," *Architectural Design*: 494–6.

Papanek, V. (1971), *Design for the Real World: Human Ecology and Social Change*, New York: Pantheon.
Pearn, J., Google https://plus.google.com/+JamesPearn/posts/VaQu9sNxJuY (accessed April 16, 2016).
Pine, B. J. and J. H. Gilmore (1998), "Welcome to the Experience Economy," *Harvard Business Review*, July–August https://hbr.org/1998/07/welcome-to-the-experience-economy (accessed April 16, 2016).
Rittel, H. (2010), *The Universe of Design*, a series of lectures given at UC Berkeley in 1963, reprint London: Routledge.
Sanders, L. (2008), "An Evolving Map of Design Practice and Design Research," *Interactions* 15 (6): 13–17.
Schön, D. (1982), *The Reflective Practitioner: How Professionals Think in Action*, New York: Basic Books.
Steve Wilcox, personal conversation between the author, July 10, 2015.
Yegge, S., "Google Platform Rant" https://plus.google.com/+RipRowan/posts/eVeouesvaVX (accessed April 16, 2016).

13

Designing things as "poor" substitutes

Carl Knappett

Close encounters of the third kind

If we are "encountering things" in this volume, then let me start by introducing readers to three things that they may not have previously encountered. They are all anthropomorphic male figurines from a Bronze Age site in east Crete (Greece) called Palaikastro, and hence c. 4,000 years old. The first two figurines come from the peak sanctuary above the town—a peak sanctuary is an open-air shrine that was located on top of a mountain. This peak sanctuary, Petsophas, would have been visited by the inhabitants of the town, which sat at the foot of the mountain—and quite regularly, judging by the large numbers of objects found there, which would have been brought by pilgrims as part of the cult activities performed in the sanctuary. We do not know what deities were worshipped, and there do not appear to be any representations thereof. What we do see, in particular, are hundreds if not thousands of these small figurines—often of everyday domesticated animals, such as sheep, goats, cattle, and pigs, as well as both male and female human forms. These figurines appear to have played some role in cult practices designed to evoke the deity to be worshipped.

This first figurine, made of clay, is quite simple (Figure 13.1). It is miniature, small enough to be held in the palm of the hand and in a "symmetrical hands to torso gesture" (Morris 2009: 183). Typically this figurine is interpreted as being a worshipper or adorant.

The second figurine is also male, made of clay, and at a comparable miniature scale (Figure 13.2). It shares with the first the same symmetrical hands to torso gesture. There is a little more detail in the modeling, and the addition of a dagger and loincloth at the waist. We also see a base on which the figure stands.

Our third male representation is usually called a figure rather than a figurine (Figure 13.1), as it is not at miniature scale, being quite a bit larger at c. 50 cm tall. It has the exact same symmetrical hands to torso gesture (Figure 13.3), and it, too, was probably set on a base. It seemingly also had a loincloth rendered in gold (MacGillivray et al. 2000). The similarities stop there, though. It was not made of clay, but of ivory, gold and stone, and hence is a composite figure, quite unlike the clay figurines. Moreover, two of these materials, the ivory and the gold, were exotic imports from the Near East, whereas the clay was abundantly available locally. And it was not found on the peak sanctuary, but in a house in the town. It is further marked out as different from the figurines in Figures 13.1 and 13.2 by its astonishing detail, with expertly

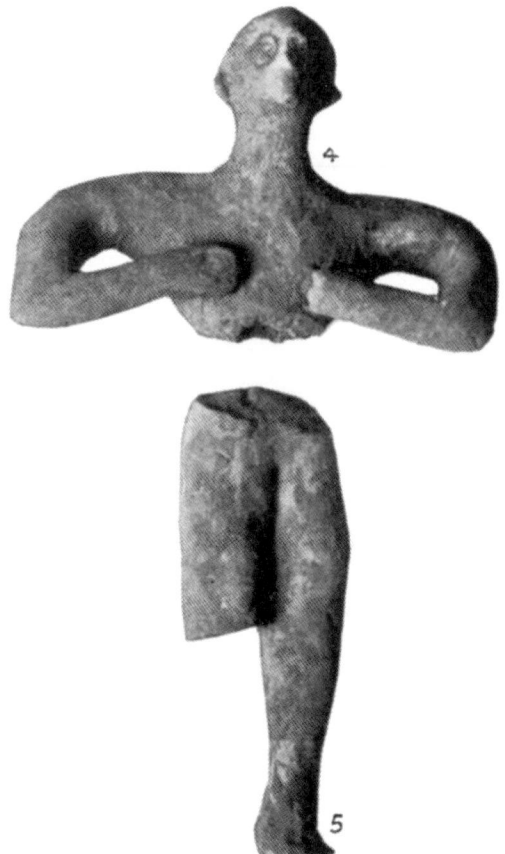
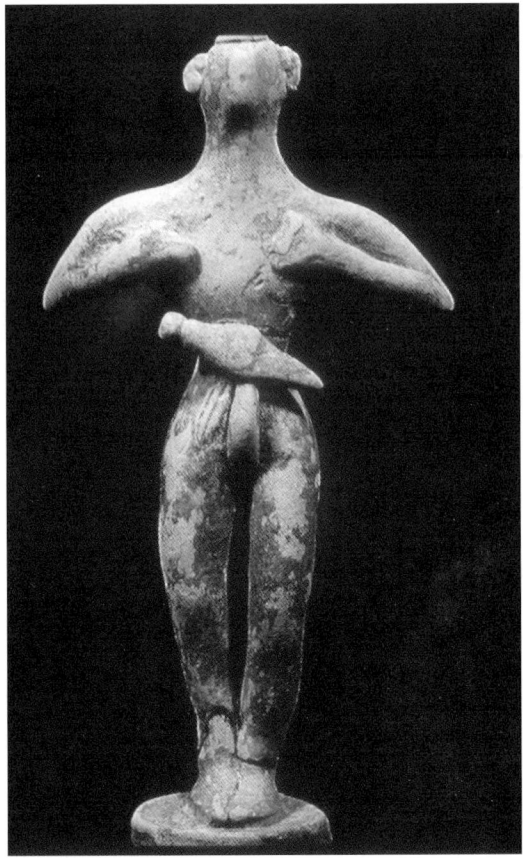

FIGURE 13.1 Male figurine from Petsophas (from Bosanquet et al. 1902–3, pl. X, 4–5). Reproduced with permission of the British School at Athens.

FIGURE 13.2 Male figurine from Petsophas. Reproduced with permission of the British School at Athens.

rendered veins on the forearms (Figure 13.4). It has been dubbed the "Palaikastro kouros" (MacGillivray et al. 2000). Unlike the clay figurines, though, it is not interpreted as a worshipper or adorant, but rather as a young god—due to its scale, exquisite materials, and stunning detail.

Figurines as substitutes

What kinds of "things" are these three figures? While they have a lot in common—their gender, gesture, and provenance—they differ in scale, materials, and detailing. Quite simply, the first two figurines are relatively "crude," their modeling in clay requiring relatively little time or expertise, while the third figure is highly refined, demanding a great deal of time, planning and skill in its creation. How can we explain such different approaches to what looks like the same kind of thing—a male figure in symmetrical hands to torso gesture?

We should start with what these things were used for. As outlined above, the figurines were found on a peak sanctuary, which we can assert with a high degree of confidence was a site

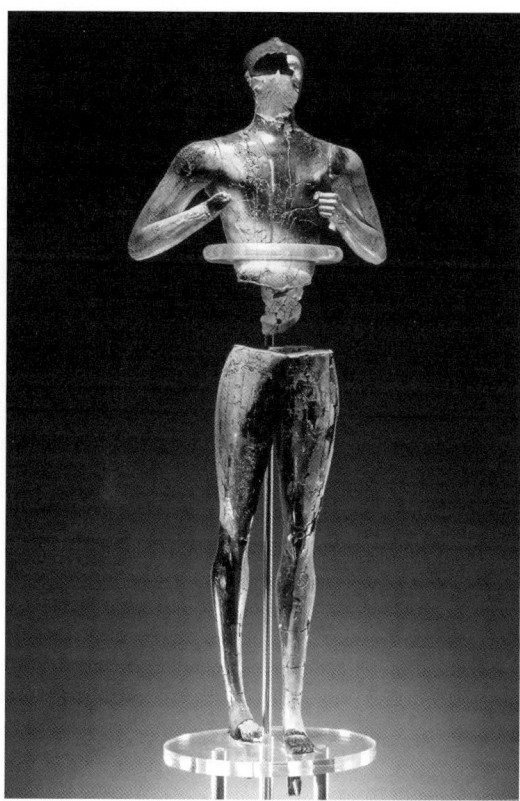

FIGURE 13.3 The Palaikastro kouros (see MacGillivray et al. 2000). Reproduced with permission of the British School at Athens.

dedicated to religious ceremonies. As we are talking about the Bronze Age, which in this part of the world is a time before any historical documents, our understanding of the religion in question is necessarily circumscribed—there is debate, for example, as to whether it was mono- or polytheistic (see Gulizio and Nakassis 2014). So we do not know precisely how the figurines were used in cult practice, though their small size and low value suggest they could quite readily have been carried up to the peak for some kind of ceremony, and then deposited there. What do they represent? Most scholars think it unlikely that they are representations of deities, but rather believe that they are representations of the worshippers. Indeed, Minoan deities seem very rarely to be directly represented in cult practice. Instead, they are indicated indirectly—as if to invite their appearance through epiphany. Whether the figurines strengthened the presence of the worshippers, or continued to stand in for them during their absence (once the worshippers had left the peak), we can understand them as *substitutes*. More generally, in numerous cases in prehistory it seems as if figurines served this kind of purpose, as simple, miniature presences standing in for absent beings in a variety of ways (Bailey 2005).

As for the ivory figure dubbed the "kouros," this was found within the settlement of Palaikastro, rather than on its peak sanctuary. Nonetheless, it is believed to have been housed in a small town shrine and so to have a cultic (and not a domestic) context. This figure, despite sharing gender and gesture with the clay figurines, is interpreted as a male deity rather than a worshipper (MacGillivray et al. 2000)—thanks to its exotic materials, exquisite craftsmanship,

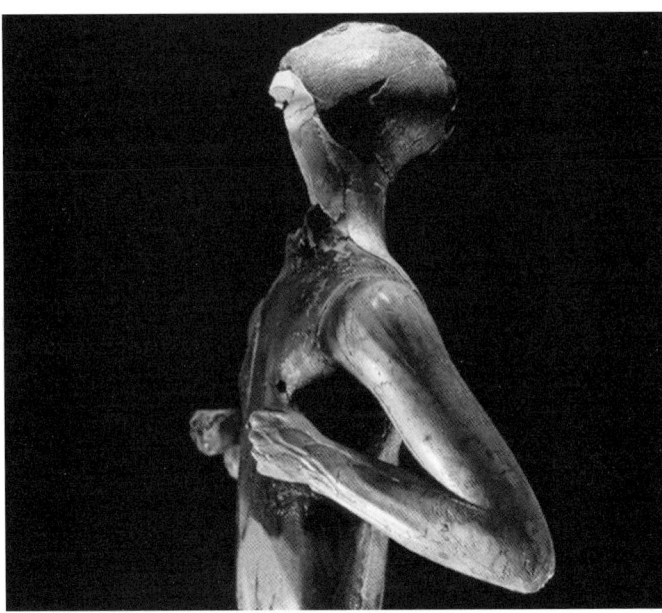

FIGURE 13.4 Detail of the Palaikastro kouros. Reproduced with permission of the British School at Athens.

and relative scale. Even if standing for a deity rather than a worshipper, or indeed a priest—and this is an interpretation rather than fact—it is still doing similar "work" to the figurines as a *substitute*.

If this hypothesis holds water—that both figurines and figure are forms of material substitute—then what we are seeing are quite different strategies for substitution. On the one hand, we have the very simple, humble forms of the figurines, and on the other, the exquisite figure of the kouros. Is it justifiable to say that the figure is a more successful substitute, being more life-like, and altogether more awe-inspiring? Can we say that this figure is a well-conceived and well-designed substitute, while the figurines are sloppy, haphazard—indeed "poor" substitutes?

This rather depends on what one means by "design." According to one oft-cited definition, design is "the human power of conceiving, planning, and making products that serve human beings in the accomplishment of their individual and collective purposes" (Buchanan 2001: 9). If we apply this definition to the ivory figure, then we certainly seem to be faced with an artifact that required considerable powers of "conceiving" and "planning." For instance, planning would surely have been necessary to acquire the raw materials themselves, with the hippopotamus ivory and gold both probably sourced from Egypt. The composite nature of the figure—with ivory having to dovetail with the stone, and gold having to be applied over ivory—also suggests a high degree of planning. Furthermore, the figure may have been carved and assembled with the help of a template, as the body appears to be divisible into an Egyptian grid of eighteen units (Weingarten 2000). Finally, the exquisite detail in the veining on the arms and feet, and in the carving of the hairstyle in stone, might also mark this out as a carefully conceived object—although it is also imaginable that some of these details emerged in the process of making itself, which we should of course recognize as an integral component of design (without necessarily going so far as to suggest that design and making are the same thing—see Ingold 2013: 70). As for the other side of the equation in Buchanan's definition—the accomplishment of purpose—we might well imagine that the figure's representational completeness is a positive design outcome that accomplishes the goal of creating an apt substitute for a deity. With heightened realism as something we have come to expect as a goal of much Western pre-modern art—and its desired effect of eliciting awe and wonder among the viewer (see Gell 1998 for this perspective on the effects of art)—the figure fits comfortably within orthodox expectations for an artwork. Surely it is such orthodox expectations that have also influenced its contemporary interpretation as a deity—what mortal figure could possibly demand such attention and planning?

In stark contrast to the kouros, the small clay figurines of the kind we show here are invariably characterized as "crude" or "roughly made" (Morris 2009: 181; Zeimbekis 2004: 360). This characterization could suggest that such figurines are somehow incomplete or lacking, as if they barely succeed in communicating to a viewer what they represent. A common accusation is that a child could have made them (or actually did). And the corollary of this assessment in design terms, following Buchanan's definition, is that they do not show much of the human power for conceiving and planning. That they are so common further adds to the sense of these figurines being rapidly churned out with little attention to detail—there are thousands known from peak sanctuaries across the island of Crete, and all of them show the same minimal level of detail. Animal figurines are common too, though one animal species can be hard to tell from another, to the extent that one can go little further than identifying them as quadrupeds. Whether human or animal, they may be considered nothing more than "poor" substitutes.

There is another way we might grasp these figurines, however, without belittling them as crude and unplanned—and that is to again turn to the second part of Buchanan's definition, i.e., the accomplishment of purpose. What if "crude and unplanned" actually contributes positively to the accomplishment of purpose? Many thousands of these figurines display a very consistent pattern of depicting human worshippers in miniature in clay, and with very little detail. Their simplicity is hardly accidental, no more so than the simplicity of the thousands of figurines in the modern art installation *Field for the British Isles* by Antony Gormley was accidental (mentioned in Morris 2009: 179). Interestingly, Gormley enlisted hundreds of volunteers to make these figurines, with very loose instructions: "the pieces were to be hand-sized and easy to hold, the eyes were to be deep and close, and the proportions of the head to the body roughly correct."[1] Therefore, each figurine was as "unplanned" as possible. The onus was on the individual volunteer just to *make*.[2] And when exhibited together in the thousands, these assembled figurines had a considerable visual and emotional impact that was perhaps hard to fathom, but which was no less striking than any single exquisite artwork, despite the crudeness of the individual pieces. Miniatures in many different contexts are quite capable of eliciting awe (see Mack 2007). Cretan peak sanctuary figurines are also often grouped together in numbers when exhibited in museum displays, and this combination of reduced scale, assembled numbers and "crude" individual form can, like the Gormley installation, have a powerful effect on viewers.

How can "poor" substitutes then have such impact? We might seek an answer to this by picking up on an interesting comment offered by Gormley regarding his *Field* project. He has described the clay figurines in *Field* as "body-surrogates."[3] What I would like to do here is link his notion of figurines as surrogates to some ideas from philosophy of mind on "material surrogacy" (Clark 2010).

Substitutes as surrogates

Philosopher Andy Clark develops a particular definition of surrogacy, or what he calls "surrogate situations," by which he means "any kind of real-world structure that is used to stand in for, or take the place of, some aspect of a certain 'target situation'" (Clark 2010: 24). Such tools are necessary because it is difficult for the human mind to grasp the conceptual—a key tenet of the extended mind hypothesis is that human cognition works most efficiently when it can piggy-back on the structure already in the world, using the world "as its own best model."[4] Let us take a simple target situation, one discussed by Clark—a child being given the "target" of locating a toy in a room. What kind of "surrogate situation" might help a child achieve this goal most effectively? According to the research on symbolic functioning in toddlers that Clark cites (DeLoach 1991), children understood certain sets of instructions about a particular goal (like locating a toy in a room), much better when the models that were used in instruction were simpler rather than richer. Apparently, the more "realistic" the detail, the less able the child is to understand the model as a symbol—he or she reacts to too many of the other affordances for action and interpretation offered by the more detailed model. So, in such cases, a model works better when it is has less detail and is more abstracted. As a result, Clark identifies two important features of surrogate situations: "the way they highlight key features by suppressing concrete detail … and … the way they relax temporal constraints on reasoning" (Clark 2010: 25). Though loss of detail need not tally with reduction in scale, often the two do co-occur: and together they serve to create a kind of incompleteness in an artifact that can positively enhance the cognitive task at hand.

Clark extends from this simple target situation to more complex ones—such as designing a building. A building that is as yet unrealized is often evoked through the use of a material surrogate, such as an architectural model. Clark cites the work of Henrik Gedenryd (1998), who documented many different ways in which designers use surrogate situations, such as prototypes, sketches, or storyboards. These (and many other) techniques are all used as steps towards the eventual realization of an outcome that, once materialized, will render the mock-ups redundant. Further insight on the different ways in which architectural models work comes from Mark Morris (2006). He describes "sketch models," too, while also using the term "process models," which "can be grouped together as seeming unfinished, fragmentary, serial and materially slipshod" (Morris 2006: 40). He is also at pains to highlight the important role played by reduction in scale. Citing Lévi-Strauss (1962), he states that scale models allow one to grasp the object as a whole right away—whereas with a "real" object one has to come to terms with the entity bit by bit, before coming to know the object as a totality. In other words, the scale model enables "a fundamentally different way of coming to know something" (Morris 2006: 11). And as a result, he suggests, a model's reduction of scale, and often detail, creates a very fruitful gap between the real and the reduced—and this gap "is one of the chief ways into architectural concepts" (2006: 12). His argument, too, like that of Gedenryd, is that model-making is a key step or moment in the creative process. Even if temporarily hard to imagine, the target situations, i.e., the buildings to be completed, are fundamentally realizable—and long before this point, the sketch or prototype becomes somewhat redundant, though having been a key part of the process.

Surrogates/models for the immaterial

But what of those target situations which are not only distal and absent in that moment of "design," but also ultimately intractable? Here we might further follow Clark's line of reasoning, which takes him towards the supernatural, and the role of religious artifacts in surrogate situations—which is where his approach becomes directly relevant to our concerns in this essay. Religious artifacts are rarely conceived as being able to deliver access to the divine—they are never going to be successful prototypes or mock-ups, because that which they are trying to evoke is fundamentally ineffable and unreachable. That does not mean, however, that the divine is utterly unapproachable—the idea being, surely, to reach part way towards the divine. Clark cites the work of Matthew Day (2004), suggesting that when anchored in religious artifacts, divine concepts that are difficult to process in the abstract may become more tractable. Ironically, current scholarship on materiality often fails to grasp that much of the significance of materiality lies in its relations with immateriality (Rose 2011). Rose's example of the materiality of the church is worth citing here:

> Like the name of God itself, the church reverberates and circulates around something that cannot be captured. The church is not built to attest and announce the presence of God—that would be impossible. Rather, what the church stands for is God's absence. It is because God is absent that the church is present. This is not to say that God is dead but that God resists presence, i.e. God resists appearing within the orbit of beings that can be comprehended, understood and/or rendered knowable. The church is a marker of God because God resists presence; it is because God fails to appear, fails to be available to mortal vision, that the church is built. (Rose 2011: 118)

The church "stands for" that which resists presence. In the reasoning of Day (2004), the church offers a tractable means for at least partially accessing the divine. A very similar idea has also been put forward by ancient historian Jean-Pierre Vernant (1991), and we may usefully quote him here:

> In the context of religious thought, every form of figuration must introduce an inevitable tension: the idea is to establish real contact with the world beyond, to actualize it, to make it present and thereby to participate intimately in the divine; yet by the same move, it must also emphasize what is inaccessible and mysterious in divinity, its alien quality, its otherness. (Vernant 1991: 153)

So, when figuration (and perhaps many other kinds of representation) is used to evoke the absent, the immaterial, and the unattainable, it should be done in such a way as to provide some handle on the absent and otherworldly, such as a particular deity, without ever suggesting that the otherworldly will ever be fully grasped. Some mystery must inevitably remain. If an artifact of whatever kind incorporates some recognition of this dilemma, then it is in some way more effective or more real than one that is oblivious to the mystery.

By considering our Bronze Age figurines as religious artifacts in much the same way, then we might also be justified in treating them as having a substitutional role within "surrogate situations," with worshippers using them as a material means for evoking their deities.

But to what extent can we properly liken such substitutions to the way that an architectural model operates in the process of design? As mentioned above, this is what Clark suggests, in drawing on the work of Gedenryd—that such models are often operating as surrogates. But is not a model of this kind quite different? Are not prototypes, sketches or storyboards acting as steps in a process towards some final product, whereas things like churches and figurines *are* finished products? One might imagine this to be a key difference, but Clark downplays such a distinction, to the extent that not just sketches but also finished products are treated together as models, if they are deemed to be cognitive supports towards some further goal. Clark's radical formulation moves us beyond treating models, prototypes and mock-ups as geared only towards achievable cognitive tasks that can be readily measured in terms of their success. As Malafouris (2013: 85) has pointed out, such a view of models risks depicting the mind as limited only to harnessing the external world as a series of props for information processing. When we start trying to include the religious artifacts that Day insists upon in his study, and the figurines we are focussed on here, then we have to include within our conception of "model" those surrogates that have some unrealizable, "immaterial" goal in mind, aimed at opening up a path to intangible and intractable religious concepts.

Crude is not poor

So if we now return to the question of why the peak sanctuary figurines are such "poor" substitutes, we might argue that a figurine *should* fail in representing an intractable deity, and that in such failure lies its success. The figurine should only point in the general direction of the otherworldly. It is thus like a mock-up in a surrogate situation—which works better when incomplete and with reduced detail. If "design" is even appropriate—and perhaps we should think more in terms of the processes of making unfolding irrespective of design intent (Ingold 2013)—the goal ought to be incompleteness. What I think is interesting to stress is how the label of "poor" substitute ascribed to crude miniatures actually then becomes a very positive attribute. So a model can function as a powerful cognitive aid to creativity by not being "perfect"—because perfection would mean an inability to comprehend the whole before the parts (see Lévi-Strauss 1962).

The crude or roughly made quality of the peak sanctuary figurines is thus an effective strategy of incompleteness to support religious thinking. All that the figurines have to do is contribute to the evocation, perhaps in a ceremony of epiphany, of the deity or deities. Moreover, the figurines may well have functioned as part of an assemblage, with a number of other small figurines, miniature vessels, and even an architectural model, creating a shrine microcosm. And so the onus of representational completeness would have been even less relevant to the individual figurine. It is also interesting to note that in Minoan religion there seem to be very few actual representations of deities, as if a direct image would be far too powerful and potentially dangerous. Rather, we see many different forms of indirect imagery through religious artifacts that only evoke a supernatural presence indirectly.[5] This indirectness and incompleteness is important because, as we noted above in the quotes from both Vernant and Rose, the divine must remain elusive and intangible. The different ways in which the materialities of Minoan cult open up a space for approaching the divine do all seem quite sensitive to the ultimate impossibility of ever attaining full access to the otherworldly. On one rare occasion when we do come across a detailed figurative representation of what might be a deity—i.e., the Palaikastro kouros—it attracts a violent reaction. This is something of a one-off occurrence for Bronze Age Crete, though there are of course many other cases of such iconoclasm in other contexts. In the Palaikastro case, its exquisite "completeness" may have brought it too close to the divine, at least in the eyes of those who violently destroyed it. Archaeologists recovered the figure's legs well inside the building, while its upper body was found scattered in tiny pieces in the small open area or court just outside the building (MacGillivray et al. 2000). The building was destroyed by a very severe fire, as was the entire settlement, and indeed almost all other settlements across the island of Crete at this time. Therefore, the archaeologists who excavated this figure saw its destruction as irrefutably tied to these destructive events; and the findspots—the places where the different parts of the figure were found—strongly suggest that someone had held the figure by the legs, smashed it against the threshold of the building, causing the upper body to break into tiny pieces and scatter across the court, before the legs were then tossed into the burning building (MacGillivray et al. 2000).

The fate of the Palaikastro kouros reminds us that emotion and belief also play a role in cognition. The line between completeness and incompleteness is not just determined by cognitive efficacy, but also by a *feeling* of how far it is acceptable to push the limits of presentation towards representation. Even within the same religion, some individuals or groups may feel that a lack of representation opens a more direct path to the divine. This is discussed by Engelke (2007) in his ethnographic study of the materiality of Bibles in apostolic Christianity in West Africa. Do Bibles help one approach God, or are they a distraction from the direct presence of God, experienced without the intervening clutter of materiality? From a cognitive standpoint, according to Day (2004), we might more commonly expect to see extensive use of religious artifacts for accessing the otherworldly, rather than their exclusion; the scenario presented by Engelke may then result from a reaction to material excesses. Presumably both the producers and the destroyers of the Palaikastro kouros shared the same Minoan "religion," and yet they may have had differing views on the appropriateness of this degree of completeness in representation.

Additional insights on incompleteness and completeness are found in Bille et al.'s (2010) fascinating edited volume on the "anthropology of absence." They oblige us to think seriously about presence and absence not as "two antonymic categories" (Bille et al. 2010: 4), but rather as having a much more ambiguous interdependency. Indeed one very relevant point that emerges from their treatment is that often absence emerges from presence in unexpected ways. If the absence created by death creates longing, then this feeling may be triggered by all kinds of everyday objects that certainly were not designed to act in that way. These objects have come to carry an emotional charge simply because of their material presence in the face of absence. We cannot reduce everything to intention in design, because things of course can have long and complex biographies. Things do not always do as we want or expect (Brown 2003).

Conclusion

Perhaps we too readily judge the merits of an artifact according to an unspoken criterion of representational completeness. An artifact that fulfills this criterion, like the Palaikastro kouros, is often assumed to be well designed, that is, made with forethought. But the flipside of this is that the "crude" clay figurines discussed above are considered incomplete, slipshod, and hence poorly designed. However, this attitude towards the crudely made neglects the utility of the incomplete—as in sketch models—in cognitive processing. A reduction in scale and detail can prove very useful in "surrogate situations." Indeed, in such situations, the external prop (i.e., model or substitute) should offer something complementary to internal mental processes (Rowlands 2010). From the perspective of situated cognition, and especially the extended mind, the thing is only one part of a system. It should then follow that the most effective artifact would be the one that best exploits the properties of the world to enable human thought and action. If we accept this proposition, then an artifact that supports action not only *need* not be representationally complete in order to be considered effective, but *ought* not to be. As it is the integrated internal-external cognitive system that has to function, it is the completeness of the design of the *system, not any individual part of it,* that should be "measured." In this light, the simple clay figurines may then very easily be viewed as more effective kinds of thing (in surrogate situations) than the detailed ivory figure.

Acknowledgments

My thanks go to Prasad Boradkar and Leslie Atzmon for the invitation to contribute to this volume, and for comments on an earlier draft. Dr. Quentin Letesson, Cristina Ichim and Rachel Dewan also all kindly provided feedback. I am grateful to the British School at Athens for permission to reproduce the images in Figures 13.1–13.4.

Notes

1. See http://www.tate.org.uk/whats-on/tate-liverpool/exhibition/antony-gormley-testing-world-view-field-british-isles (accessed December 27, 2014).
2. On this distinction between designing and making, see Ingold (2013).
3. See http://www.antonygormley.com/projects/item-view/id/245#p0 (accessed December 27, 2014).
4. In philosophy of mind, significant moves have been made in the last two decades in the domain of "situated cognition" (Robbins and Aydede 2009). Although this includes both embodied and embedded cognition, it is the more radical version, "extended mind," which is most apposite here. Advocates of this "active externalism" (Clark and Chalmers 1998; Clark 1997) contend that artifacts typically considered as external to the mind can in many circumstances actually be partially constitutive of cognitive processes. The original and oft-cited example is that of "Otto's notebook." Clark and Chalmers argued that if "Otto," who has Alzheimer's, needs his notebook in order to find his way around, and if the information in his notebook is trusted, reliable and accessible, then it is as much constitutive of his cognitive process as would be any "internal" mental mechanisms achieving the same goal. So, the mind "extends" to the notebook—it is not simply that his mental processes are embedded in an environment of which his notebook is a part. Things may act as mnemonic devices, can actively scaffold our learning, or serve as anchors for complex ideas (Tomasello 1999; Hutchins 2005; Sinha 2005).
5. Examples include horns of consecration and double axes—see Briault (2007), and Haysom (2010), for example.

Bibliography

Bailey, D. W. (2005), *Prehistoric Figurines: Representation and Corporeality in the Neolithic*, London: Routledge.

Bille, M., F. Hastrup, and T. F. Sørensen (2010), "Introduction: An Anthropology of Absence," in M. Bille, F. Hastrup, and T. F . Sørensen (eds), *An Anthropology of Absence: Materializations of Transcendence and Loss*, 3–22, New York: Springer.

Briault, C. (2007), "High Fidelity or Chinese Whispers? Cult Symbols and Ritual Transmission in the Bronze Age Aegean," *Journal of Mediterranean Archaeology* 20 (2): 239–65.

Brown, B. (ed.) (2003), *Things*, Chicago: University of Chicago Press.

Buchanan, R. (2001), "Design Research and the New Learning," *Design Issues* 17 (4): 3–23.

Clark, A. (1997), *Being There: Putting Brain, Body, and World Together Again*, Cambridge, MA: MIT Press.

Clark, A. (2010), "Material Surrogacy and the Supernatural: Reflections on the Role of Artefacts in 'Off-line' Cognition," in L. Malafouris and C. Renfrew (eds), *The Cognitive Life of Things: Recasting the Boundaries of the Mind*, 23–28, Cambridge: McDonald Institute Monographs.

Clark, A., and Chalmers, D. (1998), "The Extended Mind," *Analysis* 58 (1): 7–19.

Day, M. (2004), "Religion, Off-line Cognition, and the Extended Mind," *Journal of Cognition and Culture* 4 (1): 101–21.

DeLoache, J. S. (1991), "Symbolic Functioning in Very Young Children: Understanding of Pictures and Models," *Child Development* 62: 736–52.

Engelke, M. (2007), *A Problem of Presence: Beyond Scripture in an African Church*, Berkeley, CA: University of California Press.

Gedenryd, H. (1998), *How Designers Work: Making Sense of Authentic Cognitive Activities*, Lund: Lund University Cognitive Studies [Doctoral dissertation].

Gell, A. (1998), *Art and Agency: Towards a New Anthropological Theory*, Oxford: Clarendon Press.

Gosden, C. (2010), "The Death of the Mind," in L. Malafouris and C. Renfrew (eds), *The Cognitive Life of Things: Recasting the Boundaries of the Mind*, 39–46, Cambridge: The McDonald Institute for Archaeological Research.

Gulizio, J., and D. Nakassis (2014), "The Minoan Goddess(es): Textual Evidence for Minoan Religion," in D. Nakassis, J. Gulizio, and S. James (eds), *KE-RA-ME-JA: Studies Presented to Cynthia W. Shelmerdine*, 115–28, Philadelphia: INSTAP Academic Press.

Haysom, M. (2010), "The Double-Axe: A Contextual Approach to the Understanding of a Cretan Symbol in the Neopalatial Period," *Oxford Journal of Archaeology* 29 (1): 35–55.

Hutchins, E. (2005), "Material Anchors for Conceptual Blends," *Journal of Pragmatics*, 37: 1555–77.

Ingold, T. (2013), *Making. Anthropology, Archaeology, Art and Architecture*, London: Routledge.

Lévi-Strauss, C. (1962), *La Pensée Sauvage*, Paris: Plon.

MacGillivray, J. A., L. H. Sackett, and J. Driessen (eds), (2000), *The Palaikastro Kouros: A Minoan Chryselephantine Statuette and its Aegean Bronze Age Context*, London: British School at Athens Studies 6.

Mack, J. (2007), *The Art of Small Things*, London: British Museum Press.

Malafouris, L. (2013), *How Things Shape the Mind: A Theory of Material Engagement*, Cambridge, MA: MIT Press.

Morris, M. (2006), *Models: Architecture and the Miniature—Architecture in Practice*, London: John Wiley.

Morris, C. (2009), "Configuring the Individual: Bodies of Figurines in Minoan Crete," in A.-L. D'Agata and A. van de Moortel (eds), *Archaeologies of Cult: Essays on Ritual and Cult in Crete in Honor of Geraldine C. Gesell*, 179–87, Hesperia Supplement 42.

Robbins, P. and M. Aydede (eds), (2009), *The Cambridge Handbook of Situated Cognition*, Cambridge: Cambridge University Press.

Rose, M. (2011), "Secular Materialism: A Critique of Earthly Theory," *Journal of Material Culture* 16 (2): 107–29.

Rowlands, M. (2010), "What is Cognition? Extended Cognition and the Criterion of the Cognitive," *Proceedings of the British Academy* 158: 317–37.

Sinha, C. (2005), "Blending Out of the Background: Play, Props and Staging in the Material World," *Journal of Pragmatics* 37: 1537–54.

Tomasello, M. (1999), *The Cultural Origins of Human Cognition*, Cambridge, MA: Harvard University Press.

Vernant, J.-P. (1991), *Mortals and Immortals: Collected Essays*, F. I. Zeitlin (ed.), Princeton: Princeton University Press.

Weingarten, J. (2000), "Reading the Minoan Body: Proportions and the Palaikastro Kouros," in J. A. MacGillivray, L. H. Sackett and J. Driessen (eds), *The Palaikastro Kouros: A Minoan Chryselephantine Statuette and its Aegean Bronze Age Context*, 103–111, London: British School at Athens Studies 6.

Zeimbekis, M. (2004), "The Organisation of Votive Production and Distribution in the Peak Sanctuaries of State Society Crete: A Perspective Offered by the Juktas Animal Figurines," in G. Cadogan, E. Hatzaki, and A. Vasilakis (eds), *Knossos: Palace, City, State*, 351–61, London: BSA Studies.

14

The graphic thing

Ambiguity, dysfunction, and excess in designed objects

Phil Jones

Introduction

Defining graphic design often begins with stereotypical graphic design objects: logotypes, typefaces, books, posters, diagrams, packaging and so forth. We have learned ways of interacting with these objects. We understand how objects such as books are typically constructed and the scenarios in which they are used. From the flow of sensorimotor data presented to us, we readily produce conceptualizations such as "book" or "poster" in conscious experience. We recognize (unproblematically) individual examples of graphic design as members of categories.

In contrast, a second type of graphic artifact may not be so easy to pigeonhole. Our perception of such artifacts might be less clear than what we expect for "book," "logotype," etc. How this second type of artifact functions might be unknown, ambiguous or impaired, and our experience of their existence may be less certain and categorical. Such artifacts will consequently become a focus of attention requiring a conscious effort on behalf of their users to precisely place them within their own network of understanding.

In the first kind of experience, it is possible in the moment in which the artifacts are perceived, for the experiencer to project structure and concepts onto graphic artifacts, and for the structure and concepts to be reflected back. In the second type of artifact, it is either difficult for us to know what to project, or if we do project structure, there is dissonance between what is projected and what is reflected. The differences between these two types of graphic artifacts are similar to the differences between *objects* and *things*.

Bill Brown (2001) provides an overview of approaches used and problems encountered in trying to make sense of things. Brown foregrounds the ambiguity of things, their "specific unspecificity," as well as the ways that the term "thing" describes a particular subject-object relationship (Brown 2001: 3). The word "thing" is sometimes used to denote an aspect of the real—an entity external to human consciousness. Brown describes it thus, "Somewhere beyond or beneath the phenomena we see and touch there lurks some other life and law of things, the swarm of electrons" (2001: 6). For objects on the other hand, "there are codes by which our interpretive attention makes them meaningful, because there is a discourse of objectivity that allows us to use them as facts" (Brown 2001: 4). These particular understandings of "thing" and "object" provide a useful starting point for my discussion in this essay. There is the use of the term "thing" to label entities in our experience as having an extra-phenomenal existence (having attributes beyond the ability of our senses to detect) that is unknown or even unknowable. Then there is the use of the term "object" to label entities in our experience that are more certain and which emerge through a process of "interpretive attention" (Brown 2001: 4).

In the terminology of cognitive science this use of the term "object" suggests a "top-down" form of processing, utilizing "mechanisms that assign categories" and "prior knowledge" (Kandel 2012: 305–6). Psychologist Lawrence Barsalou summarizes it this way:

> an important family of basic cognitive processes appears to utilize a single mechanism, namely, sensory-motor representations. These processes, although related, vary along a continuum of bottom-up to top-down processing. At one extreme, bottom-up input activates sensory-motor representations in the absence of top-down processing ("pure" perception). At the other extreme, top-down processing activates sensory-motor representations in the absence of bottom-up processing (imagery and conception). In between lie processes that fuse complementary mixtures of bottom-up and top-down processing to coordinate the perception of physical entities (implicit memory, filling-in, anticipation, interpretation). (Barsalou 1999: 590)

In other words, our experience of the world is not always a question of *either* bottom up processing (using data captured by sense organs such as our eyes), *or* top down processing (using concepts and images assembled cognitively); there is a space in between where both forms of processing participate. This zone where bottom-up and top-down processing converge seems a suitable space for "thingness," to use Brown's phrase. Entities are delineated and become distinct from their surroundings in this space. But to a greater or lesser degree, the bottom-up sensorimotor data conflicts with the predictions, memories and prior knowledge activated in top-down processing. In such a situation, sensorimotor data might seem to suggest the external world is a bigger and less predictable place than we expect because it does not always conform to prior experiences.

But why should graphic design embrace the vagueness and ambiguity of a thing rather than the clarity and functionality of the object? Is it perhaps in order to elicit a surrealistic frisson of strangeness and uncertainty, or to call attention to the designed artifact itself as the thing that mediates communication between addressor and addressee? This article re-appraises some examples of graphic design that evoke, in different ways, the thingness of graphic objects.

The so-called embodied realist position, as described by linguist George Lakoff and philosopher Mark Johnson (1999), acknowledges the role of our bodies as mediators in the production of meaning. There is an external reality; however, our understanding of this reality is deeply influenced by the ways that our whole bodies and not just our brains interact with it. According to embodied realism, much of the structure that we assume exists independently in objects in the external world instead arises from the ways that the brain interacts with the rest of the body. As Lakoff and Johnson note:

embodied realism, relies on the fact that we are coupled to the world through our embodied interactions. Our directly embodied concepts…can reliably fit those embodied interactions and the understandings of the world that arise from them. (Lakoff and Johnson 1999: 93)

Embodied concepts may not exist in the outside world, but they must still be developed through our engagement with it. As scholars Francisco Varela, Evan Thompson and Eleanor Rosch (1993: 233) observe, "Mind-independent objects are challenged, but object-independent minds never are." Consequently, the authors advocate an enactive approach in which cognitive structures develop from repeated sensorimotor patterns in experience.

The external world—devoid of color, image, and schematic structure such as top and bottom or inside and outside—is the stuff with which we physically engage bodies and brains. In doing so, we make the external world meaningful in ways that are useful to us as a species. There are questions here in relation to the idea of a noumenal world: "that which exists beyond our experience, the thing-in-itself" (Boradkar 2010: 30). There may be attributes that a thing has that we may not perceive as a phenomenon, but this is not the same thing as saying that there is one true way of comprehending something to which, if only we had the requisite perceptual abilities, all life forms could universally agree. We cannot escape our embodied experience—and the language and concepts we would use to describe this noumenal world are themselves embodied. Both thing and object, therefore, should be approached as embodied mental constructs rather than unmediated representations of an external world.

The way we experience the external world is a complex and layered process involving the unconscious as well as the conscious mind. According to semiotician Per Aage Brandt (2006: 173), "When consciousness is awake and aware, our organization of what we will call *meaning* is a process that occurs on many levels simultaneously." Brandt proposes five different strata that we can imagine as five parallel streams of ongoing mental activity:

the strata of sensations, the coherent forms arising from fragments of sensorimotor data;
the strata of perceptions, dealing with objects as categories;
the strata of apperceptions, where perceptions are understood as part of an episode, situation, or broader field of knowledge;
the strata of reflections, involving descriptive or argumentative notions; and
the strata of affects, concerning the meaning of our emotional states.

The first two of these strata seem particularly relevant to our experience of things. The difference between a "sensation of forms" and a "perception of 'gestalted' and categorized objects" (Brandt 2006: 173) is suggestive of the difference between things and objects. This is because "sensation of forms" suggests a level of processing, reliant on sensorimotor data, out of which forms have emerged. A level closer to the idea of things since it deals with forms not yet paired with conceptual categories.

Issues of thingness however may emerge in other levels too: uncertainty about positioning an entity in relation to existing knowledge about a situation also suggests a degree of "thingness," for example, or evaluative reflection on the nature of the thing in question. Since we can attend to particular aspects of these different strata simultaneously, we may begin to appreciate the complexity surrounding our experience of things.

In relation to the gestalts described in Brandt's second stratum, the neural theory of language proposes that various types of neural circuits are responsible for different kinds of computations (Lakoff 2008). Here, networks of neurons activate and generate basic gestalt circuits in which a gestalt node is connected to a series of other nodes. When the gestalt node is activated, it excites all of the other nodes in the circuit; conversely, when a sufficient number of other excited nodes reach a threshold, they in turn activate the gestalt node. Perhaps there is a neural explanation that partially accounts for the phenomenological experience of thingness: if some, but not a sufficient number of the nodes in a gestalt network are activated, then is there a phenomenological experience which cannot be finally resolved to a specific gestalt? Such an experience does not benefit from the added value associated with gestalts in which the whole is greater than the sum of its parts; it remains partially unresolved. A thing is thus a "gathering" of elements to use Latour's phrase (2004: 160–1). Perhaps there is a parallel here, since for Latour the collection of proofs, gathered at the United Nations, in 2003, to make the case for a military strike against Iraq, was a thing attempting to turn into an object; matters of concern attempting to become matters of fact. At the level of neural circuitry perhaps a collection of nodes that do not trigger a gestalt is a gathering of elements that remains a thing because, unlike an object, it has not coalesced into a familiar conceptualization.

In a somewhat similar vein, linguist Joseph Grady (2005) notes that we form "schematic images" of objects like cups (which we could extend to include graphic artifacts like books, posters, web sites, and so forth). Such schematic images arise from recurring bodily and mental experiences of objects. Schematic images comprised more fundamental *image schemas*. Grady proposes that the term image schema (which has widespread use in cognitive linguistics) should be reserved for "mental representations of *fundamental units of sensory experience*" (2005: 44).

Image schemas include such basic structures as front/back, containment, source/path/goal, and balance; they too arise from embodied interaction with the world. It is easy to see, for example, how particular configurations of front/back and verticality might relate to a schematic image of a poster. The poster is fixed vertically to a wall and the front faces out toward the viewer. What happens, however, when these prototypical configurations are transgressed, when the front is pasted to the wall, or when the poster is made so thick that it becomes cuboid so that each of its six faces could conceivably be the front? Schematic images and image schemas have to be flexible enough to accommodate a wide range of different experiences, but at some point a particular configuration of one or more image schema might fall outside of the recurring pattern of experience associated with a schematic image. It is at this point that the notions of "thingness" and "thing" seem pertinent.

Perception, vagueness, and ambiguity

Although things frequently are a focus of our attention, there is an issue of their apperception and classification: they cannot be precisely located in relationship to our existing knowledge and experience. This is part of the power that things have; we may focus on them but they elude complete understanding. They are tangible in the literal sense of having a perceptible material physical existence, but intangible in the metaphorical sense of being able to resist our attempts to grasp their full meaning.

The ambiguity of things can be a question of perception—that something is too far away to discern completely—but it is not limited to such cases. We can engage closely with things, hold them and manipulate them, but may still be inclined to call them "things" rather than objects. In some cases, we might recognize that a thing is likely a part of some larger entity. A thing could be a component of an unidentifiable mechanical assembly, an element that functions within a scenario, or a segment of a sequence of events that is either unknown or not deducible from the thing in question. Paul Elliman's Found Font (Figure 14.1) is suggestive of such an experience. The typeface is composed of found debris collected from streets and roadsides. To the untrained eye, these fragments that coincidentally resemble letterforms may suggest a mechanical heritage, but the type of machine to which they belong, or the function that they once performed are unknown. Each piece is therefore at once a thing and a letterform, providing type characters with a link to a human-made physical form, but one that is ambiguous, under-specified, and uncertain. In linguist Charles Fillmore's terms (2006), we are vaguely able to distinguish the *conceptual frame* of machinery for the things (the font) confronting us, but it is difficult (especially for the less mechanically minded) to express how these things participate in this conceptual frame. The ambiguity about these shapes is compounded because they are also letters and therefore part of a second conceptual frame, that of writing.

A typeface is typically understood as a set of two-dimensional visual forms (type characters) rather than of a set of physical or material things. It can be instantiated in any number of materials, and is not fixed in size, as with contemporary production methods it is almost infinitely scalable. Its existence is spread across a range of printed objects, and every digital font carries with it the information required for its future uncorrupted reproduction. The dissemination of digital type, unlike its metal forebears, is not dependent on a unique set of master objects (letter punches and counterpunches for example). Letterforms are schematic images, shapes of the same order of things as a circle or square.

What we may call type, as we see it on the page, is a neural binding of form, substance, and sound: shapes in the form of letters, substances of ink and paper, and the phoneme conventionally associated with the letterform in context. This fusion, which occurs in our brains rather than on the page, means that to talk of type presupposes that we have already processed the relevant sensorimotor data and recognized it as type. It has therefore already passed from an unspecified thing to a more familiar object. Some typefaces are, of course, more familiar and prototypical than others.

FIGURE 14.1 Found Font, Paul Elliman. Image courtesy of and used with permission of Paul Elliman. (A version of Found Font was released by FontShop in the early 1990s as a digital typeface called Bits. Elliman was not involved in that project.)

The "thingness" of letterforms consequently provides a source of questioning and debate within graphic design. As things that stand for something else, letterforms are physical marks that most people tend to look through rather than at. Brown (2001: 4) notes that we tend to look through objects, "to see what they disclose about history, society, nature or culture—above all what they disclose about *us*." Things, on the other hand, are more opaque and can only be glimpsed. Our engagement with letterforms is complex and multi-faceted; immersed in reading prose, we might look through letters in the way described by Brown, and yet in such a situation we might also be distracted by the "thingness" of letterforms. The unusual texture of a double story "g" in a block of text, for example, might arrest our attention, breaking our concentration from the flow of prose. Like a sharp thing encountered, letterforms can interrupt us and demand our scrutiny. As Brown (2001: 4) notes, "We begin to confront the thingness of objects when they stop working for us." In addition to regarding letterforms as objects that we look through, therefore, we can also think of them as things with material qualities that impose themselves, unbidden, on our experience. But this does not exhaust the ways that we engage with letterforms. We might also choose to construct meaning by focusing on the forms and shapes of the letters, putting aside any material and phonological associations. The

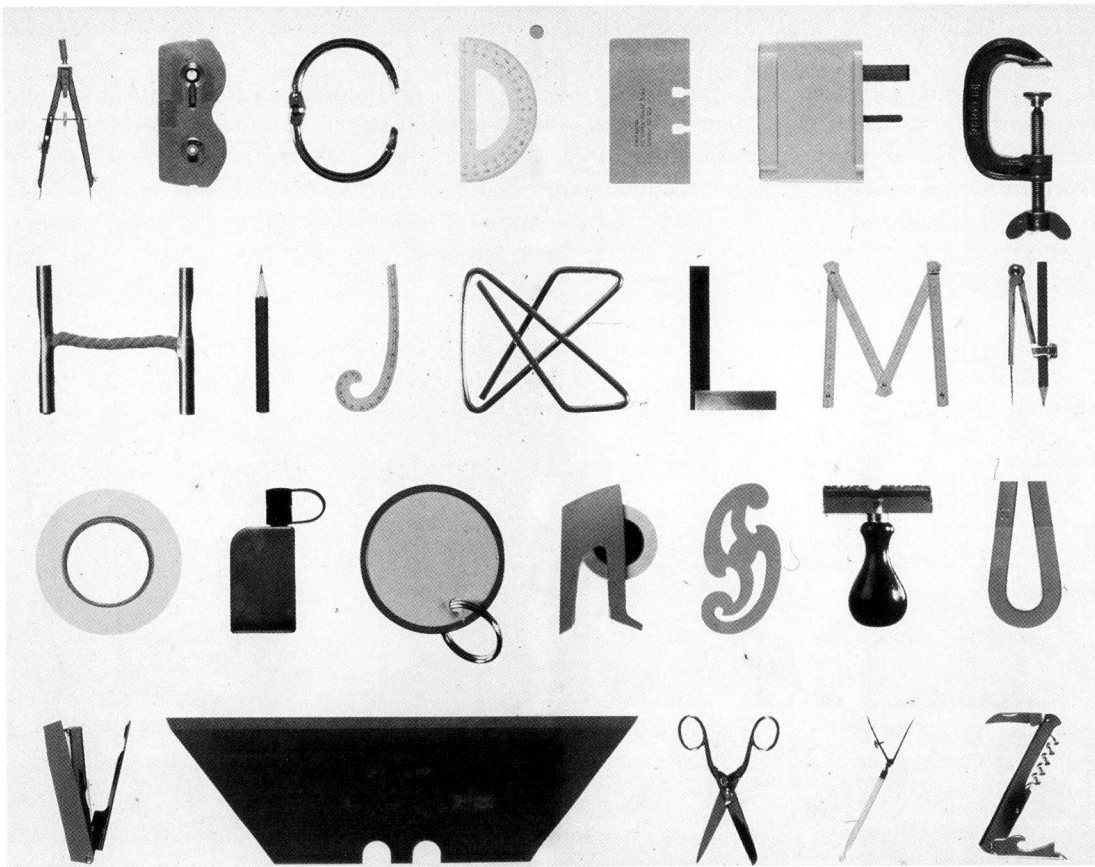

FIGURE 14.2 Krazy Kaps, Mervyn Kurlansky, 1977. Image courtesy of and used with permission of Mervyn Kurlansky.

physical forms of Elliman's letterforms suggest machines, for example, but they also possess a communicative dimension: they stand for sounds and suggest how and where they may be used.

The "thingness" of type becomes evident if we compare Elliman's letterforms with typefaces that use objects (rather than things) to form letters, such as Mervyn Kurlansky's Krazy Kaps, an alphabet fabricated from designers' tools. Kurlansky's letterforms evoke a specific reference to the designer's studio that is much less ambiguous than the suggestion of machine parts evoked by Found Font. It is important that we recognize that Kurlansky's letters are formed from functional objects, which although individually decontextualized collectively suggest a particular activity, and a certain kind of a practitioner. The evolution of the idea of letterforms projected onto objects used in a range of different activities is evident in this description by Kurlansky:

> Thinking about the task at hand with pencil poised (pre apple mac days), I became aware that the pencil could be seen as a letter i.
> So I looked about the Pentagram studio and I began to see letters of the alphabet in other objects used in the process of designing, administrating, model-making and drinking (the partners would converge on the drinks [trolley] in one of the conference rooms at 6.00 most evenings for a drink and a chat), hence the letter Z.
> (M. Kurlansky, personal communication, November 7, 2013)

For letterforms to evoke thingness, however, it is not necessary for them to point to a conceptual frame other than that of writing. As part of an undergraduate project concerned with emergence, Stephen Johnson deliberately slows down the flow of sensorimotor data available to a viewer. In this project, an apparently random homogeneous series of white dots appears sequentially on a black screen through which a structure gradually emerges. The white dots initially form the foreground, but at some point it becomes apparent to the viewer that they are in fact the background. It is during or shortly after this moment of recognition that the letters are finally resolved. The piece therefore takes us through several appreciations of the image: that of a void, of random visual noise, of an indistinct structure, and finally of an increasingly resolved depiction of an alphabet. It is the third of these four stages that is most redolent of the idea of a thing. It is at this stage that we are aware of the presence of some entity, but are also aware that it evades our ability to rely on past experiences to categorize it or make inferences about it.

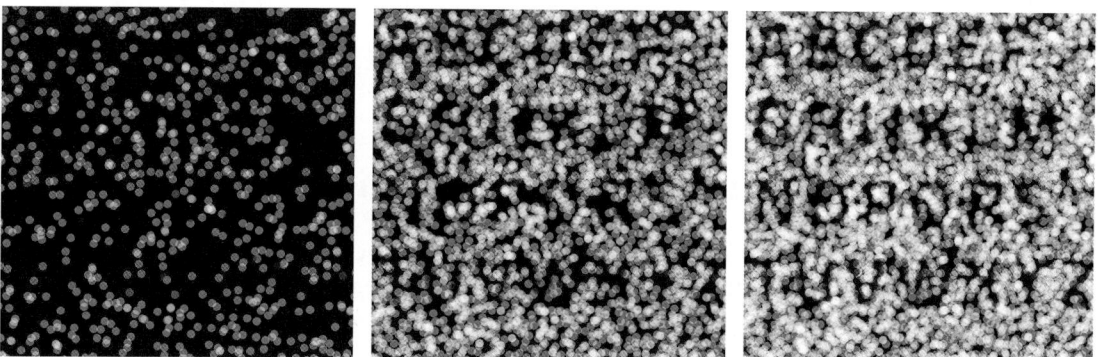

FIGURE 14.3 Undergraduate project, Stephen Johnson. Image courtesy of and used with permission of Stephen Johnson (sjohnson.co.uk).

Excess

Johnson's project relies on a sparseness of information to evoke an experience of thingness, but according to Brown things can also be imagined as:

> what is excessive in objects, as what exceeds their mere materialization as objects or their mere utilization as objects—their force as a sensuous presence. (Brown 2001: 5)

Books, such as Irma Boom's *Think Book* or Bruce Mau's *Lifestyle*, and magazines, such as the *Emigre* of the early 1990s, exert a "force as a sensuous presence" (Brown 2001: 5) by amplifying the materiality of the artifact to the extent that they begin to belong to another category. These books and magazines—which are both authored and designed by graphic designers—eschew the nomenclature of standard sizes or conventions that constrain the number of pages. Because they are bigger, thicker, or heavier they begin to over-stretch the schemata that we use to identify books or magazines, they become more palpable exerting a physical presence. They call attention to the material qualities of the paper through tactility or transparency, and they force us to reassess how we might handle and engage with them.

Books, too, like the letterforms discussed earlier, can be both looked at and looked through. As Johanna Drucker notes:

> Structures by which books present information, ideas or diversions, become habitual so that they erase, rather than foreground, their identity. One can, in other words, forget about a book even in the course of reading it. [...] But when a book calls attention to the conceits and conventions by which it normally effaces its identity, then it performs a theoretical operation. In critical parlance, one could say that such work calls attention to its own process of enunciation (the acts of speaking, representing making a work) rather than allowing a work to be enunciated (spoken as if it were naturally there). (Drucker 1994: 161–2)

Increasing or radically decreasing the size, weight and volume of graphic artifacts, so that one is (sometimes uncomfortably) reminded of their physical presence as one holds and manipulates them, draws attention to the role of the designer in the production of the artifact. Furthermore, there are also conceptual metaphors at work. Verbal expressions such as "big thoughts" and "weighty argument," use common notions of size and weight to make inferences about the thoughts and arguments in question. As physical expressions, these big, weighty things therefore make claims about the importance of both the design of the object and the texts that are imprinted on them.

Dysfunction and contradiction

Let us take the example of *Double Bind*, a book designed by Olson (cited in Smith 1984). This book is bound so that both the spine and fore-edge are sealed, denying the user access to the book's interior. This design calls attention to the book as a thing because of its inherent dysfunction and the contradiction of a binding method that prevents a user from accessing it. Close inspection suggests that this method of binding is something more than an attempt to call attention to the book as an object. The title *Double Bind* and the inherent contradiction of the binding point to double bind theory (Bateson et al. 1956), which refers to particular kinds of "unresolvable sequences of experiences" involving certain contradictory messages between, typically, parents and their offspring. The extent to which *Double Bind* precisely mirrors the complexity of double bind theory is open to debate. But it seems that this apparently dysfunctional book does have a function after all—one that is concerned with creating an experience similar to that described by double bind theory. The binding on the fore-edge that prevents us from opening the book is contradicted by the binding on the spine that grants conventional access to the book. We are held in this dichotomy by our desire to see what is printed inside the book and hidden from us.

While the above example functions in an unconventional way rather than functioning counterproductively, there are innumerable examples of dysfunctional graphic design: the column width that is too wide and makes the reader aware of her eyes jumping from one line to the next, differences in texture arising from inconsistent spacing or typeface design, setting text too small or in a too pale a tone to be legible, creating a book that is difficult to hold, and so forth. In such experiences there is the presumption that the designer is trying to present information transparently, that there is no interrogation of the form of the book, but that designed elements, through their demands on our attention, are inadvertently and inappropriately getting in the way. These dysfunctional elements have not stopped working for us entirely, just as with the example of the dirty windows that evoke the "thingness of objects" described by Brown (2001: 4). They function below the threshold of what we might expect of them and thereby become manifest. But this claim on our attention does not serve some communicative intention. Both the dirtiness of the window and the inconsistent typographic texture are irrelevant according to the definition of relevance provided by Sperber and Wilson (1995: 48) since they do not work alongside some old information allowing us to make new inferences.

In contrast, the designed-in dysfunctionality of Olson's binding is highly relevant to the title of the book allowing us to make new inferences about desire and denial. In conclusion, both Olson's book and the more mundane dysfunctionality of the poorly considered page, result in the experience of thingness for the user. In the former this experience is a way to deeper understanding of the artifact, in the latter it is an inconvenient distraction.

Namelessness

In terms of branding, the notion of namelessness seems to be counterintuitive. Naming manufactured objects adds a layer of specificity and association: the type of shoe (trainer) becomes the branded type of shoe (Nike trainer). The famous anonymity of the objects sold by Muji—their products are unbranded, their designers and manufacturers unspecified—demands a different kind of engagement by people who encounter them. Stripped of any explicit reference to a brand, it is more difficult to project predetermined values onto these goods. A more thorough evaluation of these goods as objects is therefore required if we are to compare them with other similar, but branded, objects that are on the market. Unbranded goods demand that we attend to them as entities rather than look through them as brands. And in this process, they take an admittedly small step towards becoming a thing.

Unbranded goods are, however, a different matter compared to the namelessness arising from new or hard to define subjective experiences. Whether we are confronted with a thing so new to us that it is outside any conceptual frame that we could bring to bear, or by a thing that is vaguely comprehended or remembered, this lack of information does not prevent an emotional response. Aesthetic and affective responses range from disgust, fear, or apathy, to attraction or empathy—despite the fact that our understanding of this entity may be slight or nonexistent. Although it is illusory, it is part of the mystique of things that personal meanings and feelings seem to reside in independently existing entities. As designer John Warwicker (2005) notes:

> Analysis and research can only inform and describe the effect of a work – it cannot name the "nameless thing" at its core. There are times when a piece of work resonates simply because it transcends its context, means, intention and production and just "is." (Warwicker 2005: 64)

The difficulty of capturing the feelings, meanings, and emotions generated by an artifact resonates in Mark Johnson's (2007) description of the over-arching pervasive qualities of situations. Such experiences evade, to some extent, the concepts and propositions that we employ to try to pin them down. It is the whole situation, rather than the object embedded within it, which is primary in our experience—and which is the first thing that we encounter. For Johnson, pervasive qualities account for our immediate experience of recognizing say, a Picasso rather than a Nolde. These same qualities must also enable us to discriminate between designs by Graphic Thought Facility and Stefan Sagmeister.

Conclusion

Rather than approaching "thingness" as a quality existing independently of human agency, my approach has been to reflect on the ways that experiences of "things" and "thingness" arise at different stages or levels in processes of meaning construction. There are issues of thingness in perception, for example, where the amount or quality of sensorimotor data is insufficient to completely resolve the thing in question. Conversely, when we are overwhelmed by sensorimotor data so that there is a veridical experience of the physical existence of a thing, the thing becomes "larger than life." Attention is another issue—things attract attention because they resist straightforward classification and understanding. But there is also the experience of becoming aware of the existence of something when it interrupts an activity and becomes the focus of our attention. Our experience of things also seems relevant to apperception when it is difficult or impossible to locate an entity within a conceptual frame or scenario. Undoubtedly, there are other facets of meaning construction relevant to thingness I've neglected; but this discussion gives a sense of why experiences of things can be so complex and difficult to describe.

In graphic design the experience of thingness can be detrimental to user experience—for example, in cases in which the reader's concentration is broken by some badly set type. But designers can also use this experience of thingness to call attention to the designed object, to create impact, to suggest emotional and affective states, and to foreground certain attributes and qualities so that new meaning may emerge.

Bibliography

Barsalou, L. W. (1999), "Perceptual Symbol Systems," *Behavioral and Brain Sciences* 22 (4): 577–660.

Bateson, G., D. Jackson, J. Haley, and J. Weakland (1956), "Towards a Theory of Schizophrenia," *Behavioral Science* 1 (4): 251–4.

Boradkar, P. (2010), *Designing Things: A Critical Introduction to the Culture of Objects*, Oxford: Berg.

Brandt, P. A. (2006), "Form and Meaning in Art," in M. Turner (ed.), *The Artful Mind: Cognitive Science and the Riddle of Human Creativity*, 171–88. New York and Oxford: Oxford University Press.

Brown, B. (2001), "Thing Theory," *Critical Inquiry* 28 (1): 1–22.

Drucker, J. (1994), *The Century of Artists' Books*, New York: Granary Books.

Fillmore, C. (2006), "Frame Semantics," in D. Geeraerts (ed.) *Cognitive Linguistics: Basic Readings*, 373–400. Berlin: Mouton de Gruyter.

Grady, J. E. (2005), "Image Schemas and Perception: Refining a Definition," in B. Hampe and J. E. Grady (eds), *From Perception to Meaning: Image Schemas in Cognitive Linguistics*, 35–55. Berlin: Mouton de Gruyter,.

Johnson, M. (2007), *The Meaning of the Body: Aesthetics of Human Understanding*, Chicago: University of Chicago Press.

Kandel, E. (2012), *The Age of Insight: The Quest to Understand the Unconscious in Art, Mind, and Brain, From Vienna 1900 to the Present*, New York: Random House.

Lakoff, G. (2008), "The Neural Theory of Metaphor," in R. W. Gibbs (ed.), *The Cambridge Handbook of Metaphor and Thought*, 17–38. New York: Cambridge University Press.

Lakoff, G. and M. Johnson (1999), *Philosophy of the Flesh*, New York: Basic Books.

Latour, B. (2004), "Why Has Critique Run out of Steam? From Matters of Fact to Matters of Concern," in B. Brown (ed.), *Things*, Chicago: University of Chicago Press.

Smith, K. A. (1984), *Structure of the Visual Book*, New York: Keith Smith Books.

Sperber, D., and D. Wilson (1995), *Relevance: Communication and Cognition*, Malden: Blackwell Publishing.

Varela, F. J., E. Thompson, and E. Rosch (1993). *The Embodied Mind: Cognitive Science and Human Experience*, Cambridge, MA, and London: MIT Press.

Warwicker, J. (2005), "Nameless Thing." *Eye* 15 (57): 60–4.

15

Agency and counteragency of materials

A story of copper

Prasad Boradkar

I begin with a puzzle.
It is that the ever-growing literature in anthropology and archaeology that deals explicitly with the subjects of materiality and material culture seems to have hardly anything to say about materials.

TIM INGOLD

Tambat ali

The *tambat ali* (coppersmith alley) region, nestled deep within the historic district of the city of Pune in western India, is known for the sonorous ringing of steel hammers striking copper utensils (see Plate 9). These unmistakable sounds have been filling this area of the city for over three hundred years, as generations of copper craftspeople living and working here mold sheets of malleable copper into beautiful water jugs, cooking pots and religious artifacts. In a network of narrow streets, sunny courtyards and shaded workshops, some forty coppersmiths ply an old and honorable trade, as did several generations of *tambat ali* craftspeople before them. Each copper product they make is passed through a long chain of practiced hands and machines until it ends up with experts who strike the surface with a precise hammertone pattern that gives the object its strength and lustrous beauty (see Plate 10).

In the local language, Marathi, the word *tamba* is copper, and *tambat* refers to the coppersmith. The material copper has special significance to the craftspeople living and working in *tambat ali*: not only is their name derived from the Marathi word for the metal, but it has provided subsistence to the families who have lived in *tambat ali* for generations. These craftspeople are best known for the unique hammertone texture they impart to many of the things they make such as water heaters, cookware, containers for water, candle holders, etc. Using a set of specialized hammers and anvils, as well as a range of highly practiced and precise motions, they beat row after row of even dimples into a beautiful pattern on the surfaces of the products they make.

Creating even rows of indentations with these hammer strokes, a process called *matharkam*, requires highly specialized tools, distinctive gestures, series of highly coordinated actions, manual strength, extreme concentration, and years of practice (see Plate 11). A right-handed *tambat* typically locates and stabilizes the copper product to be hammered on a specialized anvil called the *kharvai* using the toes of the left and right feet and the left hand, while holding the hammer in the right hand. A left-handed *tambat* uses toes similarly, but holds the hammer in the left hand. The product has to be indexed (rotated slightly after every hammer stroke) by the fingers of one hand, and the hammer held in the other hand has to be struck on a specific location each time so as to create a uniform line of indentations (see Plate 12).

How material is materiality?

In order to understand the significance of copper to these objects and to the *tambats*, it is useful first to examine how materials are considered in the discourse on materiality. In the introductory chapter to *Materiality*, anthropologist Daniel Miller recommends that the meaning of the word material "needs to encompass both colloquial and philosophical uses of this term" (Miller 2005: 4). The first and more mundane interpretations of the term material, Miller goes on to explain, simply foreground the "quantity of objects," "proliferation of artifacts," and so on (2005: 4). In addition to their abundance and ubiquity, though, this definition of materiality also references the physicality of things, and is therefore of critical consequence to design. This materiality of designed objects is manifested through their physical presence, which includes weight, size, proportion, texture and surface, as well as sensorial qualities such as tactility, visuality, aurality, and so on. It is through these properties of materials that we first engage objects. At the second, and philosophical level, Miller augments the definition to "consider the large compass of materiality" which stretches into "the ephemeral, the imaginary, the biological, and the theoretical; all that which would have been external to the simple definition of an artifact" (2005: 4). Materiality, in this interpretation, enlarges its conceptual boundaries "beyond the most evident category of artifacts" to include all that can be imagined to be material culture (Miller 2005: 4). However, as the idea of materiality stretches beyond the physical, it seems to lose touch with the fundamental material of which things are made. Anthropologist Tim Ingold laments this by saying that while anthropologists and archaeologists talk about materiality and material culture, they have "hardly anything to say about *materials*" themselves (2007: 1). He urges us to "take materials seriously, since it is from them that everything is made" (Ingold 2007: 14).

We are surrounded by natural and synthetic materials of all kinds—metals, alloys, woods, stones, ceramics, fabrics, plastics, fiberglass, etc.—but seldom are we actively aware of how they are the essential elements of our buildings, products, clothing, and everything with which we interact. Industrial designers, architects, engineers, polymer scientists, and other specialists engage materials regularly in their work. However, while designers and architects often think of materials in functional and aesthetic terms (considering their weight, color, texture, tactile properties, etc. for specific applications), engineers and scientists tend to think of them in terms of their mechanical properties (tensile strength, compressive strength, durability, etc.). And while more scholars in anthropology and design studies have been examining the sociocultural import of designed objects, the materials of which these objects are made have not been studied in as much detail. Though nested within the term "materiality" is the word "material," and though materiality as a concept relies on the undeniable actuality that all things are made of some kind of a material, the discussion of materials themselves—the stuff of which stuff is made—is limited in the discourse on materiality.

Material agency

In the swell of recent scholarship in the social sciences and humanities often referred to as the material turn, there is significant writing about the agency of things (Hoskins 2006; Hicks and Beaudry 2010; Verbeek 2005; Latour 2005; Gell 1998; Knappett and Malafouris 2008). The primary question in these conversations is whether non-human entities have the power and means to cause change in the world. One of the most engaging accounts of agency appears in Gell's *Art and Agency*. Gell explains that agents are the originators of series of events, and that they do so by intention (1998). He argues that "Agency is attributable to those persons (and things, see below) who/which are seen as initiating causal sequences of a particular type, that is, events caused by acts of mind or will or intention, rather than the mere concatenation of physical events" (Gell 1998: 16)). According to Gell then, an agent "causes events to happen" (1998: 16). He then offers concrete examples that include the "treachery" of cars that break down and "mines which have caused so many deaths," while also recognizing the "somewhat bizarre" nature of such attribution of intention and will to objects. While human agency is accepted as fact, the notion that things might have agency and the means of acting on their own behalf might be perceived as mildly peculiar or simply outlandish. However, making that very assertion of the intention of things is one of the explicit goals of the scholarship that has emerged in support of the material turn. Gell creates categories of primary and secondary agents to deal with this issue of intention. He explains that "social agency manifests itself, via the proliferation of fragments of [human] 'primary intentional agents' [soldiers, for instance] in their [non-living] 'secondary' artefactual forms [the mines they plant]" (1998: 21). It seems clear that for Gell intention is an essential attribute of an agent; and while non-human things cannot possess intent, they act as secondary agents because of the presence of humans, who serve as primary agents. In other words, a thing that is relegated to this position only has secondary agency because it cannot function on its own without the presence of the primary agency of the human.

I would like to suggest, however, that agency can exist without intention and the presence of humans. While intention relies on an inherent notion of aim or purpose in the mind of the agent, in case of materials, the properties that define their being can serve an agentic role. The steel, plastic, and composite materials that are used in manufacturing Gell's treacherous cars and death-causing mines are responsible for some of the agency these dangerous objects possess. In the case of materials, agency is less about *that which gives material its intention* and more about *that for which is a material is responsible*. The chassis of a car is made of steel because it has desired properties of hardness, malleability, shear strength, tensile strength, and so on. A fender is made of a copolymer because it has specific properties of moldability and impact resistance. The properties of materials are responsible for the way they behave. And it is from these properties that their primary agency emerges. The agency of things, therefore, is at least partially responsible for the agency of materials of which they are made.

For Heidegger, material is one of four aspects of responsibility and indebtedness that brings things into being, and he explains this with an example of a silver chalice: "Silver is that out of which the silver chalice is made. As this matter (*hyle*), it is co-responsible for the chalice. The chalice is indebted to, i.e. owes thanks to, the silver for that out of which it consists" (Heidegger 1977: 7). In other words, silver is "co-responsible," along with the material form of the chalice, for the "chaliceness" of the thing. Heidegger refers to this dimension as the "aspect" (*eidos*) of the chalice. Heidegger adds two other components that make a thing what it is. The third element is the context of use—in this case, the Christian ceremony of communion for which the chalice might be used—which Heidegger refers to as that which circumscribes and gives bounds (*telos*) to the thing. The fourth element is the silversmith, whose agency is co-responsible for bringing the chalice into being. The silversmith understands the "three aforementioned ways of being responsible and indebted" while creating the chalice, and this he refers to as *logos*. Materials (*hyle*), along with forms (*eidos*), contexts (*telos*) and makers (*logos*), are responsible for bringing things into the world.

While materiality is abstract, materials are concrete. If, in the discussion of materiality, we do not account for the presence of the materials, we ignore the very substrate from which the agency of things rises. It is from materials, raw or processed, that things emerge. Tangible goods like hammers and nails are visibly and evidently made from such materials as iron and wood; but even intangible things like apps need devices on which to function. Services too rely on physical infrastructure. The substance from which things materialize demands acknowledgement in the discussion of the presence and power of things.

"In urging that we take a step back, from the materiality of objects to the properties of materials," anthropologist Tim Ingold writes, "I propose that we lift the carpet, to reveal beneath its surface a tangled web of meandrine complexity" (2007: 9). In turning our attention away from the abstract notion of materiality to the more concrete properties of materials, as Ingold suggests here, we might uncover an entire network of people, products, places and practices that make up a culture. This essay is an examination of the nature of the agency of the material itself, i.e., the copper with which these craftspeople work, as a conduit and mechanism to experience *tambat ali*. The copper goods, the material itself, the craftspeople, their tools and machines, the location of this crafts cluster in Pune, and a host of other agents connected to *tambat ali* represent an extended and complex network of people, products and places.

Visible, accessible, and material

"There are times in many ethnographically observed contexts when a transformation occurs between perceiving surroundings as an agglomeration of forms or seeing them as an agglomeration of substances," according to anthropologist Adam Drazin (2015: 4). In *tambat ali*, a place named after a material, this is shockingly evident. The shiny reddish-orange material is visible everywhere—large copper sheets being dragged into factories, smaller blanks heated and hammered into vessels, finished goods drying on the streets, and scraps of the shiny metal tossed into bins. This is, as Drazin describes, "a materials world" (2015). All around *tambat ali* tools transform materials into desired shapes, converting substance into form. "An 'anthropology of materials' explores moments of manifest transformation between form and substance and their sociocultural implications," Drazin explains (2015: 27). And while the material is visible everywhere, its transformation sometimes renders it invisible. Materials transform into things under the combined agency of a variety of actors. In this transformation however, the raw materials sometimes recede, and we become less aware of them as thingly qualities of the thing emerge. Ingold writes:

> At this point materials appear to vanish, swallowed up by the very objects to which they have given birth. That is why we commonly describe materials as 'raw' but never 'cooked' – for by the time they have congealed into objects they have already disappeared. Thenceforth it is the objects themselves that capture our attention, no longer the materials of which they are made. (Ingold 2007: 9)

The inaccessibility of materials that Ingold describes also relates to the types of things into which they have metamorphosed. While the properties of the fragrant sandalwood of which a religious statue is made might still be accessible to us, the materials that comprise our electronic products are clearly less so. A printed circuit board might be made up of such materials as porcelain, mica, epoxy resin, glass fiber, copper foil, cadmium, chrome, lead, nickel, and so on—an extremely long list that disappears into the product. There is no way for us to recognize or relate to these materials. Simpler objects, though, like a porcelain mug, a leather bag, a marble table, or a copper utensil, might, to a certain extent be able to maintain their independent presence as materials and resist being subsumed into the thing.

How then do we re-connect with the materials of which things are made? Ingold suggests that it is "by engaging quite directly with the stuff we want to understand: by sawing logs, building a wall, knapping a stone or rowing a boat" that we can learn more deeply about the material nature of our world. "Could not such engagement—working practically with materials—offer a more powerful procedure of discovery than an approach bent on the abstract analysis of things already made? (Ingold 2007: 3). Over the past few years, I have been conducting ethnographic research with the *tambat* community, interviewing the craftspeople, observing their techniques, and documenting their work through audio and visual means. In addition, and to pay heed to Ingold's advice, I have asked a few of the craftsmen to teach me some of the skills that they have learned from their fathers. While I do not expect to learn this craft with a high level of expertise, I hope that in the process of doing this work repeatedly and over time, I will absorb and assimilate some of the "techniques of the body" (Mauss 1973), the highly evolved human actions that embody specific cultures. In a workshop in *tambat ali* owned and operated by Bhalchandra Kadu, an artist and craftsman himself, and under the guidance of several craftsmen who work with him, I have started to craft a few copper artifacts. While Kadu has helped me understand some of the sociotechnical aspects of the work of the *tambat* community, Shantaram Ambre, Ashok Chowgule, Nilesh Kadu, and Ganesh Lanjrekar, in his workshop, have been teaching me the specifics of copper marking, cutting, spinning, hammering, polishing, and lacquering. Each of these techniques demands a highly evolved and precise set of gestures that define the relation between the body, the material, and the tool.

Sociologist Marcel Mauss writes, "I call technique an action which is effective and traditional" (1973: 82). Mauss explains that without tradition, there is neither technique nor transmission. The techniques I am learning have been passed down through generations of *tambats* and are deeply rooted in tradition. However, it is important to note that the *tambats* have invented new processes, experimental tools, novel methods, and several new artifacts over the years. So, while there is tradition, there is also innovation. While some of the techniques of the body have significant historical precedent, some are entirely contemporary. For me, the process of acquiring the skills and knowledge of making these copper artifacts has involved absorbing into my body a long list of chronologically organized steps of material manipulation. Each step has involved a position, movement, gesture, and action of the body that has been essential in shaping these copper artifacts; because it is through these sorts of activities that the *tambats* exercise their agency on the copper (see Plate 13).

Copper: Properties, agency, and counteragency

While the craftspeople act as agents in shaping copper into specific forms, the material itself acts as an agent on account of its inherent properties. Copper is found in nature in pure form as "native copper," but also in the form of two mineral ores, chalcopyrite and chalcocite. Archaeological evidence shows that copper was known to prehistoric people and was possibly one of the first metals to be smelted, cast, alloyed, and from which everyday articles were made. Copper's mechanical and chemical properties give it agency even in the absence of humans; these are things it *does* on its own. Copper easily propels electricity through its body because it has several delocalized or free electrons in its atomic structure. And, when connected to a battery, these electrons are activated to move in the direction of the positive charge, in effect, transmitting electricity. Therefore, one of the primary uses of the material is in electrical applications; it is the metal of choice for household wiring as well as for circuit boards. Copper is also an extremely good conductor of heat. It's unique ability to draw heat away from the source and dissipate it as and where needed has made it an excellent material to be used as a heat sink in products. The color of copper, its unique property to reflect visible light of a certain wavelength, is also a form of its agency. When in pure form, copper has a reddish luster and glow. However, in certain specific conditions, it starts to bind with other elements present in the atmosphere, creating a layer of copper compounds on its surface, such as carbonates, sulphates and oxides, that give the material a range of colors and patinas from bright green to black. Copper also has the ability to "contact kill" microbes. "The antimicrobial activity of copper and copper alloys is now well established, and copper has been recently registered at the U.S. Environmental Protection Agency as the first solid antimicrobial material" (Grass et al. 2011: 1451). When microbes such as bacteria, yeast and viruses are brought into contact with copper, a thin layer of copper material dissolves on the surface of the metal and begins to damage the microorganisms by rupturing their cell membranes. The process degrades the genomic DNA of the microbes and eventually kills them. Copper therefore is considered to be a self-sanitizing material, and is used for medicinal purposes. Indian traditional medicinal practices of Ayurveda, for example, advocate storing water in and drinking water from copper vessels because of its perceived health benefits.

These properties of copper, which the material employs in the absence of humans, represent a form of fundamental or primary agency—a material agency. The material does what it does simply on account of its inherent nature as a metal with a certain atomic structure. It is also important to note that this material agency of copper (and every other material) is not a fixed entity; it changes with geographic location, weather conditions, ambient temperature, atmospheric pressure, and so on. So in order to get copper to do what they want, craftspeople will modify these conditions by heating the metal until it starts softening so that they may force it into molds and dies, hammering it to give it a specific texture, or exposing it to chemicals to build a patina of a desired color. Copper is highly ductile and malleable; which means that it will allow itself to be pulled into wires and pressed into sheets with comparative ease, in relation to other metals on the periodic table. It is too hard to be easily formed by hand, but soft enough to be pliable when subjected to the concentrated and exaggerated force of tools and machines. Though not as soft as gold, it is significantly more pliable than steel (see Plate 14).

The *tambats* have designed and developed a wide array of specialized hand tools and powered machines in response to the particular properties of copper, with which they force the material into useful things. But as humans exercise their creative agency on the material, it fights back. And in this process, it exercises a form of counteragency—a direct response to the human agency to which it is subjected. So, as the material is being shaped into things, it performs two roles—it acts as an agent, on account of its sheer properties, in aiding the transformation that is being urged upon it by the craftsperson, but it also acts as a counteragent in resisting that change. It yields and acquiesces to the agency of the human (equipped with a machine tool), but only after putting up a certain amount of defiance. All craftspeople speak to the material they work with, and it is through counteragency that the material "speaks back" (Holbraad 2011; Pels 1998). In fact, design has been characterized as a "reflective conversation with the materials of a design situation" (Schön 1992). Clearly craftspeople too engage in reflective conversations with the materials with which they work. The agency and counteragency present in the body of the material are critical to its becoming a thing. This interaction between the human agency of the craftperson and the material counteragency of copper unfold over time in a chain of events through the manufacturing process. In a series of highly choreographed movements—involving such tangible and intangible entities as people, workshops, materials, tools, machines, heat, light, pressure, money, time, and knowledge—the making of the copper utensils unfolds in *tambat ali* (see Plate 15).

Biographies of things, chains of events

Anthropologist Igor Kopytoff argues that: "Biographies of things can make salient what might otherwise remain obscure" (1986: 67). Kopytoff suggests that asking the same questions (where does a thing come from? who made it? what has happened in its life so far?) as one would of people, can potentially lead to the discovery of otherwise hidden critical cultural meanings of things. Each of the vessels that emerges from *tambat ali* travels to the market and eventually into someone's home is a repository of stories, and writing its biography can reveal social, cultural, and technical insights into its evolution from raw material to useful thing. Appadurai suggests that things have biographies because they, too, like people, have social lives. And, how do we discover these biographies and therefore the sociality of things? "We have to follow the things themselves," Appadurai contends, "for their meanings are inscribed in their forms, their uses, their trajectories. It is only through the analysis of these trajectories that we can interpret the human transactions and calculations that enliven things" (Appadurai 1986: 5). What does a biography, or a "life history" to use archaeologist Michael Schiffer's term, tell us? According to Schiffer, a biography reminds us that "artifacts begin as raw materials and are altered and assembled, transported and exchanged, used and reused, maintained, and eventually discarded, abandoned, or ritually deposited" (2011: 23). And what happens to the materials of which things are made as they progress through their journeys? This could potentially reveal the dynamics of interactions between human and material agency; it could lead to insights into the role of materials in the evolution of things; and it would shed light on the changing nature of material agency and counteragency over time. The *tambats* have been making copper water containers called *handis* for generations. As stainless steel containers and plastic buckets have appeared on the market, the use of these *handis* has declined. However, people sometimes bring back old, dented and broken *handis* to *tambat ali*, either for repair or to sell as scrap. These things bear the scars of hammering, brazing, polishing, and all other production techniques, as well as scratches and dents that appeared during use. The agency of humans (producers, as well as consumers) and the material is written on the body of the *handi*, there to be read by its biographer.

Some of the more intense and radical transformations of a material occur during the first few stages in its life history, when it still exists in raw form. In case of the copper, for example, extracting pure metal from chalcocite or chalcopyrite requires mechanical, chemical, and electrolytic processes in which the ore is drilled, blasted, crushed, melted, and exposed to a variety of powerful reagents. These operations merely convert ore embedded underneath the earth's surface into sheets and ingots of pure copper. The *tambats* acquire sheet stock from raw material dealers, and through a series of operations that make up their manufacturing process, convert them into vessels and other products for sale to consumers. This string of operations that transforms the material into a thing is often referred to as the *chaîne opératoire*. Archaelogist Catherine Perlès defines this concept as a "succession of mental operations and technical gestures, in order to satisfy a need (immediate or not), according to a preexisting project" (Sellet 1993: 106). This notion of an operational chain is derived from ethnology and the analysis of life histories of stone tools (lithic technologies), and is being applied currently in anthropology and material culture studies as a form of processual analysis of the manufacturing of things (Sellet 1993; Leroi-Gourhan,1964; Lemonnier 1983). Archaeologists Marie Soressi and Jean-Michel Geneste have, in fact, observed that "the efficacy of the '*chaîne opératoire* tool' is augmented by physical experiments performed by archaeologists using the raw materials employed by prehistoric groups to produce their stone tools, as well as by the growing number of analyses of archaeological assemblages using this methodology" (Soressi and Geneste 2011: 337). In other words, in addition to analyzing the operational chain, reproducing it oneself, as I have in *tambat ali*, can augment the process of discovery and the outcomes.

While Perlès' definition of the *chaîne opératoire* only mentions cognitive and technological factors, one cannot ignore the social forces at play in shaping objects. Schlanger explains this well:

> With the *chaîne opératoire*, it is possible to appreciate that alongside tools, raw materials, energy and various physical or environmental possibilities, technical systems are also composed of such crucial elements as the knowledge, skills, values and symbolic representations brought to bear and generated in the course of action, as well as the social frameworks (including gender, age or ethnic differentiations) implicated in the production and reproduction of everyday life. (Schlanger 2005: 21)

A *chaîne opératoire*, therefore, is formed by individual, cognitive, social, technical, material, and environmental agents and their actions. Schiffer's concept of "behavioral chain" which he defines as "the entire sequence of activities that took place during the life history of a component, product, or complex technological system" is similar (Schiffer 2011: 30). While the *chaîne opératoire* approach has traditionally focused its attention on the the manufacture of things (more specifically tools), the behavioral chain model can be more broadly applied to a range of products and activities. More recent interpretations and applications of *chaîne opératoire* have included a broader range of activities such as lifetime use, maintenance and disposal, the behavioral chain approach tends to include the entire life of the objects being analyzed.

Tracing the trajectory of any of the utilitarian, decorative, or religious things that the *tambats* have been making for generations reveals that they make complex journeys from their origins as ideas in the minds of designers and craftspeople, through raw material and manufacture, to useful life with the buyers, and finally to their disposal as garbage, hand-me-downs, or metal for recycling. Through this journey, the materials of which they are made undergo a variety of transformations, and re-constructing a *chaîne opératoire* of one of the products can help us understand how things emerge from the interactions between the various human and non-human agents and agencies involved.

The water carafe

The copper water carafe seen on Plate 16 is designed by architect and product designer Rashmi Ranade. The carafe, with its lustrous, hammered exterior, starts its life in the workshop as a dull, stained sheet of copper 4 × 4 inches in size. This product, known as Water Bearer, is manufactured from 98 percent pure copper by Studio Coppre, based in Pune, India. Ranade, the lead designer at Studio Coppre, has been working with craftspeople in *tambat ali* for a decade and carefully considers traditional manufacturing processes and human skills while designing the products. The carafe emerges from a flat sheet of copper into the usable vessel that we see here on account of the agency of the material, humans, and tools, through a series of processes that include marking, cutting, cleaning, heating, spinning, buffing, polishing, hammering, and lacquering (see Plate 18).

The first step in the making of the water carafe is cutting the large sheets of copper into smaller squares and finally into a 6-inch diameter circle using a pair of metallic shears. This disc is heated on a coal forge to soften the material and then submerged in water in a process called quenching to cool and anneal it. The process of creating the form of the carafe is undertaken over a series of progressive dies that gradually convert the flat sheet into the final form of the vessel on a spinning lathe. Spinning is a relatively slow, room temperature manufacturing process used to create radially symmetrical metal parts by pressing sheet stock against a die that is turning at high speed on a lathe. In Kadu's workshop, the dies—devices for cutting or molding metal into particular shapes—are often made from the wood of acacia trees since the material is hard, durable, and does not distort too drastically over time. Copper hardens as it is worked over on the lathe, and therefore it has to be frequently taken off the lathe and heated on the coal forge to soften it again. Here, I was able to observe human agency, as well as the agency and counteragency of the material. The natural hardness of copper that resists bending and shaping at room temperature gives in to the heat, realigns its crystalline structure, and becomes more pliable. Knowledge of how far human agency can push against the counteragency of the material is critical knowledge for the craftspeople as they mold the carafe. Once the final shape has been achieved, the craftsperson forces a curled edge (referred to as a bead) on the top of the carafe to facilitate easy drinking. The tapered neck of this carafe requires the use of a special, collapsible die that can be extracted from the vessel after it is processed on the lathe. The lid, which serves as a drinking cup, is similarly spun on the lathe with a different die (see Plate 17).

During the process of spinning, a significant amount of lubricating grease is applied on the copper and, therefore, once the final shape has been formed, the carafe is washed with tamarind paste and dilute sulfuric acid to clean the surface. It is dried again and polished to a shine on a buffing wheel. The carafe is now ready for hammering (*matharkam*).

It is *matharkam* for which the community is best known. Only a few of the craftspeople are able to create the kind of even hammertone texture on the surface of the carafe. It is critical that the rows of the dents are evenly hammered onto the carafe without deforming the product's overall shape. Doing this takes enormous skill, years of practice, knowledge of the material, familiarity with the tools, and significant strength. The carafe is positioned on the anvil (*kharvai*), held in place with toes of both feet, indexed (rotated) ever so slightly with one hand, and hammered with the other, row after row, until the entire surface is fully covered with the burnished marks. Ambre, one of the most skilled craftsmen in *tambat ali*, who taught me some of this skill, has over thirty years of experience doing this work, and has a unique gestural technique of *matharkam*. The hammertone marks on the copper between his toes and under his hammer spill out with remarkable fluidity on everything he makes. His hammer strokes do not descend vertically down on to the surface of the copper; he moves his right arm in a fluid ellipsoidal motion striking the metal almost in a swiping motion, denting the surface while simultaneously burnishing it. In addition to imparting a unique sense of beauty to the product, the process of hammering serves another important role. The hammertone texture highlights what copper can do, and in this process works as an agent in preventing the material from disappearing into the thing. Instead of being "swallowed up by the very objects to which they have given birth" (Ingold 2007: 9), the hammered dents on the carafe do the opposite and highlight the material properties of the copper (see Plate 18).

Once the hammertone is created, the product is cleaned again, buffed, and the outer surface sprayed with a clear coat to protect the surface from corrosion. The inner walls are untreated, to allow copper to come in contact with the water filled into the carafe so it can impart its antibacterial properties. In other words, this will allow copper to exercise its agency. At this stage, the material has been transformed into a thing, the human and material agency and counteragency have played out in the production of the water carafe. The other life stories of the product are yet to unfold, yet to be written.

Conclusion

"All materials have their properties which may be described but only some of these materials and their properties are significant to people. The concept of materiality is one that needfully addresses the 'social lives' of stones [and other materials] in relation to the social lives of persons," according to archaeologist Christopher Tilley (2007: 17). Materials and things circulate through people's lives and participate in (as well as enable) a variety of social and cultural rituals and human relationships. As they exercise their agencies through this trajectory of production, distribution, and consumption, they acquire and discard multiple meanings. At times, we are aware of the significance of the materials themselves, and at times, they recede into the things of which they are part. According anthropologist Susanne Küchler, there is a growing trend to "locate social processes at the stage of *material innovation* (emphasis in original) in ways that will bring notions of social relations into dialogue with the creative transformation of materials" (Küchler 2008: 103). I hope this examination of materials continues to reveal their centrality to material culture.

Bibliography

Appadurai, A. (1986), "Introduction: Commodities and the Politics of Value," in A. Appadurai, *The Social Life of Things: Commodities in Cultural Perspective*, 3–62, Cambridge: Cambridge University Press.

Drazin, A. (2015), "To Live in a Materials World," in A. Drazin, and S. Küchler, *The Social Life of Materials: Studies in Materials and Society*, 3–28, London: Bloomsbury.

Gell, A. (1998), *Art and Agency: An Anthropological Theory*, Oxford: Oxford University Press.

Grass, G., C. Rensing, and M. Solioz (2011), Metallic Copper as an Antimicrobial Surface. *Applied and Environmental Microbiology* 77 (5): 1541–7.

Heidegger, M. (1977), *The Question Concerning Technology and Other Essays*, New York: Harper & Row.

Hicks, D., and M. Beaudry (2010), "Introduction, Material Culture Studies: A Reactionary View," in D. Hicks and M. Beaudry, *The Oxford Handbook of Material Culture Studies*, 1–21, Oxford: Oxford University Press.

Holbraad, M., *Can The Thing Speak?* (O. A. Press, Producer). http://openanthcoop.net/press/: http://openanthcoop.net/press/2011/01/12/can-the-thing-speak/ (accessed January 12, 2011).

Hoskins, J. (2006), "Agency, Biography and Objects," in C. Tilley, W. Keane, S. Küchler, M. Rowlands, and P. Spyer, *Handbook of Material Culture*, 4–84, New Delhi: Sage.

Ingold, T. (2007), "Materials Against Materiality," *Archaeological Dialogues* 14 (1): 1–16.

Knappett, C., and L. Malafouris, L. (2008), *Material Agency: Towards a Non-Anthropocentric Approach*, New York: Springer Science+Business Media LLC.

Kopytoff, I. (1986), "The Cultural Biography of Things: Commoditization as Process," in A. Appadurai, *Social Life of Things: Commodities in Cultural Perspective*, 64–91, Cambridge: Cambridge University Press.

Küchler, S. (2008), "Technological Materiality: Beyond the Dualist Paradigm," *Theory Culture Society* 25: 101–20.

Latour, B. (2005), "From Realpolitik to Dingpolitik: How to Make Things Public," in B. Latour and P. Weibel, *Making Things Public: Atmospheres of Democracy*, 14–41, Cambridge: MIT Press.

Lemonnier, P. (1983), "L'Etude des Systemes Techniques: Une Urgence en Technologie Culturelle," *Techniques et Culture* 1: 11–34.

Leroi-Gourhan, A. (1964), *Le Geste et la Parole I: Technique et Language*, Paris: Albin Michel.

Mauss, M. (1973), "Techniques of the Body," *Economy and Society* 2 (1): 70–88.

Miller, D. (2005), "Materiality: An Introduction," in D. Miller, *Materiality: Politics, History, and Culture*, 1–50, Durham: Duke University Press.

Perlès, C. (1987), *Les Industries Lithiques Taillees de Franchthi, Argolide: Presentation Generate et Industries Paleolithiques*, Terre Haute: Indiana University Press.

Pels, P. (1998), "The Spirit of Matter: On Fetish, Rarity, Fact and Fancy," in P. Spyer, *Border Fetishisms: Material Objects in Unstable Places*, 91–121, New York: Routledge.

Schön, D. (1992), "Designing as Reflective Conversation with the Materials of a Design Situation," *Knowledge-Based Systems* 5 (1): 3–14.

Schiffer, M. (2011), *Studying Technological Change*, Salt Lake City, UT: University of Utah Press.

Schlanger, N. (2005), "The Chaîne Opératoire," in C. Renfrew and P. Bahn, *Archaeology: The Key Concepts*, New York: Routledge.

Sellet, F. (1993), "Chaine Operatoire: The Concept and its Applications," *Lithic Technology* 18 (1/2): 106–12.

Soressi, M. and J.-M Geneste (2011), "The History and Efficacy of the Chaîne Opératoire Approach to Lithic Analysis: Studying Techniques to Reveal Past Societies in an Evolutionary Perspective," *PaleoAnthropology*: 334–50.

Tilley, C. (2007), "Materials in Materiality," *Archaeological Dialogues*, 14 (1): 16–20.

Verbeek, P.-P. (2005), *What Things Do: Philosophical Reflections on Technology, Agency, and Design*, University Park, PA: Pennsylvania State University Press.

Afterword

Encountering design

Bill Brown

What happens when thing theory encounters design? How can the imperatives, histories, and theories of design expand the conceptualization of thingness, enabling theory to engage not just one or another object, but also that object's prehistory, a new biography of things that, say, begins with conception and preconception? Although the essays in *Encountering Things* were collected to "help make theory accessible to and relevant to design practitioners," the collection also makes design accessible and relevant to that wide range of scholars who now focus on objects and things, matter and materiality. Indeed, as Atzmon and Boradkar assert in the introduction to this volume, design is "particularly consequential to theories about things." It is consequential, on the one hand, because design can underscore Theodor Adorno's insistence that "we are not to philosophize about concrete things; we are to philosophize, rather, out of those things;"[1] and it is consequential, no less, because those concrete things so clearly turn out to be (like concrete itself) composites (made up of materials but also of ideas, signs, ideologies, aspirations and frustrations). The range of the essays—focused on posters and metal signage, needles and rockets, ancient figurines and a recent potato masher—underscores the ubiquity of design as a practice (across, time, place, and scale) and thus highlights a more august consequentiality. For of course in the twenty-first century we inhabit an object world more thoroughly designed than ever before, the designed material environment that shapes our everyday lives, individual and collective. The difference (as charted here by Boradkar and Owerko) between a group listening to music blaring from a boombox and an individual listening through earbuds could not illustrate the point more plainly. Encountering design—engaging its past, trying to illuminate its present and to anticipate its future—may give theory its best shot at being consequential.

Since publishing "Thing Theory," in 2001, I've taken the time to refine and further specify the claims I made there, to situate those claims in relation to different philosophical, anthropological, and sociological traditions (with particular attention to Gaston Bachelard, Walter Benjamin, Hannah Arendt, and Bruno Latour), and to think through particular objects (mechanical banks, Air Jordans, the World Trade Towers, Charlie McCarthy dolls, florescent lighting, white plastic chairs, clay pots).[2] But I haven't paused to write about design—even while proposing that the University of Chicago develop a Media Arts & Design Center and an Urban Architecture and Design School. Encountering the essays in this volume provides such a pause and allows me to begin, tentatively, to measure some immediate consequences that the field of design should have for that thing called *theory*. For the moment: just three points.

1   Materialisms and matter

The so-called *material turn* has emerged across several disciplines—Art History, Anthropology, Political Theory, History, Sociology, etc. At the same time, one strain of the so-called new materialism has been inspired and informed by Deleuze and Guattari's *Mille Plateaux* (1980). The simultaneity does not bespeak a necessary or obvious convergence. For Deleuze and Guattari define matter as the "unformed, unorganized, nonstratified, or destratified body and all its flows: subatomic and submolecular particles, pure intensities, prevital and prephysical free singularities."[3] Indeed, rather than addressing *matter*, they prefer to write about "matter-movement, this matter-energy, this matter-flow," about "vague essences" that must "not be confused" with any "sensible, formed and perceived thinghood" (TP: 407). On the one hand, their disposition might help you to identify the energy within the physical (and "prephysical") environment, both actual and virtual; on the other, they seem to elide objects altogether, as though sensible, perceived thinghood were beside the point, let alone the designed object world.[4]

A description of "pure intensities" may help you to fathom an alternate ontology, indeed a liberating ontology insofar as it diminishes the preponderant resistance of physical object forms (conceptually dissolved in the flow). But that description does not get you very far when it comes to understanding how a chair or a radio or a telephone has shaped the way you inhabit everyday space … or when it comes to sensing (intellectually and affectively) how new object forms might alter everyday life. For the Constructivists, after all, design strategies could help to complete the revolution; and in 2015, projekt bauhaus organized a symposium around the still relevant and much contested question, "can design change society?"[5] With conspicuous urgency, the very idea of design ought to summon a new materialism that confronts matter—physical objects—rather than, once again, theorizing matter into some remote margin. Indeed, as Boradkar makes clear when he writes about the agency of copper, finally engaging with materials is one way to make materialism new.

Which certainly isn't to argue that concrete objects are merely material; they are indeed composites. A simple and sentimental expression of the fact could be seen in Michael Brown's "An Object is Just Material," his exhibition at the Yvon Lambert Gallery in New York (2009). Like so much contemporary art, his work depends on the dynamics of re-fabrication: in this case the conversion of vinyl records into household tools—resulting in the minimalist display of a broom, a mop, a fan, a bucket, for which he had melted down stacks of records and recast the molten vinyl into broom handles, mop handles, fan blades, buckets. Moreover, he chooses iconic records—by Aretha Franklin, Elvis, Johnny Cash, the Ramones—that were part of the collection he began to amass as a teenager. Whatever sentiment he meant to evoke, the fascination of the project lies in his demediation of the acoustical medium and his remediation of it as cleaning equipment—the point being that the substance from which objects are made (the wood of a table, the marble of a column, the ceramic of the pot) has always had some other life in some other object form. To begin with, then, "just material" doesn't make much sense, except insofar as it names the threat of de-objectivization that any object lives with. (A car can become scrap metal, a barn can become lumber, the plastic bottle can be recycled into a plastic box. A kind of kinesis inheres within the object world. Indeed, in a Deleuzian accent you might say that material is perpetually in a state of becoming and unbecoming one or another form.) Moreover, the simple objects in the show depended on a complex treatment of the material and the complex conceptual work of transposition. The vinyl that once contained the record of a human voice (say Aretha singing *Natural Woman*) has become the record of Michael Brown's own fixations and aspirations, within a specific cultural context. The exhibition dramatized the way that any designed object, whatever it is, is always a *record* of the work that went into it (material and immaterial both).

When Rappaport describes the collaboration of makers and designers in the Steinway piano factory, when Golec describes the alliance between medics and designers in the technological and aesthetic development of the Eames DCM—these are accounts of the collective composition of manufactured products. No less, Hall's account of the Concorde's fall from grace, like Hadlaw's story of the American public's disappointment with Bell's candlestick telephone in the 1920s—these show how the consuming public becomes part of that collective. This is one reason why the logic of Marx's own materialism remains so relevant: he understood commodity fetishism as a pathology that prevents us from seeing the social relations that inhere in any commodity—the history of human labor that the object congeals. Of course, objects congeal much else besides—calculations and negotiations and anticipated relations to other objects—obscured by more than the commodity form. Design thinking (or thinking design) can disclose the activity that lies behind the static object. As Atzmon and Boradkar put it, "things take shape in the interstitial spaces that develop among designers, design processes, design environments and user experiences" (8). When it comes to the artefacts that surround us, what Hegel called the "community (*Gemeninschaft*)" of the "objective entity" involves far more than the entity's properties. The object serves as a kind of medium that holds that community in suspension.

2 **Autonomy vs. relationality**

This is why, in my own effort to differentiate the thing from an object I've emphasized how *thingness* can productively caption a kind of *relation*. What Hall describes as the isolation of the *object* through exhibition and glossy advertising, which belies its life as a thing among things (both objects and human subjects), can be understood as the mass cultural version of the conceptual isolation of the object. An object isn't just material. It also isn't an independent, self-same, autonomous object. And this is why, no matter how compelling Heidegger has become for those of us who mean to reengage the object world, it is important to recognize a profound yet profoundly problematic aspect of his thinking. For it was essential to Heidegger, by the time he delivered his lecture on "The Thing" in 1950, to fathom the "thing as thing" in its absolute autonomy.[6] To answer the question "what is a thing?" he turns to a jug (*Krug*), which, by his light, "stands on its own"; in its independence "the jug differs from an object" (164); its "thingly character" cannot "be defined in any way in terms of the objectness, the over-againstness of the object" ("T": 164–5). This names the kind of relation that Heidegger is determined to think beyond; only beyond the *Ding für uns* can we locate the thing's self-sameness. To answer that fundamental question— "What in the thing is thingly? What is the thing itself?"—Heidegger concentrates on what you could call the force of the jug's form: "From start to finish the potter takes hold of the impalpable void"—not a material that is present (clay), but an absence, the "void that holds" ("T": 165, 167).⁷ The philosopher then transposes that holding into a gathering, etymologically licensed by the word *Ding* having originally meant a gathering (an assembly—*dinc*, in Old High German), enabling him to say that "the thing things" (*Das Ding dingt*): a predication that lets the thing simply be in its Being, as though you were to say that *the chair chairs*. In its self-sameness the thinging thing gathers. The jug is no "object" or "*res*" or "*ens*": "The jug is a thing insofar as it things" ("T": 175). This culminates Heidegger's strategy for thinking beyond both subject and object—beyond relation ... except insofar as the gathering void poetically brings earth and sky, deities and mortals, into ringing relation to each other, thinging the world as such. Outside relation it nonetheless constitutes relations.

In this august meditation Heidegger has given up on the everyday world in which you might use the jug to pour yourself a glass of iced coffee or a little water to accompany your single malt scotch—a world in which relation is the given, and in which thingness designates a relation that has become conspicuous, incapable of being overlooked. This is why Heidegger's earlier thinking about things can seem more useful. In *Being and Time*, however anthropocentric his concern with *Dasein* may be (specifically designating human-being), his originality lies not least in his insistence that we cannot begin to appreciate what being human means without recognizing that such being is thrown (has been thrown) into a world of things. His commitment to the "average everydayness" of *Dasein*, and his description of *Dasein* as a being in the midst of what is (*inmitten des Seienden*), render things absolutely adhesive: there is no human-being without them—they are never not within Being.⁸ The things most engaged by (or in) *Dasien* Heidegger terms "equipment" (*das Zeug*), his translation of the Greek *pragmata*, all sorts of "entities which we encounter in concern," with which we involve ourselves everyday: "equipment for writing, sewing, working, transportation, measurement," for instance, but also the equipment used for unconscious tasks: "when I open the door, for instance, I use the latch" (*BT*: 96–7).⁹ But our very involvement with such things, which entails concentrating on the task rather than the tools, means that their essential characteristic—their equipmental being, their instrumentality, their "readiness-to-hand"—remains inconspicuous: should we stop to observe them we necessarily fall into a secondary mode of encounter, wherein only their "presence-at-hand" becomes apparent. Heidegger's famous case is the hammer: should you simply look at the hammer, its readiness-to-hand (*Zuhandenheit*), its specific "Thingly character," cannot be "grasped theoretically at all" (*BT*: 98, 99). But as you bodily deploy the hammer the thing disappears from *conceptual* view.¹⁰ "The peculiarity of what is proximally ready-to-hand is that, in its readiness-to-hand, it must, as it were, withdraw in order to be ready-to-hand quite authentically" (*BT*: 99).¹¹ In this case, though, Heidegger neglects the production of the hammer, its design, the practice of giving form to function, during which the equipmental being of the hammer has had to be internalized, its readiness-to-hand ... not apprehended theoretically (at a distance) perhaps, but grasped nonetheless. Like the maker (of the pot), the designer (of the hammer) has both cognitive and bodily insight into a relational thingness of things that theory should persist in acknowledging. It has been acknowledged, as Tonkinwise celebrates, by Scarry, who works at describing the materialized knowledge that informs the equipment with which we live, understanding the chair as "a sentient awareness materialized into a freestanding design." Encountering design should mean re-encountering the philosophy that shapes contemporary thought, and dilating it at just those moments when theory seems to have reached an impasse—because it too quickly isolates a single object, because it has forgotten the composite character of any human-made object (and any biological object, no less), because it would rather not face the imbrications of the material and immaterial, and because it would rather not accept the relationality of every object—indeed the fact that relation precedes the object's coming to be.

3 **Agency and narrativity**

Throughout out this volume the authors persuasively describe the vitality and agency of objects. So too, now that the object world has begun to enjoy a new kind of academic attention, various thinkers (I include myself) have perceived a secret life of things or more simply declared the vibrancy and agency of matter. We do so at some risk—the risk of overlooking the obvious: the fact that, these days, one object after another has been designed to assume a kind of agency of its own. The automated checkout counter, the automatic car (now sponsored in Pittsburgh by Uber), the drone, any number of robotic entities, the internet of things—these make one thing very clear: that the effort, *in theory*, to stop thinking about the subject, to de-privilege the human, and to flatten ontology has intersected with the *practice*, however unconscious, of rendering the human obsolete.[12]

Less melodramatically: all objects may have agency; some have more agency than others. The more patently agential among them, like the eighteenth-century automata and the contemporary Android OS that Marenko pairs, provoke "questions about the shifting boundary between the artificiality of life and the intelligence of machines." Of course, as Tonkinwise patiently charts, the conviction that "things have agency" captions a wide range of phenomena, from a range of perspectives, and it often appears as "a strategic claim." At a moment when artificial intelligence promises to supplant social media as the new focus of attention in Silicon Valley, the strategy can seem to oscillate between the ontological and the phenomenological, the epistemological and the social. For just as Guffey emphasizes how the new discourse on things began to emerge (within Anthropology) when "the relationship between the physical thing and the digital thing" became a new matter of concern for the computer culture of the mid 1980s, so too our current theoretical investment in a de-hierarchizing zone of immanence where "every entity is equally being" has emerged at a moment technology has challenged more than a few human preserves.[13] Insofar as design "breathes agency into materials" (5), design should be at the center of the theoretical conversation—as it has been, of course, in the case of Bruno Latour, who began as an anthropologist of science.

These days I often find myself speaking to an audience of archaeologists, curators, or artists, but it was literature that first mediated my own scholarly engagement with objects, as I worked to understand the *material unconscious* through which literary texts, however inconspicuously and unintentionally, register changes in material culture. Since then, I've been struck by how often literary canons anticipate topics that now enjoy considerable currency. When it comes to the vitality of matter, for instance, Homer's account of Achilles' Shield could hardly provide a more dramatic example: *there* on (or *in*) the object, armies clash within the City of War; in the City of Peace, children dance while men harvest grapes and guide their cattle. The poem emphasizes that this life resides within a crafted object—that the activity amounts to activated metal: Hephaestus "made next a herd of longhorns, / fashioned in gold and tin: away they shambled, … / Four cowherds all of gold were plodding after / with nine little dogs beside them."[14] The *Iliad* might be said to share Deleuze and Guattari's fascination with metal, the way that "metal and metallurgy" illuminate a "life proper to matter, a vital state of matter as such, a material vitalism that doubtless exists everywhere but is ordinarily hidden or covered, rendered unrecognizeable" (TP: 454). But of course in the case of Homer's epic it is design and manufacture that make the vitalism recognizable. Encountering Achilles' Shield within the *Iliad* means encountering design. This is when, as the editors to this volume put it, things can be apprehended as "vital entities that possess power to effect change through their material, formal, and functional properties" (4).

Of course, the *Iliad* is a pre-modern text. Other pre-modern writers (particularly Lucretius) have provided a conceptual resource for reanimating the material world. Indeed, Latour has quipped that "inanimism" is "the queer invention" of modernity.[15] His own conceptual resource for reanimating objects and reimagining the social has been the semiotic formalization of agency within narrative theory. A. J. Greimas's notion of the *actant*, an agential role without specific content, enables Latour to re-describe certain putatively inanimate objects (a key, a speed bump) as having agency (and no less agency than some human actor).[16] Such actants then combine and recombine into various networks.[17] Latour was once a student in Greimas's seminars. While teaching anthropology he routinely taught semiotics, with the conviction that Greimas provides "a sort of tool box" to "treat questions of agency" and "questions of the careers of objects." It's unsurprising, then, that Latour understands "literature [as] the place where the freedom of agency can be regained"; more precisely, it is narrative theory that should be "to the social sciences what mathematics is to physics."[18]

As Greimas points out, though, narrative structures are "characteristic of the human imaginary in general."[19] For one thing, the syntactic apprehension of events "is, whether we like or not, of anthropomorphic inspiration" (104). For another, the *actant* as the subject of a *doing* has already been humanized, whether human or not. Indeed, Greimas maintains that doing is "doubly anthropomorphic": "As an activity it presupposes a subject; as a message, it is objectified and implies the axis of transmission between sender and receiver" (71). But rather than emphasizing the inescapable anthropomorphism of the actant as such, I mean to underscore the inevitability—when it comes to assessing agency—of narrative. I hasten to add that Latour has had such a profound impact across fields not least because he is such a good storyteller, often telling the story of design, its success and its failure.

It is hard to make that point without noticing, thanks to the stories told in the foregoing volume, that the aspiration to give form to function is an aspiration that itself depends on a narrative imagination. Narrative might well be understood as the fundamental medium of design—the cognitive structuring though which design thinking must think. And design might well be understood as granting us the best access we have to appreciating, in practice, how actants are conceived.

In the patois of our present, particular words have less than predictably become ubiquitous. To take a notable example: one does not simply *curate* an art exhibition; one also *curates* a public conversation, a dinner party, home décor. Design has enjoyed a different kind of promiscuity: *design* has permeated quotidian speech but it has also expanded wildly as a discipline. Architectural design, urban design, landscape design, interior design, product design, graphic design, fashion design—those were just the beginning. As Dubberly recounts in his recent history of the discipline, the design of physical structures and products has morphed into "business design, interaction design, service design, social innovation design," with an eye to the "experience economy" we now inhabit. Peter Miller, Dean of the Bard Graduate Center in New York (devoted to material culture, design history, and the decorative arts) has asked whether "Design Thinking" is not the "New Liberal Arts."[20] His question focuses on Stanford's "d.school"—which grew out of the product design program but has become an autonomous site (inspired in part by IDEO) where students are taught strategies for action-oriented problem-solving. Miller too underscores the switch (so key to Apple's success) from designing products to designing experience. Eager as one might be to argue that great design has always been the design of experience, a more pressing line of thought might question (as Benjamin and Adorno did, as William James and John Dewey did) what one means by experience to begin with, and how dependent that meaning is on narrative form. Just as encountering things means encountering thingness as an experience provoked by a relation that can be cast in narrative form, so too encountering design can demonstrate how theories about things should intersect with stories about them.

Notes

1. Theodor W. Adorno (1997), *Negative Dialectics*, trans. E. B. Ashton, New York: Continuum, 33.
2. See *Other Things* (2015), Chicago: University of Chicago Press.
3. G. Deleuze and F. Guattari (1987), *A Thousand Plateaus*, trans. B. Massumi, Minneapolis: University of Minnesota Press, 1987, 43. Further references will be provided parenthetically as TP. For some sense of Deleuze and Guattari's impact on various new materialisms, see, for instance the essays collected by D. Coole and S. Frost in (2010) *New Materialisms: Ontology, Agency, and Politics*, Durham, NC: Duke University Press.
4. It is decidedly beside the point, disappointingly, for an object-oriented ontology that concerns itself not with objects but with the supposed essences of objects that perpetually withdraw, both from people and from other objects. (See, for instance, G. Harman (2005), *Guerrilla Metaphysics: Phenomenology and the Carpentry of Things*, Peru, IL: Open Court Press.) Design makes a compelling counter case for focusing on the interaction of objects with people and with other objects. Within the philosophical tradition both William James and Alfred North Whitehead make such a case, which is why both thinkers are so important to Bruno Latour.
5. See B. Arvatov (1925), "Everyday Life and the Culture of the Thing (Toward the Formulation of the Question)," trans. C. Kiaer, October, 81 (Summer 1997): 119–28; and http://projekt-bauhaus.de/en/events/symposium-can-design-change-society/ (accessed February 5, 2016).
6. M. Heidegger (2001), "The Thing," *Poetry, Language, Thought*, trans. A. Hofstadter, 178, New York: Perennial Classics. Hereafter cited parenthetically as "T."
7. This quick sleight of hand in Heidegger's lecture could be read as an allegory of the fate of objects in the field of anthropology, when Franz Boas, among others, gave up on any object-based epistemology. See S. Conn (1998), *Museums and American Intellectual Life, 1876–1926*, 31, Chicago: University of Chicago Press; see also B. Brown (2003), *A Sense of Things: The Object Matter of American Literature* Chicago: University of Chicago Press, 88–95, 118.

8   M. Heidegger, *Being and Time*, trans. J. Macquarrie and E. Robinson, New York: Harper & Row, 1962, 125–34. (Further references will be provided parenthetically as *BT*.)

9   "Concern" (*Besorgen*) includes the sense of procuring and of looking after; it is an involvement, Heidegger dilates, that can be understood as "having to do with something, producing something, attending to something and looking after it, making use of something, giving something up and letting it go, undertaking, accomplishing, evincing, interrogating, considering, discussing, determining" (*BT* 83).

10 This is to say that the thing necessarily disappears from <u>theory</u>, given that theory is a view that requires distance. For Alfonso Lingis's poignantly different account of the hammer and hammering, see *The Imperative*, 75.

11 As he epigrammatically puts it in the Work of Art essay, "the more handy a piece of equipment is, the more inconspicuous it remains" ("WA" 63).

12 See B. Brown (2015), "The Obsolescence of the Human," *Cultures of Obsolescence: History, Materiality, and the Digital Age*, B. B. Tishleder and S. Wasserman (eds), Basingstoke: Palgrave Macmillan, 19–40.

13 See G. Deleuze (2007), "Zones of Immanence," in *Two Regimes of Madness: Texts and Interviews 1975–1995*, trans. A. Hodges and M. Taormina, New York: Semiotext[e], 266–9.

14 The *Iliad* (2004), trans. R. Fitzgerald, New York: Farrar, Straus, and Giroux, 18, 661–2, 665–6

15 B. Latour (2010), "An Attempt at a 'Compositionalist Manifesto,'" *New Literary History* 41: 481–2.

16 A. J. Greimas (1973), "Actants, Actors, and Figures," *On Meaning: Selected Writings in Semiotic Theory*, trans. P. J. Perron and F. H. Collins, Minneapolis: University of Minnesota Press, 106–20. His original use of the term "actant" appeared in his effort to re-schematize Vladimir Propp's morphology of Russian folktales. What is significant for the argument at hand is that, for instance, among the oppositional actants paired along three axes, the *content* of the "helper" actant (which stands in binary opposition to the "opponent" actant) can be human (the wise man), animate but unhuman (the horse), inanimate (the sword), or abstract (courage), each of which assists the Prince in attaining his goal. See A. J. Greimas (1966), "Reflections on Actantial Models," *Structural Semantics* (1983), trans. D. McDowell, R. Schleifer, and A. Velie, Lincoln: University of Nebraska Press, Ch. 10. On the speed bump, see Latour, *Pandora's Hope*, 190; on the key, see "The Berlin Key or How to Do Words with Things," in *Matter, Materiality and Modern Culture* (2000), P. M. Graves-Brown (ed.), London: Routledge, 11–21.

17 Thus, in *The Pasteurization of France* (1988), trans. A. Sheridan and J. Law (1993), Cambridge, MA: Harvard University Press, Latour writes, "No actant is as weak that it cannot enlist another. Then the two join together and become one for a third actant, which they can therefore move more easily. An eddy is formed, and it grows by becoming many others" (159).

18 B. Latour (2009), "Where Constant Experiments Have Been Provided," interview, *Arch* 2 (Spring), http://artsci.wustl.edu/~archword/interviews/latour/interview.htm (accessed January 10, 2012). See also Latour (1993), "Pasteur on Lactic Acid Yeast: A Partial Semiotic Analaysis," *Configurations* 1: 129–45.

19 A. J. Greimas, *On Meaning*, 115. Further references to Greimas, made parenthetically, will be to this text.

20 See P. Miller, "Is 'Design Thinking' the New Liberal Arts?", *The Chronicle of Higher Education*, March 26, 2015 http://www.chronicle.com/article/Is-Design-Thinking-the-New/228779 (accessed January 25, 2016). Subsequent Miller quotations are from this article. He answers his question in the negative: design thinking, however compelling it has become, is not the new liberal arts; indeed, what such thinking needs is the "the study of past achievements" to appreciate "the complexity of human existence."

Bibliography

Adorno, T. W. (1997), *Negative Dialectics*, trans. E. B. Ashton, New York: Continuum.
Arvatov, B. (1925), "Everyday Life and the Culture of the Thing (Toward the Formulation of the Question," trans. C. Kiaer. *October* 81 (Summer 1997): 119–28.
Arvatov, B., "Can Design Change Society?," project bauhaus http://projekt-bauhaus.de/en/events/symposium-can-design-change-society (accessed September 29, 2016).
Brown, B. (2003), *A Sense of Things: The Object Matter of American Literature*, Chicago: University of Chicago Press.
Brown, B. (2015), "The Obsolescence of the Human," in B. B. Tishleder and S. Wasserman (eds), *Cultures of Obsolescence: History, Materiality, and the Digital Age*, 19–40, New York: Palgrave Macmillan.
Brown, B. (2015), *Other Things*, Chicago: University of Chicago Press.
Conn, S. (1998), *Museums and American Intellectual Life, 1876–1926*, Chicago: University of Chicago Press.
Coole, D., and S. Frost (2010), *New Materialisms: Ontology, Agency, and Politics*, Durham, NC: Duke University Press.
Deleuze, G. (2007), "Zones of Immanence," in *Two Regimes of Madness: Texts and Interviews 1975–1995*, trans. A. Hodges and M. Taormina, 266–9, New York: Semiotext[e].
Deleuze, G., and F. Guattari (1987), *A Thousand Plateaus*, trans. B. Massumi, Minneapolis: University of Minnesota Press.
Greimas, A. J. (1966), "Reflections on Actantial Models," in *Structural Semantics* (1983), trans. D. McDowell, R. Schleifer, and A. Velie, Ch. 10, Lincoln, NB: University of Nebraska Press.
Greimas, A. J. (1973) "Actants, Actors, and Figures," in *On Meaning: Selected Writings in Semiotic Theory*, trans. P. J. Perron and F. H. Collins, 106–20, Minneapolis: University of Minnesota Press.
Greimas, A. J. (1987), *On Meaning*, trans. P. J. Perron and F. H. Collins, Minneapolis: University of Minnesota Press.
Harman, G. (2005), *Guerrilla Metaphysics: Phenomenology and the Carpentry of Things*, Peru, IL: Open Court Press.
Heidegger, M. (1962), *Being and Time*, trans. J. Macquarrie and E. Robinson, New York: Harper & Row.
Heidegger, M. (2001), "The Thing," in *Poetry, Language, Thought*, trans. A. Hofstadter, New York: Perennial Classics.
Homer (2004), *Iliad*, trans. R. Fitzgerald, New York: Farrar, Straus, and Giroux.
Latour, B. ([1988] 1993), *The Pasteurization of France,* trans. A. Sheridan and J. Law, Cambridge, MA: Harvard University Press.
Latour, B. (1993), "Pasteur on Lactic Acid Yeast: A Partial Semiotic Analaysis," *Configurations* 1: 129–45.
Latour, B. (1999), *Pandora's Hope*: *Essays on the Reality of Science Studies*, Cambridge, MA: Harvard University Press, 1999.
Latour, B. (2000), "The Berlin Key or How to Do Words with Things," in *Matter, Materiality and Modern Culture*, P. M. Graves-Brown (ed.), 11–21, London: Routledge.
Latour, B. (2009), "Where Constant Experiments Have Been Provided," interview, *Arch* 2 (Spring): http://artsci.wustl.edu/~archword/interviews/latour/interview.htm (accessed January 10, 2012).
Latour, B. (2010), "An Attempt at a 'Compositionalist Manifesto'," *New Literary History* 41: 481–2.
Lingis, A. (1998), *The Imperative* (Studies in Continental Thought), Bloomington, IN: Indiana University Press.
Miller, P. (2015), "Is 'Design Thinking' the New Liberal Arts?," *The Chronicle of Higher Education*, March 26. http://www.chronicle.com/article/Is-Design-Thinking-the-New/228779 (accessed September 29, 2016).

INDEX

Achilles' Shield, 207–8
actant, 100, 119, 208, 210
actor, 9–11, 17, 58, 66, 71, 79, 96, 100, 102, 106, 111, 119–20, 125, 127–32, 156, 208
actor network, 10–11, 66, 71, 96, 100, 111, 119, 125, 127–32, 156
Actor-Network Theory (ANT), 58
    ANT, 10–11, 66, 78, 96, 100, 111–12, 115, 127, 131–2, 156
Adorno, Theodor, 203, 209, 211
aesthetic, 4–5, 8, 61, 66, 88, 113–14, 117, 133–4, 141, 188, 192, 205
aesthetics, xii, xv, 11, 33, 109, 111, 113–15, 121, 134, 143, 189
affordance, 50, 68, 119–20, 159
Age of Entanglement, 14, 162
agency, vi, 2–5, 10–12, 15–18, 47–9, 52–7, 60–2, 65–7, 71, 73, 75, 77–8, 106, 112, 133, 138, 146, 158, 177, 188, 191, 193–201, 204, 207–9, 211
agent, 4, 48, 62, 193, 196–7, 200
agential, 12, 48–50, 207–8
agricultural, 157
Akrich, Madeleine, 49, 57
algorithm, ix, 23, 32
android/Android, v, 8–9, 19–20, 22, 27–8, 30–2, 207
animate, 22–3, 25, 51–2, 62, 75, 210
animating, 12, 49–50, 80
animism, ix, 12, 33, 50, 53, 66
animistic, ix, 10, 12, 52–4, 65–6, 78
anthropology, xv, 1, 16, 33, 151, 175, 177, 191, 193–4, 198, 204, 207–9
anthropomorphic, 14, 28, 52, 146, 167, 208
anthropomorphism, 50, 52, 208
antimicrobial, 196, 201
Apollo 13, 10, 129
Appadurai, Arjun, 5–6, 11, 17, 68, 79, 82–6, 92–3, 98–9, 106–7, 111, 120, 134, 147, 197, 201

Apple, xiii, 13, 82–5, 89–93, 107, 155, 158–60, 163–4, 185, 209
Aramis, 9, 40, 44, 58
Architectural Forum, 115
architecture, xi–xii, 36, 57, 121, 151, 153, 160, 177, 203
    Architectural, xi, 11, 14, 115, 162, 164, 172–4, 209
Arendt, Hannah, 96, 203
artifact, 37, 51, 54, 79, 114, 121, 126, 136–7, 150, 170, 172–3, 175–6, 179–80, 186–8, 192
assemblage, xiii, xv, 78, 111–12, 174
assemblies, 9, 13, 57, 115, 124–5, 145
automata, 19–20, 22–3, 25, 28, 30–4, 207
autonomy, 48, 205

Babbage, Charles, vii–viii, 26–8, 32–4
Baudrillard, Jean, 73, 79
behavioral chain, 198–9
Berger, John, 36, 44, 63
Bergson, Henri, 96, 107
Bernhard, Lucian, viii, 142, 143–4
biographies, 2, 5, 9, 17, 35, 68, 175, 197
biography of things, 17, 98, 147, 201, 203
blackbox, 54
Bogost, Ian, 112, 119–20
Boom, Irma, 186
boombox, vii, xi, 59–63, 203
branding, xiv, 187
Brandt, Per Aage, 181, 189
Braudel, Fernand, 96, 107
broken needle, 66
Bronze Age, xiv, 167, 169, 173–4, 177–8
Brown, Bill, vi, xiv, 1–4, 6–10, 12, 14, 17, 34–5, 43–4, 65–6, 73, 75, 79, 82–4, 92–3, 95–6, 99, 107, 121, 123, 126, 131–4, 145, 147, 150–1, 175, 177, 179–80, 184, 186–7, 189, 203–5, 210–11
Buchanan, Richard, 159, 170–1, 177

Callon, Michel, 120, 131, 156
cam, 23
capitalism, 50, 83, 107
Cartesian subject, 36–7
chaîne opératoire, 16, 198–9
China, 71, 80, 95, 107
Chorpash, Rama, viii, 11, 103–4, 106–7
chreod, 55
circulation, 11, 71, 77, 83, 85–6, 98–9, 106
civilized knowledge, 67
Clark, Andy, 14, 171–4, 176–7
Clark, Réne, 143
clockwork, 19–20, 25, 29, 34
co-creation, 25
co-evolution, 25
co-responsible, 194
code, 23, 32, 91–2, 158
cogito ergo sum, 37
cognitive, ix, xiv, 8, 14, 23, 25, 45, 159, 172, 174–8, 180–2, 189, 198, 206, 208
cognitive science, 180, 189
commodification, 160
commodity, 11, 32, 68, 75, 95, 98–9, 106, 133–4, 137, 154–5, 205
    commodities, 13, 17, 52, 68, 73, 82–3, 93, 98–9, 106–7, 120, 147, 151, 154, 201
commodity fetishism, 205
Concorde, 9, 41, 205
concretization, 24, 129
connectivity, 9, 20, 29, 31, 112, 118
consumer, xiii, 57, 60, 77, 84, 90, 95–6, 99–100, 137, 143, 161
convenience, 49, 53–6, 58–9, 73, 135
Cooper-Hewitt National Museum of Design, 36
copper, vi–vii, 5, 15–16, 28, 139, 191–2, 194–201, 204
coppersmith, 15, 191
counteragency, vi, 15–16, 191, 193, 195–201
craft, xi, 15, 29, 68, 96–8, 101, 106, 154, 195
craft-production, 154
craftsman, vii, 98, 195
    craftsmanship, 14, 60, 169
    craftspeople, 16, 96, 98, 191, 194–7, 199–200
    craftsperson, 197, 199
Crick, Francis, 38–9
Cultural Studies, 13, 16–17, 147, 153
culture, v, ix–xiv, 1–4, 7, 9–11, 16–18, 24–5, 33–4, 40, 43, 45, 48, 53, 57–61, 63, 66–8, 73, 79–80, 82, 93, 96, 98, 100, 106–7, 111, 114, 117, 120–1, 124, 132–3, 137, 147–8, 151, 153, 177–8, 184, 189, 191–2, 194, 198, 200–1, 207, 209–11
cybernetic constructions, 22

Das Kapital, 98
Dasein, 206
Daston, Lorraine, 6, 17
Debord, Guy, 38, 44
Deleuze, Gilles, ix–x, 112, 119, 204, 208–11
dematerialization, 13, 15, 20, 28–9, 31, 82, 91–2, 159
    dematerialize, 85
Descartes, Rene, 8, 25
design education, x, 153, 159
Design Museum, 37
design object, 9–10, 67, 124, 127–8, 130
design practice, ix, xiv, 3, 6–8, 13–14, 124, 126–7, 153, 158–9, 161, 163, 165
design process, x, 2, 4, 6, 124, 127–8, 130
Design Quarterly, 15, 82, 85, 87, 120
design research, x, 6, 16, 163, 165, 177
Design Studies, ix–x, 6–7, 16–17, 193
design thinking, ix, 14, 158–9, 205, 208–11
designed object, 4, 10, 35–7, 188, 204–5
die-cut, 85–6
Difference Engine, vii–viii, 26–8
digital, ix, xi, xiii, 5, 8–10, 15, 19–20, 22, 24–5, 28, 30–3, 63, 82–5, 88–92, 101, 127, 131, 164, 183, 207, 210–11
    design, 101
    enchantment, 20, 30–1
    media, xi, 15, 28
Ding, 9, 40, 62, 124, 205–6
distribution, xiii, 5, 8, 16–17, 43, 65, 99, 109, 111–12, 114–15, 118, 121, 134, 142, 155, 158, 178, 200
DIY, 101
DNA, 38–9, 196
Do the Right Thing, vii, 59, 61–2
door-closer, 52, 57
"Does It Make Sense?", 86
DOS, 90
dot-matrix, 15, 87
double bind, 15, 186–7
drawing, 6, 14, 35, 78, 82, 88, 90–1, 127, 130, 132, 139, 159, 174
Dreyfuss, Henry, 13, 144, 147
Drucker, Johanna, 90, 92–3, 186, 189
dysfunctionality, 187

Eames, Charles and Ray Eames, v, 11, 27, 33, 109–21, 205
    Eames, Charles, viii, 109, 111, 113, 115, 116, 120, 121
    Eames, Ray, 113–15, 119, 121
ecological perception, 50
Eidos, 194
Elliman, Paul, viii, 15, 183, 185
embodied, 14–15, 24–5, 38, 51, 53, 75, 118, 125, 142, 145, 176, 180–2, 189
embodied realism, 14, 180–1
Engels, Friedrich, 98, 107
engineer, 89–90, 102–3, 106–7, 141, 143, 146
engineering, ix, 19, 43, 137, 142–7, 158
Enlightenment, 3, 8–9, 25, 29, 33–4, 38, 65, 162
entanglement, 14, 162, 164
everyday life, 16, 49, 53, 56, 58, 68, 73, 75, 114, 135, 198, 204, 209, 211
experience economy, 155, 162, 165, 209

factory, vii, xi, 11, 34, 41, 95–6, 98–104, 106–7, 139, 150, 205
    factories, 16, 95–6, 98–101, 103, 106–7, 194
failure, 10, 36, 40–1, 43–4, 65–6, 134, 140–1, 145, 174, 208
fil rouge, 20, 125
Flusser, Vilém, 96, 103, 107
font, viii, 183, 185
Ford, Henry, 44, 102, 158
    post-Fordist era, 103
form, iv, 3–5, 9–10, 12, 14–16, 25, 28–30, 35–6, 39–40, 48–9, 51, 55, 62, 65–6, 75, 77, 82–3, 85, 89, 91, 96, 109, 112, 114, 118, 127, 129, 131, 139, 141, 144–5, 153, 157–9, 162, 164, 171, 173, 180, 182–3, 185, 187, 189, 194, 196–9, 204–6, 208–9
Found Font, viii, 183, 185
French phone, 135, 139–41, 143–6
Fry, Tony, 39, 44
Fuller, Buckminster, 84, 159, 163–4
functionality, 134, 180

gathering, 10, 40, 50, 56, 62, 124, 127, 156, 161, 182, 206
Gedenryd, Henrik, 172, 174, 177
Gell, Alfred, 29–30, 33, 171, 177, 193, 201
gender, 68, 75, 168–9, 198
gendered practice, 78
Gestalt, 181–2

ghetto-blaster, 62
Gibson, James, 50, 52, 159, 163–4
globalization, 43, 101
Grady, Joseph, 182, 189
graphic design, ix–x, xiii–xiv, 5, 15, 81, 93, 153, 179–80, 184, 187–8, 209
gravity, 12, 23, 49–50, 54–5
Greiman, April, v, viii, 15, 81–93
Greimas, Algirdas Julien, 208, 210–11
Guattari, Félix, ix, 204, 209, 211
Guggenheim Museum, 37
GUI, 85, 90, 92

hammer, 35, 40, 114, 192, 200, 206, 210
hammertone, vii, 191, 200
Hari Kuyō, v, 10, 66–7, 75, 77–8
Harman, 37, 40, 44, 48, 57, 119, 209, 211
Heidegger, Martin, 9–10, 35, 38, 40, 44, 62–3, 120, 124, 131, 156, 159, 194, 201, 205–6, 209–11
Herman Miller, 117, 120
Hillis, Danny, 14, 162, 164
Hodder, Ian, 156, 162, 164
human-machine interaction, 24, 28
humanities, xiv, 6, 16–17, 45, 93, 193
Hyle, 194
hyper-rational, 40
hyperobjects, 48, 58

iconic, x, 41, 60, 82, 158, 204
ideal form, 36
ideal technology, 29
IDEO, 42, 159, 209
Ihde, Donald, 55
Iliad, 208, 210–11
image schemas, 182, 189
immaterial, 3, 13, 15, 82–4, 92, 101, 153, 161, 173–4, 205, 207
    immaterial turn, 13, 153
inanimate, 4, 8, 22, 25, 29, 31, 62, 79, 133, 145, 208, 210
    inanimism, 208
industrial design, ix–x, 36
industrial revolution, 32, 82, 99, 101, 103, 154, 157
information economy, 157
Ingold, Tim, 44, 171, 174, 176–7, 191–2, 194–5, 200–1
Internet of things, xii, 207
iron, 68, 71, 77, 102, 118, 194
Ito, Joi, 161–2, 164

Jacquard, Joseph-Marie, 25, 27–8, 32–3
jambox, 62
Japan, v, xi, 10, 65–8, 71, 77, 79–80
Jaquet-Droz, Pierre, vii, 21–2
Johnson, Mark, viii, 14–15, 93, 180–1, 188–9
Johnson, Philip, 36, 38
jug, 156, 205–6
JVC, vii, 60

Kada Awashima Shrine, 67, 77
Kaufmann, Edgar, 38
Kellogg grab-a-phone, 139
Kockelkoren, Peter, 55–6, 58
Kopytoff, Igor, 5, 17, 134, 147, 197, 201
Krazy Kaps, viii, 15, 184–5
Kubler, George, 97–8, 106–7
Kurlansky, Mervyn, viii, 15, 184–5
Kuyō, v, 10, 66–7, 75, 77–8

Lakoff, George, 14, 162, 164, 180–1, 189
Latour, Bruno, 4, 9–10, 12–13, 17, 31–3, 35, 37–45, 49, 52, 55, 57–8, 62–3, 66, 71, 77, 79, 96, 99–100, 106–7, 111–12, 119–20, 124, 130–4, 136, 145, 147, 156, 182, 189, 193, 201, 203, 207–11
Law, John, 10, 17, 57–8, 79, 120, 127, 130–2, 156, 210–11
Lemonnier, Pierre, 119–20, 198, 201
Leroi-Gourhan, André, 198, 201
letterforms, 183–6
Lévi-Strauss, Claude, 172, 174, 177
life history, 98, 197–8
liminality, 78
LisaDraw, 89
LL Cool J, vii, 60
logos, 24, 194
loom, 25, 27–8, 33

machine, 9, 20, 22–5, 27–8, 30–4, 36–7, 45, 47, 54, 62, 79, 91, 93, 102, 104, 106, 114, 119, 127, 135, 183, 185, 197
machine age, 22, 37
machine art, 36–7, 45
machine learning, 47
Macintosh, 82, 84–5, 89–91, 93
MacPaint, 89
magic, ix, 20, 22–3, 29–33
making, v, viii, x–xi, xiii, 3–4, 6–7, 11–13, 17, 20, 23, 36, 39–40, 44, 50–3, 56, 58, 63, 67–8, 71–4, 77–8, 82, 84–5, 91, 95–103, 105–7, 111–12, 117, 125–30, 132, 143, 153–4, 156–9, 161, 170, 174, 176–7, 185–6, 193, 196–9, 201, 210
making-real, 12, 52–3
making-up, 12, 52
manufacturing, vii, 5, 10–11, 36, 43, 71, 95–6, 98–103, 106–7, 112–13, 137, 143, 145, 154–5, 157–8, 193, 197–9
Marx, Karl, 32, 98–100, 106–7, 205
mass-production, 101, 113, 136, 154
material agency, 17, 193, 196–8, 200–1
material culture, x–xi, xiv, 1–2, 4, 11, 16–18, 48, 63, 82, 98, 100, 111, 120–1, 151, 153, 178, 191–2, 198, 200–1, 207, 209
Material Culture Studies, x, 1–2, 11, 17, 111, 198, 201
material surrogacy, 171, 177
material turn, 1, 3, 7, 17, 147, 153, 193, 204
material unconscious, xiv, 207
material vitalism, 208
materialism, 4, 33, 47, 83–4, 133, 147, 178, 204–5
materiality, vi, ix, xii, xiv, 1, 7–8, 13, 15, 17, 20, 23–5, 28, 30, 41, 49, 58–60, 67, 80, 82, 84, 90, 92–3, 132, 134, 149, 151, 173, 175, 186, 191–4, 200–1, 203, 210–11
materials, vi, xi, 5–6, 10, 14–15, 29, 35, 37, 67, 77, 100–1, 103, 106, 124, 127, 131, 144, 150, 154, 157, 167–70, 183, 191–5, 197–201, 203–4, 207
Matharkam, vii, 192, 200
matter for discourse, 62
matter of concern, 126, 128–9, 136–7, 139, 141, 207
matter of pertinence, 62
Mau, Bruce, 186
Mauss, Marcel, 195, 201
mechanical memory, 23
Media Studies, 93
metal, v, vii, 11, 23, 37–8, 67, 71, 77–8, 101, 106, 109, 111, 113–15, 117–18, 147, 149–50, 183, 191, 194, 196, 198–200, 203–4, 208
metaphor, x, xiv, 8, 12, 25, 33, 49, 51, 55–6, 83, 189
  Metaphorical, 47, 67, 77, 182
Metropolis, x, 41–2, 44
Miller, Daniel, 1, 4, 17–18, 111, 120, 192, 201
miniaturization, 8, 25
missing mass, 49
model, viii, 5, 8, 25, 27, 40, 88, 127, 137,

139, 144, 157, 163–4, 172–4, 176, 185, 198
modernity, 38, 41, 44, 92, 120, 208
monk(s), viii, 75, 76, 77
Morris, Mark, 167, 171–2, 177
Museum of Modern Art, 36, 45, 111, 115
   MoMA, viii, 37–8, 111, 113, 115

narrative, ix, xiii, 1, 20, 36, 41, 73, 114, 134, 208–9
NASA, 39–40
needle, viii, xi, 10, 66–9, 71–5, 77–9
needlework, 75, 78
network, x, xiv, 10–12, 17, 41, 58, 66–8, 71, 75, 77–9, 95–7, 99–100, 102, 106, 111–12, 115, 119–20, 125, 127–32, 137, 139–40, 146, 156, 158, 160, 179, 182, 191, 194
   networked, xiii, 6, 10, 49, 54, 56, 100, 155
neural theory of language, 181
no-thingness, 15, 82–4, 87–8, 92
node chair, viii, 9, 42
non-human, 3, 7, 9, 11, 29, 37–9, 65–6, 75, 96, 111–12, 129
non-human turn, 3
nonsense, 82
nothingness, v, 15, 81–3, 85, 87–9, 91–3
Noyes, Elliot, 111, 121

object-subject, 3
objectification, 32, 123–6, 128–31
ontological, 10, 22, 39, 65, 207
ontology, 204, 207, 209, 211

Palaikastro, viii, xiv, 14, 167–70, 174–5, 177–8
Papanek, Victor, 159, 163, 165
perception, 15, 20, 44, 50–1, 134, 145, 158, 163–4, 179–82, 188–9
phallic, 77–8
phenomenological, 48, 75, 130–1, 182, 207
pictographs, xii, 82, 87
pixels, 82, 89–90
platform, 28, 160, 163–5
platonic metaphysics, 36
pornographic, 81
poster, xi, xiii, 15, 81–3, 85–93, 179, 182
power, viii, 2, 4–5, 10, 19, 23, 28, 30, 37, 39, 41, 47, 55, 59–62, 66, 71, 82–4, 89–91, 97–9, 106, 120, 146, 154, 157, 170–1, 182, 193–4, 208
PowerPoint, 40, 45
Practicing, Practising, 49

pre-industrial, 20, 25, 27, 95, 101
producer, 99, 145, 158, 161, 201
product semantics, 159
product-service ecologies, vi, 13–14, 153, 155–6, 161–2
   product-service ecology, 155
production, ix, xiii, 2, 5, 8, 10–11, 14, 16–17, 29, 32, 43, 65, 68, 71, 84, 93, 95–104, 106–7, 111, 113, 119, 134–6, 142–4, 154–5, 178, 180, 183, 186, 188, 198, 200, 206
production line, 99, 101–2, 104
proto-cyborg, 23
prototype, 5, 11, 27, 103, 106, 172
Puja, 66
punch cards, 25
pushing pixels, 89–90

quasi-object, 39–41

Radio Raheem, 59, 61–2
readiness-to-hand, 206
realist, 180
reciprocity, 4, 75
recycling, 77, 199
Red Dot Museum, 37
reification, 38, 52, 129–30
relational, 2–3, 5, 37–8, 41, 48, 54, 206
relationality, ix, 205, 207
representation, xii, 11, 24, 50, 67–8, 71, 88, 90, 92, 106, 127, 167, 173–5, 177
retrofitting, 71

Saarinen, Eero, 113–15
Scarry, Elaine, 12, 51–3, 58, 206
Schiffer, Michael, 197–8, 201
Schön, Donald, 129, 131–2, 157, 163, 165, 197, 201
science, xii, xiv, 6, 17, 24, 26–8, 30, 33–4, 38–40, 43–5, 49, 79, 82, 87–8, 100, 102, 106–7, 111, 131, 133, 135, 143, 147, 151, 164, 180, 189, 201, 207, 211
scrolling, 91
semiotic, 7, 41, 48–9, 56–7, 125, 156, 208, 210–11
   semiotics, 41, 159, 208
   semiotician, 181
sense, v, viii, xv, 3–5, 7, 10, 15, 20, 22, 30, 38, 44, 48, 59, 81–9, 91–3, 103, 114, 118, 123–9, 134, 141, 145, 156, 159, 171, 177, 179–80, 182, 188, 200, 204, 209–11
Serres, Michel, 9, 32, 34–5, 38–9, 45

sewing, viii, 67–8, 70–1, 73, 75, 78–9, 102, 206
Shinto-Buddhist, 10, 65
shock-mount, 112, 115, 117–18
Shove, Elizabeth, 49, 54, 58
Shunya, 88
Simmel, George, 83, 92
Simondon, Gilbert, 23–5, 29, 33–4
simulate, 9, 22–3, 31
Siri, 23, 31
situated cognition, 176–7
sketch, 5, 172, 175
slipcase, 15, 85–7, 92
smartphones, 10, 25, 29, 155, 160
Smith, Adam, 100
social lives of things, 4–5, 11
Social Practice Theory, 49, 54
social-technical-linguistic matrix, 155
socio-technical network, 66
sociomateriality, 49
software, xiii, 5, 13, 28, 40, 83, 89–91, 127, 131, 155–6, 160, 162
space shuttle, 9, 39–40, 134
    Challenger, 9, 39
    Columbia, 9, 39–40, 134
speculative realism, 48
subject, xi, 3, 5, 9–10, 32, 36–8, 50, 65–6, 73, 78, 82, 95, 99, 117, 124–5, 128, 134, 161, 179, 206–8
subject-object, 37, 66, 95, 124–5, 179
Sunyata, 88
symbol, xi, 145, 172, 177, 189
symmetrical, 50, 111, 167–8, 199
system, iv, xii–xiii, 9–10, 13, 19, 23, 28, 31, 34, 40–1, 54, 62, 65, 73, 79, 86, 88, 90, 92, 102, 111–12, 118, 127, 137, 139, 142, 145–7, 150, 155, 158, 160, 176, 198
system of objects, 73, 79

Tamba, 16, 191
Tambat Ali, vii, 15–16, 191, 194–5, 197–200
technical objects, 23–5, 29, 34
techniques of the body, 195, 201
techno-animism, 66
technological intentionality, 55
technology, x, xii–xiii, 2, 8, 10, 14–15, 18–20, 22–5, 27, 29–34, 38–40, 43–4, 48, 53, 55, 57–9, 61–3, 66–8, 72, 74–5, 78–80, 82–3, 85, 87–90, 93, 99, 103, 115, 118–20, 132–3, 135, 139, 146, 155, 158, 162–4, 201, 207
Telos, 194
The Age of Entanglement, 162
thick things, 8, 23–4, 30–2
thing theory, xv, 1–2, 10, 17, 35, 44, 51, 66, 78–9, 82, 84–5, 92–3, 99, 107, 131, 147, 151, 189, 203
thing-power, 61–2
thingly, 9, 15, 31, 49, 55, 61–2, 159, 195, 205–6
thingness, 3, 8, 10, 12, 15, 38, 40, 43, 65, 75, 82–8, 92, 96, 99, 123, 126, 129–30, 134, 180–2, 184–8, 203, 205–6, 209
things-in-motion, 6, 85, 134
Tierney, Thomas, 53, 58
tiling, 15, 87
tool, xiii, 15, 50–1, 62, 65, 75, 82, 91, 133, 195, 197–8, 208
toolbar, 90
Tsukumogamiki, 65
turn toward things, 82–4
type, 5, 40, 48, 141, 147, 179, 183, 185, 187–8, 193
typeface(s), 5, 15, 150, 179, 183, 185, 187
typography, xiv

usables, 50
user, ix, 2, 6–8, 10, 15, 28, 56, 58, 65, 75, 82, 84–5, 90–3, 96, 159–61, 186–8, 205
utensil, vii, 195

value, 3, 5, 11, 13, 32, 36, 53, 58, 61, 67, 73, 79, 83–4, 92, 95–100, 106–7, 128, 134, 139, 147, 151, 153–5, 157, 159–61, 169, 182, 201
Vaucanson, Jacques de, 20, 22–3, 25, 27, 31–3
Verbeek, Peter-Paul, 4, 18, 55–6, 58, 159, 163–4, 193, 201
vibrant matter, 17, 57, 60, 63
vivified machines, 22

Walker Art Center, 85
Watson, James, 38–9, 58, 93
weaving, 25, 28, 32, 95
weight, v, 12, 41, 47, 49, 51–3, 55–7, 59, 73, 115, 186, 192
Wittgenstein, Ludwig, 82, 86

zero, 88